THE IRONY OF DEMOCRACY

Thomas R. Dye *Florida State University*

L. Harmon Zeigler *University of Oregon*

THE IRONY OF DEMOCRACY
AN UNCOMMON INTRODUCTION TO AMERICAN POLITICS 6TH EDITION

Brooks/Cole Publishing Company *Monterey, California*

Brooks/Cole Publishing Company
A Division of Wadsworth, Inc.

Printed in the United States of America

10 9 8 7 6 5 4 3

Library of Congress Cataloging in Publication Data

Dye, Thomas R. [Date]
   The irony of democracy.
   Includes bibliographical references and index.
     1. Elite (Social sciences)—United States.
2. United States—Politics and government.   3. Pluralism
(Social sciences)—United States.   I. Zeigler, L. Harmon
(Luther Harmon), [Date].   II. Title.
JK271.D92   1983   306'.2'0973   83-15045

ISBN 0-534-02847-0

Subject Editor: Marquita Flemming
Production Editor: Jane Stanley
Manuscript Editor: Adrienne Cordova
Permissions Editor: Carline Haga
Interior Design: Stanley Rice
Cover Design and Photo: Stanley Rice
Art Coordinator: Rebecca Ann Tait
Interior Illustration: Art by Ayxa
Cartoon Editor: Judy Blamer
Cartoon Research: Lindsay Kefauver and Lisa Young
Typesetting: Graphic Typesetting Service,
Los Angeles, California
Cover, Printing, and Binding: R. R. Donnelly & Sons Co.
Crawfordsville, Indiana

Contents

6 Elite-Mass Communication: Television, the Press, and the Pollsters 140

7 Elections: Imperfect Instruments of Accountability 158

11 The Bureaucratic Elite and Public Policy   270

12 Congress: The Legislative Elite   298

13 Courts: Elites in Black Robes   332

To the student

In asking you to read this book, your instructor wants to do more than teach about "the nuts and bolts" of American government, for this book has a "theme": only a tiny handful of people make decisions that shape the lives of all of us, and, despite the elaborate rituals of parties, elections, and interest group activity, we have little influence over these people. This theme is widely known as *elitism*. Your instructor may not believe completely in this theory but may instead believe that many groups of people share power in America, that competition is widespread, that we have checks against the abuse of power, and that the individual citizen can personally affect the course of national events by voting, supporting political parties, and joining interest groups. This theory, widely known as *pluralism*, characterizes virtually every American government textbook now in print—except this one. Your instructor, whether personally agreeing with the "elitist" or with the "pluralist" perspective, is challenging you to confront our arguments and to deal directly with some troubling questions about democracy in America.

It is far easier to teach "the nuts and bolts" of American government—the constitutional powers of the president, Congress, and courts; the functions of parties and interest groups; the key cases decided by the Supreme Court; and so on—than to tackle the question, How democratic is American society? It is easier to teach the "facts" of American government than to search for their explanations. While this book does not ignore such facts, its primary purpose is to interpret them—to help you understand *why* American government works *as it does*.

Pluralism portrays the American political process as competition, bargaining, and compromise among a multitude of interest groups vying for the rewards distributed by the political system. Anyone who wants such rewards can effectively gain them only by joining (or organizing) such a group. Moreoover, pluralists argue, most individuals are members of more than one kind of organized group. Thus they believe the multiplicity of such groups and the overlap of their memberships are insurance against one group's eventual emergence as a dominant elite.

While pluralists highly value individual dignity, they nevertheless accept giant concentrations of power as inevitable in a modern, industrial, urban society. Realizing that the individual is no match for giant corporate bureaucracy, pluralists hope that countervailing centers of power will balance each other and thereby protect individuals from abuse. Through organized groups and coalitions of groups (parties), individuals gain access to the political system and ensure that government is held responsible. Pluralism contends that the American system is open and accessible to the extent that any interest of a significant portion of the populace can find expression through one or more groups.

Elitist theory, on the other hand, contends that all organizations are subject to the rule of a small minority of their membership and that the backgrounds and values of all these leaders tend to be similar—so similar, in fact, that they constitute an American sociopolitical elite. The members of this elite determine the society's values and control its resources. They act as much—if not more—on their elite identities as they do on their specific group attachments. Thus rather than viewing organized groups as a balance of power, elitists see organized interest groups as platforms of power from which the elite effectively governs the nation. These leaders accommodate each other more than they compete. They share a basic consensus about preserving the system essentially as it is, and members of their groups do not really hold them accountable. Members have little or nothing to say about policy decisions. In fact, leaders influence followers far more than followers influence leaders. These assertions conflict with pluralist beliefs.

A generation or more of Americans have been educated in the pluralist tradition. We do not claim that they have been educated poorly (if for no other reason than that we are among them); nor do we argue that pluralism is either "wrong" or "dead," for clearly it contains much of value and commands many perceptive adherents. Thus we did not write this book to "attack the pluralists." Our primary concern is to make available to students and teachers of political science an introductory analysis of American politics that is not based on pluralist theory.

The Irony of Democracy explains American political life by an elitist theory of democracy. In organizing historical and social science evidence from the American political system, we have sacrificed some breadth of coverage to present a coherent exposition of the elitist theory. You will find encyclopedic presentations of the "facts" of American government elsewhere. Nor do we present a "balanced," or theoretically eclectic, view of American politics. Students can find democratic-pluralist interpretations of American politics everywhere.

The Irony of Democracy is not necessarily "antiestablishment." This book challenges the prevailing pluralistic view of democracy in America, but it neither condemns nor endorses American political life, America's governance by a small, homogeneous elite is subject to favorable or unfavorable interpretation according to one's personal values. Each reader is free to decide whether we as a society should preserve, reform, or restructure the political system described in these pages.

To the Instructor

The sixth edition of *The Irony of Democracy* continues as the leading thematic introduction to American government. Despite the near-universal acceptance of pluralist ideology in American political science and American government textbooks, we remain unrepentant. *The Irony of Democracy* remains an *elitist* introduction to American government.

This edition includes several new contributions to our elitist interpretation of American politics. In chapter 1, we view "The Reaganauts in Perspective" by analyzing the elite composition of the Reagan cabinet and comparing it with past Democratic and Republican cabinets. Borrowing on important new data sources, we also trace elites in American history in chapter 3. Chapter 4 adds information on neoconservative ideology and Reaganomics. Our coverage of mass politics in chapter 5 now includes a discussion of the "New Right." And we have strengthened our argument about the role of the mass media with new sections on the political functions of the mass media and the media and political campaigning in chapter 6.

Chapter 7 considers on elections as imperfect instruments of accountability, and chapter 8 reviews American political parties as a System in decay. Both chapters outline politics in the 1980s and the Reagan presidency. We have extended our discussion of an increasingly important topic—campaign finance. In these chapters we also trace variations in the power and prestige of the presidency from the days of Camelot, through the Great Society, Vietnam, Watergate, the Carter presidency, and the early victories and later setbacks of Ronald Reagan. Our interest-group chapter (chapter 9) now contains a case study of the most potent of lobbies, the National Rifle Association. Chapter 11, on the bureaucracy, adds a new theoretical focus on "incrementalism" and a new case study on incrementalism and Reagan's budget cuts. Our chapter on Congress (chapter 12) gives more attention to voting coalitions, especially the southern "boll weevils."

In our section on protest groups in chapter 15, we continue to emphasize our belief that like *all* social movements, the civil rights and women's movements are led largely by upper- and upper-middle-class people. We discuss the much-publicized "gender gap" in women's and men's attitudes and voting patterns and offer conclusions that challenge current popular beliefs.

Our epilogue now discusses the relationships of freedom, wealth, and equality in a global context. We offer this new material so that students can understand that the dilemmas of American politics are not unique. We present a critical view of American politics, but we would apply the same standards in assessing any other country. By offering a comparative perspective, we trust that we can erase any suspicion that we would prefer other political systems to our own.

Nevertheless we cannot offer the students of the 1980s any advice that we did not offer the students of the 1970s. We warn of the inevitability of elites and the bitterness that can result from unrealistic expectations of changing the world overnight. Thus a plea for realism continues to guide our modest recommendations in the book's final pages.

In addition, we express our gratitude to the people who reviewed the book in the preparation of the sixth edition: Samuel T. Bookheimer, University of Kentucky; Douglas A. Brown, Arizona Western College; James L. Gibson, University of Wisconsin; Peter Nelson, University of Dayton; Delbert Ringquist, Central Michigan University; Henry Steck, Cortland State University; and Richard Vengroff, Texas Tech University.

Thomas R. Dye
L. Harmon Zeigler

THE IRONY OF DEMOCRACY

1 The Irony of Democracy

Elites, not masses, govern America. In an industrial, scientific, and nuclear age, life in a democracy, just as in a totalitarian society, is shaped by a handful of people.

Government is always government by the few, whether in the name of the few, the one, or the many.

—Harold Lasswell, The Comparative Study of Elites, *1952*

Elites, not masses, govern America. In an industrial, scientific, and nuclear age, life in a democracy, just as in a totalitarian society, is shaped by a handful of people. Despite differences in their approach to the study of power in America, political scientists and sociologists agree that "the key political, economic, and social decisions are made by 'tiny minorities.'"[1]

An *elite* is the few who have power; the *masses* are the many who do not. Power is deciding who gets what, when, and how; it is participation in the decisions that allocate values for a society. Elites are the few who participate in the decisions that shape our lives; the masses are the many whose lives are shaped by institutions, events, and leaders over which they have little direct control. Harold Lasswell writes, "The division of society into elite and mass is universal," and even in a democracy "a few exercise a relatively great weight of power, and the many exercise comparatively little."[2]

Elites need not be conspiracies that oppress or exploit the masses. On the contrary, elites may be very "public regarding" and deeply concerned with the welfare of the masses. Membership in an elite may be relatively open to ambitious and talented individuals from the masses, or it may be closed to all except top corporate, financial, military, civic, and government leaders. Elites may be competitive or noncompetitive; they may agree or disagree over the direction of foreign and domestic policy. Elites may form a pyramid, with a top group exercising power in many sectors of the society; or they may be plural elites that divide power, with separate groups making key decisions about different issues. Elites may be responsive to the demands of the masses and influenced by the outcome of elections, or they may be unresponsive to mass movements and unaffected by elections. But whether elites are public-minded or self-seeking, open or closed, competitive or consensual, pyramidal or pluralistic, responsive or unresponsive, they, not the masses, govern the modern nation.

Democracy is government "by the people," but the survival of democracy rests on the shoulders of elites. This is the irony of democracy: elites must govern wisely if government "by the people" is to survive. If the survival of the American system depended on an active, informed, and enlightened citizenry, then democracy in America would have disappeared long ago, for the masses of America are apathetic and ill-informed about politics and public policy. Moreover, they have a surprisingly weak commitment to democratic values of individual dignity, equal opportunity, the right to dissent, freedom of speech and press, religious toleration, and due process of law. But fortunately for these values and American democracy, the American masses do not lead; they follow. They respond to the attitudes, proposals, and behavior of elites.

Although the symbols of American politics grow out of democratic political thought, *elite theory* is often more useful in understanding the reality of American politics. Elite theory poses questions vital to politics: Who governs America? What roles do elites and masses play in American politics? How do people acquire power? How are economic and political power related? How open and accessible are American elites? How do American elites change over time? How widely is power shared in America? Do elites compete with each other, or do they generally agree on values and directions in public policy? What is the basis of elite consensus? How do elites and masses differ? How responsive are elites to mass sentiments? How much influence do masses have over policies decided by elites? How do elites accommodate themselves to mass movements?

This book, *The Irony of Democracy*, attempts to explain American political life using elite theory. It aims to organize systematically the evidence of American history and contemporary social science to come to grips with the central questions posed by elite theory. But before we examine American political life, we must understand more about *elitism*, *democracy*, and *pluralism*.

Meaning of elitism

The central proposition of elitism is that all societies are divided into two classes: the few who govern and the many who are governed. The Italian political scientist Gaetano Mosca expressed this basic concept as follows:

> In all societies—from societies that are very underdeveloped and have largely attained the dawnings of civilization, down to the most advanced and powerful societies—two classes of people appear—a class that rules and a class that is ruled. The first class, always the less numerous, performs all of the political functions, monopolizes power, and enjoys the advantages that power brings, whereas the second, the more numerous class, is directed and controlled by the first, in a manner that is now more or less legal, now more or less arbitrary and violent.[3]

For Mosca it was inevitable that elites and not masses would govern all societies. Elites are not a product of capitalism, or socialism, or industrialization, or technological development. All societies—socialist and capitalist, agricultural and industrial, traditional and advanced—are governed by elites. All societies require leaders, and leaders acquire a stake in preserving the organization and their position in it. This motive gives leaders a perspective different from that of the organization's members. An elite, then, is inevitable in any social organization. As the French political scientist Roberto Michels put it, "He who says organization, says oligarchy."[4] The same is true for societies as a whole. According to political scientist Harold Lasswell, "The discovery that in all large-scale societies the decisions at any given time are typically in the hands of a small number of people" confirms a basic fact: "Government is always government by the few, whether in name of the few, the one, or the many."[5]

Elitism also asserts that the few who govern are not typical of the masses who are governed. Elites control more resources: power, wealth, education, prestige, status, skills of leadership, information, knowledge of political processes, ability to communicate, and organization. Elites in America are drawn disproportionately from among wealthy, educated, prestigiously employed, socially prominent, white, Anglo-Saxon, and Protestant groups in society. They come from society's upper classes, those who own or control a disproportionate share of the societal institutions: industry, commerce, finance, education, the military, communications, civic organizations, and law.

Elitism, however, does not necessarily bar individuals of the lower classes from rising to the top; elite theory admits of some social mobility that enables nonelites to become elites. In fact, a certain amount of "circulation of elites" (upward mobility) is essential for the stability of the elite system. Openness in the system siphons off potentially revolutionary leadership from the lower classes, and an elite system strengthens when talented and ambitious individuals from the masses enter governing circles. However, social stability requires that the individuals' movement from nonelite to elite positions be a slow, continuous assimilation rather than a rapid or revolutionary change. Moreover, only those nonelites who have demonstrated their commitment to the elite system itself and to the system's political and economic values can be admitted to the ruling class.

Elites share a *consensus* about the fundamental norms of the social system. They agree on the basic rules of the game, as well as on the importance of preserving the social system. The stability of the system, and even its survival, depends upon this consensus. According to David Truman, "Being more influential, they [the elites] are privileged; and being privileged, they have, with few exceptions, a special stake in the continuation of the system in which their privileges rest."[6] Elite consensus does not prevent elite members from disagreeing or competing

© Ed Fischer/ROTHCO.

"What I want to know is, when the century of the common man is going to be over."

with each other for preeminence; indeed, a society in which elites do not compete is highly unlikely. But competition takes place within a very narrow range of issues, and elites agree on more matters than they disagree on. Disagreement usually occurs over *means* rather than *ends*.

In America, the bases of elite consensus are the sanctity of private property, limited government, and individual liberty. Richard Hofstadter writes about American elite struggles:

> The fierceness of political struggles has often been misleading; for the range of vision embodied by the primary contestants in the major parties has always been bounded by the horizons of property and enterprise. However much at odds on specific issues, the major political traditions have shared a belief in the rights of property, the philosophy of economic individualism, the value of competition; they have accepted the economic virtues of capitalist culture as necessary qualities of man.[7]

Elitism implies that public policy does not reflect demands of "the people" so much as it reflects the interests and values of elites. Changes and innovations in public policy come about when elites redefine their own values. However, the general conservatism of elites—that is, their interest in preserving the system—means that changes in public policy will be incremental rather than revolutionary. Public policies are often modified but seldom replaced.

Basic changes in the political system occur when events threaten it. Elites, acting on enlightened self-interest, institute reforms to preserve the system and their place in it. Their motives are not necessarily self-serving; their values may be very "public regarding," and the welfare of the masses may be an important element in elite decision making. Nor does elitism mean that public policy will ignore or oppose the welfare of the masses; it means only that the responsibility for the mass welfare rests with elites, not with the masses.

Finally elitism assumes that the masses are largely passive, apathetic, and ill-informed. Mass sentiments are manipulated by elites more often than elite values are influenced by the sentiments of the masses. For the most part, communication between elites and masses flows downward. Masses seldom decide government policies through elections or through evaluation of political parties' policy alternatives. For the most part, these "democratic" institutions—elections and parties—have only symbolic value: they help tie the masses to the political system by giving them a role to play on election day and a political party with which they can identify. Elitism contends that the masses have at best only an indirect influence over the decision-making behavior of elites.

Americans frequently misunderstand elitism because they take their prevailing myths and symbols from democratic theory rather than elite theory. Therefore it is as important to emphasize what elitism is *not* and to restate briefly what it *is*.

Elitism does not mean that power holders continually lock horns with the masses or that they always achieve their goals at the expense of the public interest. Elitism is not a conspiracy to oppress the masses. It does not imply that power is held by a single, impenetrable, monolithic body or that power holders always agree on public issues. It does not prevent power from shifting over time or prohibit the emergence of new elites. Elites may be more or less monolithic and cohesive or more or less pluralistic and competitive. Power need not rest exclusively on the control of economic resources; it may rest instead on other leadership resources—organization, communication, or information. Elitism does not prevent the masses from influencing the attitudes of elites; it holds only that elites influence masses more than masses influence elites.

The following points summarize elite theory:

1. Society is divided into the few who have power and the many who do not. Only a small number of people allocate values for society; the masses do not decide public policy.

2. The few who govern are not typical of the masses who are governed. Elites are drawn disproportionately from the upper socio-economic strata of society.

3. The movement of nonelites to elite positions must be slow and continuous to maintain stability and avoid revolution. Only nonelites who have accepted the basic elite consensus enter governing circles.

4. Elites share a consensus on the basic values of the social system and the preservation of the system. They disagree only on a narrow range of issues.

5. Public policy does not reflect the demands of masses but the prevailing values of the elite. Changes in public policy will be incremental rather than revolutionary.

6. Active elites are subject to relatively little direct influence from the apathetic masses. Elites influence masses more than masses influence elites.

Meaning of democracy

Ideally democracy brings individual participation in the decisions that affect one's life. John Dewey wrote, "The keynote of democracy as a way of life may be expressed as the necessity for the participation of every mature human being in formation of the values that regulate the living of men together."[8]

Traditional democratic theory has valued popular participation as an opportunity for individual self-development: responsibility for governing one's own conduct develops one's character, self-reliance, intelligence, and moral judgment—in short, one's dignity. The classic democrat would reject even a benevolent despot who could govern in the public interest. The English political philosopher J. S. Mill asked, "What development can either their thinking or active faculties attain under it?" The argument for citizen participation in public affairs depends not on its policy outcomes but on the belief that such involvement is essential to the full development of human capacities. Mill argued that people can know truth only by discovering it for themselves.[9]

Procedurally, a society achieves popular participation through majority rule and respect for the rights of minorities. Self-development means self-government, and self-government comes about only by encouraging each individual to contribute to the development of public policy and by resolving conflicts over public policy through majority rule. Minorities who have had the opportunity to influence policy but whose views have not won majority support accept the decisions of majorities. In return, majorities permit minorities to attempt openly to win majority support for their views. Freedom of speech and press, freedom to dissent, and freedom to form opposition parties and organizations are essential to ensure meaningful individual participation. This freedom of expression is also critical in ascertaining the majority's real views.

The underlying value of democracy, then, is individual dignity. Human beings, by virtue of their existence, are entitled to life, liberty, and property. A "natural law," or moral tenet, guarantees every person liberty and the right to property, and this natural law is morally superior to human law. John Locke, the English political philosopher whose writings most influenced America's founding elites, argued that even in a "state of nature"—that is, a world of no governments—an individual possesses inalienable rights to life, liberty, and property. Locke meant that these rights are independent of government; governments do not give them to individuals, and no government may legitimately take them away.[10]

Locke believed that a government's purpose is to protect individual liberty. People form a "social contract" with each other in establishing a government to help protect their rights; they tacitly agree to accept government activity to better protect life, liberty, and property. Implicit in the social contract and the democratic notion of freedom is the belief that government activity and social control over the individual must be minimal. This belief calls for removing external restrictions, controls, and regulations on the individual that do not violate the freedom of other citizens.

Moreover, since government is formed by the consent of the governed to protect individual liberty, it follows that government cannot violate the rights it was established to protect. Its authority is limited. Locke's ultimate weapon to protect individual dignity against abuse by government was the right of revolution. According to Locke, whenever governments violate the natural rights of the governed, they forfeit the authority placed in them under the social contract.

Another vital aspect of classic democracy is a belief in the equality of all people. The Declaration of Independence states that "all men are created equal." Even the Founding Fathers believed in equality for all persons *before the law*, regardless of their personal circumstances. A democratic society cannot judge a person by social position, economic class, creed, or race. Many early democrats also believed in *political equality:* equal opportunity of individuals to influence public policy. Political equality is expressed in the concept of "one man, one vote."

Over time, the notion of equality has also come to include *equality of opportunity* in all aspects of American life: social, educational, and economic, as well as political. Political scientist Roland Pennock writes:

> The objective of equality is not merely the recognition of a certain dignity of the human being as such, but it is also to provide him with the opportunity—equal to that guaranteed to others—for protecting and advancing his interests and developing his powers and personality.[11]

Thus the notion of equal opportunity has spread beyond political life to include education, employment, housing, recreation, and public accommodations. Each person has an equal opportunity to develop his or her capacities to their natural limits.

Remember, however, that the traditional democratic creed has always stressed *equality of opportunity* to education, wealth, and status and not *absolute equality*. Thomas Jefferson recognized a "natural aristocracy" of talent, ambition, and industry, and liberal democrats since Jefferson have always accepted inequalities that arise from individual merit and hard work. Absolute equality, or "leveling," is not part of liberal democratic theory.

In summary, democratic thinking reflects the following ideas:

1. Popular participation in the decisions that shape the lives of individuals in a society.
2. Government by majority rule, with recognition of the rights of minorities to try to become majorities. These rights include the freedom of speech, press, assembly, and petition and the freedom to dissent, to form opposition parties, and to run for public office.
3. A commitment to individual dignity and the preservation of the liberal values of life, liberty, and property.
4. A commitment to equal opportunity for all individuals to develop their capacities.

Meaning of pluralism

Political rhetoric in America emphasizes citizen participation in decision making, majority rule, protection of minorities, individual rights, and equality of opportunity. Nevertheless, no scholar or commentator, however optimistic about life in the United States, would contend that the American political system has fully realized these goals. No one contends that citizens participate in all decisions shaping their lives or that majority preferences always prevail. Nor does anyone argue that the system always protects the rights of minorities, always preserves the values of life, liberty, and property, or provides every American with an equal opportunity to influence public policy.

Modern pluralism seeks to reaffirm that American society is democratic by asserting that:

1. Although citizens do not directly participate in decision making, their many leaders make decisions through a process of bargaining, accommodation, and compromise.
2. Competition among leadership groups helps protect individuals' interests. Countervailing centers of power—for example, com-

petition among business leaders, labor leaders, and government leaders—can check each other and keep each interest from abusing its power and oppressing the individual.

3. Individuals can influence public policy by choosing among competing elites in elections. Elections and parties allow individuals to hold leaders accountable for their actions.

4. Although individuals do not participate directly in decision making, they can exert influence through participating in organized groups.

5. Leadership groups are open; new groups can form and gain access to the political system.

6. Although political influence in society is unequally distributed, power is widely dispersed. Access to decision making is often determined by how much interest people have in a particular decision; and because leadership is fluid and mobile, power depends on one's interest in public affairs, skills in leadership, information about issues, knowledge of democratic processes, and skill in organization and public relations.

7. Multiple leadership groups operate within society. Those who exercise power in one kind of decision do not necessarily exercise power in others. No single elite dominates decision making in all issues.

8. Public policy does not necessarily reflect majority preference but is an equilibrium of interest interaction—that is, competing interest group influences are more or less balanced, and the resultant policy is therefore a reasonable approximation of society's preferences.

Pluralism, then, is the belief that democratic values can be preserved in a system of multiple, competing elites who determine public policy through bargaining and compromise, in which voters exercise meaningful choices in elections and new elites can gain access to power.

Pluralism versus democracy

Pluralism, even if it accurately describes American society, is not the same as classical democracy. First, the pluralist notion of decision making by elite interaction is not the same as the democratic ideal of direct individual participation in decision making. Pluralists recognize that individual participation in decision making is not possible in a complex, urban, industrial society and that it inevitably must give way to interaction—bargaining, accommodation, and compromise—among leaders of the society's institutions and organizations. The political system represents individuals only if they are members of institutions or organizations whose leaders participate in policy making. Society's leaders, not individual citizens, hold government responsible. The principal actors are leaders of corporations and financial institutions, elected and appointed government officials, the top ranks of military and governmental bureaucracies, and leaders of large organizations in labor, agriculture, and the professions.

Yet decision making by elite interaction, whether it succeeds in protecting the individual or not, fails to contribute to individual growth and development. Here modern pluralism diverges sharply from classic democracy, which emphasizes as a primary value personal development through active participation in decisions that affect the individual's life.

Pluralism emphasizes that power is fragmented throughout society and that public opinion and elections influence the behavior of elites. But this fragmentation of power is different from the democratic ideal of political equality. Who rules, in the pluralist view of America? According to political scientist Aaron Wildavsky, the people who rule come from "different small groups of interested and active citizens in different issue areas with some overlap, if any, by public officials, and occasional intervention by a larger number of people at the polls."[12] This is not government by the people. While citizen influence can be felt through leaders who anticipate the reaction of citizens, decision making is still in the hands of the leaders—the elites. According to the pluralists, multiple elites decide public policy in America, each in its own sphere of interest.

Traditional democratic theory envisions public policy as the rational choice of individuals with equal influence, who evaluate their needs and reach a decision with due regard for the rights of others. This traditional theory does not view public policy as a product of elite interaction or interest group pressures. In fact, classical democratic theorists viewed interest groups and even political parties as intruders into an individualistic brand of citizenship and politics.

Several other problems show that pluralism is not necessarily the legitimate heir to classical democratic theory. First, can pluralism ensure that membership in organizations and institutions is really an effective form of individual participation in policy making? Robert Presthus argues that the organizations and institutions on which pluralists rely "become oligarchic and restrictive insofar as they monopolize access to government power and limit individual participation."[13] Henry Kariel writes, "The voluntary organizations or associations, which the early theorists of pluralism relied upon to sustain the individual against a unified omnipotent government, have themselves become oligarchically governed hierarchies."[14] Individuals may provide the numerical strength for organizations, but what influence does each have on the leadership? Rarely do corporations, unions, armies, churches, government bureaucracies, or professional associations have any internal democratic mechanisms. They are usually run by a small elite of officers and activists.

Leaders of corporations, banks, labor unions, churches, universities, medical associations, and bar associations remain in control year after year. Very few people attend meetings, vote in organizational elections, or make their influence felt within their organization. The pluralists offer no evidence that the giant organizations and institutions in American life really represent the views or interests of their individual members.

Also, can pluralism really assume that elite competition protects the dignity of the individual? Since pluralism contends that different groups of leaders make decisions about different issues, why should we assume that these leaders compete with each other? More likely, each group of leaders allows other groups of leaders to govern their own spheres of influence without interference. Accommodation, rather than competition, may be the prevailing style of elite interaction: "You scratch my back and I'll scratch yours."

Pluralists hope that the power of diverse institutions and organizations in society will roughly balance out and prevent the emergence of a power monopoly. They assure us that no interest can ever emerge the complete victor in political competition. Yet inequality of power among institutions and organizations is commonplace. Examples abound of narrow, organized interests achieving their goals at the expense of the broader, unorganized public. Furthermore, producer interests, bound together by economic ties, usually dominate less organized consumer groups and groups based on noneconomic interests. Pluralists offer no evidence that political competition prevents monopoly or oligopoly in political power.

Finally, pluralism must explain how private, nongovernment elites can be held accountable to the people. Even if government elites can be held accountable through elections, how can corporation elites, union leaders, and other kinds of private leadership be held accountable? Pluralism usually dodges this important question by focusing primary attention on *public*, government-elite decision making and largely ignoring *private*, nongovernment-elite decision making. Pluralists focus on rules and orders enforced by *governments*, but certainly citizens' lives are vitally affected by decisions made by private institutions and organizations, among them, corporations, banks, universities, medical associations, and newspapers. In an ideal democracy, individuals participate in all decisions that significantly affect their lives; but pluralism largely excludes individuals from participation in many vital decisions by claiming that these decisions are "private" in nature and not subject to public accountability.

Thus pluralism diverges from classical democratic theory in these ways:

1. Decisions are made by elite interaction—bargaining, accommodation, compromise—rather than by direct individual participation.

2. Key political actors are leaders of institutions and organizations rather than individual citizens.
3. Power is fragmented, but inequality of political influence among power holders is common.
4. Power is distributed among government and nongovernment institutions and organizations, but these institutions and organizations are generally governed by oligarchies rather than by their members in democratic fashion.
5. Institutions and organizations divide power and presumably compete among themselves, but this competition does not necessarily guarantee political equality or protect individual dignity.
6. *Government* elites are presumed to be accountable to the masses through elections, but many important decisions affecting individuals' lives are made by *private* elites, who are not directly accountable to the masses.

Confusion often arises in distinguishing pluralism from elitism. Pluralists say that the system they describe is a reaffirmation of democratic theory in a modern, urban, industrial society. They offer pluralism as a "practical solution" to the problem of achieving democratic ideals in a large, complex social system in which direct individual participation and decision making is simply not possible. But many critics of pluralism assert that pluralism is a disguised form of elitism—that pluralists are closer to the elitist position than to the democratic tradition they revere. Thus political scientist Peter Bachrach describes pluralism as "democratic elitism."[15]

Threats to democracy

Mass threats

Democratic theory assumes that mass political participation best protects the fundamental values of individual dignity, equality of opportunity, the right of dissent, freedom of speech and press, religious toleration, and due process of law. Historically the masses, not elites, have been considered the guardians of liberty. For example, in the eighteenth and nineteenth centuries, the threat of tyranny arose from corrupt monarchies and decadent churches. But in the twentieth century, the masses have been most susceptible to the appeals of totalitarianism.

The irony of democracy in America is that elites, not masses, are most committed to democratic values. Despite a superficial commitment to the symbols of democracy, the American people have a surprisingly weak commitment to individual liberty, toleration of diversity, and freedom of expression for those who would challenge the existing order. Social science research reveals that most people are not deeply attached to the causes of liberty, fraternity, or equality. On the contrary, support for free speech and press, for freedom of dissent, and for equality of opportunity for all is associated with high educational levels, prestigious occupations, and high social status. Authoritarianism is stronger among the working classes in America than among the middle and upper classes.

Democratic values have survived because elites, not masses, govern. Elites in America—leaders in government, industry, education, and civic affairs; the well educated, prestigiously employed, and politically active— give greater support to basic democratic values and "rules of the game" than do the masses. And it is because masses in America respond to the ideas and actions of democratically minded elites that liberal values are preserved.[16] In short, the common person, not the elite, is most likely to respond to antidemocratic ideology; and the elite, not the common person, is the chief guardian of democratic values.

If elites are to fulfill their role as guardians of liberty and property, they must be insulated from the antidemocratic tendencies of the masses. Too much mass influence over elites threatens democratic values. Mass behavior is highly unstable. Usually, established elites can depend on mass apathy, but occasionally the masses mobilize, and their activism is extremist, unstable, and unpredictable. Mass activism is usually an expression of resentment against the established order, and it usually occurs in times of crisis when a "counterelite" (demagogue) emerges from the masses to mobilize them against the established elites.

Democracies, in which elites are dangerously accessible to mass influence, can survive only if the masses are absorbed in the problems of everyday life and are involved in groups that distract their attention from mass politics. The masses are stable when they are absorbed in their work, family, neighborhood, trade union, hobby, church, recreational group, and other activities. When the masses become alienated from their home, work, and community—when existing ties to social organizations and institutions weaken—mass behavior becomes unstable and dangerous. At such a time a demagogue, or counterelite, can capture and direct the attention and activity of the masses. The demagogue can easily mobilize for revolution those elements of the masses who have few ties to the existing social and political order.[17]

Counterelites are mass-oriented leaders who express hostility toward the established order and appeal to mass sentiments: extremism, intolerance, racial identity, anti-intellectualism, egalitarianism, and violence. *Elites*, whether liberal or conservative, support the fundamental values of the system—individual liberty, majority rule, due process of law, limited government, and private property; *counterelites*, whether "left" or "right," are antidemocratic, extremist, impatient with due process, contemptuous of law and authority, and violence prone. The

"I came dashing in here thirty years ago yelling 'Death to the ruling classes'
. . . . liked it, and decided to stay . . ."

only significant difference between "left" and "right" counterelites is
their attitude toward change. "Right" counterelites express mass reaction against change—political, social, economic, technological—while
"left" counterelites demand radical and revolutionary change.[18]

All counterelites claim to speak for "the people," and both "left"
and "right" assert *the supremacy of "the people"* over law, institutions,
procedures, or individual rights. Right-wing counterelites, including
fascists, justify their policies as "the will of the people," while left-wing
radicals cry "all power to the people" and praise the virtues of "people's
democracies."

Extremism is another characteristic of mass politics: the view that
compromise and coalition building are immoral. Indeed extremists view
"politics" and "politicians" with hostility as potential threats to mass
demands.[19] Occasionally counterelites will make cynical use of politics,
but only as a short-term tactical means to other goals.

Counterelites frequently charge that a deliberate *conspiracy* exists
among established elites to perpetuate evil upon the people. The "left"
counterelite charges that the established order knowingly exploits and
oppresses the people for its own benefit and amusement; the "right"
counterelite charges that the established order is falling prey to an inter-

national communist conspiracy whose goal is to deprive the people of their liberty and property and to enslave them. Richard Hofstadter refers to this phenomenon as "the paranoid style of politics."[20] A related weapon in the arsenal of the counterelite is *scapegoatism*—the designation of particular minority groups in society as responsible for the evils suffered by the people. American history has seen a number of scapegoats, among them Catholics, immigrants, Jews, blacks, communists, intellectuals, Wall Street bankers, and arms manufacturers.

The masses define politics in *simplistic* terms. They want simple answers to society's problems, regardless of how complex these problems may be. Thus black counterelites charge that "white racism" is responsible for the complex problems of undereducation, poverty, unemployment, crime, delinquency, ill health, and poor housing of ghetto dwellers. In a similar fashion white counterelites dismiss ghetto disturbances as "communist agitation." These simplistic answers are designed to relieve both black and white masses of any difficult thinking about social issues and to place their problems in simple, emotion-laden terms. Anti-intellectualism and antirationalism are important parts of mass politics.

In summary, elite theory views the critical division in American politics as the division between elites and masses. "Left" and "right" counterelites are similar. Both appeal to mass sentiments; assert the supremacy of "the people" over laws, institutions, and individual rights; reject compromise in favor of extremism; charge that established elites are a conspiracy; designate scapegoat groups; define social problems in simple emotional terms and reject rational thinking; express egalitarian sentiments and hostility toward those who have achieved success within the system.

Elite threats

Elites are more committed to democratic values than the masses, but they frequently abandon these values in crisis periods and become repressive. Antidemocratic mass activism has its counterpart in elite repression. Both endanger democratic values.

Mass activism and elite repression frequently interact to create multiple threats to democracy. Mass activism—riots, demonstrations, extremism, violence—generates fear and insecurity among elites, who respond by curtailing freedom and strengthening security. Convincing themselves that they are preserving liberal democratic values, elites may cease tolerating dissent, censor the news media, curtail free speech, jail potential counterelites, and strengthen police and security forces in the name of "national security" or "law and order." Ironically, these steps make society less democratic rather than more so.

Repressive behavior is typical of elites who feel threatened in crises as some notable events in American history show. The Alien and Sedition

Acts (1798), passed in the administration of John Adams, closed down Jeffersonian newspapers and jailed their editors. Abraham Lincoln suspended due-process rights and imposed military law in many areas, both North and South, where citizens opposed his efforts to preserve the Union. The "Red scare" of 1919–1920 resulted in the roundup of suspected Bolsheviks in the administration of Woodrow Wilson, even after the end of World War I. During World War II the Roosevelt administration imprisoned thousands of Japanese American families in West Coast detention camps. And during the Truman and Eisenhower administrations, suspected communists and "fellow travelers" were persecuted by dismissal from their jobs, blacklisting, and occasionally jailing. Moreover, federal security agencies have long used such practices as wiretapping, monitoring mail, use of paid informants, surveillance of suspected subversives, infiltration of radical organizations, and "surreptitious entry" (burglary). Investigations of the domestic intelligence activities of the Federal Bureau of Investigation, Central Intelligence Agency, National Security Agency, and Internal Revenue Service confirmed that these practices began with the Roosevelt administration and continued through the Truman, Eisenhower, Kennedy, Johnson, and Nixon years.[21] These agencies frequently used illegal methods to monitor antiwar organizations, civil rights advocates, and other individuals and groups who were not the objects of criminal investigations. They used covert tactics to corrupt and discredit these groups and collected derogatory information to pass on to other government agencies, the president, and private employers. The FBI made a special effort to expose the personal life of Martin Luther King, Jr. while Robert F. Kennedy was attorney general.

The Watergate affair is a dramatic illustration of elite reaction to mass unrest and the tendency of elites to resort to repression when they feel threatened. The events of Watergate (the break-in at Democratic party headquarters in the Watergate apartments, Washington, D.C., in June 1972, and subsequent White House attempts at a coverup of those involved) grew out of a more general atmosphere of fear and repression that surrounded the White House in the early 1970s. No evidence suggests that the major figures participated in Watergate for personal financial gain. Rather they appeared to genuinely believe that the political system was in jeopardy and that only extraordinary measures could preserve it. The mass media, the Democratic opposition, and the academic community may contend that the Nixon administration was especially blameworthy among presidential administrations; we do not dispute this contention. But Watergate clearly has precedents and is not unique. Elite repression is a continuing threat to democratic values. And this threat to democratic values will always be greatest in periods of mass unrest when elites believe that their repressive acts are necessary to preserve the political system.

Thus neither elites nor masses in America are totally and irrevocably committed to democratic values. Elites are generally more committed to democratic procedures than are the masses for several reasons. First, people successful at the game of democratic politics are more amenable to abiding by the rules of the game than those who are not. Second, many elite members have internalized democratic values learned in childhood. Finally, the achievement of high position may bring a sense of responsibility for, and an awareness of, societal values. However, elites can and do become repressive when they perceive threats to the political system and their position in it.

Case study: The Reaganauts in elite perspective

Each new presidential administration promises dramatic change in government—change in personnel as well as policy. Indeed, "pluralists" often portray the American political system as a struggle between broad coalitions of groups, represented by the Republican and Democratic parties, to capture control of government and to determine personnel and policy. According to this interpretation, a change in the party in power should bring significant change in interest group representation as well as in programs and policies.

Critics of this pluralist view contend that changes in administration do not bring different kinds of people to Washington and in fact bring only incremental changes in policy. According to this "elitist" interpretation, a change in the party in power may bring new faces into high office but that new personnel will rarely differ from past administrations in their social backgrounds, corporate ties, educational credentials, Ivy League connections, and government experience.

As usual in these debates, evidence is available to support each position. Consider the credentials of the nineteen cabinet-level officials in the Reagan administration—thirteen secretaries, together with the vice-president, UN ambassador, CIA director, director of the Office of Management and the Budget (OMB), national security advisor, and chairman of the Council of Economic Advisors (CEA).

- Eleven (57.9%) have Ivy League educations and two others are West Point graduates.
- Thirteen (68.4%) have advanced degrees; three have Ph.D.s, five have law degrees, and five have master's degrees.
- Fourteen (73.7%) have served as officers or directors of corporations, banks, or investment firms.
- Thirteen (68.4%) have prior government experience.
- Their average age upon taking office was fifty-five.
- The top team has only one black (HUD Secretary Samuel R. Pierce) and one woman (UN Representative Jeanne Kirkpatrick).

Yet the Reagan team is no more "elitist" than other presidential administrations. In eight presidential administrations since World War II (Tru-
(continued)

Case study (*continued*)

man, Eisenhower, Kennedy, Johnson, Nixon, Ford, Carter, Reagan), cabinet-level appointees have possessed extensive educational, corporate, and governmental experience: 47.8 percent had Ivy League educations; 69.4 percent had advanced degrees (18.6% had Ph.D.s and 39.5% had law degrees); 60.4 percent had served as officers or directors of corporations, banks, or investment firms before their appointment; and their average age upon taking office was fifty-two. Only 3.7 percent of cabinet-level appointees were black, and only 3.7 percent were women. The Carter administration had more blacks (two) and women (two) in the cabinet than did any other administration.

The political significance of these observations can be debated. One might argue, for example, that social background, educational experience, and corporate ties are poor predictors of decision-making behavior. Even if top administrative officials have homogeneous backgrounds, they often view policy questions very differently. The link between social backgrounds and decision-making behavior is very weak.

Nonetheless, it is an interesting comment on the recruitment process that characteristics of top cabinet officials do not change very much from one administration to the next. Names and faces change, but characteristics of top leaders remain the same.

Given the different social bases of the Democratic and Republican parties, we might expect modest differences in the composition of Democratic and Republican cabinets. But in fact few significant differences exist between members of the four Democratic administrations (Truman, Kennedy, Johnson, Carter) and the four Republican administrations (Eisenhower, Nixon, Ford, Reagan) since World War II. The Republicans are only slightly more "Ivy-League" than the Democrats (55.1% versus 40.0%), and the Democrats tend to recruit more lawyers than the Republicans (44.6% versus 34.8%). The greatest party difference is the Republicans' tendency to call upon corporate directors (71.0% of cabinet-level appointees). While Democratic presidents also call upon corporate directors (49.2% of cabinet-level appointees), the difference is statistically significant.

The occupational backgrounds of cabinet-level appointees confirm the homogeneity of Democratic and Republican administrations. About one-quarter of the top posts generally go to lawyers. Almost one-quarter go to corporate executives, with Republican appointees more likely to be corporate executives (30.4%) than Democratic appointees (15.4%). About 15 percent of the Republican appointees have based their careers on public office; Democratic appointees are more likely to have centered their careers in government (20.0%) than are Republican appointees (11.6%).

Universities have contributed about 18 percent of cabinet-level appointees since World War II, nearly all of whom earned a Ph.D. Economics is the leading field of study among academics in cabinet-level positions. The Carter administration had more Ph.D.s (seven) than any other; the Truman administration had none. Reagan has already accepted the resignation of one of his academics (National Security Advisor Richard Allen); his others are UN Representative Jeanne Kirkpatrick and CEA Chairman Murray Weidenbaum.

(*continued*)

Cabinet-level recruitment in the Reagan administration clearly fits the-pattern of other administrations. We may lament the absence of pluralism in the social character of the nation's elites, but the Reaganauts are no different than previous administrators in their corporate ties, government experience, Ivy League connections, and educational credentials. (See table 1-1.)

TABLE 1-1   The Reaganauts in perspective

	Reaganauts	Total	Democratic	Republican
Previous government posts	68.4%	79.1%	81.5%	76.8%
Previous corporate posts	73.7	60.4	49.2	71.0
Education				
Advanced degree	68.4	69.4	76.9	65.2
Law degree	26.3	39.5	44.6	34.8
Ivy League	57.9	47.8	40.0	55.1
Harvard	26.3	23.9	23.1	24.6
Ph.D.s	15.8	18.6	20.0	18.2
No degree	0	0	0	0
Average age	55.1	52.5	50.4	54.5
Women	5.3	3.7	3.1	4.4
Blacks	5.3	3.7	4.6	3.0
Occupation				
Law	11.1	28.3	32.3	24.6
Big business	26.3	23.1	15.4	30.4
Small business	5.3	5.2	1.5	9.1
Government/public office	15.8	15.7	20.0	11.6
Academia	15.8	18.6	21.5	15.9
Agriculture	5.3	2.2	1.5	3.0
Military	5.3	3.0	3.1	3.0
Other	5.3	3.7	4.6	3.0

NOTES

1. Robert A. Dahl, "Power, Pluralism, and Democracy: A Modest Proposal," paper delivered at American Political Science Association annual meeting, 1964, p. 3. See also Peter Bachrach, *The Theory of Democratic Elitism* (Boston: Little, Brown, 1967).
2. Harold Lasswell and Abraham Kaplan, *Power and Society* (New Haven, Conn.: Yale University Press, 1950), p. 219.
3. Gaetano Mosca, *The Ruling Class* (New York: McGraw-Hill, 1939), p. 50.
4. Roberto Michels, *Political Parties: A Sociological Study of the Oligarchical Tendencies of Modern Democracies*, 1915, reprint (New York: Free Press, 1962), p. 70.
5. Harold Lasswell and Daniel Lerner, *The Comparative Study of Elites* (Stanford, Calif.: Stanford University Press, 1952), p. 7.
6. David Truman, "The American System in Crisis," *Political Science Quarterly* 74 (December 1959):489.
7. Richard Hofstadter, *The American Political Tradition* (New York: Knopf, 1948), p. viii.
8. John Dewey, "Democracy and Educational Administration," *School and Society*, April 3, 1937.
9. John Stuart Mill, *Representative Government* (New York: Dutton, Everyman's Library), p. 203.

10. For a discussion of John Locke and the political philosophy underlying democracy, see George Sabine, *A History of Political Theory* (New York: Holt, Rinehart & Winston, 1950), pp. 517–541.

11. Roland Pennock, "Democracy and Leadership," in *Democracy Today*, eds. William Chambers and Robert Salisbury (New York: Dodd, Mead, 1962), pp. 126–127.

12. Aaron Wildavsky, *Leadership in a Small Town* (Totowa, N.J.: Bedminster Press, 1964), p. 20.

13. Robert Presthus, *Men at the Top* (New York: Oxford University Press, 1964), p. 20.

14. Henry Kariel, *The Decline of American Pluralism* (Stanford, Calif.: Stanford University Press, 1961), p. 74.

15. Bachrach, *The Theory of Democratic Elitism: A Critique* (Boston: Little, Brown, 1967), p. xi.

16. Ibid., pp. 47–48.

17. William Kornhauser, *The Politics of Mass Society* (Glencoe, Ill.: Free Press, 1959), p. 99.

18. See Seymour Martin Lipset and Earl Raab, *The Politics of Unreason* (New York: Harper & Row, 1970).

19. See John H. Bunzel, *Anti-Politics in America* (New York: Knopf, 1967).

20. Richard Hofstadter, *The Paranoid Style of American Politics* (New York: Knopf, 1965).

21. Report of the Senate Select Committee on Intelligence, April 23, 1976 (Washington, D.C.: U.S. Government Printing Office, 1976).

SELECTED READINGS

Bachrach, Peter. *The Theory of Democratic Elitism: A Critique.* Boston: Little, Brown, 1967. In addition to giving a good review of classical elitist literature, Bachrach discusses the distinctions among democracy, pluralism, and elitism. He observes that whereas pluralists claim that their model is the practical adaptation of democratic theory to the modern, technological state, pluralism in fact makes so many alterations in democratic theory as to render it unrecognizable. Bachrach coins a new term for the model produced by the combination of democratic theory with group theory; he calls it "democratic elitism." We call it "pluralism."

Bachrach, Peter, and Baratz, Morton. "Two Faces of Power." *American Political Science Review* 56 (1962):947–952. The authors argue that power is tied to decision making but that power also comes from preventing a decision (called a "nondecision"). Thus power has two faces.

Dahl, Robert A. "A Critique of the Ruling Elite Model." *American Political Science Review* 58 (1958):369–463. This essay has become a classic critique of elitism from a pluralist point of view.

Dahl, Robert A. *Pluralist Democracy in the United States: Conflict and Consensus.* Chicago: Rand McNally, 1967. This book is one of the few recent theoretical extensions of pluralism on the national level. Most of Dahl's important theoretical work has been at the community level. This book fills an important gap in pluralist literature.

Debman, Geoffrey. "Nondecisions and Power." *American Political Science Review* 69 (1975):889–900. This article defends pluralism from attacks by "neoelitists" who claim that non–decision making is an important technique of elite dominance. A reply by "neoelitists" Peter Bachrach and Morton S. Baratz follows the article.

Michels, Roberto. *Political Parties: A Sociological Study of the Oligarchical Tendencies of Modern Democracies.* New York: Free Press, 1962. This book first appeared in

1911 in German. Michels was a disciple of Mosca. Like Mosca, he sees elitism as an outcome of social organization. Michels argues that the very fact of organization in society leads inevitably to an elite. His often-quoted thesis is, "Who says organization, says oligarchy." Political scientists have called this "the iron law of oligarchy."

Mosca, Gaetano. *The Ruling Class.* Edited by A. Livingston. New York: McGraw-Hill, 1939. This book was first published in 1896 in Italy. Mosca added to it later in a 1923 edition that reflects the impact of World War I on his ideas. Along with the work of Vilfredo Pareto, Mosca's *Ruling Class* forms the basis of "classical elitism."

Pareto, Vilfredo. *The Mind and Society: Treatise of General Sociology.* New York: Harcourt, Brace & World, 1935 (originally published in 1915–1916 in four volumes). Pareto begins with a very broad definition of elite. He suggests that in any human activity, those who are the top practitioners are the elite in that activity. Thus he groups elites into two classes—the governing elite and the nongoverning elite—depending on whether the activity of which they are a top practitioner is important to government. Pareto also introduces psychological notions into his work. He speaks of "residues," which are human instincts, sentiments, or states of mind, that remain constant over time and from state to state.

Parry, Geraint. *Political Elites.* New York: Praeger, 1969. This book is an excellent discussion of classical elitism. It includes extensive treatment of Mosca, Pareto, Michels, Max Weber, James Burnham, C. Wright Mills, and other elitist writers.

Ricci, David M. *Community Power and Democratic Theory: The Logic of Political Analysis.* New York: Random House, 1971. Here is an excellent review of past and current philosophical, ideological, and methodological differences between elitists and pluralists of each theory, including the contributions of Joseph Schumpeter ("process" theory of democracy), David Truman ("group" theory of democracy), Floyd Hunter ("reputational" theory of elitism), C. Wright Mills ("positional" theory of elitism), and Robert Dahl ("pluralist" theory of democracy). The text also offers an excellent discussion of the present scholarly impasse between advocates of each point of view and an annotated bibliography of relevant literature.

Walker, Jack L. "A Critique of the Elitist Theory of Democracy." *American Political Science Review* 60 (1966):285–295. This critique treats elitism and pluralism as if they were variations of the same theory. Walker argues that both make too many changes in classical democratic theory to allow either to serve as a meaningful model for government.

2 The Founding Fathers: The Nation's First Elite

It was the existence of a national elite and its agreement on the fundamentals of politics that enabled the American government to be founded.

All communities divide themselves into the few and the many. The first are the rich and well-born, the other the masses of people.

—Alexander Hamilton, Records of the Federal Convention of 1787

The Founding Fathers—those fifty-five men who wrote the Constitution of the United States and founded a new nation—were a truly exceptional elite, not only "rich and wellborn" but also educated, talented, and resourceful. When Thomas Jefferson, then the nation's minister in Paris, first saw the list of delegates to the Constitutional Convention of 1787, he wrote to John Adams, the minister to London, "It is really an assembly of demigods."[1] The men at the Convention belonged to the nation's intellectual and economic elites; they were owners of landed estates, important merchants and importers, bankers and financiers, real estate and land speculators, and government bond owners. Jefferson and Adams were among the nation's very few notables who were not at the Constitutional Convention.

The Founding Fathers were not representative of the four million Americans in the new nation, most of whom were small farmers, debtors, tradespeople, frontier dwellers, servants, or slaves. However, to say that these men were not representative of the American people, or that the Constitution was not a very democratic document, does not discredit the Founding Fathers or the Constitution. To the aristocratic society of eighteenth-century Europe, the Founding Fathers were dangerous revolutionaries who were establishing a government in which men with the talent of acquiring property could rise to political power even though not born into the nobility. And the Constitution has survived the test of time, providing the basic framework for an ever-changing society.

Elites and masses in the new nation

Many visitors from the aristocratic countries of Europe noted the absence of an American nobility and commented on the spirit of equality that prevailed. Yet class lines existed in America. At the top of the social structure, a tiny elite dominated the social, cultural, economic, and political life of the new nation. The French chargé d'affaires reported in 1787 that America had "no nobles" but that certain "gentlemen" enjoyed "preeminence" because of "their wealth, their talents, their education, their families, or the offices they hold."[2] Some of these prominent gentlemen were Tories who fled America after the Revolution; but Charleston still had its Pinckneys and Rutledges; Boston its Adamses, Lowells, and Gerrys; New York its Schuylers, Clintons, and Jays; Philadelphia its Morrises, Mifflins, and Ingersolls; Maryland its Jenifers and Carrolls; and Virginia its Blairs and Randolphs.

Below this thin layer of educated and talented merchants, planters, lawyers, and bankers was a substantial body of successful farmers, shopkeepers, and independent artisans—of the "middling" sort, as they were known in Revolutionary America. This early middle class was by no means a majority in the new nation; it stood considerably above the masses of debt-ridden farmers and frontier dwellers who made up most of the population. This small middle class had some political power, even at the time of the Constitutional Convention; it was entitled to vote, and its views were represented in governing circles, even if they did not prevail at the Convention. The middle class was especially well represented in state legislatures and was championed by several men of prominence in the Revolutionary period—Patrick Henry, Luther Martin, and Thomas Jefferson.

The great mass of white Americans in the Revolutionary period were "freeholders," small farmers who worked their own land, scratching out a bare existence for themselves and their families. They had little interest in, or knowledge of, public affairs. Usually the small farmers who were not barred from voting by property-owning or tax-paying qualifications were too preoccupied with debt and subsistence, or too isolated in the wilderness, to vote anyway. Nearly 8 out of 10 Americans made a marginal living in the dirt; 1 in 10 worked in fishing or lumbering; and 1 in 10 worked in commerce in some way, whether as a dockhand, sailor, lawyer, or merchant.

At the bottom of the white social structure in the new Republic were indentured servants and tenant farmers; this class, which was perhaps 20 percent of the population, apparently exercised little, if any, political power. Finally, still further below, were the black slaves. Although they made up almost another 20 percent of the population and were an important component of the American economy, they were considered property, even in a country that proclaimed the natural rights and equality of "all men."

Elite dissatisfaction with the confederation

In July 1775, Benjamin Franklin proposed to the Continental Congress a plan for a "perpetual union"; and, following the Declaration of Independence in 1776, the Congress appointed a committee to consider the

Franklin proposals. The committee, headed by John Dickinson, made its report in the form of the Articles of Confederation, which the Congress debated for more than a year before finally adopting them on November 15, 1777. The Articles of Confederation were not to go into effect until every state approved; Delaware withheld its consent until 1779, Maryland until 1781.

The Articles of Confederation, effective from 1781 to 1789, established a "firm league of friendship" among the states "for their common defense, the security of their liberties, and their mutual and general welfare." The document reassured each state of "its sovereignty, freedom, and independence, and every power, jurisdiction, and right, which is not by this confederation expressly delegated to the United States, in Congress assembled." The confederation's delegated powers included power to declare war, to send and receive ambassadors, to make treaties, to fix standards of weights and measures, to regulate the value of coins, to manage Indian affairs, to establish post offices, to borrow money, to build and equip an army and navy, and to make requisitions (requests) to the several states for money and people. Certain powers remained with the states, including two of the most important ones of government: to regulate commerce and to levy taxes. Moreover, Congress had no authority to compel the states to honor its requisitions for revenues. Since Congress could not regulate commerce, the states were free to protect local trade and commerce even at the expense of the emerging national economy.

Thus the United States under the Articles of Confederation was comparable to an international organization of thirteen separate and independent governments. At this time Americans viewed the national government as an alliance of separate *states*, not a government "of the people"; and the powers of the national government depended on state governments.

The Founding Fathers were very critical of the first government of the United States under the Articles of Confederation, but the government was not a failure. Between 1774 and 1789, the American Confederation declared its independence from the world's most powerful colonial nation, fought a successful war, established a viable peace, won powerful allies in the international community, created a successful army and navy, established a postal system, created a national bureaucracy, and laid the foundations for national unity.

But despite the successes of the confederation in war and diplomatic relations, the American elites found the political arrangements under the Articles unsatisfactory, even threatening. Generally the Founding Fathers most lamented the "weaknesses" of the Articles that allowed political arrangements threatening the interests of merchants, investors, planters, real estate developers, and owners of public bonds and securities.

The inability of Congress to levy taxes under the Articles of Confederation was a serious threat to those patriots who had given financial backing to the new nation during the Revolutionary War. The Continental Congress and the states had financed the war with money borrowed through the issuance of government bonds. Congress was unable to tax the people to pay off these debts; and the states became less and less inclined, as time passed, to meet their obligations to the central government. The states paid only one-tenth the sums requisitioned by Congress under the Articles; and during the last years of the Articles, the United States was unable even to pay interest on its debt. As a result, the bonds and notes of the U.S. government lost most of their value, sometimes selling on the open market for only one-tenth their original value. Investors who had backed the American war effort were left with nearly worthless bonds.

Without the power to tax and with the credit of the United States ruined, the prospects of the central government for future financial support—and survival—looked dim. Naturally the rich planters, merchants, and investors who owned government bonds had a direct financial interest in helping the U.S. government acquire the power to tax and to pay off its debts.

The inability of Congress under the Articles to regulate commerce among the states and with foreign nations, and the states' practice of laying tariffs on the goods of other states as well as on those of foreign nations, created havoc among commercial and shipping interests. "In every point of view," Madison wrote in 1785, "the trade of this country is in a deplorable condition."[3] The American Revolution had been fought, in part, to defend American commercial and business interests from oppressive regulations by the British government. Now the states themselves were interfering with the development of a national economy. Merchants and shippers with a view toward a national market and a high level of commerce were vitally concerned that the U.S. government acquire the power to regulate interstate commerce and to prevent the states from imposing crippling tariffs and restrictions on interstate trade.

State governments under the Articles posed a serious threat to investors and creditors through issuing cheap paper money and passing laws impairing contractual obligations. Paper money issued by the states permitted debtors to pay off their creditors with money worth less than the money originally loaned. Even the most successful farmers were usually heavily in debt, and many of these farmers were gaining strength in state legislatures. They threatened to pass laws delaying the collection of debts and even abolishing the prevailing practice of imprisonment for unpaid debts. Obviously creditors had a direct financial interest in establishing a strong central government that could prevent the states from issuing public paper or otherwise interfering with debt collection.

A strong central government would help protect creditors against social upheavals by the large debtor class in America. In several states, debtors had already engaged in open rebellion against tax collectors and sheriffs attempting to repossess farms on behalf of creditors. The most serious rebellion broke out in the summer of 1786 in Massachusetts, when bands of insurgents—composed of farmers, artisans, and laborers—captured the courthouses in several western districts and briefly held the city of Springfield. Led by Daniel Shays, a veteran of Bunker Hill, the insurgent army posed a direct military threat to the governing elite of Massachusetts. Shays's Rebellion was put down by a smaller mercenary army, paid for by well-to-do citizens who feared a wholesale attack on property rights.

The states' growing radicalism intimidated the propertied classes, who began to advocate a strong central government to "insure domestic tranquility," guarantee "a republican form of government," and protect property "against domestic violence." The American Revolution had disturbed the masses' tradition of deferring to those in authority. Extremists, like Thomas Paine, who reasoned that it was right and proper to revolt against England because of political tyranny might also call for revolt against creditors because of economic tyranny. If debts owed to British merchants could be legislated out of existence, why not also the debts owed to American merchants? Acts of violence, boycotts, tea parties, and attacks on tax collectors frightened all propertied people in America.

A strong central government with enough military power to oust the British from the Northwest and to protect western settlers against Indian attacks could open the way for the development of the American West. In addition, the protection and settlement of western land would cause land values to skyrocket and make land speculators rich.

Men of property in early America very actively speculated in western land. George Washington, Benjamin Franklin, Robert Morris, and even the popular hero Patrick Henry were involved in land speculation. During the Revolutionary War, the Congress had often paid the Continental soldiers with land certificates. After the war, most of the ex-soldiers sold these certificates to land speculators at very low prices. The confederation's military weakness along its frontiers had kept the value of western lands low, for ravaging Indians discouraged immigration to the lands west of the Alleghenies, and the British threatened to cut off westward expansion by continuing to occupy (in defiance of the peace treaty) seven important fur-trading forts in the Northwest. The British forts were also becoming centers of anti-American influence among the Indians.

The development of a strong American navy was also important to American commercial interests, for the states seemed ineffective in preventing smuggling, and piracy was a very real danger and a vital concern of American shippers.

Manufacturing was still in its infant stages during the Revolutionary era in America, but farsighted investors were anxious to protect infant American industries against the import of British goods. Although all thirteen states erected tariff barriers against foreign goods, state tariffs could

© Bo Brown/ROTHCO.

"We probably won't live here . . . we just want it for an investment!"

not provide the same protection for industry as a strong central government with a uniform tariff policy, because the state tariff system allowed low-tariff states to bring in foreign goods and circulate them throughout the country.

Finally, a strong sense of nationalism appeared to motivate America's elites. While the masses focused on local affairs, the educated and cosmopolitan leaders in America were concerned about the weakness of America in the international community. Thirteen separate states failed to manifest a sense of national purpose and identity. The United States were held in contempt not only by Britain, as evidenced by the violations of the Treaty of Paris, but even by the lowly Barbary states. Hamilton expressed the indignation of America's leadership over its inability to swing weight in the world community:

> There is something . . . diminutive and contemptible in the prospect of a number of petty states, with the appearance only of union, jarring, jealous, and perverse, without any determined direction, fluctuating and unhappy at home, weak and insignificant by their dissentions in the eyes of other nations.[4]

In short, America's elite wanted to assume a respectable role in the international community and exercise power in world affairs.

Formation of a national elite

In the spring of 1785, delegates from Virginia and Maryland met at Alexandria, Virginia, to resolve certain difficulties that had arisen between the two states over the regulation of commerce and navigation on the Potomac River and Chesapeake Bay. It was fortunate for the new nation that the most prominent man in America, George Washington, took a personal interest in this meeting. As a rich planter and land speculator, who owned over 30,000 acres of western lands upstream on the Potomac, Washington was keenly aware of commercial problems under the Articles. He lent great prestige to the Alexandria meeting by inviting participants to his home at Mount Vernon. Out of this conference came the idea for a general economic conference for all of the states. The Virginia legislature issued a call for such a convention to meet at Annapolis in September 1786.

Judged by its publicly announced purpose—securing interstate agreement on matters of commerce and navigation—the Annapolis Convention was a failure; only twelve delegates appeared, representing five commercial states: New York, New Jersey, Pennsylvania, Delaware, and Virginia. But these twelve men saw the opportunity to use the Annapolis meeting to achieve greater political successes. Alexander Hamilton, with masterful political foresight, persuaded the others in attendance to strike out for a full constitutional solution to America's ills. The Annapolis Convention adopted a report, written by Hamilton, that outlined the defects in the Articles of Confederation and called upon the states to send delegates to a new convention to suggest remedies for these defects. The new convention was to meet in May 1787 in Philadelphia. Rumors at the time suggested that Hamilton, with the behind-the-scenes support of James Madison in the Virginia legislature, had intended all along that the Annapolis Convention fail in its stated purposes and that it provide a stepping-stone to larger political objectives.

Shays's Rebellion was very timely for men like Hamilton and Madison, who sought to galvanize America's elite into action. Occurring in the fall of 1786, after the Annapolis call for a new convention, the rebellion convinced men of property in Congress and state legislatures that there was cause for alarm.

On February 21, 1787, Congress confirmed the call for a convention to meet in Philadelphia

for the sole and express purpose of revising the Articles of Confederation and reporting to Congress and the several legislatures such alterations and provisions therein as shall, when agreed to in Congress and confirmed by the states, render the federal Constitution adequate to the exigencies of government and the preservation of the union.

Delegates to the Convention were appointed by the legislatures of every state except Rhode Island, the only state in which the debtor classes had won political control.

The fifty-five men who met in the summer of 1787 to establish a new national government quickly chose George Washington, their most prestigious member—indeed the most prestigious man on the continent—to preside over the assembly. Just as quickly, the Convention decided to hold its sessions behind closed doors and to keep all proceedings a carefully guarded secret. Delegates adhered closely to this decision and informed neither close friends nor relatives of the nature of the discussions. Apparently the Founding Fathers were aware that elites are most effective in negotiation, compromise, and decision making when operating in secrecy.

The Convention was quick to discard its congressional mandate to "revise the Articles of Confederation"; and without much hesitation, it proceeded to write an entirely new constitution. Only men confident of their powers and abilities, men of principle and property, could proceed in this bold fashion. Thus let us examine the characteristics of the nation's first elite more closely.

One cannot overestimate the prestige of George Washington at this time in his life. As the commander in chief of the successful Revolutionary army and founder of the new nation, he had overwhelming charismatic appeal among both elites and masses. Preeminent not only as a soldier, statesman, and founder of the nation, he was also one of the richest men in the United States. Despite all the years that he had spent in the Revolutionary cause, he had refused any payment for his services. He often paid his soldiers from his own fortune. In addition to his large estate on the Potomac, he possessed many thousands of acres of undeveloped land in western Virginia, Maryland, Pennsylvania, Kentucky, and the Northwest Territory. He owned major shares in the Potomac Company, the James River Company, the Bank of Columbia, and the Bank of Alexandria. And he held large amounts in U.S. bonds and securities. Washington stood at the apex of America's elite structure.

The Founding Fathers had extensive experience in governing. These same men had made all the key decisions in American history from the Stamp Act Congress to the Declaration of Independence to the Articles of Confederation. They controlled the Congress of the United States and had conducted the Revolutionary War. Eight delegates had signed the Declaration of Independence. Eleven delegates had served as officers in Washington's army. Forty-two of the fifty-five Founding Fathers had already served in the U.S. Congress. Even at the moment of the Convention, more than forty delegates held high offices in state governments; Franklin, Livingston, and Randolph were governors. The Founding Fathers were unsurpassed in political skill and experience.

In an age when no more than a handful of men on the North American continent had gone to college, the Founding Fathers were conspicuous for their educational attainment. Over half the delegates had been educated at Princeton, Yale, Harvard, Columbia, Pennsylvania, or William and Mary, or in England. The tradition of legal training for political decision makers, which has continued in America to the present, was already evident. About a dozen delegates were still active lawyers in 1787, and about three dozen had legal training.

The fifty-five men at Philadelphia formed a major part of the nation's economic elite as well. The personal wealth represented at the meeting was enormous. It is difficult to determine accurately who were the richest men in America at this time because the finances of the period were chaotic and because wealth assumed a variety of forms—land, ships, credit, slaves, business inventories, bonds, and paper money of uncertain worth (even George Washington had difficulty at times converting his land wealth into cash). But at least forty of the fifty-five delegates were known to be holders of government bonds; fourteen were land speculators; twenty-four were money-lenders and investors; eleven were engaged in commerce or manufacturing; and fifteen owned large plantations.[5] (See table 2-1.)

Robert Morris was perhaps the foremost business and financial leader in the nation in 1787. This Philadelphia merchant owned scores of ships

TABLE 2-1   Founding Fathers' known membership in elite groups

| Holders of public security interests | | Real estate and land speculators | Lenders and investors | Merchants, manufac- turers, and shippers | Planters and slaveholders |
Major	Minor				
Baldwin	Bassett	Blount	Bassett	Broom	Butler
Blair	Blount	Dayton	Broom	Clymer	Davie
Clymer	Brearley	Few	Butler	Ellsworth	Jenifer
Dayton	Broom	Fitzsimons	Carroll	Fitzsimons	A. Martin
Ellsworth	Butler	Franklin	Clymer	Gerry	L. Martin
Fitzsimons	Carroll	Gerry	Davie	King	Mason
Gerry	Few	Gilman	Dickinson	Langdon	Mercer
Gilman	Hamilton	Gorham	Ellsworth	McHenry	C.C. Pinckney
Gorham	L. Martin	Hamilton	Few	Mifflin	C. Pinckney
Jenifer	Mason	Mason	Fitzsimons	G. Morris	Randolph
Johnson	Mercer	R. Morris	Franklin	R. Morris	Read
King	Mifflin	Washington	Gilman		Rutledge
Langdon	Read	Williamson	Ingersoll		Spaight
Lansing	Spaight	Wilson	Johnson		Washington
Livingston	Wilson		King		Wythe
McClurg	Wythe		Langdon		
R. Morris			Mason		
C.C. Pinckney			McHenry		
C. Pinckney			C.C. Pinckney		
Randolph			C. Pinckney		
Sherman			Randolph		
Strong			Read		
Washington			Washington		
Williamson			Williamson		

that traded throughout the world; he engaged in iron manufacturing, speculated in land in all parts of the country, and controlled the Bank of North America in Philadelphia, probably the nation's largest financial institution at the time. He earned his title "the patriot financier" by underwriting a large share of the debts of the United States during and after the Revolutionary War. Later in his life, his financial empire collapsed, probably because of overspeculation, and he died in debt. But at the time of the Convention, he stood at the apex of America's financial structure.

Perhaps what most distinguished the men at Philadelphia from the masses was their cosmopolitanism. They approached political, economic, and military issues from a "continental" point of view. Unlike the masses, members of the elite extended their loyalties beyond their states; they experienced the sentiment of nationalism half a century before it would begin to seep down to the masses.[6]

Elite consensus in 1787

By focusing on the debates within the Convention, many historical scholars have overemphasized the differences of opinion among the Founding Fathers. True, the convention was the site of many conflicting views and innumerable compromises; yet the more striking fact is that the delegates were in almost complete accord on essential political questions.

Protecting liberty and property

They agreed that the fundamental end of government is the protection of liberty and property. They accepted without debate many of the precedents set by the English constitution and by the constitutions of the new states. Reflecting the advanced ideas of their times, the Founding Fathers were much less religious than most Americans today. Yet they believed in a law of nature with rules of abstract justice to which human laws should conform. They believed that this law of nature endowed each person with certain inalienable rights essential to a meaningful existence—the rights to life, liberty, and property—and that these rights should be recognized and protected by law. They believed that all people were equally entitled to respect of their natural rights regardless of their station in life. Most Founding Fathers were even aware that this belief ran contrary to the practice of slavery and were embarrassed by this inconsistency in American life.

But "equality" did *not* mean to the Founding Fathers that people were equal in wealth, intelligence, talent, or virtue. They accepted inequalities in wealth and property as a natural product of human diversity. They did not believe that government had a responsibility to reduce these inequalities; in fact, they saw "dangerous leveling" as a serious violation of the right to property and the right to use and dispose of the fruits of one's own industry. On the contrary, they felt it was the very function of government to protect property and to prevent "leveling" influences from reducing the natural inequalities of wealth and power.

Government as contract

The Founding Fathers agreed that the origin of government is an implied contract among people. They believed that people pledge allegiance and obedience to government in return for protection of their natural rights, the maintenance of peace, and protection from foreign invasion. They felt that the ultimate legitimacy of government—sovereignty—rests with the people themselves and not with gods or kings and that the basis of government is the consent of the governed.

Republicanism

The Founding Fathers believed in republican government. They opposed hereditary monarchies, the prevailing form of government in the world at the time. Although they believed that people of principle and property should govern, they were opposed to an aristocracy or a governing nobility. To them, a "republican government" was a representative, responsible, and nonhereditary government. But they certainly did *not* mean mass democracy, with direct participation by the people in decision making. They expected the masses to consent to government by men of principle and property, out of recognition for their abilities, talents, education, and stake in the preservation of liberty and order. The Founding Fathers believed that the masses should have only a limited role in selecting government leaders. They bickered over how much direct participation is appropriate in selecting decision makers and they bickered over the qualifications of public office, but they generally agreed that the masses should have only a limited, indirect role in selecting decision makers and that decision makers themselves should be men of wealth, education, and proven leadership ability.

Limited government

The Founding Fathers believed in limited government that could not threaten liberty or property. Since the Founding Fathers believed that power is a corrupting influence and that the concentration of power is dangerous, they believed in dividing government power into separate bodies capable of checking, or thwarting, each other should any one branch pose a threat to liberty or property. Differences of opinion among honest people, particularly differences among elites in separate states, could best be resolved by balancing representation of these several elites in the national government and by creating a decentralized system that permits local elites to govern their states as they see fit, with limited interference from the national government.

The laissez-faire principles of Adam Smith were *not* part of elite consensus in 1787. Quite the contrary, the men who wrote the Constitution believed that government had the obligation not only to protect private property but also to nourish it. They expected government to foster trade and commerce, protect manufacturing, assist in land development, and provide other positive economic assistance. And to protect the rights of property, they expected government to enforce contracts, maintain a stable money supply, punish thievery, assist in the collection of debts, record property ownership in deeds, punish counterfeiting and piracy, protect copyrights and patents, regulate the value of money, establish courts, and regulate banking and commerce.

Nationalism

Finally, and perhaps most importantly, the Founding Fathers believed that only a strong national government, with power to exercise its will directly on the people, could "establish justice, insure domestic tranquility, provide for the common defense, promote the general welfare, and secure the blessings of liberty."

This consensus on fundamentals dwarfed the differences requiring compromise in the Convention. It was the existence of a national elite and its agreement on the fundamentals of politics that made possible the formation of the American government. If the elites had faced substantial divisiveness in 1787, any substantial competition or conflict, or any divergent centers of influence, a new government would never have emerged from the Philadelphia convention. Elite consensus in 1787 was profoundly conservative; it wished to preserve the status quo in the distribution of power and property in America. Yet at the same time, this elite consensus was radical compared with the beliefs of other elites in the world at this time. Nearly every other government adhered to the principles of hereditary monarchy and privileged nobility, while American elites were committed to republicanism. Other elites asserted the divine right of kings, while American elites talked about government by the consent of the governed. While the elites in Europe rationalized and defended a rigid caste system, American elites believed in equality in inalienable human rights.

An elite in operation: conciliation and compromise

On May 25, 1787, sessions of the Constitutional Convention opened in Independence Hall, Philadelphia. After the delegates selected Washington as president of the Convention and decided to keep the proceedings of the Convention secret, Governor Edmund Randolph, speaking for the Virginia delegation, presented a draft of a new constitution.*

Representation compromise

The Virginia plan gave little recognition to the states in its proposed composition of the national government. The plan suggested a two-house legislature, the lower house to be chosen by the people of the states, with representation according to the population. The upper house was to be chosen by the first house. This Congress would have power to "legislate in all cases in which the separate states are incompetent, or in which the harmony of the United States may be interrupted by the exercise of individual legislation." Moreover, Congress would have the authority to nullify state laws that it felt violated the Constitution, thus ensuring national supremacy. The Virginia plan also proposed a parliamentary form of government, with Congress choosing members of the executive and judiciary branches.

The most important line of cleavage at the Convention was between elites of large states and elites of small states over the representation scheme in the Virginia plan. This question was not one of economic interest or ideology, since delegates from large and small states did not divide along economic or ideological lines. But the Virginia plan did not provide certainty that elites from small states would secure membership in the upper house of the legislature.

After several weeks of debate over the Virginia plan, delegates from the small states presented a counterproposal in a report by William Paterson of New Jersey. The New Jersey plan may have been merely a tactic by the small state elites to force the Convention to compromise on representation, for the plan was set aside after only a week of debate with little negative reaction from the small state delegates. The New Jersey plan proposed to retain the representation scheme outlined in the Articles of Confederation, which granted each state a single vote. But the plan went further to propose separate executive and judiciary branches and expansion of the powers of Congress to include the right to levy taxes and regulate commerce.

The New Jersey plan was not an attempt to retain the confederation. Indeed the plan included words that later appeared in the Constitution itself as the famous national supremacy clause that provided that the U.S. Constitution and federal law superseded each state's constitution and laws. Thus even the small states did not envision a confederation.

*James Madison kept secret notes on the Convention, which he published many years later. Most of our knowledge about the Convention comes from Madison's notes. See Max Ferrand, ed., *The Records of the Federal Convention of 1787* (New Haven, Conn.: Yale University Press, 1911).

Both the Virginia and New Jersey plans were designed to strengthen the national government; they differed only on how much to strengthen it and on its system of representation.

On June 29, William Samuel Johnson of Connecticut proposed the obvious compromise: *that representation in the lower house of Congress be based upon population, whereas representation in the upper house would be equal—two senators from each state.* The Connecticut compromise also provided that equal representation of states in the Senate could not be abridged, even by constitutional amendment.

Slavery compromises

The next question requiring compromise was that of slavery and the role of slaves in the system of representation, an issue closely related to economic differences among America's elite. It was essentially the same question that seventy-five years later divided that elite and pro-voked the nation's bloodiest war. Planters and slaveholders generally believed that wealth, particularly wealth in slaves, should count in apportioning representation. Nonslaveholders felt that "the people" should include only free inhabitants. The decision to apportion direct taxes among the states in proportion to population opened the way to compromise, since the attitudes of slaveholders and nonslaveholders reversed when counting people in order to apportion taxes. The result was the famous three-fifths compromise: *three-fifths of the slaves of each state would be counted for the purposes both of representation and appor-tioning direct taxes.*

A compromise was also necessary on the question of trading in slaves. On this issue, the men of Maryland and Virginia, states already well supplied with slaves, were able to indulge in the luxury of conscience and support proposals for banning the further import of slaves. But the less-developed southern states, particularly South Carolina and Geor-gia, could not afford this posture since they still wanted additional slave labor. Inasmuch as the southern planters were themselves divided, the ultimate compromise permitted Congress to *prohibit slave trade—but not before the year 1808.* This twenty-year delay would allow the undevel-oped southern states to acquire all the slaves they needed before the slave trade ended.

Export tax compromise

Agreement between southern planters and northern merchants was still relatively easy to achieve at this early date in American history. But latent conflict was evident on issues other than slavery. Although all elite groups agreed that the national government should regulate inter-state and foreign commerce, southern planters feared that the unre-stricted power of Congress over commerce might lead to the imposition of export taxes. Export taxes would bear most heavily on the southern states, which depended on foreign markets to buy indigo, rice, tobacco, and cotton. However, planters and merchants were able to compromise again in resolving this issue: *articles exported from any state should bear no tax or duty.*

Voter qualification compromise

Another important compromise, one that occupied much of the Convention's time (though it has received little recognition from later writers), concerned qualifications for voting and holding office in the new government. Although no property qualifications for voters or office-holders appear in the text of the Constitution, the debates revealed that members of the Convention generally favored property qualifications for officeholding. The delegates showed little enthusiasm for mass participation in democracy. Elbridge Gerry of Massachusetts declared that "the evils we experience flow from the excess of democracy." Roger Sherman protested that "the people immediately should have as little to do as may be about the government." Edmund Randolph continually deplored the turbulence and follies of democracy, and George Clymer's notion of republican government was that "a representative of the people is appointed to think for and not with his constituents." John Dickinson considered property qualifications a "necessary defense against the dangerous influence of those multitudes without property and without principle, with which our country like all others, will in time abound." Gouverneur Morris also insisted upon property qualifications: "Give the votes to the people who have no property and they will sell them to the rich who will be able to buy them." Charles Pinckney later wrote to Madison, "Are you not . . . abundantly depressed at the theoretical nonsense of an election of Congress by the people; in the first instance, it's clearly and practically wrong, and it will in the end be the means of bringing our councils into contempt." Many more such elitist statements appear in the records of the Convention.[7]

Given these views, how do we explain the absence of property qualifications in the Constitution? Actually a motion was carried in the Convention instructing a committee to fix property qualifications for officeholding, but the committee could not agree upon the qualifications to be imposed. Various propositions to establish property qualifications met defeat on the floor, not because delegates believed they were inherently wrong but, interestingly enough, because the elites at the Convention represented different kinds of property holdings. Madison pointed out this fact in the July debate, noting that a land ownership requirement would exclude from Congress the mercantile and manufacturing classes, who would hardly be willing to turn their money into landed property just to make them eligible for a seat in Congress. Madison rightly observed that "landed possessions were no certain evidence of real wealth. Many enjoyed them to a great extent who were more in debt than they were worth." The objections by merchants and investors defeated the "landed" qualification for congressional representatives. The delegates also struck down a motion to disqualify from public office people with "unsettled accounts" with the United States (an early-day version of a conflict-of-interests law).

Thus the Convention approved the Constitution *without property qualifications on voters, except those that the states themselves might see fit to impose.* Failing to come to a decision on this issue of suffrage, the delegates merely returned the question to state legislatures by providing that "the electors in each state should have the qualifications requisite for electors of the most numerous branch of the state legislatures." At the time, this expedient course of action did not seem likely to produce mass democracy. Only one branch of the new government, the House of Representatives, was to be elected by popular vote. The other three controlling bodies—the president, the Senate, and the Supreme Court—were removed from direct voter participation. The delegates were reassured that nearly all the state constitutions then in force included property qualifications for voters.

Finally, the Constitution did not recognize women as legitimate participants in government. For nearly one hundred years, no state accorded women the right to vote. (The newly formed Wyoming Territory first gave women the right to vote and hold public office in 1869.) Not until 1920 was the U.S. Constitution amended to guarantee women the right to vote.

The Constitution as an elitist document

The text of the Constitution, together with interpretive materials in *The Federalist* papers written by Hamilton, Madison, and Jay, provides ample evidence that elites in America benefited both politically and economically from the adoption of the Constitution. Although both elites and nonelites—indeed all Americans—may have benefited from the Constitution, elites benefited more directly and immediately than did nonelites. And we can infer that the elites would not have developed and supported the Constitution if they had not stood to gain substantially from it.

Elite philosophy

We can discover the elitist consensus by examining the underlying philosophy of government contained in the Constitution. According to Madison in *The Federalist*, "the principal task of modern legislation" was to control factions.[8] A *faction* is a number of citizens united by a common interest averse to the interest of other citizens or of the community as a whole. The causes of factions lie in human diversity:

> A zeal for different opinions concerning religion, concerning government, and many other points, as well of speculation as of practice; an attachment to different leaders ambitiously contending for preeminence and power; or to persons of other descriptions whose fortunes have been interesting to human passions.

Factions arise primarily because of inequality in the control of economic resources:

> But the most common and durable source of factions has been the various and unequal distribution of property. Those who hold and those who are without property have ever formed distinct interests in society. Those who are creditors and those who are debtors fall under like discrimination. A landed interest, a manufacturing interest, a mercantile interest, a monied interest, with many lesser interests, grow up of necessity in civilized nations, and divide them into different classes, actuated by different sentiments and views. [*Federalist* Number 10]

In Madison's view, a national government is the most important protection against mass movements that might threaten property. By creating such a government, encompassing a large number of citizens and a great expanse of territory,

> you take in a greater variety of parties and interests; you make it less probable that a majority of the whole will have a common motive to invade the rights of other citizens; or if such a common motive exists it will be more difficult for all who feel it to discover their own strength, and to act in unison with each other.

The structure of the new national government should ensure suppression of "factious" issues (those that would generate factions). And Madison did not hedge in naming these factious issues: "A rage for paper money, for an abolition of debts, for an equal division of property, or any other improper or wicked project." Note that Madison's factious issues are all challenges to the dominant economic elites. His defense of the new Constitution was that its republican and federal features would help keep certain threats to property from ever becoming public issues. In short, the Founding Fathers deliberately designed the new American government to make it difficult for any mass political movement to challenge property rights.

Impact of the Constitution on elites

Now let us examine the text of the Constitution itself and its impact on American elites. Article I, Section 8, grants seventeen types of power to Congress, followed by a general grant of power to make "all laws which shall be necessary and proper for carrying into execution the foregoing powers."

Levying taxes. The first and perhaps most important power is the "power to lay and collect taxes, duties, imposts, and exercises." The taxing power is the basis of all other powers, and it enabled the national government to end its dependence upon states. This power was essential to the holders of public securities, particularly when combined with the provision in Article VI that "all the debts contracted and engagements entered into before the adoption of this Constitution shall be valid against the United States under this Constitution as under the Confederation." Thus the national government must pay off all those investors who hold bonds of the United States, and the taxing power would enable it to do this on its own.

The text of the Constitution suggests that the Founding Fathers intended Congress to place most of the tax burden on consumers in the form of custom duties and excise taxes rather than direct taxes on individual income or property. Article I, Section 2, states that government can levy direct taxes only on the basis of population; it follows that it could not levy such taxes in proportion to wealth. This provision prevented the national government from levying progressive income taxes; not until the Sixteenth Amendment in 1913 did this protection for wealth disappear from the Constitution.

Southern planters, whose livelihoods depended on the export of indigo, rice, tobacco, and cotton, strenuously opposed giving the national government the power to tax exports. Article I, Section 9, offered protection for their interests: "No tax or duty shall be laid on goods exported from any state." However, Congress was given the power to tax imports so that northern manufacturers could erect a tariff wall to protect American industries against foreign goods.

Regulating commerce.   Congress also had the power to "regulate commerce with foreign nations and among the several states." The interstate commerce clause, together with the provision in Article I, Section 9, prohibiting the states from taxing either imports or exports, created a free trade area over the thirteen states. This was a very beneficial arrangement for American merchants.

Protecting money and property.   Following the powers to tax and spend, to borrow money, and to regulate commerce in Article I, is a series of specific powers designed to enable Congress to protect money and property. Congress is given the power to make bankruptcy laws, to coin money and regulate its value, to fix standards of weights and measures, to punish counterfeiting, to establish post offices and post roads, to pass copyright and patent laws to protect authors and inventors, and to punish piracies and felonies committed on the high seas. Each of these powers is a specific asset to bankers, investors, and shippers, respectively. Obviously the Founding Fathers felt that giving Congress control over currency and credit in America would result in better protection for financial interests than would leaving the essential responsibility to the states. Similarly, they believed that control over communication and transportation (by establishing post offices and post roads) was too essential to trade and commerce to be left to the states.

Creating the military.   The remaining powers in Article I deal with military affairs: raising and supporting armies; organizing, training, and calling up the state militia; declaring war; suppressing insurrections; and repelling invasions. These powers in Article I—together with the provisions in Article II making the president the commander in chief of the army and navy and of the state militia when called into the federal service; and giving the president power to make treaties with the advice and consent of the Senate, and to send and receive ambassadors—all combined to centralize diplomatic and military affairs at the national level. Article I, Section 10, confirms this centralization of diplomatic-military power by prohibiting the states from entering into treaties with foreign nations, maintaining ships of war, or engaging in war unless actually invaded.

Clearly the Founding Fathers had little confidence in the state militia, particularly when it was under state control; General Washington's painful experiences with state militia during the Revolutionary War were still fresh in his memory. The militia had proven adequate when defending their own states against invasion, but when employed outside their own states, they were often a disaster. Moreover, if western settlers were to be protected from the Indians and if the British were to be persuaded to give up their forts in Ohio and open the way to westward expansion, the national government could not rely upon state militia but must have an army of its own. Similarly, a strong navy was essential to the protection of American commerce on the seas (the first significant naval action under the new government was against the piracy of the Barbary states). Thus a national army and navy were not so much protection against invasion (for many years the national government continued to rely primarily upon state militia for this purpose) as they were protection and promotion of the government's commercial and territorial ambitions.

Protecting against revolution.   A national army and navy, as well as an organized and trained militia that could be called into national service, also provided protection against class wars and debtors' rebellions. In an obvious reference to Shays's Rebellion, Hamilton warned in *The Federalist* Number 21:

> The tempestuous situation from which Massachusetts has scarcely emerged evinces that dangers of this kind are not merely speculative. Who could determine what might have been the issue of her late convulsions if the malcontents had been headed by a Caesar or a Cromwell? A strong military force in the hands of the national government is a protection against revolutionary action.

Further evidence of the Founding Fathers' intention to protect the governing classes from revolution is found in Article IV, Section 4, where the national government guarantees to every state "a republican form of government" as well as protection against "domestic violence." Thus in addition to protecting western land and commerce on the seas, a strong army and navy would enable the national government to back up its pledge to protect governing elites in the states from violence and revolution.

Protection against domestic insurrection also appealed to the southern slaveholders' deep-seated fear of a slave revolt. Madison drove this point home in *The Federalist* Number 23:

> I take no little notice of an unhappy species of population abounding in some of the states who, during the calm of regular government were sunk below the level of men; but who, in the tempestuous seeds of civil violence, may emerge into human character and give a superiority of strength to any party with which they may associate themselves.

Protecting slavery.   As we have noted, the Constitution permitted Congress to outlaw the import of slaves after 1808. But most southern planters were more interested in protecting their existing property and slaves than they were in extending the slave trade, and the Constitution provided an explicit advantage to slaveholders in Article IV, Section 2:

> No person held to service or labor in one state, under the laws thereof, escaping into another, shall, in consequence of any law or regulation thereof, be discharged from such service or labor, but shall be delivered upon claim of the party to whom such service or labor may be due.

This provision was an extremely valuable protection for one of the most important forms of property in America at the time. Although slave trade lapsed in America after twenty years, slavery itself, as a domestic institution, was better safeguarded under the new Constitution than under the Articles.

Limiting states in monetary affairs.   The restrictions placed upon state legislatures by the Constitution also provided protection to economic elites in the new nation. States could not coin money, issue paper money, or pass legal-tender laws that would make any money other than gold or silver coin tender in the payment of debts. This restriction would prevent the states from issuing cheap paper money, which debtors could use to pay off creditors with less valuable currency. Moreover, the states were prohibited from passing legal-tender laws obliging creditors to accept paper money in payment of debts.

Limiting states in business affairs.   The Constitution also prevents states from passing any law "impairing the obligation of contracts." The structure of business relations in a free-enterprise economy depends on government enforcement of private contracts, and economic elites seek to prevent government from relieving people of their contractual obligations. If state legislatures could relieve debtors of their contractual obligations, or relieve indentured servants of their obligations to their masters, or prevent creditors from foreclosing on mortgages, or declare moratoriums on debt, or otherwise interfere with business obligations, the interests of investors, merchants, and creditors would be seriously damaged.

Elitism and the structure of the national government

National supremacy.   The heart of the Constitution is the supremacy clause of Article VI:

> This Constitution, and the laws of the United States which shall be made in pursuance thereof, and all treaties made, or which shall be made, under the authority of the United States, shall be the supreme Law of the Land; and the judges in every state shall be bound thereby, anything in the Constitution or laws of any state to the contrary notwithstanding.

This sentence made it abundantly clear that laws of Congress would supersede laws of the states, and it made certain that Congress would control interstate commerce, bankruptcy, monetary affairs, weights and measures, currency and credit, communication, transportation, and foreign and military affairs. Thus the supremacy clause ensures that the decisions of the national elite will prevail over those of the local elites in all vital areas allocated to the national government.

Republicanism.   The structure of the national government—its republicanism and its system of separated powers and checks and balances—was also designed to protect liberty and property. To the Founding Fathers, a republican government meant the delegation of powers by the people to a small number of citizens "whose wisdom may best discern the true interest of their country, and whose patriotism and love of justice will be least likely to sacrifice it to temporary or partial consideration."[9] Madison explained, in classic elite fashion, "that the public voice, pronounced by representatives of the people, will be more consonant to the public good than if pronounced by the people themselves." The Founding Fathers clearly believed that representatives of the people were more likely to be enlightened persons of principle and property than the voters who chose them, and would thus be more trustworthy and dependable.

Voters also had a very limited voice in the selection of decision makers. Of the four major decision-making bodies established in the Constitution—the House of Representatives, the Senate, the presidency, and the Supreme Court—the people were to elect only one. The other bodies were to be at least twice removed from popular control. In the

Constitution of 1787, the people elected only U.S. House members, and for short terms of only two years. In contrast, state legislatures were to elect U.S. senators for six-year terms. Electors, selected as state legislatures saw fit, selected the president. The states could hold elections for presidential electors, or the state legislatures could appoint them. The Founding Fathers hoped that presidential electors would be prominent men of wealth and reputation in their respective states. Finally, federal judges were to be appointed by the president for life, thus removing these decision makers as far as possible from popular control.

These republican arrangements make it unfair to brand the Founding Fathers "conservative." In 1787, the idea of republicanism was radical since few other governments provided for any popular participation in government, or even for a limited role in the selection of representatives. While the Founding Fathers believed that government ultimately rested on the will of the people, they hoped that republicanism could reduce the influence of the masses and help ensure government by elites.

Separation of powers and checks and balances. The Founding Fathers also intended the system of separated powers in the national government—separate legislative, executive, and judicial branches—as a bulwark against majoritarianism (government by popular majorities) and an additional safeguard for elite liberty and property. The doctrine derives from the French writer, Montesquieu, whose *Spirit of Laws* was a political textbook for these eighteenth-century statesmen. *The Federalist* Number 51 expressed the logic of the system of checks and balances:

> Ambition must be made to counteract ambition. . . . It may be a reflection on human nature, that such devices should be necessary to control the abuses of government. But what is government itself, but the greatest of all reflections on human nature? If men were angels, no government would be necessary. If angels were to govern men, neither external nor internal controls on government would be necessary. In framing a government which is to be administered by men over men, the great difficulty lies in this: you must first enable the government to control the governed; and in the next place oblige it to control itself.

The Constitution states the separation-of-powers concept in the opening sentences of the first three articles:

> All legislative powers herein granted shall be invested in the Congress of the United States. . . . The Executive power shall be vested in a President of the United States. . . . The Judicial power shall be vested in one Supreme Court and such inferior courts as Congress may from time to time ordain and establish.

Insofar as this system divides responsibility and makes it difficult for the masses to hold government accountable for public policy, it achieves one of the purposes intended by the Founding Fathers. Each of the four major decision-making bodies of the national government is chosen by different constituencies. Because the terms of these decision-making bodies are of varying length, a complete renewal of government at one stroke is impossible. Thus the people cannot wreak havoc quickly through direct elections. To make their will felt in all the decision-making bodies of the national government, they must wait years.

Moreover, each of these decision-making bodies has an important check on the decisions of the others. No bill can become law without the approval of both the House and the Senate. The president shares in the legislative power through the veto and the responsibility to "give to the Congress information of the state of the union, and recommend to their consideration such measures as he shall judge necessary and expedient." The president can also convene sessions of Congress. But the appointing power of the president is shared by the Senate; so is the power to make treaties. Also Congress can override executive vetoes. The president must execute the laws but cannot do so without relying on executive departments, which Congress must create. The executive branch can only spend money appropriated by Congress. Indeed, "separation of powers" is really a misnomer, for we are really talking about sharing, not separating, power; each branch participates in the activities of every other branch.

Even the Supreme Court, which was created by the Constitution, must be appointed by the president with the consent of the Senate, and Congress may prescribe the number of judges. More importantly, Congress must create lower and intermediate courts, establish the number of judges, fix the jurisdiction of lower federal courts, and make "exceptions" to the Supreme Court's jurisdiction over appeals.

Those who criticize the U.S. government for its slow, unwieldy processes should realize that the government's founders deliberately built in this characteristic. These cumbersome arrangements—the checks and balances and the fragmentation of authority that make it difficult for government to realize its potential power over private interests— aim to protect private interests from government interference and to shield the government from an unjust and self-seeking majority. If the system handcuffs government and makes it easy for established groups to oppose change, then the system is working as intended.

This system of intermingled powers and conflicting loyalties is still alive today. Of course, some aspects have changed; for example, voters now elect senators directly, and the president is more directly responsible to the voters than was originally envisioned. But the basic arrangement of checks and balances endures. Presidents, senators, representatives, and judges are chosen by different constituencies; their terms of office vary, and their responsibilities and loyalties differ. This system makes majority rule virtually impossible.

Judicial review. Perhaps the keystone of the system of checks and balances is the idea of *judicial review*, an original contribution by the

Founding Fathers to the science of government. In *Marbury* v. *Madison* in 1803, Chief Justice John Marshall argued convincingly that the Founding Fathers intended the Supreme Court to have the power to invalidate not only state laws and constitutions but also any laws of Congress that came in conflict with the Constitution. Marshall reasoned (1) that the Supreme Court is the reigning judicial power, (2) that historically the judicial power included the power to interpret the law, (3) that the supremacy clause made the Constitution the "Supreme Law of the Land," (4) that laws of the United States should be made "in pursuance thereof," (5) that judges swear to uphold the Constitution, and (6) that judges must therefore declare void any legislative act that they feel conflicts with the Constitution.

The text of the Constitution nowhere specifically authorizes federal judges to invalidate acts of Congress; at most, the Constitution implies this power. (But Hamilton apparently thought that the Constitution contained this power, since he was careful to explain it in *The Federalist* Number 78 before the ratification of the Constitution.) Thus, the Supreme Court stands as the final defender of the fundamental principles agreed upon by the Founding Fathers against the encroachments of popularly elected legislatures.

Ratification: An exercise in elite political skills

When its work ended on September 17, 1787, the Constitutional Convention sent the Constitution to New York City, where Congress was then in session. The Convention suggested that the Constitution "should afterwards be submitted to a convention of delegates chosen in each state by the people thereof, under the recommendation of its legislature for their assent and ratification." Convention delegates further proposed that ratification by nine states be sufficient to put the new constitution into effect. On September 28, Congress sent the Constitution to the states without further recommendations.

The ratification procedure suggested by the Founding Fathers was a skillful political maneuver. Since Convention proceedings had been secret, few people knew that the delegates had gone beyond their instructions to amend the Articles of Confederation to create a whole new scheme of government. Their ratification procedure was a complete departure from what was then the law of the land, the Articles of Confederation. The Articles provided that Congress make amendments only with the approval of *all* states. But since Rhode Island was firmly in the hands of small farmers, the unanimity required by the Articles was obviously out of the question; and the Founding Fathers felt obligated to act outside of the existing law.

The Founding Fathers also called for special ratifying conventions in the states rather than risk submitting the Constitution to the state legislatures. This extraordinary procedure gave clear advantage to supporters of the Constitution since submitting the plan to the state legislatures would weaken its chances for success. Thus the struggle for ratification began under ground rules designed by the national elite to give them the advantage over any potential opponents.

In the most important and controversial study of the Constitution to date, Charles A. Beard compiled a great deal of evidence supporting the hypothesis "that substantially all of the merchants, moneylenders, security holders, manufacturers, shippers, capitalists and financiers, and their professional associates are to be found on one side in support of the Constitution, and that substantially all of the major portion of the opposition came from the non-slaveholding farmers and debtors."[10] While historians disagree over the solidarity of class divisions in the struggle for ratification, most concede that only about 160,000 people voted in elections for delegates to state ratifying conventions and that not more than 100,000 of these voters favored the adoption of the Constitution. This figure represents about one in six of the adult males in the country, and no more than 5 percent of the general population. Thus, whether Beard is correct about class divisions in the struggle for ratification, it is clear that the number of people who participated in any fashion in ratifying the Constitution was an extremely small minority in the population.*

Some men of property and education did oppose the new Constitution. These were men who had greater confidence in their ability to control state governments than to control the new federal government. They called themselves "Anti-Federalists" and they vigorously attacked the Constitution as a counterrevolutionary document that could undo much of the progress made since 1776 toward freedom, liberty, and equality. According to the opponents of the Constitution, the new government would be "aristocratic," all powerful, and a threat to the "spirit of republicanism" and the "genius of democracy." They charged that the new Constitution created an aristocratic upper house and an almost monarchical presidency. The powers of the national government could trample the states and deny the people of the states the opportunity to

---

*Beard's economic interpretation differs from an elitist interpretation in that Beard believes that the economic elites supported the Constitution and the masses opposed it. Our elitist interpretation asserts only that the masses did not participate in writing or adopting the Constitution and that elites benefited directly from its provisions. Our interpretation does not depend upon showing that the masses opposed the Constitution but merely that they did not participate in its establishment. Attacks on Beard appear in Forrest McDonald, *We the People: The Economic Origins of the Constitution* (Chicago: University of Chicago Press, 1963); and Robert E. Brown, *Charles Beard and the Constitution* (Princeton, N.J.: Princeton University Press, 1956). Lee Benson provides a balanced view in *Turner and Beard: American Historical Writing Reconsidered* (New York: Free Press, 1960).

handle their own political and economic affairs. The Anti-Federalists repeatedly asserted that the Constitution removed powers from the people and concentrated them in the hands of a few national officials who were largely immune from popular control; moreover, they attacked the undemocratic features of the Constitution and argued that state governments were much more representative of the people. Also under attack were the secrecy of the Constitutional Convention and the actions of the Founding Fathers, both contrary to the law and the spirit of the Articles of Confederation.

While the Anti-Federalists deplored the undemocratic features of the new Constitution, their most effective criticism centered on the absence of any bill of rights. The omission of a bill of rights was particularly glaring since the idea was very popular at the time, and most new state constitutions contained one. It is an interesting comment on the psychology of the Founding Fathers that the idea of a bill of rights did not come up in the Convention until the final week of deliberations; even then it received little consideration. The Founding Fathers certainly believed in limited government, and they did write a few liberties into the body of the Constitution such as protection against bills of attainder and *ex post facto* laws, a guarantee of the writ of *habeas corpus*, a limited definition of treason, and a guarantee of jury trial. However, they did not create a bill of rights labeled as such.

When the states' criticism about the absence of a bill of rights began to mount, supporters of the Constitution presented an interesting argument to explain this deficiency: (1) the national government was one of enumerated powers and could not exercise any powers not expressly delegated to it in the Constitution; (2) the power to interfere with free speech or press or otherwise to restrain liberty was not among the enumerated powers in the Constitution; (3) it was therefore unnecessary to deny the new government this power specifically. But this logic was unconvincing; the absence of a bill of rights seemed to confirm the suspicion that the Founding Fathers were more concerned with protecting property than with protecting the personal liberties of the people. Many members of the elite and nonelite alike were uncomfortable with the thought that personal liberty depended on a thin thread of inference from enumerated powers. Supporters of the Constitution thus had to retreat from their demand for unconditional ratification; the New York, Massachusetts, and Virginia conventions agreed to the new Constitution only after receiving the Federalists' solemn promise to add a bill of rights as amendments. Thus the fundamental guarantees of liberty in the Bill of Rights were political concessions by the nation's elite. While the Founding Fathers deserved great credit for the document that they produced at Philadelphia, the first Congress to meet under that Constitution was nonetheless obliged to submit twelve amendments to the states, ten of which were ratified by 1791.

Summary

Elite theory provides us with an interpretation of the U.S. Constitution and the basic structure of American government. Our analysis of constitutional politics centers on the following propositions:

1. The Constitution of the United States was not "ordained and established" by "the people." Instead it was written by a small, educated, talented, wealthy elite in America, representative of powerful economic interests: bondholders, investors, merchants, real estate owners, and planters.

2. The Constitution and the national government that it established had its origins in elite dissatisfaction with the inability of the central government to pay off its bondholders, the interference of state governments with the development of a national economy, the threat to investors and creditors posed by state issuance of cheap paper money and laws relieving debtors of contractual obligations, the threat to propertied classes arising from post-Revolutionary War radicalism, the inability of the central government to provide an army capable of protecting western development or a navy capable of protecting American commercial interests on the high seas, and the inability of America's elite to exercise power in world affairs.

3. The elite achieved ratification of the Constitution through its astute political skills. The masses of people in America did not participate in the writing of the Constitution or in its adoption by the states, and they probably would have opposed the Constitution had they the information and resources to do so.

4. The Founding Fathers shared a consensus that the fundamental role of government is the protection of liberty and property. They believed in a republican form of government by men of principle and property. They opposed an aristocracy or a governing nobility, but they also opposed mass democracy with direct participation by the people in decision making. They feared mass movements seeking to reduce inequalities of wealth, intelligence, talent, or virtue. "Dangerous leveling" was a serious violation of men's rights to property.

5. The structure of American government was designed to suppress "factious" issues—threats to dominant economic elites. Republicanism, the division of power between state and national governments, and the complex system of checks and balances and divided power were all designed as protections against mass movements that might threaten liberty and property.

6. The text of the Constitution contains many direct and immediate benefits to America's governing elite. Although all Americans, both

elite and mass, may have benefited by the adoption of the Constitution, the advantages and benefits for America's elite was their impelling motive for supporting the new Constitution.

NOTES

1. Lester Cappon, ed., *The Adams-Jefferson Letters* (Chapel Hill: University of North Carolina Press, 1959), vol. I, p. 106.
2. Max Farrand, ed., *The Records of the Federal Convention of 1787* (New Haven, Conn.: Yale University Press, 1937), vol. III, p. 15.
3. Ibid., p. 32.
4. See Clinton Rossiter, *1787, The Grand Convention* (New York: Macmillan, 1966), p. 45.
5. Charles A. Beard, *An Economic Interpretation of the Constitution of the United States* (New York: Macmillan, 1913), pp. 73–151.
6. John P. Roche, "The Founding Fathers: A Reform Caucus in Action," *American Political Science Review* 55 (December 1961):799.
7. See especially Beard, *Economic Interpretation.*
8. James Madison, Alexander Hamilton, and John Jay, *The Federalist* (New York: Modern Library, 1937).
9. Ibid.
10. Beard, *Economic Interpretation,* pp. 16–17.

SELECTED READINGS

Beard, Charles A. *An Economic Interpretation of the Constitution of the United States.* New York: Macmillan, 1913. The Free Press issued a paperback edition in 1965. Much of this chapter reflects data presented by Beard in this classic work. Beard traces the events leading up to the writing of the Constitution and the events surrounding ratification from an economic point of view. He discovers that economic considerations played a major, if not central, role in the shaping of the Constitution.

For several critiques of Beard, see:
1. Benson, Lee. *Turner and Beard: American Historical Writing Reconsidered.* New York: Free Press, 1960.
2. Beale, Howard K., ed. *Charles A. Beard: An Appraisal.* Lexington: University of Kentucky Press, 1954.
3. McDonald, Forrest. *We the People: The Economic Origins of the Constitution.* Chicago: University of Chicago Press, 1958.

Corwin, Edward S., and Peltason, J. W. *Understanding the Constitution,* 6th ed. New York: Holt, Rinehart & Winston, 1973. Of the many books that explain parts of the Constitution, this paperback is one of the best. It contains explanations of the Declaration of Independence, the Articles of Confederation, and the Constitution. The book is written clearly and is well suited for undergraduate as well as graduate and faculty use.

Lipset, Seymour Martin. *The First New Nation.* Garden City, N.Y.: Doubleday, Anchor Books, 1963. This book offers a comparative treatment of the factors necessary for the development of a new nation. Lipset argues that any new nation must develop legitimacy of government, national identity, national unity, opposition rights, and citizen payoffs. The book is important because it examines the United States as the first "new nation" in light of these five factors and then compares it to other developing nations.

Madison, James, Hamilton, Alexander, and Jay, John. *The Federalist*. New York: Modern Library, 1937. This collection of the articles published in support of the Constitution offers perhaps the most important contemporary comments available on the Constitution.

Rossiter, Clinton L. *1787, The Grand Convention*. New York: Macmillan, 1966. This readable and entertaining account of the men and events of 1787 contains many insights into the difficulties the Founding Fathers had writing the Constitution.

Wills, Gary. *Explaining America*. New York: Penguin Books, 1982. This book is a rigorous examination of *The Federalist* and the intellectual influences on its authors.

3 The Evolution of American Elites

America's political leadership over the years has been essentially conservative in that it has accepted the basic consensus underlying the American political and economic system.

The fierceness of political struggles has often been misleading; for the range of vision embodied by the primary contestants in the major parties has always been bounded by the horizons of property and enterprise.

—*Richard Hofstadter,* The American Political Tradition, *1948*

A stable elite system depends on the movement of talented and ambitious individuals from the lower strata into the elite. An open elite system providing for "a slow and continuous modification of the ruling classes" is essential for continuing the system and avoiding revolution. Of course, only those nonelites who accept the basic consensus of the system can be admitted into the ruling class. Although popular elections, party competition, and other democratic institutions in America have not enabled the masses to govern, these institutions have helped keep the elite system an open one. They have assisted in the circulation of elites, even if they have never been a means of challenging the dominant elite consensus.

In this chapter, a historical analysis of the evolution of American elites, we show that American elite membership has evolved slowly, without any serious break in the ideas or values underlying the American political and economic system. America has never experienced a true revolution that forcefully replaced governing elites with nonelites. Instead American elite membership has been open to those who acquire wealth and property and who accept the national consensus about private enterprise, limited government, and individualism. Industrialization, technological change, and new sources of wealth in the expanding economy have produced new elite members, and America's elite system has permitted the absorption of the new elites without upsetting the system itself.

America's political leadership over the years has been essentially conservative in that it has accepted the basic consensus underlying the American political and economic system. Whatever the popular political label—"Federalist," "Democrat," "Whig," "Republican," "Progressive," "Conservative," or "Liberal"—American leadership has remained committed to the same values and ideas that motivated the Founding Fathers. No drastic revisions of the American system have ever been contemplated by the American elites.

Drawing by Donald Reilly; © 1974 The New Yorker Magazine, Inc.

"Religious freedom is my immediate goal, but my long range plan is to go into real estate."

Changes in public policy and innovations in the structure of American government over the decades have been *incremental* (step-by-step) rather than revolutionary. Elites have modified public policies but seldom replaced them. They have made structural adaptations in the constitutional system designed by the Founding Fathers but have kept intact the original framework of American constitutionalism.

Policy changes in America have not come about through demands by the people. Instead changes and innovations in public policy have occurred when elites have perceived threats to the system and have instituted reforms to preserve the system and their place in it. Reforms have been designed to strengthen the existing social and economic fabric of society with a minimum of dislocation for governing elites. Political conflict in America has centered on a very narrow range of issues. Only once, in the Civil War, have American elites been deeply divided over the nature of American society. The Civil War reflected a deep cleavage between Southern elites—dependent upon a plantation economy, slave labor, and free trade—and Northern industrial and commercial elites, who prospered under free labor and protective tariffs.

Hamilton and the nation's first public policies

The most influential figure in George Washington's administration was Alexander Hamilton, secretary of the treasury. More than anyone else, Hamilton was aware that the new nation had to win the lasting confidence of business and the financial elites in order to survive and prosper. Only if the United States were established on a sound financial basis could it attract investors at home and abroad and expand its industry and commerce. Great Britain remained the largest source of investment capital for the new nation, and Hamilton was decidedly pro-British. He also favored a strong central government as a means of protecting property and stimulating the growth of commerce and industry.

Paying the national debt

Hamilton's first move was to refund the national debt at face value. Most of the original bonds were no longer in the hands of the original owners but had fallen to speculators who had purchased them for only a fraction of their face value. Since these securities were worth only about 25 cents on the dollar, the Hamilton refund program meant a 300 percent profit for the speculators. Hamilton's program went beyond refunding the debts owed by the United States; he also undertook to pay the debts incurred by the states themselves during the Revolutionary War. His object was to place the creditor class under a deep obligation to the central government.

Establishing a national bank

Hamilton also acted to establish a Bank of the United States, which would receive government funds, issue a national currency, facilitate the sale of national bonds, and tie the national government even more closely to the banking community. The Constitution did not specifically grant Congress the power to create a national bank, but Hamilton was willing to interpret the "necessary and proper" clause broadly enough to include the creation of a bank to help carry out the taxing, borrowing, and currency powers enumerated in the Constitution. Hamilton's broad construction of the "necessary and proper" clause looked in the direction of a powerful central government that would exercise powers not specifically enumerated in the Constitution. Thomas Jefferson, who was secretary of state in the same cabinet with Hamilton, expressed growing concern over Hamilton's tendency toward national centralization. Jefferson argued that Congress could not establish the bank because the bank was not strictly "necessary" to carry out delegated functions. But Hamilton won out, with the support of President Washington; and in 1791 Congress voted to charter the Bank of the United States. For twenty years the bank was very successful, especially in stabilizing the currency of the new nation.

Expanding the "necessary and proper" clause

Not until 1819 did the Supreme Court decide the constitutionality of the Bank of the United States. In the famous case of *McCulloch* v. *Maryland*, the Supreme Court upheld the broad definition of national power suggested by Hamilton under the "necessary and proper" clause. At the same time, the Court established the principle that a state law that interferes with a national activity is unconstitutional.[1] "Let the end be legitimate," Chief Justice John Marshall wrote, "let it be within the scope of the Constitution, and all means which are appropriate, which are plainly adopted to that end, which are not prohibited, but consistent with the letter and spirit of the Constitution, are constitutional." The *McCulloch* case firmly established the principle that Congress has the right to choose any appropriate means for carrying out the delegated powers of the national government. The "necessary and proper" clause is now sometimes called the "implied powers" clause or the "elastic" clause because it gives to Congress many powers that the Constitution does not explicitly grant. Of course, Congress must still trace all its activities to some formal grant of power, but this task is usually not difficult.

Rise of the Jeffersonians

The centralizing effect of Hamilton's programs and their favoring of merchants, manufacturers, and shipbuilders aroused serious opposition in elite circles. Southern planters and large landowners benefited very little from Hamilton's policies, and they were joined in their opposition by local and state elites who feared that a strong central government threatened their own powers. These agrarian groups were first called "Anti-Federalists," and later "Republicans" and "Democratic Republicans" when these terms became popular after the French Revolution. When Thomas Jefferson resigned from Washington's cabinet in protest of Hamilton's program, opposition to the Federalists began to gather around Jefferson.

Jefferson as a wealthy plantation owner

Historians portray Jefferson as a great democrat and champion of the "common man." And in writing the Declaration of Independence, the Virginia Statute for Religious Freedom, and the famous *Notes on Virginia* Jefferson indeed expressed concern for the rights of all "the people" and a willingness to trust in their wisdom. But when Jefferson spoke warmly of the merits of "the people," he meant those who owned and managed their own farms and estates. He firmly believed that only those who owned their own land could make good citizens. Jefferson disliked aristocracy, but he also held the urban masses in contempt. He wanted to see the United States become a nation of free, educated, land-owning farmers. Democracy, he believed, could be founded only on a propertied class in a propertied nation.

Jefferson shared the Founding Fathers' concern about unrestrained rule by the masses. He was willing to base republican government on large and small landowners, but he distrusted merchants, manufacturers, laborers, and urban dwellers. His belief that land ownership is essential to virtuous government explains in part his Louisiana Purchase, which he hoped would provide the American people with land "to the hundredth and thousandth generation."[2]

The dispute between Federalists and Anti-Federalists in early America was not between elites and masses. It was a dispute within elite circles between two propertied classes: merchants and bankers on one side, and plantation owners and slaveholders on the other.[3]

Rise of political parties

The Anti-Federalists, or "Republicans," did not elect their first president, Thomas Jefferson, until 1800. John Adams, a Federalist, succeeded Washington in the election of 1796. Yet the election of 1796 was an important milestone in the development of the American political system. For the first time, two candidates, Adams and Jefferson, campaigned not as individuals but as members of political parties. For the first time, the candidates for the electoral college announced themselves before the election as either "Adams's men" or "Jefferson's men." Most importantly, for the first time, American political leaders realized the importance of molding mass opinion in organizing the masses for political action. The Republican party first saw the importance of working among the masses to rally popular support. The Federalist leaders made the mistake of assuming that they could maintain the unquestioning support of the less educated and less wealthy without bothering to mold their opinions.

Rather than try, as the Republicans did, to manipulate public opinion, the Federalists tried to outlaw public criticism of the government by means of the Alien and Sedition Acts of 1798. Among other things, these acts made it a crime to conspire to oppose the legal measures of the government or to interfere with their execution, or to publish any false or malicious writing directed against the president or Congress, or to "stir up hatred" against them. These acts directly challenged the newly adopted First Amendment guarantee of freedom of speech and press.

In response to the Alien and Sedition Acts, Jefferson and Madison put forward their famous Kentucky and Virginia resolutions. These measures proposed that the states assume the right to decide whether Congress has acted unconstitutionally and, furthermore, that the states properly "interpose" their authority against "palpable and alarming infractions of the Constitution." The Virginia and Kentucky legislatures passed these resolutions and declared the Alien and Sedition Acts "void and of no force" in these states.

Republicans in power: The stability of public policy

In the election of 1800, the Federalists went down to defeat; Thomas Jefferson and Aaron Burr were elected over John Adams and C. C. Pinckney. Only the New England states, New Jersey, and Delaware, where commercial and manufacturing interests were strongest, voted Federalist. Because the vast majority of American people won their living from the soil, the landed elites were able to mobilize these masses behind their bid for control of the government. The Federalists failed to recognize the importance of agrarianism in the nation's economic and political life. Another half-century would pass and America's industrial revolution would be in full swing before manufacturing and commercial elites would reestablish their dominance.

But the real importance of the election of 1800 is *not* that landed interests gained power in relation to commercial and industrial interests. The importance of 1800 is that for the first time in America's history, control of the government passed peacefully from the hands of one faction to an opposition faction. Even today few nations in the world see government office change hands in an orderly or peaceful fashion. The fact that an "out" party peacefully replaced an "in" party is further testimony to the strength of the consensus among the new nation's elite. Despite bitter campaign rhetoric, Federalists and Republicans agreed to abide by the basic "rules of the game," to view an opposition faction as legitimate, and to accept the outcome of an election. The Federalists relinquished control of the government without fear that the fundamental values of the American society would be destroyed by a new governing faction. Clearly American leaders agreed more than they disagreed.*

*The original text of the Constitution did not envision an opposition faction. Presidential electors could cast two votes for president, with the understanding that the candidate with the second highest vote total would be vice-president. Seventy-three Republican

The "Virginia dynasty"—Thomas Jefferson, James Madison, and finally James Monroe—governed the country for six presidential terms, nearly a quarter of a century. Interestingly, once in office, the Republicans made few changes in Federalist and Hamiltonian policy. (The only major pieces of legislation repealed by the Republicans were the Alien and Sedition Acts. And it seems clear that in these acts the Federalists had violated elite consensus. Even John Marshall, who was elected as a Federalist congressman in 1798, pledged to support repeal of these acts.) The Republicans did not attack commercial or industrial enterprise; in fact commerce and industry prospered under Republican rule as never before. They did not attempt to recover money paid out by Hamilton in refunding national or state debts. They allowed public land speculation to continue. Instead of crushing the banks, Republicans soon supported the financial interests they had sworn to oppose.

Jefferson was an ardent expansionist; to add to America's wealth in land, he purchased the vast Louisiana Territory. Later a stronger army and a system of internal roads were necessary to help develop western land. Jefferson's successor, James Madison, built a strong navy and engaged in another war with England, the War of 1812, to protect American commerce on the high seas. The Napoleonic wars and the War of 1812 stimulated American manufacturing by depressing trade with Britain. In 1816 Republicans passed a high tariff in order to protect domestic industry and manufacturing from foreign goods. As for Republican tax policies, Jefferson wrote in 1816:

> To take from one, because it is thought his own industry and that of his fathers has acquired too much, in order to spare to others, who, or whose fathers, have not exercised equal industry and skill, is to violate arbitrarily the first principle of association, "the guarantee to everyone of free exercise of his industry and the fruits acquired by it."[4]

In short, the Republicans had no intention of redistributing wealth in America. Indeed before the end of Madison's second term in 1817, the Republicans had taken over the whole complex of Hamiltonian policies: a national bank, high tariffs, protection for manufacturers, internal improvements, western land development, a strong army and navy, and

electors pledged to Jefferson and sixty-five Federalists pledged to Adams went to the electoral college. Somewhat thoughtlessly, all the Republicans cast one vote for Jefferson and one vote for Aaron Burr, his running mate, with the result that each man received the same number of votes for the presidency. Because of the tie vote, the decision went to the Federalist-controlled House of Representatives, where a movement was begun to elect Burr, rather than Jefferson, in order to embarrass the Republicans. But Alexander Hamilton used his influence in Congress to swing the election to his old political foe Jefferson, suggesting again that their differences were not so deep that either would deliberately undermine the presidency to strike at the other. Once in power, the Republicans passed the Twelfth Amendment to the Constitution, providing that each presidential elector should thereafter vote separately for president and vice-president. Both Federalists and Republicans in the states promptly agreed with this reform and ratification was completed by the election of 1804.

a broad interpretation of national power. So complete was the elite consensus that by 1820 the Republicans had completely driven the Federalist party out of existence, largely by taking over its programs.

Rise of western elites

According to Frederick Jackson Turner, "The rise of the New West was the most significant fact in American history."[5] Certainly the American West had a profound impact on the political system of the new nation. People went west because of the vast wealth of fertile lands that awaited them there; nowhere else in the world could one acquire wealth so quickly as in the new American West. Because aristocratic families of the eastern seaboard seldom had reason to migrate westward, the western settlers were mainly middle- and lower-class immigrants. With hard work and good fortune, penniless migrants could become wealthy plantation owners or cattle ranchers in a single generation. Thus the West offered rapid upward social mobility.

New elites arose in the West and had to be assimilated into America's governing circles. This assimilation had a profound effect on the character of America's elites. No one exemplifies the new entrants into America's elite better than Andrew Jackson. Jackson's victory in the presidential election of 1828 was not a victory of the common man against the propertied classes but rather one of the new western elites against established Republican leadership in the East. Jackson's victory forced America's established elites to recognize the growing importance of the West and to open their ranks to the new rich west of the Alleghenies.

The "natural aristocracy"

Since Jackson was a favorite of the people, it was easy for him to believe in the wisdom of the common man. But Jacksonian democracy was by no means a philosophy of leveling egalitarianism. The ideal of the frontier society was the self-made man, and people admired wealth and power won by competitive skill. Wealth and power obtained only through special privilege offended the frontiersmen, however. They believed in a *natural aristocracy* rather than an aristocracy by birth, education, or special privilege. Jackson himself best expressed this philosophy in his famous message vetoing the bill to recharter the national bank:

> Distinctions in society will always exist under every just government. Equality of talents, of education, or wealth cannot be produced by human institutions. In the full enjoyment of the gifts of heaven and the fruits of superior industry, economy, and virtue, every man is equally entitled to protection

by law; but when the laws undertake to add to these natural and just advantages artificial distinctions, to grant titles, gratuities, and exclusive privileges, to make the rich richer and the potent more powerful, the humble members of society—the farmers, mechanics, and laborers—who have neither the time nor the means for securing like favors to themselves, have a right to complain of the injustice of their government.[6]

Thus Jacksonians demanded not absolute equality but a more open elite system—a greater opportunity for the rising middle class to acquire wealth and influence through competition.

Expansion of the electorate

In their struggle to open America's elite system, the Jacksonians appealed to mass sentiment. Jackson's humble beginnings, his image as a self-made man, his military adventures, his frontier experience, and his rough, brawling style endeared him to the masses. As beneficiaries of popular support, the new elites of the West developed a strong faith in the wisdom and justice of popular decisions. The new western states that entered the Union granted universal white male suffrage, and gradually the older states fell into step. Rising elites, themselves often less than a generation away from the masses, saw in a widened electorate a chance for personal advancement that they could never have achieved under the old regime. Therefore the Jacksonians became noisy and effective advocates of the principle that all men should have the right to vote and to hold public office. They also successfully attacked the congressional caucus system of nominating presidential candidates. After his defeat in Congress in 1824, Jackson wished to sever Congress from the nominating process. In 1832, when the Democrats held their first national convention, they renominated Andrew Jackson by acclamation.

Character of the elite

Nonetheless, the changes in the character of elites, from the administration of John Adams through Thomas Jefferson to Andrew Jackson, were very minor. Sociologist Sidney H. Aronson's historical research reveals that, contrary to the general assumption, Jackson's administration was clearly upper class, college educated, prestigiously employed, professionally trained, and probably wealthy. (See table 3-1.) In fact, the class character of Jackson's administration was not much different from that of Thomas Jefferson or even that of the Federalist John Adams. Over half of Jackson's top appointees were born into America's distinguished upper-class families, and three-quarters enjoyed high class standing before their appointment either through birth or achievement.

TABLE 3-1   Social class characteristics of three presidents' appointments

Characteristics	Adams (N = 96)	Jefferson (N = 100)	Jackson (N = 127)
Father political officeholder	52%	43%	44%
Father college educated	17	13	12
Class I family social position[a]	62	58	51
High-ranking occupation	92	93	90
Political officeholder before appointment	91	83	88
Class I social position[a]	86	74	74
Family in America in seventeenth century	55	48	48
College educated	63	52	52
Professionally trained	69	74	81
Relative an appointive elite	40	34	34

[a]"Class I" is the highest of the following four classes:
Class I: "national and international aristocracy";
Class II: "prosperous and respectable";
Class III: "respectable";
Class IV: "subsistence or impoverished."

Breakdowns by each class are as follows:
Adams: I: 62%; II: 19%; III: 5%; IV: 1%; unknown: 13%.
Jefferson: I: 58%; II: 15%; III: 6%; IV: 1%; unknown: 20%.
Jackson: I: 51%; II: 25%; III: 11%; IV: 2%; unknown: 11%.
Source: Sidney H. Aronson, *Status and Kinship in the Higher Civil Service* (Cambridge, Mass.: Harvard University Press, 1964), p. 195. Reprinted by permission.

Elite cleavage: The Civil War

During the nation's first sixty years, America's elites substantially agreed about the character and direction of the new nation. Conflicts over the national bank, the tariff, internal improvement (such as roads and harbors), and even the controversial war with Mexico in 1846 did not threaten the basic underlying consensus. In the 1850s, however, the status of blacks in American society—the most divisive issue in the history of American politics—drove a wedge into America's elites and ultimately led to the nation's bloodiest war. The American political system was unequal to the task of negotiating a peaceful settlement to the slavery problem because America's elites divided deeply over the question.

Southern elites

In 1787 the Southern elites—cotton planters, landowners, exporters, and slave traders—foresaw an end to slavery; but after 1820, the demand for cotton became insatiable, and Southern planters could not profitably produce cotton without slave labor. Cotton accounted for over half the value of all American goods shipped abroad before the Civil War. Although Virginia did not depend on cotton, it sold great numbers of slaves to the cotton states, and "slave raising" itself became immensely profitable. The price of a good slave for the fields increased from $300 in 1820 to over $1,000 in 1860, even though the slave population grew from about a million and a half to nearly four million during this period.

It was the white *elites* and not the white *masses* of the South who had an interest in the slave and cotton culture. On the eve of the Civil War, probably no more than four hundred thousand Southern families—approximately one in four—held slaves, and many of these families held only one or two slaves each. The number of great planters—men who owned fifty or more slaves and large holdings of land—was probably not more than seven thousand, yet their views dominated Southern politics.

Northern elites

The Northern elites were merchants and manufacturers who depended on free labor, yet they had no direct interest in abolishing slavery in the South. Some Northern manufacturers made good profits from Southern trade; with higher tariffs, they could make even higher profits. Abolitionist activities imperiled trade relations between North and South, and even Northern social circles often looked upon them with irritation. But both Northern and Southern elites realized that control of the West was the key to future dominance of the nation. Northern elites wanted a West composed of small farmers who produced food and raw materials for the industrial and commercial East and provided a market for eastern goods. Southern planters feared the voting power of a West composed of small farmers and wanted western lands for expansion of the cotton and slave culture. Cotton ate up the land and, because it required continuous cultivation and monotonous rounds of simple tasks, was suited to slave labor. Thus to protect the cotton economy, it was essential to protect slavery in western lands. This conflict over western land eventually precipitated the Civil War.

Attempts at compromise

Despite these differences, the underlying consensus of American elites was so great that they devised compromise after compromise to maintain unity. The Missouri Compromise of 1820 divided the land in the Louisiana Purchase exclusive of Missouri between free territory and slave territory at 36°30' and admitted Maine and Missouri as free and slave states, respectively. After the war with Mexico, the elaborate Compromise of 1850 caused one of the greatest debates in American legislative history, with Senators Henry Clay, Daniel Webster, John C. Calhoun, Salmon P. Chase, Stephen A. Douglas, Jefferson Davis, Alexander H. Stevens, Robert Tombs, William H. Seward, and Thaddeus Stevens all participating. Elite divisiveness was apparent, but it was not yet so destructive as to split the nation. Congress achieved a compromise admitting California as a free state; creating two new territories, New

Mexico and Utah, out of the Mexican cession; enacting a drastic fugitive slave law to satisfy Southern planters; and prohibiting slave trade in the District of Columbia. Even the Kansas-Nebraska Act of 1854 was to be a compromise; each new territory would decide for itself whether to be slave or free, with the expectation that Nebraska would vote free and Kansas slave. But gradually the spirit of compromise gave way to cleavage and conflict.

Elite cleavage

Beginning in 1856, proslavery and antislavery forces fought it out in "bleeding Kansas." Intemperate language in the Senate became commonplace, with frequent threats of secession, violence, and civil war.

In 1857 the Supreme Court decided, in *Dred Scott* v. *Sandford*, that the Missouri Compromise was unconstitutional because Congress had no authority to forbid slavery in any territory.[7] The Constitution protected slave property, said Chief Justice Roger T. Taney, as much as any other kind of property.

In 1859 John Brown and his followers raided the U.S. arsenal at Harpers Ferry as a first step to freeing the slaves of Virginia by force. Brown was captured by Virginia militia under the command of Colonel Robert E. Lee, tried for treason, found guilty, and executed. Southerners believed that Northerners had tried to incite the horror of slave insurrection, while Northerners believed that Brown had died a martyr.

The conflict between North and South led to the complete collapse of the Whig party and the emergence of a new Republican party composed exclusively of Northerners and westerners. For the first time in the history of American parties, one of the two major parties did not spread across both sides of the Mason-Dixon line; 1860 was the only year in American history that four major parties sought the presidency. The nation was so divided that no party came close to winning the majority of popular votes. Lincoln, the Republican candidate, and Douglas, the Democratic candidate, won most of their votes from the North and West, while John C. Breckinridge (Kentucky), the Southern Democratic candidate, and John Bell (Tennessee), the Constitutional Union candidate, received most of their votes from the South.

More important, the cleavage had become so deep that many prominent Southern leaders announced that they would not accept the outcome of the presidential election if Lincoln won. Threats of secession were not new, but this time it was no bluff. For the first and only time in American history, prominent elite members were willing to destroy the American political system rather than compromise their interests and principles. Shortly after the election, on December 20, 1860, the state of South Carolina seceded from the Union. Within six months, ten other Southern states followed.

Lincoln and slavery

Even in the midst of this disastrous conflict, both Northern and Southern elites showed continued devotion to the principles of constitutional government and private property. They made many genuine efforts at compromise and conciliation. Abraham Lincoln never attacked slavery in the South; his exclusive concern was to halt the spread of slavery in the western territories. He wrote in 1845, "I hold it a paramount duty of us in the free states, due to the union of the states, and perhaps to liberty itself (paradox though it may seem), to let the slavery of the other states alone."[8] Throughout his political career, he consistently held this position. On the other hand, with regard to the western territories he said, "The whole nation is interested that the best use shall be made of these territories. We want them for homes and free white people. This they cannot be, to any considerable extent, if slavery shall be planted within them."[9] In short, Lincoln wanted to tie the western territories economically and culturally to the Northern system. As for Lincoln's racial views, as late as 1858 he said:

> I will say, then, that I am not, nor ever have been, in favor of bringing about in any way the social and political equality of the white and black races; that I am not, nor ever have been, in favor of making voters or jurors of Negroes, nor qualifying them to hold office, nor to intermarry with white people . . . and in as much as they cannot so live while they do remain together, there must be a position of superior and inferior; and I as much as any other man am in favor of having the superior position assigned to the white race.[10]

Lincoln's political posture was essentially conservative. He wished to preserve the long-established order and consensus that had protected American principles and property rights so successfully in the past. He was not an abolitionist, and he did not want to destroy the Southern elites or to alter the Southern social fabric. His goal was to bring the South back into the Union, to restore orderly government, and to establish the principle that the states cannot resist national authority with force.

Emancipation as political opportunism

As the war continued and casualties mounted, Northern opinion toward Southern slaveowners became increasingly bitter. Many Republicans joined the abolitionists in calling for emancipation of the slaves simply to punish the "rebels." They knew that the South's power depended on slave labor. Lincoln also knew that if he proclaimed that the war was being fought to free the slaves, foreign intervention was less likely. On September 22, 1862, Lincoln issued his preliminary Emancipation Proclamation. Claiming his right as commander in chief of the army and navy, he promised that "on the first day of January 1863, all persons held as slaves within any state or designated part of a state, the people whereof shall then be in rebellion against the United States shall be then, thence forward, and forever free." Thus one of the great steps toward freedom in this nation, the Emancipation Proclamation, did not come about as a result of demands by the people and certainly not as a result of demands by the slaves themselves. It was a political and military action by the president intended to help preserve the Union. It was not a revolutionary action but a conservative one.

Rise of the new industrial elite

The Civil War's importance to America's elite structure lies in the commanding position that the new industrial capitalists won in the course of struggle. Even before 1860, Northern industry had been altering the course of American life; the economic transformation of the United States from an agricultural to an industrial nation reached the crescendo of a revolution in the second half of the nineteenth century. Canals and steam railroads had been opening new markets for the growing industrial cities of the East. The rise of corporations and of stock markets for the accumulation of capital upset old-fashioned ideas of property. The introduction of machinery in factories revolutionized the conditions of American labor and made the masses dependent on industrial capitalists for their livelihood. Civil War profits compounded the capital of the industrialists and placed them in a position to dominate the economic life of the nation. Moreover when the Southern planters were removed from the national scene, the government in Washington became the exclusive domain of the new industrial leaders.

Social Darwinism

The new industrial elite found a new philosophy to justify its political and economic dominance. Drawing an analogy from the new Darwinian biology, Herbert Spencer undertook to demonstrate that just as nature selected its elite through evolution, so also society selects natural social elites through free economic competition. In defense of the new capitalists, Herbert Spencer argued, "There cannot be more good done than that of letting social progress go on unhindered; an immensity of mischief may be done in . . . the artificial preservation of those least able to care for themselves."[11] Spencer hailed the accumulation of new industrial wealth as "the survival of the fittest." The social Darwinists found in the law of survival of the fittest an admirable defense for the emergence of a ruthless ruling elite, an elite that defined its own self-interest more narrowly perhaps than any other in American history. It was a philosophy that permitted the conditions of the masses to decline to the lowest depths in American history.

Industrial capitalism

After the Civil War, businessmen became more numerous in Congress than at any other time in American history. They had little trouble voting high tariffs and hard money (made of or backed by gold), both of which heightened profits. The legislators allowed very little effective regulatory legislation to reach the floor of Congress. After 1881 the Senate came under the spell of Nelson Aldrich, son-in-law of John D. Rockefeller, who controlled Standard Oil. Aldrich served thirty years in the Senate. He believed that geographic representation in the Senate was old-fashioned and openly advocated a Senate composed officially of representatives from the great business constituencies—steel, coal, copper, railroads, banks, textiles, and so on.

As business became increasingly national in scope, only the strongest or most unscrupulous of the competitors survived. Great producers tended to become the cheapest ones, and little companies tended to disappear. Industrial production rose rapidly, while the number of industrial concerns steadily diminished. Total capital investment and total output of industry vastly increased, while ownership became concentrated. One result was the emergence of monopolies and near monopolies in the major industries of America. Another result was the accumulation of great family fortunes.[12] (See table 3-2, compiled from 1924 tax returns. Admittedly it fails to record other great personal fortunes, such as Armour and Swift in meat packing, Candler in Coca-Cola, Cannon in textiles, Fleischmann in yeast, Pulitzer in publishing, Golet in real estate, Harriman in railroads, Heinz in foods, Manville in asbestos, Cudahy in food processing, Dorrance in Campbell's Soup, Hartford in A&P, Eastman in film, Firestone in rubber, Sinclair in oil, Chrysler in automobiles, Pabst in beer, and others.)

Rockefeller.   Typical of the great entrepreneurs of industrial capitalism was John D. Rockefeller. By the end of the Civil War, Rockefeller had accumulated a modest fortune of $50,000 in wholesale grain and meat. In 1865, with extraordinary good judgment, he invested his money in the wholly new petroleum business. He backed one of the first oil refineries in the nation and continually reinvested his profits in his business. In 1867, backed by two new partners—H. M. Flagler and F. W. Harkness—Rockefeller founded the Standard Oil Company of Ohio, which in that year refined 4 percent of the nation's output. By 1872, with monopoly as his goal, he had acquired twenty of the twenty-five refineries in Cleveland and was laying plans to bring him control of over 90 percent of the country's oil refineries within a decade. Rockefeller bought pipelines, warehouses, and factories and was able to force railroads to grant him rebates. In 1882 he formed a giant trust, the Standard Oil Company, with a multitude of affiliates. Thereafter the Standard Oil Company became a prototype of American monopolies. As Rockefeller himself put it, "The day of combination is here to stay. Individualism

TABLE 3-2. The great industrial fortunes, 1924

Ranking by 1924 income tax	Family	Primary source of wealth
1	Rockefeller	Standard Oil Co.
2	Morgan Inner Group (including Morgan partners and families and eight leading Morgan corporation executives)	J. P. Morgan & Co., Inc.
3	Ford	Ford Motor Co.
4	Harkness	Standard Oil Co.
5	Mellon	Aluminum Company
6	Vanderbilt	New York Central Railroad
7	Whitney	Standard Oil Co.
8	Standard Oil Group (including Archbold, Bedford, Cutler, Flagler, Pratt, Rogers, and Benjamin, but excepting others)	Standard Oil Co.
9	duPont	E. I. duPont de Nemours
10	McCormick	International Harvester Co. and Chicago Tribune, Inc.
11	Baker	First National Bank
12	Fisher	General Motors
13	Guggenheim	American Smelting and Refrigerating Co.
14	Field	Marshall Field & Co.
15	Curtis-Bok	The Curtis Publishing Company
16	Duke	American Tobacco Co.
17	Berwind	Berwind-White Coal Co.
18	Lehman	Lehman Brothers
19	Widener	American Tobacco and Public Utilities
20	Reynolds	R. J. Reynolds Tobacco Company
21	Astor	Real estate
22	Winthrop	Miscellaneous
23	Stillman	National City Bank
24	Timken	Timken Roller Bearing Company
25	Pitcairn	Pittsburgh Plate Glass Company

has gone, never to return." A series of antitrust cases inspired by President Theodore Roosevelt culminated in the Supreme Court decision *U.S.* v. *Standard Oil Co.* (1911), which forced the Rockefellers to divide the company into several separate corporations: Exxon Corporation, Standard Oil Co. of California, Standard Oil Co. (Indiana), Standard Oil Co. (Ohio), Atlantic Richfield Company, Mobil Corporation, and Marathon Oil Company. The Rockefellers continue to hold large blocks of stock in these companies.

Morgan. At the apex of America's new corporate and industrial elite stood J. Pierpont Morgan, master of industrial finance. In 1901 Morgan knit together the United States Steel Corp., America's first bil-

TABLE 3-2.   The great industrial fortunes, 1924 (*continued*)

Ranking by 1924 income tax	Family	Primary source of wealth
26	Warburg	Kuhn, Loeb & Company
27	Metcalf	Rhode Island textile mills
28	Clark	Singer Sewing Machine Company
29	Phipps	Carnegie Steel Company
30	Kuhn	Kuhn, Loeb & Company
31	Green	Stocks and real estate
32	Patterson	Chicago Tribune, Inc.
33	Taft	Real estate
34	Deering	International Harvester Co.
35	De Forest	Corporate law practice
36	Gould	Railroads
37	Hill	Railroads
38	Drexel	J. P. Morgan & Company
39	Thomas Fortune Ryan	Stock market
40	H. Foster (Cleveland)	Auto parts
41	Eldridge Johnson	Victor Phonograph
42	Arthur Curtiss James	Copper and railroads
43	C. W. Nash	Automobiles
44	Mortimer Schiff	Kuhn, Loeb & Company
45	James A. Patten	Wheat market
46	Charles Hayden	Stock market
47	Orlando F. Weber	Allied Chemical & Dye Corp.
48	George Blumenthal	Lazard Freres & Co.
49	Ogden L. Mills	Mining
50	Michael Friedsam	Merchandising
51	Edward B. McLean	Mining
52	Eugene Higgins	New York real estate
53	Alexander S. Cochran	Textiles
54	Mrs. L. N. Kirkwood	
55	Helen Tyson	
56	Archer D. Huntington	Railroads
57	James J. Storrow	Lee Higgins & Co.
58	Julius Rosenwald	Sears, Roebuck and Co.
59	Bernard M. Baruch	Stock market
60	S. S. Kresge	Merchandising

Source: Ferdinand Lundberg, *America's Sixty Families* (Secaucus, N.J.: Citadel Press, 1937). Reprinted by permission.

lion-dollar corporation, by merging Carnegie Steel, the Tennessee Coal and Iron Company, the Illinois Steel Company, and Colorado Fuel and Iron. He later established International Harvester Co. During World War I, J. P. Morgan & Company was the Allies' purchasing agent in America at a commission of 1 percent. Morgan was not the wealthiest person in America, but his firm derived unprecedented power from the combined resources of many families and corporations in which it had an interest, including American Telephone and Telegraph Corporation, United States Steel Corp., General Electric Co., Consolidated Edison Co., International Telephone and Telegraph Corporation, General Motors Corp., E. I. duPont de Nemours, and many others. The combined Morgan commercial banks outweighed all other banking interests in total assets, deposits, and resources. A 1932 estimate placed the Morgan interests, with their vary-ing degrees of control, dominance, and influence, at more than one-quarter of all American corporate wealth.

Political dominance of the industrial elite

The condition of the masses during the age of great industrial expansion was perhaps the lowest in American history. At the turn of the century, American workers earned, on the average, between $400 and $500 a year (or only $5,000 a year by today's standards). Unemployment was fre-quent, and unemployment benefits did not exist. A workday of ten hours, six days a week, was normal. Accidents among industrial employees were numerous and lightly regarded by employers. Employment of women and children in industry tended to hold down wages but was a necessity for many families. Child labor was ruthlessly exploited in the cotton mills of the South, in the sweatshops of the East, and in the packing plants of the West. Very few people owned their own homes; from 80 percent to 90 percent rented their dwellings.

The Republican and Democratic parties both reflected the domi-nance of the industrial elites. The Democratic party under Grover Cleve-land was little different from the Republican—except perhaps that Cleveland called upon businessmen to improve their morals and become trustees of the public interest. Nevertheless Cleveland used federal troops to break the Pullman strike in 1894 and to help keep down the urban working class. He supported the gold standard and alienated the debt-ridden farmers of the West. He even negotiated a much-publicized gold purchase loan from J. P. Morgan. Hofstadter remarks, "Out of heartfelt conviction he gave to the interests what many a lesser politician might have sold them for a price."[13]

The only serious challenge to the political dominance of eastern capital came over the issue of "free silver." Leadership of the "free silver" movement came from mine owners in the silver states of the Far West. Their campaigns convinced thousands of western farmers that the unrestricted coinage of silver was the answer to their economic distress. The western mine owners did not care about the welfare of small farm-ers, but the prospect of inflation, debt relief, and expansion of the supply of money and purchasing power won increasing support among the masses in the West and South.

When William Jennings Bryan delivered his famous Cross of Gold speech at the Democratic convention in 1896, he undid the Cleveland "Gold Democrats'" control of the Democratic party. Bryan was a west-erner, a talented orator, an anti-intellectual, and a deeply religious man; he was antagonistic to the eastern industrial interests and totally com-mitted to the cause of free silver. Bryan tried to rally the nation's have-nots to his banner; he tried to convince them that Wall Street was exploiting them. Yet he did not severely criticize the capitalist system, nor did he call for increased federal regulatory powers. In his acceptance speech he declared, "Our campaign has not for its object the reconstruction of society. . . . Property is and will remain the stimulus to endeavor and the compensation for toil."[14]

The Republican campaign, directed by Marcus Alonzo Hanna of Standard Oil, aimed to persuade the voters that what was good for business was good for the country. Hanna raised an unprecedented $16 million campaign fund from his wealthy fellow industrialists (an amount unmatched in presidential campaigns until the 1960s) and advertised his candidate, William McKinley, as the man who would bring a "full dinner pail" to all.

Bryan's attempt to rally the masses was a dismal failure; McKinley won by a landslide. Bryan ran twice again under the Democratic banner, in 1900 and 1908, but he lost by even greater margins. Although Bryan carried the South and some western states, he failed to rally the masses of the populous eastern states or of America's growing cities. Republicans carried working-class, middle-class, and upper-class neighborhoods in the urban industrial states.

Liberal establishment: Reform as elite self-interest

In 1882 William H. Vanderbilt of the New York Central Railroad expressed the ethos of the industrial elite: "The public be damned." This first generation of great American capitalists had little sense of public responsibility. They had built their empires in the competitive pursuit of profit. They believed that their success arose from the immutable laws of natural selection, the survival of the fittest; and they believed that society was best served by allowing these laws to operate freely.

Wilson's early warning

In 1910 Woodrow Wilson, forerunner of a new elite ethos, criticized America's elite for its lack of public responsibility. At a widely publicized lecture to a meeting of bankers, with J. P. Morgan sitting at his side, Wilson declared:

> The trouble today is that you bankers are too narrow-minded. You don't know the country or what is going on in it and the country doesn't trust you. . . . You take no interest in the small borrower and the small enterprise which affect the future of the country, but you give every attention to the big borrower and the rich enterprise which has already arrived. . . . You bankers see nothing beyond your own interests. . . . You should be broader-minded and see what is best for the country in the long run.[15]

Wilson urged America's elite to value the welfare of others, especially that of "the community," as an aspect of its own long-run welfare.

Wilson did not wish to upset the established order; he merely wished to develop a sense of public responsibility within the establishment. He believed that the national government should see that industrial elites operate in the public interest, and his New Freedom program reflected these high-minded aspirations. The Federal Reserve Act (1914) placed the nation's banking and credit system under public control. The Clayton Antitrust Act (1914) attempted to define specific business abuses, such as charging different prices to different buyers, granting rebates, or making false statements about competitors. Wilson's administration also established the Federal Trade Commission (1914) and authorized it to function in the "public interest" to prevent "unfair methods of competition and unfair and deceptive acts in commerce." Congress established an eight-hour day for railroad workers in interstate commerce (1914); and passed the Child Labor Act (1914) in an attempt to eliminate the worst abuses of children in industry (the Supreme Court, much less "public regarding," declared this act unconstitutional, however). Wilson's program aimed to preserve competition, individualism, enterprise, opportunity—all considered vital in the American heritage. But he also believed fervently that elites must function in the public interest and that some government regulation might be required to see that they do so.

America's participation in World War I pushed Wilson's New Freedom into the background, and the postwar reaction to reform largely wiped out its gains. During the 1920s America's elite rejected Wilsonian idealism. The established order clung to the philosophy of rugged individualism and rejected Wilson's appeal to a higher public interest.

The Great Depression

Herbert Hoover was the last great advocate of the rugged individualism of the old order. The economic collapse of the Great Depression undermined the faith of both elites and nonelites in the ideals of the old order. Following the stock market crash of October 1929, and despite elite assurances that prosperity lay "just around the corner," the American economy virtually stopped. Prices dropped sharply, factories closed, real estate values declined, new construction practically ceased, banks went under, wages dropped drastically, and unemployment figures mounted. By 1932 one out of every four persons was unemployed, and one out of every five persons was on welfare. People who had never known unemployment before lost their jobs, used up their savings or lost them when banks folded, cashed in their life insurance, gave up their homes and farms because they could not continue the mortgage payments. Economic catastrophe struck far up into the ranks of the middle classes. A person who lost a job could not find another. Tramps abounded, panhandlers plied the streets, transients slept on the steps of public buildings, on park benches, on lawns, or on highways. Mines were no longer worked; steel mills, iron foundries, and every variety of industrial plant put out only a fraction of the goods that they could produce; trains ran with only a handful of passengers; stores lacked customers, and many closed their doors; ships stayed in port; hospitals were empty, not because they were unneeded but because people could not afford them.

Elite reform

The election of Franklin Delano Roosevelt to the presidency in 1932 ushered in a new era in American elite philosophy. The Great Depression did not bring about a revolution or the emergence of new elites, but it did have an important impact on the thinking of America's governing elites. The economic disaster that had befallen the nation caused American elites to consider the need for economic reform. The depression also gave force to Wilson's advice that elites acquire a greater public responsibility. The victories of fascism in Germany and communism in the Soviet Union and the growing restlessness of the masses in America combined to convince America's elite that reform and regard for the public welfare were essential to the continued maintenance of the American political system and their dominant place in it.

Roosevelt sought a New Deal philosophy that would permit government to devote much more attention to the public welfare than did the philosophy of Hoover's somewhat discredited "rugged individualism." The New Deal was not new or revolutionary but rather a necessary reform of the existing capitalist system. It had no consistent unifying plan; it was a series of improvisations, many of them adopted very suddenly and some of them even contradictory. Roosevelt believed that government needed to undertake more careful economic planning to adapt "existing economic organizations to the service of the people." And he believed that the government must act humanely and compassionately toward those who were suffering hardship. Relief, recovery, and reform, not revolution, were the objectives of the New Deal.

"Noblesse oblige"

For anyone of Roosevelt's background, it would have been surprising indeed if he had tried to do other than preserve the existing social and economic order. Roosevelt was a descendant of two of America's oldest elite families, the Roosevelts and the Delanos, patrician families whose wealth predated the Civil War and the industrial revolution. The Roosevelts were not schooled in social Darwinism or the survival of the fittest or the scrambling competition of the new industrialists. From the beginning Roosevelt expressed a public-regarding philosophy. In Hofstadter's words:

At the beginning of his career he took to the patrician reform thought of the progressive era and accepted a social outlook that can best be summed up in the phrase "noblesse oblige." He had a penchant for public service, personal philanthropy, and harmless manifestos against dishonesty in government; he displayed a broad easy-going tolerance, a genuine liking for all sorts of people; he loved to exercise his charm in political and social situations.[16]

Roosevelt's personal philosophy of noblesse oblige—elite responsibility for the welfare of the masses—soon became the prevailing ethos of the new liberal establishment.

In the New Deal, American elites accepted the principle that the entire community, through the agency of the national government, had a responsibility for mass welfare. In Roosevelt's second inaugural address he called attention to "one third of a nation, ill-housed, ill-clad, ill-nourished." Roosevelt succeeded in saving the existing system of private capitalism and avoiding the threats to the established order posed by fascism, socialism, communism, and other radical movements.

Of course, some capitalists were unwilling to be "saved" by the New Deal. Roosevelt was genuinely hurt by criticisms from American industrialists, whom he felt he had protected with his reforms; he was angry at the "economic royalists" who challenged his policies. He believed that the economic machinery of the nation had broken down and that the political fabric of America was beginning to unravel. He believed he had stabilized the economy and returned politics safely to its normal democratic course. He believed that his relief and reform measures were those that any wise and humane conservative would agree are necessary.

Emergence of the liberal establishment

Eventually Roosevelt's philosophy of noblesse oblige won widespread acceptance within America's established leadership. The success of Roosevelt's liberal philosophy was in part a product of the economic disaster of the Great Depression and in part a tribute to the effectiveness of Roosevelt himself as a mobilizer of opinion among both elites and masses. But the acceptance of liberal establishment ideas may also be attributed in part to the changes taking place in the economic system.

One such change was a declining rate of new elite formation. Most of America's great entrepreneurial families had built their empires before World War I. The first-generation industrialists and entrepreneurs were unfriendly toward philosophies of public responsibility and appeals to the public interest. But among the children and grandchildren of the great empire builders, these ideals won increasing acceptance. Those who are born to wealth seem to accept the idea of noblesse oblige more than those who must acquire wealth for themselves, and available evidence indicates that more self-made men were around in 1900 than in 1950. Figure 3-1 shows that only 39 percent of America's richest men in

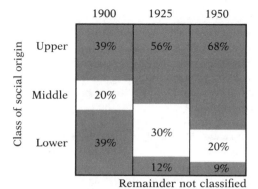

Remainder not classified

Figure 3–1   Social Origins of America's Richest Men, 1900–1950

Note: The percentages are derived from biographies of the 275 people who were and are known to historians, biographers, and journalists as the richest people living in the United States—the ninety richest of 1900, the ninety-five of 1925, and the ninety of 1950. At the top of the 1900 group is John D. Rockefeller; at the top in 1925 is Henry Ford I; at the top of the 1950 is H. L. Hunt.

Source: Data based on C. Wright Mills, *The Power Elite* (New York: Oxford University Press, 1956). pp. 104–105.

1900 came from the upper classes, while 68 percent of the nation's richest men in 1950 were born to wealth. Moreover, 39 percent of the richest men in 1900 had struggled up from the bottom, whereas only 9 percent of the richest men of 1950 had done so. These data suggest that America's elite in the mid-twentieth century was more receptive to the ideas of responsibility for the common good and concern for the welfare of the masses. Wilson's appeals for elite responsibility fell on the deaf ears of John D. Rockefeller in 1910, but a sense of public responsibility motivated the careers of his grandsons: Nelson Rockefeller, former governor of New York and vice-president of the United States (appointed); Winthrop Rockefeller, former governor of Arkansas; David Rockefeller, chairman of the board of the Chase Manhattan Bank of New York; and John D. Rockefeller III, former chairman of the board of the Lincoln Center for Performing Arts in New York City.

Case study: Elites in American history

What has been the relationship between economic elites and governmental leadership in American history? Political scientist Phillip H. Burch has explored this central question in a three-volume study evaluating the social and economic backgrounds of top cabinet-level and diplomatic appointments from the administration of President George Washington to that of President Jimmy Carter.* Burch defines an "economic elite" as a person who has held an important post (executive or director) in a major business enterprise or corporate law firm and/or whose family owned great wealth

(continued)

Case study (*continued*)

or occupied an important corporate position. This economic elite never constituted over 1 percent of the U.S. population. Yet according to Burch, over the years since 1789 they constituted 78.7 percent of top governmental leaders.

According to Burch, the accompanying table shows that "the United States has certainly not been a land of equality of political opportunity. Rather, it has been an elitist-dominated nation." Nonetheless, economic elites occupied fewer top governmental posts in some periods than in others. During the New Deal years and World War II, President Roosevelt brought many non-economic-elites into top government posts, although Roosevelt himself possessed the very highest elite credentials. In earlier periods of American political history, government was almost exclusively directed by economic elites (95.8 percent elite dominated in the pre–Civil War period, compared with 74.4 percent in more recent years).

Overall, nearly 80 percent of the nation's top appointed leaders have been elite figures, a considerably higher percentage than the proportion of presidents with elite backgrounds (only 58 percent by Burch's estimate). Burch concludes: "Regardless of its changing form, America has almost always been dominated by some form of wealth."**

*Phillip H. Burch, Jr., *Elites in American History*, 3 vols. (New York: Holmes and Meier, 1980).
**Ibid., Vol. III, p. 388.

Elites in Government 1789–1980

	Elite cabinet and diplomatic appointees %
Federalist period (1789–1801)	100.0
Jeffersonian Republican years (1801–1829)	95.7
Jacksonian era (1829–1841)	93.8
Pre–Civil War decades (1841–1861)	95.2
Pre–Civil War period (1789–1861)	95.8
Civil War and Reconstruction (1861–1877)	81.1
Late nineteenth-century period (1877–1897)	86.8
McKinley-Taft years (1897–1913)	91.7
Wilson regime (1913–1921)	57.1
Harding-Hoover years (1921–1933)	80.9
Post–Civil War to New Deal period (1861–1933)	83.5
New Deal years (1933–1940)	47.4
World War II years (1940–1945)	57.9
Truman years (1945–1953)	55.6
Eisenhower years (1953–1961)	81.1
Kennedy-Johnson years (1961–1969)	62.7
Nixon-Ford years (1969–1977)	68.6
Carter years (1977–1980)	65.4
New Deal to Carter period (1933–1980)	64.4
Overall (1789–1980)	78.7

Note: An elite appointee is a person who has held a prior important position (executive or director) in a major business enterprise or corporate law firm and/or whose family has considerable wealth or an important corporate link.

Source: Phillip H. Burch, Jr., *Elites in American History*, Vol. III (New York: Holmes and Meier, 1980), p. 383. Reprinted by permission.

Summary

According to elite theory, the movement of nonelites into elite positions must be slow and continuous to maintain stability and avoid revolution. Furthermore potential elite members must demonstrate their commitment to the basic elite consensus before being admitted to elite positions. Elite theory recognizes competition among elites but contends that elites share a broad consensus about preserving the system essentially as it is. It views public-policy changes as a response to elite redefinition of its own self-interest rather than as a product of direct mass influence. Finally elite theory views changes in public policy as incremental rather than revolutionary. America's political history supports these propositions:

1. America's elite membership evolved slowly with no serious break in the ideas or values of the American political and economic system. When the leadership of Hamilton and Adams—Federalists—shifted to that of Jefferson, Monroe, and Madison—Republicans—the policies of American government changed very little because of the fundamental consensus among elite members.

2. As new sources of wealth opened in an expanding economy, America's elite membership opened to new groups and individuals who acquired wealth and property and who accepted the national consensus about private enterprise, limited government, and individualism. The West produced new elites, who were assimilated into America's governing circle. Public policies changed but were not replaced. The Jacksonians wanted a more open elite system in which the newly wealthy could acquire influence, but they were no more in favor of "dangerous leveling" than were the Founding Fathers.

3. The Civil War reduced Southern planters' influence in America's elite structure and paved the way for the rise of the new industrial capitalists. The industrial revolution produced a narrowly self-interested elite of industrial capitalists. Mass movements resulted—chiefly free silver—but they met with failure.

4. America's elites have divided deeply on the nature of American society only once. This division produced the Civil War, the nation's bloodiest conflict. The Civil War was a conflict between Southern elites—dependent on a plantation economy, slave labor, and free trade—and Northern industrial commercial elites—who prospered under free labor and protective tariffs. But before, during, and after the Civil War, Northern and Southern elites continued to strive for compromise in recognition of shared consensus on behalf of liberty and property.

5. Although industrial elites were never ousted from power, they were prevailed upon to assume a more public-regarding attitude toward

the welfare of the masses. Economic collapse undermined the faith of elites and nonelites in the rugged individualism of the nineteenth-century industrial elite. But even economic collapse brought neither revolution nor the emergence of new elites. Instead the Great Depression, the victories of fascism in Germany and communism in the Soviet Union, and growing restlessness of the American masses combined to convince America's elites that a more public-regarding philosophy was essential to preserving the American political system and their prominent place in it.

6. The new liberal establishment sought to preserve the existing social and economic order, not to overthrow it. Eventually Franklin D. Roosevelt's philosophy of noblesse oblige—elite responsibility for the welfare of the masses—won widespread acceptance within America's established leadership.

7. Political conflict in America has centered on a narrow range of issues. Consensus rather than conflict has characterized America's elite history. Political rhetoric and campaign slogans should not obscure the fundamental consensus of America's elites. Whatever the popular political label has been—"Federalist," "Democratic," "Whig," "Republican," "Progressive," "Conservative," or "Liberal"—America's leadership has been essentially conservative.

8. Policy changes, even those seemingly as revolutionary as the New Deal, did not cause any serious break in the ideals and values of the American system; nor did they result from demands by "the people." Instead policy changes, including the New Deal, occurred when events threatened the system; governing elites—acting on the basis of enlightened self-interest—instituted reforms to preserve the system. Even the reforms and welfare policies of the New Deal were designed to strengthen the existing social and economic fabric of society while minimally dislocating elites.

NOTES

1. *McCulloch* v. *Maryland*, 4 Wheaton 316 (1819).
2. See Richard Hofstadter, *The American Political Tradition* (New York: Knopf, 1948), pp. 18–44.
3. Ibid., pp. 32–33.
4. Ibid., p. 38.
5. Frederick Jackson Turner, "The West and American Ideals," in *The Frontier in American History* (New York: Holt, Rinehart and Winston, 1921).
6. See Hofstadter, op cit., pp. 45–67.
7. *Dred Scott* v. *Sandford*, 19 Howard 393 (1857).
8. Hofstadter, op. cit., p. 109.
9. Ibid., p. 113.
10. Ibid., p. 116.
11. Herbert Spencer, *Social Statics* (1851).

12. See Gustavus Myers, *A History of the Great American Fortunes*, 3 vols. (Chicago: Kerr, 1910).
13. Hofstadter, op. cit., p. 185.
14. V. O. Key, Jr., *Politics, Parties, and Pressure Groups* (New York: T. Y. Crowell, 1942), pp. 189–191.
15. Hofstadter, op cit., p. 251.
16. Ibid., pp. 323–324.

SELECTED READINGS

Beard, Charles A. *The Economic Basis of Politics*. New York: Knopf, 1947. Beard provides a brief reinterpretation of American political history from the perspective of economic determinism. America's foremost historian and political scientist first published this essay in 1916.

Hartz, Louis. *The Liberal Tradition in America*. New York: Harcourt, Brace & World, 1955. The absence of a feudal aristocracy in America obstructed the development of social class consciousness, which in turn prevented the emergence of socialism in this country. America as a nation was "born free," and most Americans consider themselves middle class.

Hofstadter, Richard. *The American Political Tradition*. New York: Knopf, Vintage Books, 1948. This book is an important political history from an elite perspective. Hofstadter traces the development of American political elites and their philosophies from Jefferson and the Founding Fathers through Jackson, Bryan, Wilson, and Franklin Roosevelt. He emphasizes that at every stage of American history, elites have been in considerable agreement over major issues (with the possible exception of the Civil War). Finally Hofstadter discusses the elite practice of incrementalism: that elite leaders have always moved to preserve the established order with as little change in the system as possible.

Lundberg, Ferdinand. *America's Sixty Families*. New York: Citadel Press, 1937. This book is a classic work on elites that systematically traces the development of the entrepreneurial elite of the late nineteenth and early twentieth centuries.

4 Positions of Power in America

Power in America is organized into large institutions: corporate, governmental, military, religious, professional, occupational. We include the major private institutions—in industry, finance, law, and other "nongovernmental institutions"—because we believe that they allocate values for our society and shape the lives of all Americans.

The leading men in each of the three domains of power—the warlords, the corporation chieftains, the political directorate—tend to come together to form the power elite of America.

—C. Wright Mills, The Power Elite, *1959*

Power in America is organized into large institutions—corporate, government, educational, military, religious, professional, occupational. Positions at the top of the major institutions in American society are sources of great power. True, not all power is anchored in and exercised through institutions, and the potential power of giant institutions is not always exercised by the leadership, but institutional positions nevertheless provide a continuous and important base of power. Sociologist C. Wright Mills described the relationship between institutional authority and power in this way:

> If we took the one hundred most powerful men in America, the one hundred wealthiest, and the one hundred most celebrated away from the institutional positions they now occupy, away from their resources of men and women and money, away from the media of mass communication that are now focused upon them—then they would be powerless and poor and uncelebrated. For power is not of a man. Wealth does not center in the person of the wealthy. Celebrity is not inherent in any personality. To be celebrated, to be wealthy, to have power, requires access to major institutions, for the institutional positions men occupy determine in large part their chances to have and to hold these valued experiences.[1]

In this chapter we describe the people who occupy high positions in the major private and governmental institutions of American society. We include the major *private* institutions—in industry, finance, law, and other "nongovernmental institutions"—because we believe that they allocate values for our society and shape the lives of all Americans. Remember, we defined an elite member as anyone who participates in decisions that allocate values for society, not just those who participate in decision making as part of the government. The decisions of steel companies to raise prices, of defense industries to develop new weapons, of banks to raise or lower interest rates, of electrical companies to market new products, of the mass media to determine what is "news," and of schools and colleges to decide what shall be taught—all affect the lives of Americans as much as do government decisions. Moreover these private institutions have the power and resources to enforce their decisions.

Nondecisions

Nondecisions occur when individuals or institutions limit the scope of decision making to exclude issues that disturb established elites. Keeping issues *out* of politics is an important aspect of power, one that is just as important (perhaps more so) as deciding the issues that *are* presented to public officials. So power really has two manifestations: decisions and nondecisions. Power is not only deciding the issues but also deciding what the issues will be.

Nondecisions can occur (1) when influential elites act directly to exclude an issue from the political arena; (2) when subordinates anticipate the negative reaction of elites and ignore proposals or suggestions that would "cause trouble"; or (3) when the underlying values of society and its institutional structure prevent serious consideration of alternative programs and policies.

In nondecision making, those at the top of institutional structures need not exercise their power overtly; their subordinates who carry on the day-to-day business of industry, finance, government, and so on know the values of the top elite and understand the great potential for power that the top elite possesses. These subordinates obtained their jobs in part because they reflected dominant values in their thinking and actions. Whether consciously or unconsciously, their decisions reflect the values of those at the top.

The institutional structure of society also exercises power when it limits the scope of public decision making to issues that are relatively harmless to the elite. Institutions support the achievement of some values while obstructing the achievement of others. For example, we already know that the Founding Fathers deliberately constructed the American government system to suppress certain values and issues. James Madison, in *The Federalist* Number 10, defended the structure of the new American government, particularly its republican and federal features, on the grounds that it would suppress "factious issues." And Madison named outright the factious issues that must be avoided: "a rage for paper money, for an abolition of debts, for an equal division of property, or any other improper or wicked project."[2] Note that all the issues Madison wished to avoid involved challenges to the dominant economic interests. As a nongovernment example, consider the following: by placing owners of large blocks of company stock on governing boards of directors and by increasingly allocating large blocks of stock to top management personnel, American corporations tend to encourage the values of profit and investment security in corporate decision making. The structure of the American corporation deters it from pursuing a policy of public welfare at the expense of profit.

The fact that institutional structures maximize certain values (private enterprise, limited government, the profit system) while obstructing other values (absolute equality or "leveling," government ownership of industry) is an important aspect of American politics. It is another reason for examining the major institutions of society and those who occupy high positions in them.

Governing elites

Politicians specialize in office seeking. They know how to run for office, but they may not know how to run the government. After victory at the polls, wise politicians turn to experienced executive elites to run the government. Both Democratic and Republican presidents select essentially the same type of executive elite to staff the key positions in their administrations. These top government executives—cabinet members, presidential advisers, department officers, special ambassadors—are frequently people who have occupied key posts in private industry, finance, or law, or who have held influential positions in education, in the arts and sciences, or in social, civic, and charitable associations. They move easily in and out of government posts from their positions in the corporate, financial, legal, and educational world. They often assume government jobs at a financial sacrifice, and many do so out of a sense of public service.

Obviously the top leadership in America overlaps to some extent, but it is difficult to measure precisely how much. The pluralist model of power (described in chapter 1) suggests very little overlap, with *different* groups exercising power in different sectors of American life. In contrast, the elitist model of power envisions extensive overlap, with a single group of people exercising power in many different sectors of American life. To understand position overlap among American elites, examine the career backgrounds of several key government executives in recent Democratic and Republican presidential administrations.

Secretaries of State

John Foster Dulles: 1953–1960; partner of Sullivan and Cromwell (one of twenty largest law firms on Wall Street); member of the board of directors of the Bank of New York, the Fifth Avenue Bank, the American Bank Note Company, the International Nickel Company of Canada, Babcock and Wilson Corporation, Gold Dust Corporation, the Overseas Security Corporation, Shenandoah Corporation, United Cigar Stores, American Cotton Oil Company, United Railroad of St. Louis, and European Textile Corporation; a trustee of the New York Public Library, the Union Theological Seminary, the Rockefeller Foundation, and the Carnegie Endowment for International Peace; a delegate to the World Council of Churches.

Dean Rusk: 1961–1968; former president of the Rockefeller Foundation.

William P. Rogers: 1969–1973; U.S. attorney general during Eisenhower administration; senior partner in Royall, Koegal, Rogers, and Wells (one of the twenty largest Wall Street law firms).

Henry Kissinger: 1973–1977; former special assistant to the president for national security affairs; former Harvard professor of international affairs and project director for Rockefeller Brothers Fund and for the Council on Foreign Relations.

Cyrus Vance: 1977–1980; senior partner in New York law firm of Simpson, Thatcher, and Bartlett; a director of IBM and Pan American World Airways; a trustee of Yale University and chairman of the board of trustees of the Rockefeller Foundation, and a member of the Council on Foreign Relations; former secretary of the army and undersecretary of defense; U.S. negotiator in the Paris Peace Conference on Vietnam.

Edward S. Muskie: 1980–1981; the only "political" figure to serve in this office in recent times. U.S. senator (D-Maine), 1959–1980, and chairman of the Senate Budget Committee. Former Governor of Maine, 1955–1959; member of Maine House of Representatives, 1947–1951. Small-town attorney.

Alexander M. Haig, Jr.: 1981–1982; president of United Technologies and former four-star general, U.S. Army; former supreme allied commander NATO; former White House chief of staff under President Richard Nixon; former deputy assistant for national security affairs under Henry Kissinger.

George P. Schultz: 1982– ; president of Bechtel Corporation, the world's largest construction company; former secretary of treasury and secretary of labor; former dean of the Graduate School of Business of the University of Chicago; a director of J. P. Morgan & Company, Morgan Guaranty Trust Co., Sears Roebuck and Co., and the Alfred P. Sloan Foundation.

Secretaries of Defense

Charles E. Wilson: 1953–1957; president and member of the board of directors of General Motors Corporation.

Neil H. McElroy: 1957–1959; former president and member of the board of directors of Procter & Gamble Co.; member of the board of directors of General Electric Co., Chrysler Corporation, and Equitable Life Insurance Company; member of the board of trustees of Harvard University, the National Safety Council, and the National Industrial Conference.

Thomas S. Gates: 1959–1960, and secretary of the navy, 1957–1959; chairman of the board and chief executive officer, Morgan Guaranty Trust Co. (J. P. Morgan, New York); member of the board of directors of General Electric Co., Bethlehem Steel Corp., Scott Paper Co., Campbell Soup Co., Insurance Co. of North America, Cities Service Co., Smith, Kline and French (pharmaceuticals), and the University of Pennsylvania.

Robert S. McNamara: 1961–1967; president and member of the board of directors of the Ford Motor Co.; member of the board of directors of Scott Paper Co.; president of the World Bank, 1967 to 1982.

Clark Clifford: 1967–1969; senior partner of Clifford and Miller (Washington law firm); member of the board of directors of the National Bank of Washington and the Sheridan Hotel Corporation; special counsel to the president, 1949–1950; member of the board of trustees of Washington University in St. Louis.

Melvin Laird: 1969–1973; former Republican congressman from Wisconsin.

James R. Schlesinger: 1973–1977; former director, Central Intelligence Agency; former chairman, Atomic Energy Commission; former economics professor and research associate, Rand Corporation.

Harold Brown: 1977–1981; former president, California Institute of Technology; member of the board of directors of IBM Corp. and the Times-Mirror Corporation; former secretary of the Air Force under President Lyndon Johnson; and U.S. representative to the Strategic Arms Limitation Treaty talks under President Richard Nixon.

Caspar W. Weinberger: 1980– ; former vice-president of Bechtel Corporation, former secretary of health, education, and welfare; former director of Office of Management and Budget; former chairman of Federal Trade Commission; a director of Pepsico and Quaker Oats Co., former San Francisco attorney and California state legislator.

Secretaries of the Treasury

George M. Humphrey: 1953–1957; former chairman of the board of directors of the M. A. Hanna Company; member of the board of directors of National Steel Corp., Consolidated Coal Company, Canada and Dominion Sugar Company; a trustee of the Massachusetts Institute of Technology.

Robert B. Anderson: 1957–1961; secretary of the navy, 1953–1954; deputy secretary of defense, 1954–1955; member of the board of directors of the Goodyear Tire & Rubber Company; member of the executive board of the Boy Scouts of America.

Douglas Dillon: 1961–1965; chairman of the board of Dillon, Reed, and Company (Wall Street investment firm); member of the New York Stock Exchange; director of U.S. and Foreign Securities Corporation and of U.S. International Securities Corporation; member of the board of governors of the New York Hospital and of the Metropolitan Museum.

Henry H. Fowler: 1965–1969; senior partner, Washington law firm of Fowler, Leva, Hawes, and Symington; former undersecretary of the treasury, 1961–1964; member of the Council on Foreign Relations.

David Kennedy: 1969–1971; president and chairman of the board of Continental Illinois Bank and Trust Company; a director of International Harvester Company, Commonwealth Edison, Pullman Company, Abbott Laboratories, Swift and Company, U.S. Gypsum, and Communications Satellite Corporation; and a trustee of the University of Chicago, the Brookings Institution, the Committee for Economic Development, and George Washington University.

John B. Connally: 1971–1972; former secretary of the navy, governor of Texas, administrative assistant to Lyndon B. Johnson; attorney for Murcheson Brothers Investment (Dallas); former director of New York Central Railroad.

George P. Schultz: 1972–1974; former secretary of labor and director of the Office of Management and Budget; former dean of the University of Chicago Graduate School of Business; former senior partner of Salmon Brothers (one of Wall Street's largest investment firms) and Stein, Roe and Farnham (investments).

William E. Simon: 1974–1977; former director, Federal Energy Office, and former deputy secretary of the treasury; formerly a senior partner of Salmon Brothers.

Werner Michael Blumenthal: 1977–1979; former president of the Bendix Corporation; a trustee of Princeton University and member of the Council on Foreign Relations.

G. William Miller: 1979–1981; chairman and chief executive officer of the Textron Corporation; formerly a partner in the prestigious New York law firm of Cravath, Swaine, and Moore; a director of Allied Chemical and Federated Department Stores; former chairman of the Council of Economic Advisors.

Donald T. Regan: 1981– ; former chairman of Merrill Lynch & Co., the nation's largest investment firm; former vice-chairman of the New York Stock Exchange; a trustee of the University of Pennsylvania, Committee for Economic Development, and the Business Roundtable.

The administrations of presidents Kennedy, Johnson, Nixon, Ford, Carter, and Reagan included top business leaders, experienced corporate lawyers, and intellectuals from prestigious universities. The mixture of career backgrounds represented in each of these administrations showed only slight variation. For example, Kennedy's secretary of defense was Robert McNamara, president of Ford Motor Co., while Eisenhower's secretary of defense was Charles E. Wilson, president of General Motors Corp. Kennedy brought into government as special assistant to the president for national security, McGeorge Bundy, who was formerly dean of arts and sciences at Harvard University. The Nixon administration replaced Harvard dean McGeorge Bundy with Harvard professor Henry

Kissinger. The Carter administration replaced Harvard professor Henry Kissinger with Columbia professor Zbigniew Brzezinski. The Rockefeller Foundation supported the intellectual careers of both Kissinger and Brzezinski. The Bechtel Corporation supplied its president and vice-president, George Schultz and Caspar Weinberger, to serve the nation as secretaries of state and defense in the Reagan administration.

Corporate elites

Formal control of the nation's economic life rests in the hands of the presidents, vice-presidents, and boards of directors of the nation's corporate institutions. This concentration has occurred chiefly because the economic enterprise has increasingly consolidated into a small number of giant corporations. The following statistics only suggest the scale and concentration of modern corporate enterprise in America.

More than two hundred thousand industrial corporations exist in the United States, but the one hundred corporations listed in table 4-1 control 52 percent of all industrial assets in the nation. The five largest industrial corporations (Exxon Corporation, General Motors Corp., Mobil Corporation, Ford Motor Co., and International Business Machines Corp.) control 10 percent of the nation's industrial assets themselves. Concentration in utilities, transportation, and communications is even greater.

The financial world is equally concentrated. Of thirteen thousand five hundred banks serving the nation, the fifty largest banks control 48 percent of all banking assets; three banks (Bank of America, Citicorp, and Chase Manhattan) control 14 percent of all banking assets. (See table 4-2.)

Control of these corporate resources is officially entrusted to the presidents and directors of these corporations. Approximately thirty-six hundred people are listed as presidents or directors of these top corporations. Collectively these people control half of the nation's industrial assets and nearly half of all banking assets.

A. A. Berle, Jr., a corporation lawyer and corporate director who has written extensively on the modern corporation, explains that corporate power rests with these corporations' directors and with the holders of large control blocks of corporate stock:

> The control system in today's corporations, when it does not lie solely in the directors as in the American Telephone & Telegraph Company, lies in a combination of the directors of a so-called control block (of stock) plus the directors themselves. For practical purposes, therefore, the control or power element in most large corporations rests in its group of directors, and it is autonomous—or autonomous if taken together with a control block. . . . This is a self-perpetuating oligarchy.[3]

Drawing by Stan Hunt; ©1975 The New Yorker
Magazine, Inc.

*"The People want integrity?
Big deal. We'll give them integrity."*

Corporate power thus does not rest in the hands of the masses of corporate employees or even in the hands of the millions of middle- and upper-middle-class Americans who own corporate stock.

Corporate power is further concentrated by a system of interlocking directorates and by a corporate ownership system in which control blocks of stock are owned by financial institutions rather than by private individuals. Interlocking directorates, in which a director of one corporation also sits on the boards of other corporations, enable key corporate elites to wield influence over a large number of corporations. It is not uncommon for top members of an elite to hold four, five, or six directorships.

Economist Gabriel Kolko summarizes what we know about corporate power in America:

> The concentration of economic power in a very small elite is an indisputable fact.... A social theory assuming a democratized economic system—or even a trend in this direction—is quite obviously not in accord with social reality. Whether the men who control industry are socially responsive or trustees of the social welfare is quite another matter: it is one thing to speculate about their motivations, another to generalize about economic facts. And even if we assume that these men act benevolently toward their workers and the larger community, their actions still would not be the result of social control through a formal democratic structure and group

TABLE 4-1.   The 100 largest industrial corporations (ranked by sales)

1 Exxon	51 Armco
2 Mobil	52 General Foods
3 General Motors	53 W. R. Grace
4 Texaco	54 Minnesota Mining & Mfg.
5 Standard Oil of California	55 Allied
6 Ford Motor	56 Union Pacific
7 Standard Oil (Indiana)	57 Lockheed
8 International Business Machines	58 Coca-Cola
9 Gulf Oil	59 Coastal
10 Atlantic Richfield	60 Nabisco Brands
11 General Electric	61 Gulf & Western Industries
12 E.I. duPont de Nemours	62 Raytheon
13 Shell Oil	63 Consolidated Foods
14 International Telephone and	64 Farmland Industries
Telegraph	65 Deere
15 Phillips Petroleum	66 Sperry
16 Tenneco	67 Georgia-Pacific
17 Sun	68 Johnson & Johnson
18 Occidental Petroleum	69 Honeywell
19 U.S. Steel	70 Signal Companies
20 United Technologies	71 TRW
21 Standard Oil (Ohio)	72 Colgate-Palmolive
22 Western Electric	73 Ralston Purina
23 Getty Oil	74 Continental Group
24 Dow Chemical	75 Charter
25 Procter & Gamble	76 General Dynamics
26 Chrysler	77 International Paper
27 Union Oil of California	78 Aluminum Co. of America
28 Eastman Kodak	79 Litton Industries
29 Dart & Kraft	80 General Mills
30 Union Carbide	81 American Can
31 Boeing	82 Greyhound
32 R. J. Reynolds Industries	83 Dresser Industries
33 Amerada Hess	84 Weyerhaeuser
34 Westinghouse Electric	85 Borden
35 Ashland Oil	86 Bendix
36 Marathon Oil	87 Republic Steel
37 Caterpillar Tractor	88 Firestone Tire & Rubber
38 Goodyear Tire & Rubber	89 CPC International
39 Cities Service	90 BATUS
40 LTV	91 Texas Instruments
41 Beatrice Foods	92 IC Industries
42 Xerox	93 American Home Products
43 Philip Morris	94 National Steel
44 RCA	95 United Brands
45 McDonnell Douglas	96 American Brands
46 International Harvester	97 Champion International
47 Bethlehem Steel	98 Owens-Illinois
48 Rockwell International	99 Anheuser-Busch
49 Pepsico	100 Agway
50 Monsanto	

Source: *Fortune*, May 1982.

TABLE 4-2.   The 50 largest commercial-banking companies (ranked by assets)

1 BankAmerica Corp.	26 Seafirst Corp.
2 Citicorp	27 European American Bancorp.
3 Chase Manhattan Corp.	28 NCNB Corp.
4 Manufacturers Hanover Corp.	29 Republic New York Corp.
5 J. P. Morgan & Co.	30 Harris Bankcorp.
6 Continental Illinois Corp.	31 Pittsburgh National Corp.
7 Chemical New York Corp.	32 Union Bank
8 First Interstate Bancorp.	33 Mercantile Texas Corp.
9 Bankers Trust New York Corp.	34 Southeast Banking Corp.
10 First Chicago Corp.	35 Philadelphia National Corp.
11 Security Pacific Corp.	36 Wachovia Corp.
12 Wells Fargo & Co.	37 Northern Trust Corp.
13 Crocker National Corp.	38 Michigan National Corp.
14 Marine Midland Banks	39 DETROITBANK Corp.
15 Mellon National Corp.	40 Valley National Corp.
16 Irving Bank Corp.	41 National Bank of North America
17 InterFirst Corp.	42 Rainier Bancorp.
18 First National Boston Corp.	43 U.S. Bancorp.
19 Northwest Bancorp.	44 Ameritrust Corp.
20 First Bank System	45 BancOhio Corp.
21 Texas Commerce Bancshares	46 Barnett Banks of Florida
22 Republic of Texas Corp.	47 National City Corp.
23 First City Bancorp. of Texas	48 Centerre Bancorp.
24 NBD Bancorp.	49 First Union Corp.
25 Bank of New York Co.	50 First Pennsylvania Corp.

Source: *Fortune*, July 1982.

participation, which are the essentials for democracy; they would be an arbitrary noblesse oblige by the economic elite. When discussing the existing corporate system, it would be more realistic to drop all references to democracy.[4]

Wealth in America

Income inequality is and has always been a significant component of the American social structure.[5] The top fifth (20 percent) of income recipients in America receives over 40 percent of all income in the nation, while the bottom fifth receives only about 5 percent. (See table 4-3.) However, the income share of the top fifth has declined since the pre–World War II years. And the income share of the top 5 percent of families has declined dramatically from 30.0 to 15.7 percent. But the bottom fifth of the population still receives a very small share of the national income. The only significant rise in income distributions has occurred among the middle classes, in the second, third, and fourth income fifths. Many people believe that the progressive income tax substantially levels incomes, but this is not really so. The best available evidence suggests that taxation has not altered the unequal distribution of income.

Millionaires in America are no longer considered rich. Over two million people have net worths exceeding $1 million. To be truly rich

TABLE 4-3.   Distribution of family income in America

Quintiles	By quintiles and top 5 percent								
	1929	1936	1944	1950	1956	1962	1972	1975	1980
Lowest	3.5	4.1	4.9	4.8	4.8	4.6	5.5	5.4	5.2
Second	9.0	9.2	10.9	10.9	11.3	10.9	12.0	12.0	11.6
Third	13.8	14.1	16.2	16.1	16.3	16.3	17.4	17.5	17.5
Fourth	19.3	20.9	22.2	22.1	22.3	22.7	23.5	24.1	24.2
Highest	54.4	51.7	45.8	46.1	45.3	45.5	41.6	41.0	41.5
Total	100.0	100.0	100.0	100.0	100.0	100.0	100.0	100.0	100.0
Top 5 percent	30.0	24.0	20.7	21.4	20.2	19.6	14.4	15.3	15.7

Source: U.S. Bureau of the Census, *Current Population Reports;* data for early years from Edward C. Budd, *Inequality and Poverty* (New York: Norton, 1967).

today, one must be a *centimillionaire*—worth more than $100 million. In 1982, *Forbes* magazine identified "The *Forbes* Four Hundred"—400 Americans with individual net worth of at least $100 million.[6] In 1957 *Fortune* identified 45 centimillionaires, and in 1968 the magazine identified 153; the *Forbes* Four Hundred in 1982 points up the rate at which the nation's rich are increasing. Most of the nation's wealthy are reluctant to reveal their net worth; thus any listing is only an estimate.

Great wealth is not necessary to live well in the United States; one can purchase a nice estate for as little as $2.5 million, a new Rolls Royce for $115,000, a modest yet comfortable yacht for $500,000. Most centimillionaires enjoy a personal lifestyle no more lavish than a family with $5–$10 million. The fortunes listed in *Forbes* include many familiar names: Annenberg, Bechtel, Cabot, Chandler, Cox, Dorranee, duPont, Duke, Ford, Haas, Heinz, Hearst, Hunt, Houghton, Kennedy, Kleberg, Kroc, Lykes, McCormick, Mellon, Pew, Phipps, Pitcairn, Pulitzer, Pritzker, Rockefeller, Uihlein, Upjohn, Weyerhaeuser.

Despite hundreds of centimillionaires in America, however, *personal* wealth is insignificant next to *institutional* wealth. Individuals may control millions, but institutions control billions. A president of a major corporation may receive an annual salary of $300,000 or $500,000 and possess a net worth of $5 million, but these amounts are insignificant when compared to the monies that the same president may control— perhaps annual revenues of $5 billion and assets worth $10 billion or $20 billion. The contrast between individual wealth and institutional wealth is even greater when we consider that a bureaucrat in the federal government may make only $50,000 but control an annual budget of $50 billion.

Thus by far the greatest inequalities are between institutional wealth and personal wealth. Even if the government confiscated the entire personal wealth of every centimillionaire, the resulting revenue (about $80 billion) would be only 10 percent of the federal budget for a single year.

The greatest disparities in America are not between the rich and poor but between individuals and institutions. Wealth and power are concentrated in large corporate and government institutions. The people who control power and wealth in this nation do so by virtue of their high positions in these institutions, not because of their personal wealth or income.

Managerial elites

Today the requirements of technology and planning have greatly increased industry's need for specialized talent and organizational skill. Corporations can now supply their own capital. Approximately three-fifths of industrial capital comes from retained earnings of corporations; another one-fifth is borrowed, chiefly from banks. Although the remaining one-fifth comes from "outside" investments, most such investments come from large insurance companies, mutual funds, and pension trusts rather than from individual investors. Thus the individual capitalist investor is no longer essential to capital accumulation and therefore no longer in a dominant position.

American capital is administered and expended primarily by managers of large corporations and financial institutions. Power in the American economy has shifted from capital to organized intelligence, and we can reasonably expect that the deployment of power in society at large will reflect a similar shift.

Theoretically, stockholders have ultimate power over management, but in fact individual stockholders seldom have any control over the activities of the corporations they own. Usually a corporation's managers select "management slates" for the board of directors and stockholders automatically approve them. Occasionally banks and financial institutions and pension trust or mutual fund managers will get together to replace a management-selected board of directors. But more often than not, banks and trust funds will sell their stock in corporations whose management they distrust rather than use the voting power of their stock to replace management. Generally banks and trust funds vote their stock for the management slate. This inaction by institutional investors allows the directors and managements of corporations essentially to appoint themselves and to become increasingly unchallengeable; this policy freezes absolute power in the corporate managements.

Corporations, banks, insurance companies, mutual funds, investment companies, and pension trusts own most capital in America. Of course, the profit motive is still important to corporate managers, since profits are the basis of capital formation within the corporation. The more capital corporate managers have at their disposal, the more power they have; losses decrease the capital available to the managers and decrease their power (perhaps spelling eventual extinction of the organization).

Management today may be more public regarding than were capitalist entrepreneurs of a few decades ago. The management class is more sympathetic to the philosophy of the liberal establishment, to which it belongs; it is concerned with the public interest and expresses devotion to the "corporate conscience." As Berle explains:

> This is the existence of a set of ideas, widely held by the community and often by the organization itself and the men who direct it, that certain uses of power are "wrong," that is, contrary to the established interest and value system of the community. Indulgence of these ideas as a limitation on economic power, and regard for them by the managers of great corporations, is sometimes called—and ridiculed as—the "corporate conscience." The ridicule is pragmatically unjustified. The first sanction enforcing limitations imposed by the public consensus is a lively appreciation of that consensus by corporate managements. This is the reality of the "corporate conscience."[7]

Management fears loss of prestige and popular esteem. While the public has no direct economic control over management, and government control is more symbolic than real, withholding prestige is one of society's oldest methods of enforcing its values upon individuals and groups. Moreover, corporate managers themselves have internalized most values of the prevailing liberal consensus and have come to believe in a public-regarding philosophy.

Corporate and financial elites have access to government officials that ordinary citizens could never hope to acquire. Several years ago Herbert P. Patterson, then president of Chase Manhattan Bank, bemoaned his heavy schedule in Washington and listed a single day's appointments on Capitol Hill:

8:30 A.M.	Arrive National Airport
9:15 A.M.	Sen. Ernest Hollings of South Carolina
9:45 A.M.	Rep. William Widnall of New Jersey
10:30 A.M.	Sen. Warren Magnuson of Washington
11:00 A.M.	Sen. Alan Cranston of California
11:45 A.M.	Rep. Gerald Ford of Michigan, House Minority Leader. (I'm asked to note that if he's delayed at a White House conference the appointment will be rescheduled for 3:45 P.M.)
Noon	Luncheon in House dining room with Rep. Leslie Arends of Illinois, the House Minority Whip, and Rep. Harold Collier of Illinois.
1:30 P.M.	Sen. Henry Jackson of Washington
2:00 P.M.	Sen. Wallace Bennett of Utah
2:30 P.M.	Sen. Robert Packwood of Oregon
3:15 P.M.	Rep. Hale Boggs of Louisiana, the House Majority Leader
3:45 P.M.	Rep. Gerald Ford (who was delayed at the White House).

Also on the schedule, if time permitted and they could break free, were Congressman Benjamin Blackburn of Georgia and Senator William Brock of Tennessee.[8] Not many other Americans could schedule meetings with so many members of Congress in a lifetime, let alone in a single day.

Military-industrial complex

In his farewell address to the nation in 1961, President Dwight D. Eisenhower warned of "an immense military establishment and a large arms industry." He observed:

> In the councils of government, we must guard against the acquisition of unwarranted influence, whether sought or unsought, by the military-industrial complex. The potential for the disastrous rise of misplaced power exists and will persist. We must never let the weight of this combination endanger our liberties or democratic processes. We should take nothing for granted. Only an alert and knowledgeable citizenry can compel the proper meshings of the huge industrial and military machinery of defense with our peaceful methods and goals, so that security and liberty may prosper together.[9]

These words reflect Eisenhower's personal feelings about the pressures that had been mounting during his administration from the military and from private defense contractors for increased military spending. *Military-industrial complex* refers to the armed forces, the Defense Department, military contractors, and Congress members who represent defense-oriented constituencies.

Although some left-wing groups view the military-industrial complex as a conspiracy to promote war and imperialism, it is not quite so easy to describe. John Kenneth Galbraith, a liberal, portrays the military-industrial complex as a far more subtle interplay of forces in American society:

> It is an organization or a complex of organizations and not a conspiracy. . . . In the conspiratorial view, the military power is a coalition of generals and conniving industrialists. The goal is mutual enrichment; they arrange elaborately to feather each other's nests. The industrialists are the deus ex machina; their agents make their way around Washington arranging the payoff.[10]

What are the facts about the military-industrial complex? Military spending runs about $230 billion per year—only 30 percent of the federal budget and about 5 percent of the gross national product. Social welfare spending (welfare and social security) amounts to nearly 40 percent of the federal budget. Adding Medicare and Medicaid, the total health and welfare bill is over half the federal budget and nearly twice the size of the defense budget. The one hundred largest industrial corporations in the United States depend on military contracts for less than 10 percent of their sales. In other words, American industry does *not* depend upon war or the threat of war for any significant proportion of its income or sales.

Nonetheless a few companies do depend heavily on defense contracts: Lockheed Aircraft, General Dynamics, McDonnell Douglas, Boeing Co., and Rockwell International, for example. But in the world of corporate giants, these firms are only medium sized. While General Electric and American Telephone & Telegraph, among the corporate giants, also account for a large number of defense contracts, their military sales are only a small proportion of total sales. Yet the scope of their military business is still sufficient to concern certain companies, the people who work for them, the communities in which they are located, and the legislators and other public officials who represent these communities.

A frequent criticism of the military-industrial complex is that defense-oriented industries have become dependent on military hardware orders. Since any reduction in military spending would be a severe economic setback for these industries, they apply great pressure to keep defense spending high. The military, always pleased to receive new weapons, joins with defense industries in recommending to the government that it purchase new weapons. Finally, legislators from constituencies with large defense industries and giant military bases will usually join with the armed forces and defense industries in support of increased defense spending for new weapons.

But American business as a whole is not interested in promoting war or international instability. The business community considers the defense industry an unstable enterprise—a feast-or-famine business for industrial companies. The price-earnings ratios for military-oriented companies are substantially lower than for civilian-oriented companies. More importantly, corporate America seeks planned, stable growth, secure investments, and guaranteed returns. War disrupts these conditions. The stock market, reflecting the aspirations of business, goes *up*, not *down*, when peace is announced.

A more rational critique of the relationship between government and business centers on the gradual blurring of private and public activity in the economy. In *The New Industrial State*, Galbraith argues effectively that the military-industrial complex is part of a general merger of corporate and government enterprise into what he terms a giant "technostructure." Corporate planning and government planning are replacing market competition in America. Corporations avoid vigorous price competition, and the government also tries to fix overall prices. Both corporations and governments seek stable relations with large labor unions. Solid, prosperous growth is the keynote of the planned economy, without undue, disruptive, old-style competition. Wars, depressions, or overheated inflations are to be avoided in the interest of stable growth. Big government, big industry, and big labor organizations share in this consensus. Within this consensus, the big quietly grow bigger and more powerful. Government protects the secure, stable world of corporate giants, unless they abuse the accepted standards of behavior or openly try to aggrandize their positions.

Elite recruitment: Getting to the top

How do people at the top get there? Certainly we cannot provide a complete picture of the recruitment process in all sectors of society, but we can learn whether the top leadership in government comes from the corporate world or whether the two worlds depend on separate and distinct channels of recruitment.

Biographical information on individuals in positions of authority in top institutions in each sector of society reveals separate paths to authority. Figure 4-1 shows the principal lifetime occupational activity of individuals at the top of each sector of society. (This categorization depends largely on the way they identified their principal occupation in *Who's Who*.)

It turns out that the corporate sector supplies a majority of the occupants of top positions in only the corporate sector (89.1 percent). The corporate sector supplies only 37 percent of the top elites in the public interest sector and only 16.6 percent of government elites. Top leaders in government are recruited primarily from the legal profession (56.1 percent); some have based their careers in government itself (16.7 percent) and education (10.6 percent). This finding is important. Government and law apparently provide independent channels of recruitment for high public office. High position in the corporate world is *not* a prerequisite to high public office.

What do we know about those who occupy authoritative positions in American society? A number of excellent social-background studies of political decision makers,[11] federal government executives,[12] military officers,[13] and corporate executives[14] consistently show that top busi-

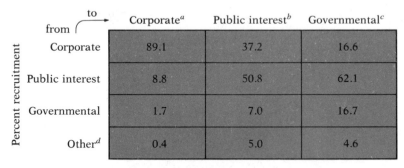

		Corporate[a]	Public interest[b]	Governmental[c]
	Corporate	89.1	37.2	16.6
Percent recruitment	Public interest	8.8	50.8	62.1
	Governmental	1.7	7.0	16.7
	Other[d]	0.4	5.0	4.6

FIGURE 4-1.   Recruitment to top institutional positions.

[a] Presidents and directors of the largest corporations in industry, communication, transportation, utilities, banking, and insurance. (See listings in previous tables.) $N = 3,572$.

[b] Trustees of prestigious private colleges and universities; directors of twelve largest private foundations; senior partners of top law firms, directors of trustees of twelve prestigious civic and cultural organizations. $N = 1,345$.

[c] President and vice-president; secretaries and under secretaries and assistant secretaries of all executive departments; White House presidential advisers; congressional leaders, committee chairpersons, and ranking minority members; Supreme Court justices; Federal Reserve Board; Council of Economic Advisers; all four-star generals and admirals. $N = 286$.

[d] Labor, press, religion, and so forth.

ness executives and political decision makers are *atypical* of the American public. They are recruited from the well-educated, prestigiously employed, older, affluent, urban, white, Anglo-Saxon, upper- and upper-middle-class male population. (See table 4-4.)

Age

The average age of the corporate leaders (directors and chief executive officers) identified in one study was sixty-one.[15] Leaders in foundations, law, education, and civic and cultural organizations were slightly older; here the average age was sixty-four. Top positions in government are filled by slightly younger people.

Sex

The female segment of the population is seriously underrepresented at the top of America's institutional structure.[16] Male dominance in top positions is nearly complete in the corporate world. A very few women have entered corporate boardrooms in recent years; fewer than 2 percent of the directors of large corporations are women. The same is true in government: only one woman served in the cabinet under President Gerald Ford; three served in the cabinet under President Jimmy Carter;

TABLE 4-4. Social characteristics of corporate, public interest, and government elites

	Corporate	Public interest	Government
Average age	61 years	64 years	58 years
Female	0.3%	7.2%	1.4%
Schools			
Public	81.8	73.2	90.9
Private	7.0	8.8	3.0
Prestigious[a]	11.2	18.0	6.1
Colleges			
Public	31.8	12.8	43.9
Private	13.3	8.4	12.1
Prestigious[b]	55.0	78.8	43.9
Education			
College educated	90.1	95.7	100.0
Advanced degree	49.2	75.7	77.4
Urban	89.0	84.9	69.7

[a]Andover, Buckley, Cate, Catlin, Choate, Cranbrook, Country Day, Deerfield, Exeter, Episcopal, Gilman, Groton, Hill, Hotchkiss, Kingswood, Kent, Lakeside, Lawrenceville, Lincoln, Loomis, Middlesex, Milton, St. Andrew's, St. Christopher's, St. George's, St. Mark's, St. Paul's, Shatluck, Taft, Thatcher, Webb, Westminister, Woodbary Forest.

[b]Harvard, Yale, Chicago, Stanford, Columbia, M.I.T., Cornell, Northwestern, Princeton, Johns Hopkins, University of Pennsylvania, and Dartmouth.

one has served as U.S. ambassador under President Ronald Reagan. In 1981 Reagan appointed Sandra Day O'Connor as the first woman Supreme Court justice, but no woman has yet served on the Council of Economic Advisors or the Federal Reserve Board. Only in civic and cultural affairs, education, and foundations can one find women among the top position holders.

Race

Of seven thousand positions of authority surveyed in top-ranked institutions in the 1980s, blacks occupied only twenty.[17] One was Thurgood Marshall, an associate justice of the Supreme Court, former solicitor general of the United States, and former director of the Legal Defense and Educational Fund of the National Association for the Advancement of Colored People (NAACP). Only one black served in the cabinet under President Gerald Ford, and one black, Patricia Roberts Harris, served in the Carter cabinet. Andrew Young, former congressman from Atlanta, an early associate of Martin Luther King, Jr., and now mayor of Atlanta, served as U.S. ambassador to the United Nations. President Reagan's cabinet includes one black, Samuel R. Pierce, secretary of housing and urban development. Other blacks in top positions include: William T. Coleman, a director of IBM, Chase Manhattan, Pepsico, Brookings Institution, and the Council on Foreign Relations; Andrew F. Brimmer, a director of BankAmerica, United Airlines, DuPont, and the Council on Foreign Relations; and Vernon Jordan, a director of Bankers Trust New York, Celanese, J.C. Penney, and Xerox. Nonetheless, still very few blacks are in positions of authority in America.

Education

Nearly all U.S. top leaders are college educated, and more than half hold advanced degrees. About 25.8 percent hold law degrees, and 31.1 percent hold advanced academic or professional degrees (earned degrees only, not honorary degrees). Government leaders are somewhat more likely than corporate leaders to hold advanced degrees.

A glance at the precollegiate education of our top elites reveals that many are "preppies": 11 percent of corporate leaders and 6 percent of government leaders attended one of the thirty prestigious preparatory schools in America—Groton, Hotchkiss, Exeter, Loomis, Choate, and so on.[18] Needless to say, only an infinitesimal proportion of the population receives an education at a prestigious preparatory school. Even more impressive, 55 percent of corporate leaders and 44 percent of government leaders are alumni of twelve prestigious, heavily endowed private universities: Harvard, Yale, Chicago, Stanford, Columbia, MIT, Cornell, Northwestern, Princeton, Johns Hopkins, University of Pennsylvania, and Dartmouth. Elites in America are notably "Ivy League" (see table 4-4).

These social-background characteristics suggest that more corporate elites come from the upper class than do government elites. The proportion of prestigious preparatory school graduates and Ivy Leaguers is slightly lower among governmental leaders than among corporate or public interest sector leaders. Moreover, government leaders tend to have more advanced professional education.

The liberal establishment

Elites in America share a consensus about the fundamental values of private property, limited government, individual liberty, and due process of law. Moreover, since the Roosevelt era, American elites have generally supported liberal, public-regarding, social welfare programs, including social security, fair labor standards, unemployment compensation, a graduated income tax, a federally aided welfare system, government regulation of public utilities, and countercyclical fiscal and monetary policies. Today elite consensus also includes a commitment to equality of opportunity for black Americans and a desire to end direct, lawful discrimination. Finally, elite consensus includes a desire to exercise influence in world affairs, to oppose the spread of communism, to maintain a strong national defense, and to protect pro-Western governments from internal subversion and external aggression.

The prevailing philosophy of America's elite is liberal and public regarding, with a willingness to take the welfare of others into account as part of one's own well-being and a willingness to use government power to correct perceived wrongs done to others. It is a philosophy of noblesse oblige—elite responsibility for the welfare of the poor and downtrodden, particularly blacks. Today's liberal elite believes that it can change citizens' lives—end discrimination, abolish poverty, eliminate slums, ensure employment, uplift the poor, eliminate sickness, educate the masses, and instill dominant culture values in everyone. America's masses do not widely share this philosophy.

Leadership for liberal reform has always come from America's upper social classes—usually from established old family segments of the elite, rather than the newly rich, self-made segments. Before the Civil War, abolitionist leaders were "descended from old and socially dominant Northeastern families" and were clearly distinguished from the new industrial leaders of that era.[19] Later when the children and grandchildren of the rugged individualists of the industrial revolution inherited positions of power, they turned away from the Darwinist philosophy of their parents and moved toward the more public-regarding ideas of the New Deal. Liberalism was championed not by the working class but by men like Franklin D. Roosevelt (Groton and Harvard), Adlai Stevenson

(Choate School and Princeton), Averell Harriman (Groton and Yale), and John F. Kennedy (Choate School and Harvard).

The liberal, public-regarding character of America's elite defies simplistic Marxian interpretations of American politics; wealth, education, sophistication, and upper-class cultural values foster attitudes of public service and do-goodism. Liberal elites are frequently paternalistic toward segments of the masses they define as "underprivileged," "culturally deprived," and "disadvantaged," but they are seldom hostile toward them. Indeed hostility toward blacks is more characteristic of white masses than of white elites.

The liberal philosophy of noblesse oblige leads inevitably to a sense of national responsibility for the welfare of the world, which in turn involves the United States in war. The missionary spirit of liberalism strives to bring freedom—self-determination, civil liberty, limited government, and private enterprise—to all the peoples of the world. America's major wars of the twentieth century occurred during the administrations of liberal Democratic presidents: Wilson (World War I), Roosevelt (World War II), Truman (Korea), and Johnson (Vietnam). Is it accidental that wars occurred during these administrations? Or is it this element of the liberal philosophy that propels the nation toward international involvement and war?

The United States fought both world wars to "make the world safe for democracy." Following World War II, the nation embarked upon a policy of worldwide involvement in the internal and external affairs of nations in an effort to halt the expansion of communism. The "containment policy," as it came to be known, was a commitment by America's liberal elite to halt revolutionary communist movements and to support noncommunist governments attempting to resist revolutionary influences either within or outside their borders.

The "good" that America's liberal leadership seeks to do throughout the world is neither appreciated nor understood by the elites and masses of many nations. The result has been a great deal of bloodshed and violence committed by well-meaning liberal administrations for the finest of motives. An American field commander in Vietnam summed up the liberal dilemma: "It was necessary to destroy the village in order to save it."[20]

The failure of America's liberal leadership to achieve victory in Vietnam seriously undermined the legitimacy of the established elite. Many Americans, both elites and masses, view the original decision to commit American troops to a land war in Vietnam as a serious military and political mistake. The obvious errors in judgment, the heavy loss of life over a prolonged period, the humiliation of the military establishment in a war with a third-rate power, the revelations of incompetency and brutality, and the moral and philosophical questions posed by American involvement in a distant war all combined to spawn serious criticism of the established leadership.

The Neoconservatives

The war in Vietnam, President Lyndon Johnson's Great Society, urban rioting, campus unrest, Watergate, and inflation all raised doubts in the 1960s and 1970s about the size and scope of government power. A mood of disillusionment has penetrated elite circles and dampened the elites' enthusiasm for government intervention in society. Elite interest in liberal reforms has been tempered by the failures and costs of well-meaning yet ineffective (and sometimes harmful) public programs. Elites have learned that government cannot solve society's problems simply by passing a law, creating a new bureaucracy, and spending a few billion dollars. War, poverty, ill-health, discrimination, joblessness, inflation, crime, ignorance, pollution, and unhappiness have afflicted society for a long time. Elites no longer assume that these problems can be erased from society by finding and implementing the "right" public policies.

The "neoconservatives" among America's elite continue to be liberal, reformist, and public regarding, but they oppose the paternalistic state. They are not as confident or ambitious (bordering on arrogant) as the liberals of the 1960s. They have more faith in the free market system and less confidence that government regulations will be effective. They have more respect for traditional values and institutions, including religion, family, and the community. They believe in equal opportunity for everyone, but they do not believe in absolute equality, whereby the government ensures that everyone gets equal shares of everything. Finally, neoconservatives believe that the United States must maintain a strong national defense and that American democracy cannot survive for long in a world that is overwhelmingly hostile to American values.[21]

Neoconservatives, like all liberals, disapprove of unequal treatment of racial minorities, but they generally oppose affirmative action and busing programs that involve racial quotas. Neoconservatives are skeptical that laws, bureaucracies, regulations, and public spending can improve the nation's health, guarantee employment, or protect the environment. They do not want government to be "overloaded" with tasks they feel should be left to the individual, the family, the church, or the free-market system. According to the neoconservative philosophy, government has attempted to do too much for its citizens and has lost respect and legitimacy by failing to meet its promises. Neoconservatives see the war in Vietnam as a "tragic error" rather than as a national "crime." They want the United States to regain its military power and remain a force for good in the world.[22]

Neoconservatism does not alter the underlying commitment to liberal, reformist values. But it represents a more realistic view of what government can achieve and a more traditional view of the importance of personal initiative, enterprise, work, and family. This view does not reside solely in the Reagan administration; it enjoys wide acceptance among the nation's top leaders in every sector of society.

Understanding Reaganomics

"The failed policies of the past"

Since the Great Depression of the 1930s, America's established leadership has believed that government could stabilize the economy through "countercyclic" fiscal and monetary policies. The government-elite believed that the government could manipulate aggregated demand levels for goods and services and increase demand in a recession by raising government spending, lowering taxes, expanding debt, and increasing the money supply. When faced with inflation, government could reduce demand by reducing its own spending, increasing taxes, reducing debt, and contracting the money supply. The ideas of British economist John M. Keynes prevailed. In the short run at least, U.S. leaders viewed society's productive capacity—its ability to supply goods and services—as fixed. Keynes focused on government stimulation of demand as the key to maintaining prosperity.

But forty years of Keynesian economics produced "stagflation" in the 1970s: inflation and high interest rates, and stagnant economic growth rates. While politicians had no difficulty increasing spending during recessions, they found it impossible to reduce spending during inflation periods. The result was continued government deficit spending during both recession and inflation, runaway "double-digit" (over 10 percent) annual inflation rates, and declining economic growth rates. President Reagan labeled Keynesian economics "the failed policies of the past."

"Supply-side" economics

By 1980, the United States had experienced its worst decade-long inflation in history. Personal savings were disappearing rapidly. Uncertainty clouded investor decisions. Factories and machines were rapidly becoming outmoded. U.S. products (particularly steel, autos, and heavy machinery) could no longer compete with products from Europe and Japan in the world (and even U.S.) market. Americans as a whole spent too much and saved too little. Federal tax and budget policies promoted immediate consumption over investment in the future.

Business and financial elites became concerned about declining economic growth rates, increasing inflation rates, and increasing tax rates:

- *Declining growth.* Real per capita GNP (actual growth in the economy after controlling for inflation) averaged only 1.2 percent per year in the 1970s compared to 3.2 percent per year in the 1960s.
- *Inflation.* The consumer price index (the average prices paid by consumers) rose 112 percent in the 1970s compared to 31 percent in the 1960s.

• *Tax rates.* Federal taxes rose from 20 percent of total personal income in 1960 to 24 percent in 1980.

Supply-side economists argue that long-term economic growth is more important than short-term manipulation of demand. Economic growth requires greater productive capacity. Economists argue that higher productivity requires an increase in one or more of (1) natural resources, (2) labor, (3) capital, or (4) technology. Economic growth requires finding and developing the nation's natural resources, improving the productivity of the labor force, providing incentives for savings and capital investment, and improving technology through continued research and development.

Supply-side economics holds that economic growth increases the overall supply of goods and services, thereby holding down prices, and reduces or eliminates inflation. More importantly, everyone's standard of living improves with the availability of more goods and services at stable prices. Government revenues even increase over the long run, according to this theory.

Most supply-side economists believe that the free market is better equipped than government to lower prices and increase supplies of what people need and want. Government, they argue, is the problem, not the solution. Government taxing, spending, and monetary policies have promoted immediate consumption instead of investment in the future. High taxes penalize hard work, creativity, investment, and savings. They believe that government should provide tax incentives to encourage investment and savings; lower tax rates in middle and high income brackets to encourage work and savings; hold down spending, if possible reducing the government proportion of the GNP over time; minimize government regulations to increase productivity and growth. Overall, then, supply-side economics holds that government should act to stimulate production and supply rather than demand and consumption.

"A program for economic recovery"

The Reagan administration came into office with a comprehensive program for economic growth, which it designated "A Program for Economic Recovery." Unofficially, this program has become known as Reaganomics.

Reaganomics, which heavily borrows from supply-side economics, arises from the belief that past Keynesian policies have failed. According to President Reagan, past government attempts to increase demand have caused high taxes, inflation, and stagnant economic growth. He believes that the most important cause of the nation's economic problems—inflation, unemployment, low productivity, low investment—is the government itself: "The federal government through taxes, spending, regulating, and monetary policies, has sacrificed long-term growth and price stability for ephemeral, short-term goals."[23] Government efforts to reduce unemployment simply add to inflation.

The Program for Economic Recovery sets forth a package of four sweeping policy directions:

1. Budget reform to cut the growth rate of federal spending.
2. Tax reductions of 25 percent over three years on personal income and additional tax reductions to encourage business investment.
3. Relief from government regulations that cost industry large amounts of money for small increases in safety or environmental protection.
4. Slower growth of the money supply, to be achieved with the cooperation of the Federal Reserve Board.

These policies aim to provide incentives for Americans to work, save, and invest. Theoretically, the economy will grow more rapidly if Americans can keep more of their earnings. Producing more goods will bring inflation under control, Americans will save a greater proportion of their incomes, and business will build new plants and provide new jobs.

Reducing taxes and stimulating growth

Central to supply-side economics is the belief that high tax rates and oversized government reduce economic output and productivity. The theory holds that people will prefer leisure time over extra work if, for example, income taxes "snatch away" 50 percent of the money they earn through extra work. People will not risk their money in new business investments if, for example, income tax takes away 50 percent of the investment income. High marginal tax rates also encourage people to seek out "tax shelters"—special tax law provisions that reduce personal income taxes. These shelters direct money to special investments (municipal bonds, commercial property, movies, horse farms, and so on) that are not critical to the nation's economic health. In addition, a large "underground economy" flourishes when tax rates are high; in the "underground economy" people hide their real incomes and/or trade goods and services rather than conduct transactions out in the open where they will be subject to taxation.

Taxes discourage work, productivity, investment, and economic growth, according to Reaganomics. If government reduces tax rates, the paradoxical result may be to increase government revenue because more people will work harder and start new businesses if they know they can keep a larger share of their earnings. Tax cuts will stimulate increased economic activity, and this increased activity will produce more government revenue even though tax rates are lower.

The Economic Recovery Tax Cut Act of 1981, pushed through Congress by President Reagan, reduced personal income taxes by 25 percent over a three-year period. The act reduces marginal tax rates from a range of 14 to 70 percent to a range of 12 to 50 percent; this reduction is minor for people in the lowest income brackets but significant for people in the highest income brackets. In addition, the act grants many new investment incentives for business and "indexes" taxes against inflation in future years.

The impact of Reaganomics

The "Reagan recession" (1981–1982) was the deepest since the Great Depression of the 1930s. For the first time since then, unemployment reached "double-digit" levels, exceeding 10 percent. Total output declined, steel and automobile plants operated at less than half capacity, home building came to a standstill, and business bankruptcies reached new highs. Personal income grew very slowly and corporate profits declined, while government unemployment compensation payments soared. The result was the largest peace-time federal deficit in history.

In American politics it is traditional to blame the "in" party when the economy falters. Yet the recession of 1981–1982 was already under way before the Economic Recovery Tax Cut Act of 1981 took effect. The recession stems from high interest rates that slowed capital investment, and high interest rates stem from runaway inflation in the 1970s. The Reagan administration claims that the recession would have been worse without its economic recovery program and tax cuts. Throughout the recession, members of the Reagan administration believed that their economic recovery program would eventually bring economic growth, more jobs, and stable prices, if America would "stay the course."

Case study: Elite competition—Sun Belt "Cowboys" and established "Yankees"

With the multiple structures of power in American society—industry, utilities, finance, law, government, education, the news media, and others—some competition among them is inevitable. In any society, various leaders will compete with each other for power and preeminence. Moreover, new members admitted to elite circles bring slightly different interests and experiences to their roles than do the older established elites. Elite theory does *not* rule out conflict, competition, and factionalism among elites.

A major source of factionalism among America's elite today is the division between the newly rich, southern and western Cowboys and the established, eastern, liberal Yankees. This factional split transcends partisan squabbling between Democrats and Republicans or traditional rifts between Congress and the president, or petty strife among organized interest groups. The conflict between Cowboys and Yankees derives from differences in their sources of wealth and the newness of the elite status of the Cowboys.

(continued)

Case study *(continued)*

The Cowboys are new-money people who acquired their wealth in the post–World War II era of erratic growth and expansion. Their wealth and power come from independent oil and natural gas exploration and development; real estate operations in the population-boom areas running from southern California and Arizona through Texas, and from the "New South" to Florida; aerospace and defense contracting and allied businesses; and in some cases, from new commercial inventions. In contrast, Yankees' fortunes have grown out of the great corporate and financial institutions established in the nineteenth century. Many Yankees are themselves second-generation descendants of the great entrepreneurial families of the industrial revolution (the Rockefellers, Fords, Mellons, duPonts, Kennedys, and Harrimans, for example). Other Yankees have been recruited through established corporate institutions, Wall Street and Washington law firms, eastern banking and investment firms, prestigious foundations, and Ivy League universities.

The Cowboys do not fully share in the liberal, public-regarding values of the dominant eastern establishment. Nor, however, do they exercise power in any way proportional to the overwhelming hegemony of the established Yankees. The Cowboys may have gained influence in recent years—and much of the petty political fighting reported in today's press has its roots in Cowboy–Yankee factionalism—but the liberal establishment remains dominant. However, Cowboys and Yankees agree on the overriding importance of preserving political stability and a healthy free-enterprise economy.

The Cowboys are self-made people who acquired wealth and power in an intense competitive struggle that continues to shape their outlook on life. Their upward mobility, their individualism, and their competitive spirit influence their view of society and the way they perceive their new elite responsibilities. In contrast, Yankees either inherit great wealth or attach themselves to established institutions of great wealth, power, and prestige. The Yankees are socialized, sometimes from childhood, into the responsibilities of wealth and power. They are secure in their upper-class membership because they are born into it. They are highly principled in their relationships with others and public regarding in their exercise of elite responsibilities.

The Cowboys are new to their position; they lack old school ties, and they are not particularly concerned with the niceties of ethical conduct. The Yankees frequently regard the Cowboys with disdain as uncouth and opportunistic gamblers and speculators, shady wheeler-dealers and influence peddlers, and uncultured and selfish boors.

The Cowboys have newly risen from the masses; many had very humble beginnings. But it is their experience in rising from the masses, rather than their mass origins, that shapes their philosophy. The Cowboys, being less public regarding and less oriented to the social welfare than the Yankees, favor individualistic solutions to social problems; they place primary responsibility for solving life's problems on the individual. Cowboys believe that they became successful themselves through initiative and hard work, and they believe that anyone else who wants more out of life can get it the same way they did. Cowboys do not feel guilty about poverty or discrimination; neither they nor their ancestors were responsible for these condi-

Case study *(continued)*

tions. No one gave them their wealth and position; they earned it themselves, and they have no apologies for their accomplishments. They support the political and economic system that helped them rise to the top; they are patriotic, sometimes vocally anticommunist, and moderate to conservative on most national policy issues.

Cowboys rose to the top echelons of government in the Democratic administrations of Lyndon B. Johnson and the Republican administrations of Richard Nixon and Ronald Reagan. Johnson, Nixon, and Reagan were themselves self-made men from the South and West. They devoted many years to convincing established eastern elites of their trustworthiness: Johnson in the U.S. Senate as a leader in civil rights and poverty legislation, Nixon as vice-president and Wall Street corporation lawyer, and Reagan as a paid spokesman for General Electric Co. Yet those who attack these presidents often criticize their closeness to the newly wealthy among America's elite and their inability to win the full trust of influential segments of the eastern liberal establishment.*

Representative of the swashbuckling style of the true Sun Belt cowboys is the father and son construction team heading the Bechtel Corporation. Steven D. Bechtel and his son, Steven D. Bechtel, Jr., control a little-known, family-held, corporate colossus, which is the world's largest construction company. The senior Bechtel never obtained a college degree, but he acquired engineering know-how as a builder of the Hoover Dam. Bechtel conceived and built the San Francisco Bay Area Rapid Transit system and the Washington, D.C., METRO subway system. Bechtel is building an entire industrial city—Jubayl in Saudi Arabia; establishing a copper industry, including mines, railroads, and smelters in Indonesia; and constructing the world's largest hydroelectric system in Ontario, Canada. Bechtel was fired as the contractor for the Trans-Alaska pipeline when the project first showed cost overruns; but it seems in retrospect that Bechtel would have done a more cost-effective job if he had been allowed to complete the work. The Bechtel Corporation remains family owned and therefore refuses to divulge to the Securities Exchange Commission or other prying bureaucracies its real worth.

Cowboy influence in the Reagan administration begins with the president himself but extends to key members of the cabinet. Secretary of State George Shultz was president of the Bechtel Corporation before joining the Reagan team, and Secretary of Defense Caspar Weinberger was a vice-president of Bechtel.

---

*Yankee distrust of Cowboys may have begun with the assassination of President John F. Kennedy in Dallas, Texas, and the rash of conspiracy theories linking the assassination to reactionary Texas oil interests. President Johnson acted decisively to discredit these rumors by appointing the prestigious Warren Commission, composed mainly of eastern liberals, to investigate the assassination. The commission determined that Kennedy's death was the act of a lone gunman, which calmed the liberal establishment, as well as the rest of the nation. Eastern liberals in both parties charged that President Nixon had surrounded himself with southern and western Sun Belt "wheeler-dealers" whose opportunism and lack of ethics created the milieu for Watergate. The prestigious *New York Times*, voice of the eastern establishment, published an article blaming Watergate on the Cowboys.

(continued)

Case study *(continued)*

Nonetheless, the Yankee establishment continues to exercise great power in America. Yankees continue to dominate the nation's largest and most prestigious corporations, banks, law firms, newspapers, television networks, foundations, and civic and cultural organizations.[24] Moreover, they even hold many key positions in the Reagan administration. No one better represents the established Yankees than Vice-President George Bush. Bush is a Phillips (Andover) Academy "preppy" and Yale graduate, whose father was a U.S. senator from Connecticut. Bush went to Houston at age twenty-five as vice-president of Dresser Industries, an oil drilling equipment firm of which his father was a director. Later Bush formed his own company, Zapata Petroleum, and became a multimillionaire. He entered politics as a Republican congressman from a wealthy suburban Houston district and later served in many key government posts: UN ambassador, U.S. envoy to the People's Republic of China, director of the CIA. He fought Reagan and the Cowboys in the 1980 Republican presidential primaries. Reagan chose Bush as his vice-presidential running mate in order to unite the eastern establishment and Sun Belt Cowboy elements in the Republican party. Bush has been a team player in the Reagan administration.

Summary

Elite theory does not limit its definition of elites to those who participate in *government* decision making. An elite member is anyone who participates in decisions that allocate values for society. Power in America is organized into large institutions, private as well as public: corporations, banks and financial institutions, universities, law firms, churches, professional associations, and military and government bureaucracies. This chapter develops several propositions in analyzing power and the institutional structure of America:

1. The giant institutions and bureaucracies of American society carry great potential for power.

2. The institutional structure of American society concentrates great authority in a relatively small number of positions. About thirty-five hundred presidents and directors of the nation's largest corporations have formal authority over half the nation's industrial assets, half its assets in communications, transportation, and utilities, nearly half of all banking assets, and two-thirds of all insurance assets.

3. Wealth in America is unequally distributed. The top fifth of income recipients receive over 40 percent of all income in the nation, while the bottom fifth receives about 5 percent. Inequality is lessening only very slowly over time.

4. Managerial elites are replacing owners and stockholders as the dominant influence in American corporations. Most capital investment

comes from the retained earnings of corporations and bank loans rather than from individual investors.

5. Despite concentration of institutional power, different elite segments tend to exercise their power in separate sectors of society. Fewer than 20 percent of top government officeholders come from the corporate world. Most come from the legal profession; some have based their career in government itself and in education. Thus separate channels of recruitment lead to top elite positions.

6. American elites disproportionately represent the well-educated, prestigiously employed, older, affluent, urban, white, Anglo-Saxon, upper- and upper-middle-class male population.

7. Elites in America share a consensus about the fundamental values of private enterprise, due process of law, liberal and public-regarding social-welfare programs, equality of opportunity, and opposition to the spread of communism. The prevailing impulse of the "liberal establishment" is to do good, to perform public services, and to use government power to change lives. In world affairs, this missionary spirit has involved the United States in a great deal of bloodshed and violence, presumably in pursuit of high motives: the self-determination of free peoples resisting aggression and suppression.

8. Disagreement among elites occurs within this framework of consensus on fundamental values. The range of disagreement among elites is relatively narrow and is generally confined to means rather than ends.

9. A major source of factionalism among America's elite today is the division between the newly rich, southern and western Sun Belt Cowboys and the established, eastern, liberal Yankees. Their differences in style derive from differences in sources of wealth and the newness of the elite status of the Cowboys. The establishment Yankees remain overwhelmingly dominant in national affairs, but new southern and western elites have gained influence in recent years.

NOTES

1. C. Wright Mills, *The Power Elite* (New York: Oxford University Press, 1956), pp. 10–11.
2. James Madison, Alexander Hamilton, and John Jay, *The Federalist* Number 10 (New York: Modern Library, 1937).
3. A. A. Berle, Jr., *Economic Power and the Free Society* (New York: Fund for the Republic, 1958), p. 10.
4. Gabriel Kolko, *Wealth and Power in America* (New York: Praeger, 1962), pp. 68–79.
5. Ibid. See also Clair Wilcox, *Toward Social Welfare* (Homewood, Ill.: Irwin, 1969), pp. 7–24.
6. Harold Seneker, "The Forbes Four Hundred," *Forbes* (September 11, 1982):100–185.
7. A. A. Berle, Jr., *Power without Property* (New York: Harcourt, Brace & World, 1959), pp. 90–91.

8. Herbert P. Patterson in *Nation's Business* (February 1971):61.
9. Excerpt from "Farewell to the Nation" speech by President Dwight D. Eisenhower, delivered over radio and television, January 17, 1961.
10. John Kenneth Galbraith, *How to Control the Military* (New York: Signet Books, 1969), pp. 23–31.
11. Donald R. Matthews, *The Social Background of Political Decision-Makers* (New York: Doubleday, 1954).
12. David T. Stanley, Dean E. Mann, and Jameson W. Doig, *Men Who Govern* (Washington, D.C.: Brookings, 1967).
13. Morris Janowitz, *The Professional Soldier: A Social and Political Portrait* (New York: Free Press, 1960).
14. Lloyd Warner and James C. Abegglen, *Big Business Leaders in America* (New York: Harper & Brothers, 1955).
15. Thomas R. Dye, *Who's Running America: The Reagan Years* (Englewood Cliffs, N.J.: Prentice-Hall, 1983).
16. See Thomas R. Dye and Julie Strickland, "Women at the Top," *Social Science Quarterly* 63 (March 1982).
17. See Dye, op cit.
18. See Lisa Birnback, ed. *The Official Preppy Handbook* (New York: Workman, 1980).
19. David Donald, *Lincoln Reconsidered* (New York: Knopf, 1956), p. 33.
20. See David Halberstam, *The Best and the Brightest* (New York: Random House, 1973), for a full account of how U.S. involvement in Vietnam grew out of the "good" motives of "good" men.
21. Irving Kristol, "What Is a Neoconservative?" *Newsweek* (January 19, 1976), p. 87.
22. Peter Steinfels, *The Neoconservative* (New York: Simon and Schuster, 1979).
23. Office of the President, *A Program for Economic Recovery* (Washington, D.C.: General Printing Office, February 18, 1981).
24. See Dye, op cit.

SELECTED READINGS

Amory, Cleveland. *Who Killed Society?* New York: Pocket Books, 1960. This popularly written book is the account of the "decline of high society" by an "insider." Amory is also the author of *The Proper Bostonians,* of which he is one. In *Who Killed Society?* he discusses the early sources of society in America, the most important families, and the supposed decline of society in recent years. G. William Domhoff (cited below) disagrees with this last aspect of Amory's work.

Andreano, Ralph L., ed. *Superconcentration/Supercorporation: A Collage of Opinion on the Concentration of Economic Power.* Andover, Mass.: Warner Modular Publications, 1973. The articles in this edited reader present a wide variety of opinions of the nature and implications of corporate concentration of economic power in America. The collection includes articles from such diverse sources as *Ramparts,* the *American Economic Review,* and *Hearings before Antitrust Subcommittee on the Judiciary, House of Representatives.* As a result, the articles vary widely in rhetoric, scholarship, factual content, and methodology, and they present an interesting collage of opinions.

Baltzell, E. Digby. *Philadelphia Gentlemen: The Making of a National Upper Class.* Glencoe, Ill.: Free Press, 1958. *The Protestant Establishment: Aristocracy and Caste in America.* New York: Random House, Vintage Books, 1964. The first of these books details how a national and associational upper class replaced the local and communal gentry in America between the close of the Civil War and 1940. The second book considers another question: will the Anglo-Saxon-Protestant caste that evolved into a national upper class remain intact, or will the descendants of newer immigrants gain access to upper-class status? Baltzell concludes that this caste is still powerful but has lost its position as an authoritative aristocracy, leaving it in an uneasy state with an uncertain future.

Berle, Adolf A., Jr. *Power without Property*. New York: Harcourt, Brace & World, Harvest Book, 1959. This work by a corporate lawyer and upper-class "insider" presents some interesting views of the American corporate economy. Berle argues that control of the corporate economy has passed from the hands of owners into the hands of managers. The effect of this change will be a return of the corporation to public accountability. This view has been widely debated. See, for example, the Kolko book cited below.

Domhoff, G. William. *Who Rules America?* Englewood Cliffs, N.J.: Prentice-Hall, Spectrum Books, 1967. *The Higher Circles*. New York: Random House, Vintage Books edition, 1970. In both books, Domhoff argues that there is a governing class in America. By this he means the part of the national upper class that holds positions of power in the federal government and industry and their upper-middle-class hired executives. He spends a great deal of time in both books developing the notion of social indicators. In *Who Rules America?* he examines elite control of the federal government, while in *The Higher Circles*, he develops in detail the role of private planning organizations in the formation of foreign and domestic policy.

Dye, Thomas R. *Who's Running America? Institutional Leadership in the United States*. Englewood Cliffs, N.J.: Prentice-Hall, 1976. This book studies five thousand top institutional leaders in industry, banking, utilities, government, the media, foundations, universities, civic and cultural organizations. The book names names, studies concentration of power and interlocking at the top, examines recruitment and social backgrounds, discusses elite values, examines cohesion and competition among leaders, and outlines the policy-making process. *Who's Running America? The Reagan Years* (1983) updates this original work.

Epstein, Edwin M. *The Corporation in American Politics*. Englewood Cliffs, N.J.: Prentice-Hall, 1969. This book is a good introduction to the interdependence of government and corporations. It contains a historical overview of corporate political activities, discusses the types and general methods of corporate political involvement, and discusses pluralism versus elitism.

Galbraith, John Kenneth. *The New Industrial State*. Boston: Houghton Mifflin, Sentry Books, 1969. Galbraith presents the notion of an intimate partnership between government officials and corporate specialists, which produces general national goals (which Galbraith observes are "trite"). This atmosphere of interrelationship between government and business is the context for many decisions. Needs and interests of the industrial system are "made to seem coordinate with the purposes of society" (p. 379).

Halberstam, David. *The Best and the Brightest*. Greenwich, Conn.: Fawcett Publications, 1973. This book assesses the men who advised presidents Kennedy and Johnson on conduct of the war in Vietnam. Based on interviews conducted by the author, a former *New York Times* Vietnam correspondent, the book reveals an excellent view of the men and processes responsible for decision making at the highest levels of the federal executive branch.

Keller, Suzanne. *Beyond the Ruling Class*. New York: Random House, 1963. Keller presents an essentially pluralist group theory argument. She adopts Pareto's notion of a series of elites, one for each type of human activity. The ones that are important to governmental and societal policy making, "strategic elites," are becoming more specialized and more isolated from one another, according to Keller. Thus she disagrees sharply with C. Wright Mills, who argues that interinstitutional elite movement is becoming easier and more common.

Kolko, Gabriel. *Wealth and Power in America*. New York: Praeger, 1962. Kolko discusses the distribution of wealth and income in America, the inequality of taxation, and the concentration of corporate power. He considers these questions: Does a small group of very wealthy people have the power to guide industry, and thereby much of the total economy, toward ends compatible with their own interests; and do they own and control the major corporations? He answers yes to both questions and then relates these facts to the problem of poverty in America.

Lundberg, Ferdinand. *The Rich and the Super Rich*. New York: Lyle Stuart, 1968. This book is an extensive, well-documented, popularly written but unsystematic discussion of both the corporate-governmental power partnership and elite life-styles. Lundberg is the author of the more systematically written but dated book, *America's Sixty Families* (1937).

Mills, C. Wright. *The Power Elite*. New York: Oxford University Press, 1956. This book is a classic of elite literature. Mills takes an institutional approach to roles within an "institutional landscape." Three institutions—the big corporations, the political executive, and the military—are of greatest importance. The individuals who fill the positions within these institutions form a power elite. These higher circles share social attributes (such as similar life-styles, preparatory schools, and clubs) as well as positions of power. Thus Mills's power elite is relatively unified. It is also practically free from mass accountability, which leads Mills to complain of the "higher immorality" of the power elite.

Rose, Arnold M. *The Power Structure*. New York: Oxford University Press, Galaxy Book, 1967. Rose offers a direct and systematic critique of elite literature, as well as a restatement of pluralist theory. He presents the notion of "multi-influence" groups headed by elites. This notion is similar to Keller's strategic elite hypotheses. Rose asserts that the "power structure is highly complex and diversified," "that the political elite is ascendant over and not subordinate to the economic elite," and "that the political system is more or less democratic" (p. 492).

5 Elites and Masses: the Shaky Foundations of Democracy

It is the irony of democracy that democratic ideals survive because authoritarian masses are generally apathetic and inactive. Thus, the capacity for intolerance, authoritarianism, scapegoatism, racism, and violence of the American lower classes is seldom translated into organized, sustained political movements.

Let us transport ourselves into a hypothetical country that, in a democratic way, practices the persecution of Christians, the burning of witches, and the slaughtering of Jews. We should certainly not approve of these practices on the ground that they have been decided on according to the rules of democratic procedure.

—*Joseph Schumpeter,* Capitalism, Socialism, and Democracy, *1942*

Many people believe that the survival of democracy depends on widespread agreement among the American people on the principles of democratic government. However, only a small portion of the people is committed to those principles of freedom of speech and press, tolerance of diversity, due process of law, and guarantees of individual liberty and dignity. Although most people voice superficial agreement with abstract statements of democratic values, they do not translate them into actual patterns of behavior. The question is not whether most Americans agree with the principles of democracy; the question is how democracy and individual freedom can survive in a country where most people do not support these principles in practice.

Antidemocratic attitudes among the masses

The mass public is generally willing to restrict the civil rights of deviant groups. As early as 1937 the majority of voters favored banning communist literature and denying communists the right to hold public office, or even to hold public meetings.[1] During World War II, when the United States and the Soviet Union were allies, tolerance of the rights of communists rose somewhat; nevertheless, two of five Americans would have prohibited Communist party members from speaking on the radio. This proportion rose during the cold war years; it was 77 percent by 1952 and 81 percent by 1954.[2] Willingness and, occasionally, eagerness to abridge the civil liberties of groups other than communists is also common.

In 1955 sociologist Samuel Stouffer was the first to systematically examine the intolerant frame of mind.[3] Stouffer conducted his surveys of attitudes toward communism and other unpopular causes. He argued, however, that he was focusing not on transient opinions but on deeper attitudes. For example, he measured popular support for freedom of speech, a fundamental democratic value. Stouffer asked a national sample of Americans whether various groups, such as communists and atheists, should be allowed to "speak in your community." He did not ask respondents to approve sabotage or espionage, only whether these minorities should have the right to speak. Twenty-one percent would not permit a person to speak if his or her loyalty had been questioned before a congressional committee, even if the person swore he or she was not a communist. Nearly 33 percent of Stouffer's sample would not permit a socialist to speak; 60 percent would not permit an atheist to speak; and fully 66 percent would not permit a communist to speak. This important study indicated that the American masses are not willing to extend democratic rights to unpopular minorities even for legitimate activities.

Mass support for the liberties of despised groups was no greater in the 1960s; only the target groups changed. For example, a replication of the Stouffer study found substantial increases in the willingness of the masses to tolerate nonconformists as defined by the original study.[4] Thus the threat of communists and "fellow-travelers" subsided, but the masses continued to oppose lawful activities of "extremists," including demonstrators and protesters of all kinds. Protesting blacks and student radicals replaced communists as "the enemy"; "law and order" became the phrase that mobilized mass support for repression. Revulsion against street demonstrations was widespread, even among those who sympathized with the protesters' stated goals. A substantial majority disapproved of civil disobedience and lawful protest: "Before 1950 a maximum of 49 percent would have allowed an extremist to speak freely. During the 1950s permissiveness towards radicals never climbed above 29 percent. Since 1960 only two in ten would approve free expression to an extreme view."[5]

But what are the attitudes of members of elites? Stouffer's study found community leaders (mayors, school board presidents, political party leaders, and others) *more willing than the general public to tolerate nonconformists.* A 1973 replication of the study found virtually identical results. While the study classified only half the general public as "tolerant," it classified 82 percent of the community leaders as such.[6] Whatever the focus of hostility, one consistent pattern emerges: elites support tolerance more than masses do.

In the 1970s and 1980s, however, those with faith in the common people found cause for rejoicing. Another replication found that large majorities would allow communists and atheists freedom of speech, except in the classroom. Responses to groups not mentioned in the original Stouffer study also indicate that the dark ages may be over: respondents were willing to tolerate homosexuals and people with the controversial belief that blacks are genetically inferior, as long as these groups did not attempt to influence young people's minds. (See figure 5-1.) The study still found a link between level of education and degree of tolerance, but the relationship is apparently not as direct as sociologists once thought.

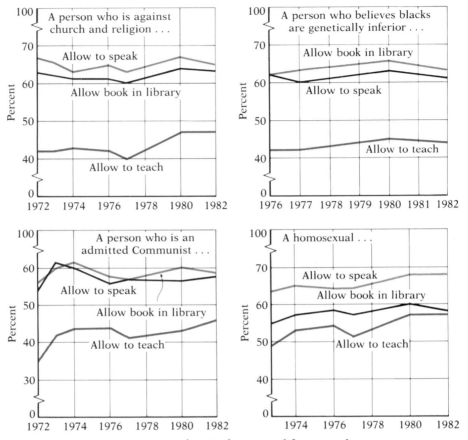

FIGURE 5-1. Americans' attitudes toward free speech.

Source: The National Opinion Research Center, General Social Surveys, latest that of February–April 1982. From *Public Opinion*, October/November 1982, p. 35.

Social class and democratic attitudes

The evidence seems quite clear that "a large proportion of the electorate has failed to grasp certain of the underlying ideas and principles on which the American political system rests."[7] We are left asking why the system survives.

The distribution of antidemocratic attitudes among various social classes may provide part of an answer. Upper social classes (from which members of elites are largely recruited) give greater, more consistent support to democratic values than do lower social classes. Political sociologist Seymour Martin Lipset has observed that "extremist and intolerant movements in modern society are more likely to be based on the lower classes than on the middle and upper classes."[8] Analyzing the ideologies of the lower classes, Lipset notes:

The poorer strata everywhere are more liberal or leftist on economic issues; they favor more welfare state measures, higher wages, graduated income taxes, support of trade unions, and so forth. But when liberalism is defined in noneconomic terms—as support of civil liberties, internationalism, and so forth—the correlation is reversed. The more well-to-do are more liberal; the poorer are more intolerant.[9]

Working-class authoritarianism

Many surveys show that intolerance concentrates disproportionately in the lower classes. One study tested for a "cultural intolerance factor": a measure of intolerance of values and beliefs differing from one's own. (See figure 5-2.) Cultural intolerance is greatest among the poorly educated and economically impoverished and among those who define their own social-class standing (under "Subjective Class" in the figure) as low.

From such findings Lipset formulated the concept of *working-class authoritarianism*. (Authoritarianism is belief in the need for a strong central authority that compels submission.) Lipset observed that only 30 percent of the manual workers in Stouffer's study were tolerant, whereas 66 percent of the professionals were. Lipset argued that several aspects of lower-class life contribute to an authoritarian or antidemocratic personality, among them low education, low participation in

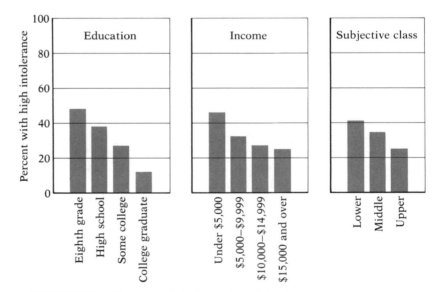

FIGURE 5-2. Factors related to cultural intolerance.

Source: Data based on Seymour Martin Lipset and Earl Raab, *The Politics of Unreason* (New York: Harper & Row, 1971), p. 447.

political organizations, little reading, economic insecurity, and rigid family patterns.

Many features of the working- and lower-class subculture support the idea of a class-linked, antidemocratic pattern. For example, lower-class child-rearing patterns are substantially more authoritarian than those of the middle and upper classes. Also, the work life of the lower classes is depressing; unskilled workers are far less satisfied with their jobs than are skilled workers and, as a partial result, have a more fatalistic attitude toward life. Workers who feel little control over their lives tend to view the social and political worlds as unchangeable. Unskilled workers are also more likely to view both big business and big government as cynically manipulative. Most important, the skill level in manual jobs is related to mental health. Mental health scores consistently show that people working in unskilled jobs have greater anxiety, hostility, negative self-feelings, and social alienation than do people in skilled occupations.[10] Lipset provides the following summary of the lower-class individual:

> He is likely to have been exposed to punishment, lack of love, and a general atmosphere of tension and aggression since early childhood—all experiences which tend to produce deep-rooted hostilities expressed by ethnic prejudices, political authoritarianism, and chiliastic transvaluational religion. His educational attainment is less than that of men with higher socioeconomic status, and his association as a child with others of similar background not only fails to stimulate his own intellectual interests but also creates an atmosphere which prevents his educational experience from increasing his general social sophistication and his understanding of different groups and ideas. Leaving school rather early, he is surrounded on the job by others with a similarly restricted cultural, educational, and family background.[11]

Social class, education, and commitment to democracy

The circumstances of lower-class life, then, make commitment to democratic ideas very difficult. But how much each of these circumstances—family life, work, and education—contributes to the making of the antidemocratic personality is not clear. Clearly, Americans' level of education is related to their degree of tolerance, as is illustrated by figure 5-3. Each increment of education adds to the respondents' willingness to allow racists, communists, or homosexuals to teach. In two of three examples, only those groups educated above the high school level contain tolerant majorities.

Lipset suggested that lack of education might be more important than any other characteristic of lower-class life. By examining the responses of people of various educational and occupational strata, he found that within each occupational level, higher educational status makes for greater tolerance. He also found that increases in tolerance

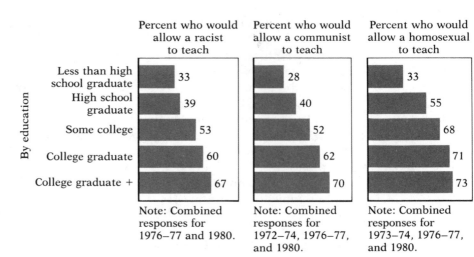

By education	Percent who would allow a racist to teach	Percent who would allow a communist to teach	Percent who would allow a homosexual to teach
Less than high school graduate	33	28	33
High school graduate	39	40	55
Some college	53	52	68
College graduate	60	62	71
College graduate +	67	70	73

Note: Combined responses for 1976–77 and 1980.

Note: Combined responses for 1972–74, 1976–77, and 1980.

Note: Combined responses for 1973–74, 1976–77, and 1980.

FIGURE 5-3.   Education levels and tolerance.

Source: *Public Opinion*, October/November 1980, p. 27.

associated with educational level are greater than those related to occupation. No matter what the occupation, tolerance and education were strongly related.

Numerous other studies also closely relate educational levels to commitment to free speech. College graduates are far more tolerant of unpopular minorities' free speech than are persons with only a grade school or high school education. Kornhauser found that within a given occupation (auto workers), the better the education, the less authoritarian the person.[12]

Examining many surveys, Lewis Lipsitz finds that the upper and middle classes are less authoritarian primarily because they are more likely to have post–high school education. When education is constant, very few other relationships between class and authoritarianism remain strong. Thus the greater authoritarianism of the working classes is largely a product of their low levels of education.[13]

It is instructive to isolate the effects of education by simultaneously examining education and income. This can be accomplished by looking at attitude variations according to education within selected income categories. Looking at one indicator of tolerance—willingness to accept the legitimacy of lawful protest—reveals that education has an *independent*, strong effect (table 5-1). Within each income group, tolerance increases significantly with education. It is also true, however, that within each education group, tolerance increases with income, but the increases are far less dramatic.

Education affects tolerance by influencing the individual's ability to apply an abstract principle to a concrete situation. It is one thing to

TABLE 5-1.   Joint effects of income and education on support for lawful protest

Family income	Education					
	Non-high school graduate		High school graduate		Some college	
Under $6,000	27%	(214)	33%	(76)	55%	(61)
$6,000–9,999	29	(113)	41	(143)	48	(103)
$10,000 and over	39	(57)	44	(140)	71	(181)

Source: Robert S. Erikson and Norman R. Luttberg, *American Public Opinion: Its Origins, Content, and Import* (1973), p. 176. Used with permission of John Wiley & Sons, Inc.

agree that peaceful demonstrations are legitimate; it is quite another to allow an unpopular demonstration. For instance, about 66 percent of those with a college education agree that "people should be allowed to hold a protest demonstration to ask the government to act on some issue," while 37 percent of those with grade school education agree. Of that 37 percent, however, 94 percent would allow an antipollution demonstration by a group of neighbors, but two-thirds would prohibit a demonstration in favor of legalizing marijuana. Thus the amount of tolerance shown by the few poorly educated people who are tolerant depends on the cause behind the demonstration. The highly educated do not shift attitudes as radically; of the two-thirds who support the right to demonstrate, 97 percent would allow a neighborhood antipollution demonstration and 81 percent would allow a promarijuana demonstration:

> Consistency in applying a general norm does increase with education. . . . College educated respondents rarely abandon their tolerant general norm. . . . Among the less educated, however, inconsistency is far more common. . . . The less educated are . . . considerably more likely than others to abandon a tolerant general norm.[14]

The key, then, to variations in tolerance is education.

However, recent findings contradict, or at least modify, early Jeffersonian assumptions that education alone is enough to ensure increased tolerance. The idea of *threat* is one complicating factor. People who feel that a particular group is threatening or dangerous may become intolerant because of a genuine (though inaccurate) belief that the "target group" endangers society. They are not simply annoyed that they must put up with a few harmless loonies but are truly frightened. Studies that take into account such perceptions of threat find that the relationship between education and tolerance virtually disappears.[15] The groups perceived as threatening vary, of course, with the subjects' education: well-educated people are less threatened by atheists or communists than are poorly educated people. But when well-educated people are threatened, they too become intolerant; threat reduces tolerance regardless of its source. Elites may not feel threatened by as many groups, but once threatened, they can respond to threats with as much vigor as can masses.

Generally, however, the behavior of active elites is more benign. Active involvement in the political process is also related to tolerance: the more active the person, the more tolerant he or she is likely to be. But since education is also related to political participation, which "causes" the tolerance? Education appears to be the stronger force, although both are contributors. College graduates who are not active in politics tend to be more tolerant than poorly educated people who are active, for example. The combination of advanced education and high political participation yields the highest proportion of tolerant people. (See table 5-2.)

Are the masses becoming more tolerant?

If education reduces intolerance, the United States should be experiencing an explosion of tolerance. Each year the proportion of high school graduates entering college increases, pushing the median education of the population upward. Additionally when elites send clear signals that an "out-group" is no longer a legitimate target of hostility, masses gradually pick up the signals. The status of blacks is a good example. Not only has federal legislation moved consistently toward equality, but also political candidates—Democrats and Republicans, liberals and conservatives—all accept the premise that blacks and whites deserve equal treatment.

Television entertainment—the medium of elite mass communication—reinforces tolerance. For example, television police shows portray only 7 percent of criminals as black, whereas in reality blacks account for 30 percent of all criminal arrests. Further, approximately half the blacks on network television appear to be middle class, again a distortion of reality.[16]

Because mass opinion generally follows that of elites, racial tolerance should be increasing. Such is the case. In 1968 the National Advi-

TABLE 5-2. Tolerance and participation, controlled for education (percent "more tolerant")

	Participation		
	Low	*Medium*	*High*
Grade school	4	8	0
High school	8	10	22
Some college	21	15	33
College graduate	25	35	45
N	58	68	100

Source: Sullivan et al., 1982.

sory Commission on Civil Disorders (the Kerner Commission) found that 33 percent of whites felt they had the right to keep blacks out of their neighborhoods. In 1978 only 5 percent agreed; an overwhelming 93 percent believed that blacks should be able to live wherever they could afford to. In 1968 a majority of whites believed that blacks themselves (rather than discrimination) were to blame for their poor economic position, compared to only 40 percent in 1978.[17]

Huge majorities would vote for a black for president, believe in school integration, and would not be distressed if blacks moved into their neighborhoods. Nonetheless, the problem of prejudice against blacks has not gone away. Despite growing tolerance, white parents also show an increasing reluctance to send their children to schools where half or more of the students are black. Stereotypes remain: a significant number of people believe that blacks are less ambitious than whites (49 percent) and that they want to live on handouts (36 percent). (See figure 5-4.)

Increased educational levels account for only a portion of these changes. Other factors include a large proportion of younger respondents and, as we suggest, elite communication to the masses about appropriate attitudes. Yesterday's out-groups are now accepted. The initial research about tolerance identified a variety of out-groups relevant at that time. In addition to racial minorities, special attention was given to the rights of political and religious nonconformists to exercise First Amendment freedoms. In 1954 Stouffer found scant support for the rights of atheists and communists to express their beliefs publicly. By 1977 tolerance of these ideas had increased substantially. Only with regard to atheists' and communists' being allowed to teach did a majority of respondents appear intolerant.[18]

It appears, then, that increasing levels of education and the elimination of prejudice against selected out-groups in the mass media have increased the tolerance of the masses. However, the relation between education and tolerance still exists. While the undereducated are more tolerant toward atheists, communists, and blacks than they were a generation ago, they are substantially less tolerant than more educated citizens are. Although "it is no longer socially acceptable to voice racial prejudice," a majority of whites would move from their neighborhoods if blacks in "great" numbers came to live in the neighborhood. Only 36 percent approve of mixed marriages.[19] Moreover, overwhelming majorities oppose affirmative-action programs and busing to achieve racial equality.

Changing targets of intolerance

We are accustomed to radical "right" groups seeking to control the instruction and reading in public schools by removing literature that they consider offensive from the libraries and classrooms. For decades,

FIGURE 5-4.   A decade of progress, yet stereotypes remain.

Black Friends

Question: *How strongly would you object if a member of your family wanted to bring a (negro/black/white) friend home to dinner? Would you object strongly, mildly, or not at all?* (1972, 1973, 1974, 1976, 1977 asked of non-blacks only about "negro/black friend"; 1980 and 1982 asked of all respondents—asked blacks about "white friend" and asked non-blacks about "negro/black friend")

Question: *Here are some opinions other people have expressed in connection with (negro/black)—white relations. Which statement on the card comes closest to how you, yourself feel. . . . (Agree strongly, Agree slightly, Disagree slightly, Disagree strongly)? . . . White people have a right to keep (negroes/blacks) out of their neighborhoods if they want to, and (negroes/blacks) should respect that right.* (1972, 1976, 1977 asked of non-blacks only; 1980 and 1982 asked of all respondents)

Question: *If your party nominated a (negro/black) for president, would you vote for him if he were qualified for the job?* (1972, 1975, 1977 asked of non-blacks only; 1974, 1978, 1982 asked of all respondents)

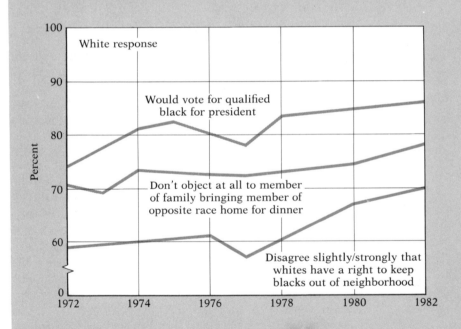

Note: The percentage of blacks saying they "didn't object at all to a member of the family bringing a member of the opposite race home for dinner" was 96% in 1980, and 94% in 1982. The percentage of blacks saying they "disagreed slightly/strongly that whites have a right to keep blacks out of the neighborhood" was 86% in 1980, and 91% in 1982. The percentage of blacks saying they would vote for a black for president were: 1974, 96%; 1978, 96%; 1982, 97%.

From *Public Opinion*, October/November, 1982, p. 34.

FIGURE 5-4. *continued*

Integrated Schools

Question: *Do you think white students and Negro students should go to the same schools or to separate schools?*

Note: Question not asked for blacks by NORC until 1972.

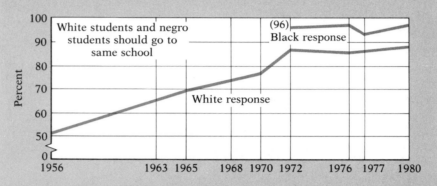

SOURCE: Surveys by the National Opinion Research Center, 1956–1970; National Opinion Research Center, General Social Surveys, 1972, 1976, 1977, 1980.

From *Public Opinion*, April/May, 1981, p. 34.

Black Neighbors

Question: *Would it upset you personally a lot, some but not a lot, only a little, or not at all if blacks moved into this neighborhood?*

Note: For comparison purposes the response "already in neighborhood (vol.)" which appeared only in 1978 was calculated out.

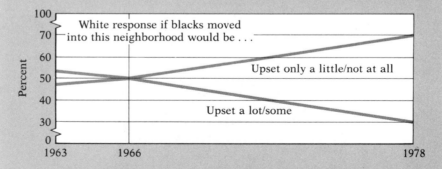

SOURCE: Surveys by Louis Harris and Associates, conducted for *Newsweek*, 1963 and 1966; Louis Harris and Associates, conducted for the National Conference of Christians and Jews, October 6–November 8, 1978. From *Public Opinion*, April/May, 1981, p. 34.

FIGURE 5-4. *continued*

Classroom Makeup

Question: (Asked of white parents) *Would you, yourself, have any objection to sending your children to a school where a few of the children are colored? Where half of the children are colored? Where more than half of the children are colored?* 1958, 1966 (In 1980, the word "black" was substituted for "colored.")

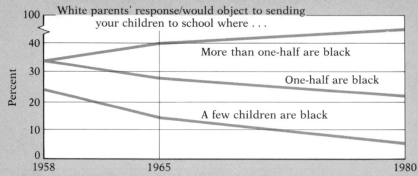

Note: Respondents who had no objection to sending their children to a school where a few children are black were asked if they had any objection to sending their children to a school where half of the children are black. Respondents who had no objection to sending their children to a school where half of the children were black were asked if they had any objection to sending their children to a school where more than half of the children are black.

SOURCE: Surveys by the Gallup Organization, latest that of December 5–8, 1980.

From *Public Opinion*, April/May, 1981, p. 33.

Generalizations about Blacks

Question: *Now let me ask you some questions about blacks as people, leaving aside the whole question of civil rights and laws. I'd like to know how you feel as an individual. Here are some statements people sometimes make about black people. For each statement, please tell me whether you personally tend to agree or disagree with that statement. . . .*

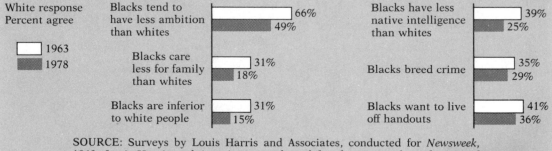

SOURCE: Surveys by Louis Harris and Associates, conducted for *Newsweek*, 1963; Louis Harris and Associates, conducted for the National Conference of Christians and Jews, October 6–November 8, 1978. From *Public Opinion*, April/May, 1981, p. 34.

such groups have sought to eliminate science books with an evolutionary bias, sex education materials judged to be threatening to the institution of marriage, political literature judged to be anti-American, and economic material assessed as hostile to capitalism. Now, however, liberal groups are becoming equally vocal on behalf of censorship. These groups seek to remove sexist and racist literature in schools and to reduce the display of violence on television. Television networks and public schools both report increased activity by liberal groups seeking to impose their values.

In short, the targets of legitimate discrimination are changeable; they vary with the times. In the 1950s when U.S. foreign policy was vigorously anticommunist and cold war mentality was official, the masses' fear of communist activity led them to reject the legitimacy of communists' speaking, writing, or seeking public office. In the 1960s many people saw internal social protest as the greatest threat. The percentage of people who believed that members of the Communist party were harmful to the "American way of life" decreased modestly from 1965 to 1969, while the percentage believing student demonstrators were harmful increased from 65 to 72 percent, only to decline to 48 percent by 1973. During the same period, increased fear of crime led to growing mass conservatism about the rights of accused criminals. In the aftermath of the demonstrations and violence of the 1960s, the masses sought a harsher penal system. In 1966, 44 percent of the public thought the criminal justice system was too lenient, a figure that reached two-thirds by 1970 and three-fourths by 1973.

Public opinion is reactive; it fears what it is supposed to fear: "Fear is transferred to new objects."[20] Attitudes toward homosexuals illustrate this concept. Whereas elite views about other out-groups is clear, it is ambiguous about homosexuals. In the late 1970s, starting with Miami, six cities held referenda on the right of homosexuals to enjoy the same freedoms from discrimination previously granted to blacks and to women. All six voted down the idea of "gay rights." Prominent leaders of the women's movement supported the cause of homosexuals. However, elite activity was not consensual, nor did media coverage spell out the "proper" position as it had with blacks and women. The consequences are predictable. While the abstract idea of equal rights of homosexuals gains majority approval in public opinion polls, equally strong majorities believe that homosexuals should not be hired as doctors, ministers, or elementary school teachers.

To discover the nature of intolerance, one needs to find targets not yet legitimated by elites or targets (such as racists or sexists) sanctioned as legitimate. Recent research bears out the effectiveness of this approach. One study allowed respondents to identify the group they most strongly opposed and then asked them whether a member of this group, whatever its cause, should be allowed to seek political office, teach, make a speech, hold public rallies, and the like. The conclusion was that "over half of

the ... respondents ... believe that their least liked group should be outlawed, hardly consistent with the recent conclusion that the mass public is increasingly tolerant."[21]

Thus tolerance has neither increased much nor declined but has simply found new targets. While the mass public is more tolerant of groups such as communists and atheists that have faded from attention as threats, other targets have emerged to take their place. This changeableness of mass attitudes suggests that, given the right circumstances, effective counterelites could mobilize people against a particular scapegoat, as has occurred in the past. Intolerance is still more concentrated in the lower classes: "there seems to be a somewhat greater willingness to limit the rights of *any* deviants whose ideas may endanger 'the American way of life,' at least as it is defined in the minds of manual workers."[22]

If, as indicated in table 5-3, two-thirds of the sample wanted to outlaw the group named as least liked, then perhaps we should know which groups people hate. Hatred tends to vary with individual ideology. As we can see in table 5-4, self-identified liberals hate the radical right, and self-identified conservatives hate communists and socialists.

How does democracy survive?

The irony of democracy is that democratic ideals survive because authoritarian masses are generally apathetic and inactive. Thus the lower classes' capacity for intolerance, authoritarianism, scapegoatism, racism, and violence seldom translates into organized, sustained political movements.

Moreover, the survival of democracy does not depend on mass support for democratic ideals. It is apparently not necessary that most people commit themselves to a democracy; all that is necessary is that they fail to commit themselves actively to an antidemocratic system. Though

TABLE 5-3. Tolerance toward least liked group (percent tolerant)

Member of least liked group . . .	
should be allowed to become president	28
Should be allowed to teach	26
Should not be outlawed	33
Should be allowed to make a speech in this city	70
Should be allowed to hold public meetings	57

Source: Sullivan et al., p. 65.

TABLE 5-4. Personal ideology and least liked group

	Liberal	Moderate	Conservative
Communists/socialists	21%	32%	44%
New Left	7%	15%	21%
Radical right	59%	34%	17%
Others	8%	11%	7%
N	293	512	372

Source: Sullivan et al., p. 276.

this fact suggests that American democracy is on shaky foundations, the masses' tendency to avoid political activity makes their antidemocratic attitudes less destructive. Those with the most dangerous attitudes are the least involved in politics.[23]

Conditions for mass activism

Occasionally, however, mass apathy gives way to mass activism. Reflecting the masses' antidemocratic, extremist, hateful, and violence-prone sentiments, this activism seriously threatens democratic values.

Mass activism tends to occur in crises—defeat or humiliation in war, economic depression and unemployment, or threats to public safety. Social psychologist William Kornhauser correctly observes:

> There appears to be a close relation between the severity of crises and the extent of mass movements in Western societies. The more severe the depression in industrial societies, the greater the social atomization, and the more widespread are mass movements (for example, there is a high [inverse] association between level of employment and increase in the extremist electorate). The stronger a country's sense of national humiliation and defeat in war, the greater the social atomization, and the greater the mass action (for example, there is a close association between military defeat and the rise of strong mass movements).[24]

Defeat in war, or even failure to achieve any notable victories in a protracted military effort, reduces mass confidence in established leadership and makes the masses vulnerable to the appeals of counterelites. Both fascism in Germany and communism in Russia followed on the heels of national humiliation and defeat in war. The antiestablishment culture of the late 1960s and early 1970s owes a great deal to the mistakes and failures of the nation's leadership in Vietnam.

Mass anxiety and vulnerability to counterelites also increase in periods of economic dislocation—depression, unemployment, or technological change—that threaten financial security. Poverty alone causes less anxiety than does change or the threat of change in people's level of affluence. Another source of anxiety among the masses is their perceived level of personal safety. Crime, street violence, and terrorism can produce disproportionately strong anxieties about personal safety. Historically, masses that believe their personal safety is threatened have turned to vigilantes, the Ku Klux Klan, and "law and order" movements.

The masses are most vulnerable to extremism when they are alienated from group and community life and when they feel their own lives are without direction or purpose.[25] Mass participation in the established organizations of the community—church groups, PTAs, Little League, fraternal orders—provide a sense of participation, involvement, and self-esteem. This involvement shields the masses from the despairing appeals of demagogues who play on latent mass fears and hatreds. People who are socially isolated are likely to become mobilized by totalitarian movements. Thus a thriving group and community life very much serves the interest of elites; it helps protect them from the threat of demagogues who wish to challenge the established system of values.

Counterelites: The demagogue as voice of the people

Threats to established elite values occur periodically, from both "left" and "right." The counterelite pattern is similar regardless of the ideology behind it. Both "left" and "right" counterelite movements appeal to the desire of the "powerless" to overthrow the established elite.

Although "left" counterelites in America are just as antidemocratic, extremist, and intolerant as "right" counterelites are, their appeal is not as broadly based as is the appeal to the "right." "Left" counterelites have no mass following among workers, farmers, or middle-class Americans. In contrast, "right" counterelites have mobilized broad mass followings. Many changes in American society have contributed to the popular appeal of "right" counterelites: shifts in power and prestige from the farms to the cities, from agriculture to industry, from the North to the West; shifts away from individual enterprise toward collective action; shifts away from racial segregation toward special emphasis on opportunities for blacks; shifts from old values to new, from religion to secularism, from work to leisure; shifts in scale from small to large, from personal to impersonal, from individual to bureaucratic; increases in crime, racial disorder, and threats to personal safety. Any genuine "people's" revolution in America would undoubtedly take the form of a right-wing nationalist, patriotic, religious-fundamentalist, antiblack, anti-intellectual, antistudent, "law and order" movement.[26]

The New Right and social issues

Generally lurking beneath the elites' "legitimate" agenda is a more radical agenda known as the "New Right," that appeals to the masses. Though the label is new, radical right influence is not new in American history. The New Right's political ancestors are centuries old: the "Know Nothings" of the nineteenth century (who opposed immigration and Catholicism), the turn-of-the-century populists led by William Jennings Bryan (who opposed all forms of social liberalism, especially the teaching of evolution), George Wallace's popularity a decade ago, and the "taxpayers' revolt" of the late 1970s.

Today's mass movement, proposed by the New Right, champions a variety of causes. Unlike mass movements of the past, it has also placed some of its adherents in institutionally powerful positions: Senator Jesse Helms (R.–N.C.) and Senator Jeremiah Denton (R.–Alabama) have consistently sought to move their agenda into the mainstream of elite politics. The New Right vigorously pursues such goals as a constitutional amendment allowing prayers in schools, a constitutional amendment prohibiting abortion, and legislation prohibiting busing to achieve racial balance in schools. The movement characterizes these goals as "the social agenda."

Many people believed that Ronald Reagan's election was a boost for the New Right, for New Right leaders (such as Richard Viguerie of the National Conservative Political Action Committee and Jerry Falwell of the Moral Majority) enthusiastically supported Reagan's presidency and expected substantial executive support for their agenda. Moreover, the less affluent and less educated portions of the population provided mass support for New Right causes. Normally at a disadvantage, the New Right saw the existence of a symbolically sympathetic president and two powerful allies in the Senate as a valuable opportunity to formalize its agenda. Yet the very disparity of its goals caused the New Right to lose momentum. According to Jerry Falwell, for example, the New Right includes the following diverse groups: "hard-working citizens sick and tired of high taxes and ever-rising inflation; small businessmen angry at excessive government regulations and federal red tape; born again Christians disturbed about sex on TV and in movies; parents opposed to forced busing; supporters of the right to life and against federal financing of abortions; middle class Americans tired of Big Government, Big Business, Big Labor and Big Education telling us what to do and what not to do; pro-defense citizens alarmed by appeasement and weakness in U.S. foreign policy."[27] Substantial majorities of the population indeed agree with some of these goals: most people are worried about inflation and taxes, oppose forced busing, and favor a strong military establishment. However, as is common to mass movement goals, these goals are not easy to achieve. Beyond certain general areas of agreement, the movement is more symbol than substance.

Soon after he took office, President Reagan, while not disavowing New Right goals, placed them well below his economic reform package in priority. He spoke about the Soviet threat, the stranglehold of government bureaucracy, and the need for government to stop meddling in Americans' lives; however, his lobbying activity did nothing to achieve these goals. Despite shouts of "betrayal" from his New Right supporters, Reagan did as all presidents do: he tried to accomplish the possible and ignore the pointless. Moreover, the New Right agenda had less congressional support than originally thought. The mood of the country, prompted by the cues of established elites, was one that did not lend much hope to the New Right. Tax cuts, reduction of spending for social programs, and the military buildup were Reagan's—and hence Congress's—priority. The emotional issues related to the family, school, and community, were in the hands of the New Right senators, who met as much opposition from traditional conservatives as from liberals. Indeed, established conservatives like Senator Barry Goldwater (R.–Arizona) spoke out against the New Right.

Organizationally very visible (the often colorful, outspoken New Right attract media coverage), the movement wanted so much so soon that it lost patience with its nominal supporters in government. Executive lobbying was brisk and effective, but New Right lobbying was weakened by infighting and the inability to compromise. As the New Right squabbled, the time for success began to pass. Candidates in the 1982 congressional elections found little to gain from pushing New Right causes. As the recession continued, few people worried about the issues of passionate concern to New Right leaders. As a result, fifteen New Right representatives lost their seats.

This rise and fall of the New Right is typical of counter elite movements. They can generate substantial support in the short run and can occasionally make a showing at the polls. But in the long run, the national agenda belongs to the established conservatives and liberals of the two major parties. The New Right will continue to receive some symbolic gratification, and some large segments of the public will find the simplicity of the New Right program attractive. However, the New Right, like its predecessors, is likely to fail in translating its emotional slogans into public policy.

Summary

Elite theory suggests that attitudes and values, as well as socioeconomic background, distinguish elites from masses. Elites give greater support to the principles and beliefs underlying the political system. Our analysis of elite and mass attitudes suggests the following propositions:

1. Elites give greater support to democratic values than do masses. Elites are also more consistent than masses in applying general principles of democracy to specific individuals, groups, and events.
2. Extremist and intolerant movements in modern society are more likely to arise from the lower classes than from the middle and upper classes. The poor may be more liberal on economic issues, but on noneconomic issues—support for civil liberties, for example—the upper classes are more liberal and the lower classes more conservative. Masses demonstrate antidemocratic attitudes more often than elites do. The masses are less committed to democratic rules of the game than elites are and are more likely to go outside these rules and engage in violence. Mass movements exploit the alienation and hostility of lower classes by concentrating on scapegoats.
3. The survival of democracy depends on elite rather than mass commitment to democratic ideals.
4. Political apathy and nonparticipation among the masses contribute to the survival of democracy. Fortunately for democracy, the antidemocratic masses are generally more apathetic than elites are. Only an unusual demagogue or counterelite can arouse the masses from their apathy and create a threat to the established system.
5. Occasionally mass apathy turns into mass activism, which is generally extremist, intolerant, antidemocratic, and violence prone. Conditions that encourage mass activism include defeat or humiliation in war, economic dislocation, and perceived threats to personal safety.
6. Counterelites appeal to mass sentiments and express hostility toward the established order and its values. Both "left" and "right" counterelites are antidemocratic, extremist, impatient with due process, contemptuous of law and authority, and violence prone. Counterelites express racial prejudice, populism, egalitarianism, anti-intellectualism, and simplistic solutions to social problems.
7. Although "left" counterelites are as antidemocratic as "right" counterelites are, their appeal is not as broadly based as is the appeal to the "right". "Right" counterelites have mobilized mass support among large numbers of farmers, workers, and middle-class Americans. Jeremiah Denton and Jesse Helms (leaders of the "New Right") are typical mass counterelites in their appeal to simplistic emotionalism and to other mass values.
8. Although more committed to democratic values than are masses, elites may abandon these values in crises. When war or revolution threatens the existing order, elites themselves may deviate from democratic values to maintain the system. They may then cease tolerating the

dissent, censor mass media, curtail free speech, jail counterelites, and strengthen police and security forces.

NOTES

1. *Fortune* (June 1940).
2. Herbert H. Hyman and Paul B. Sheatsley, "Trends in Public Opinion on Civil Liberties," *Journal of Social Issues* 9 (1953):6–16.
3. Samuel A. Stouffer, *Communism, Conformity, and Civil Liberties;* 1955, reprint (New York: Wiley, 1966).
4. J. Allen Williams, "Communism, Confirmity, and Civil Liberty: Highlights of a 1973 Replication of Stouffer's 1955 Study," paper presented at the Southwestern Sociological Association Convention, Dallas, March 1974.
5. Hazel Erskine, "The Polls: Freedom of Speech," *Public Opinion Quarterly* 34 (February 1970):484.
6. Williams, op cit., p. 6.
7. Herbert McClosky, "Consensus and Ideology in American Politics," *American Political Science Review* 58 (June 1964):361–382.
8. Seymour Martin Lipset, *Political Man* (Garden City, N.Y.: Doubleday, 1963), p. 87.
9. Ibid., p. 92.
10. Lewis Lipsitz, "Work Life and Political Attitudes: A Study of Manual Workers," *American Political Science Review* 58 (December 1964):959.
11. Lipset, op cit., p. 114.
12. Ibid., p. 110.
13. Lewis Lipsitz, "Working-Class Authoritarianism: A Reevaluation," *American Sociological Review* 30 (1965):108–109.
14. David G. Lawrence, "Procedural Norms and Tolerance: A Measurement," *American Political Science Review* 70 (March 1976):89.
15. John L. Sullivan, James Pierson, and George E. Marcus, *Political Tolerance and American Democracy* (Chicago: University of Chicago Press, 1982), p. 193.
16. Michael Robinson, "Prime Time Chic: Between Newsbreak and Commercials, the Values Are L.A. Liberal," *Public Opinion* 2 (March–May 1979):44–45.
17. "The Kerner Commission, Ten Years Later," *Public Opinion* 1 (May–June 1978):36.
18. James A. Davis, "Communism, Conformity, Cohorts, and Categories: American Tolerance in 1954 and in 1972–1973," *American Journal of Sociology* 81 (1975):491–513; David Lawrence, "Procedural Norms and Tolerance: A Reassessment," *Political Science Review* 70 (1975):80–100; Clyde A. Nunn, Harry J. Crockett, and J. Allen Williams, *Tolerance for Nonconformity* (San Francisco: Jossey-Bass, 1978).
19. Hazel Erskine and Richard L. Siegel, "Civil Liberties and the Public," *Journal of Social Issues* 31 (1975):20; and *Gallup Opinion Index* (November 1978):27.
20. Ibid., p. 22.
21. John Sullivan, James Pierson, and Gregory Marcus, "An Alternative Conceptualization of Political Tolerance," *American Political Science Review* 73 (September 1979):788.
22. Edward G. Grabb, "Working Class Authoritarianism and Tolerance of Outgroups: A Reassessment," *Public Opinion Quarterly* (Spring 1979):42.
23. Herbert H. Hyman, "England and America: Climates of Tolerance and Intolerance, 1962," in Daniel Bell, ed., *The Radical Right* (Garden City, N.Y.: Doubleday, 1963), p. 229.
24. William Kornhauser, *The Politics of Mass Society* (Glencoe, Ill.: Free Press, 1959), p. 174.

25. Ibid., p. 33.
26. Seymour Martin Lipset and Earl Raab, *The Politics of Unreason* (New York: Harper & Row, 1970), p. 348.
27. Jerry Falwell, Introduction to Richard A. Viguerie, *The New Right—We're Ready to Lead* (Falls Church, Va.: The Viguerie Co., 1980).

SELECTED READINGS

Abramson, Paul R. *Political Attitudes in America* (San Francisco: W. H. Freeman, 1983). Chapter 14 contains a balanced discussion of changes in tolerance.

Davis, James A. "Communism, Conformity, Cohorts, and Categories: American Tolerance in 1954 and in 1972–1973." *American Journal of Sociology* 81 (1975):491–513. This replication of the original Stouffer study argues that tolerance is increasing.

Devine, Donald J. *The Political Culture of the United States*. Boston: Little, Brown, 1972. Devine provides an exhaustive analysis of the content of mass ideologies.

Edelman, Murray. *The Symbolic Uses of Politics*. Chicago: University of Illinois Press, Illini Books, 1967. Edelman discusses the general uses of symbols in society and then specifically the uses of political phenomena as symbols. He points out that myth and symbolic reassurance have become key elements in the governmental process and argues that the masses are generally uninterested in and inattentive to political phenomena as symbols. Only when the masses perceive symbolic or real threats or reassurances do they notice things political. Masses react to stimuli. Therefore, it is political actions that "shape men's political wants and 'knowledge,' not the other way around" (p. 172). Edelman also argues that mass demands, when they are articulated, are most often met with "symbolic" rather than "tangible" rewards.

Erikson, Robert S., and Luttberg, Norman R. *American Public Opinion: Its Origins, Content, and Impact*. New York: Wiley, 1973. Erikson and Luttberg have brought together and updated through 1970 several aspects of American public opinion research, including the formulation and content of opinion and the linkage between opinion and public officials. Especially important for the argument made in *Irony* are the chapters on political socialization, the potential of elections for "popular" control, and the impact of voter opinion on the policy choices of government officials.

Fromm, Eric. *Escape from Freedom*. New York: Avon Books, 1941. Fromm examines the notion of authoritarianism as an escape from the isolation produced by a large society. Written primarily from a popular psychoanalytic point of view, the book offers interesting comparative reading with the political science and sociological works on authoritarianism.

Grabb, Edward G. "Working Class Authoritarianism and Tolerance of Outgroups: A Reassessment." *Public Opinion Quarterly* 3 (Spring 1979):36–47. The relation between education and tolerance among the masses remains as strong as ever.

Kornhauser, William. *The Politics of Mass Society*. Glencoe, Ill.: Free Press, 1959. This book argues that a mass society occurs when elites are accessible to masses and masses are vulnerable to elites. This situation produces a threat of tyranny. To prevent this situation, Kornhauser suggests that intermediate groups are necessary to distract the attention of the masses from elite activities, to give the masses a sense of security and belonging at the local level, and to prevent demagogic manipulation of the masses by the elite.

Lane, Robert E. *Political Ideology*. New York: Free Press, 1962, and *Political Life*. New York: Macmillan, Free Press edition, 1965. *Political Ideology* is a series of case studies, using in-depth interviews of fifteen randomly selected "common men" in "Eastport." Lane attempts to probe the nature and extent of their political ideas. He finds that they do support the democratic ideal but that their political beliefs are a subpart of their job orientation and beliefs. *Political Life*, originally published in 1959, is a diverse book that includes sections on the historical development of suffrage, conditions for the success of democracy, and political behavior of the American people. Perhaps the most interesting sections are those on the sociopsychological factors that affect political behavior. Lane discusses not only the determinants of political life but also the effects of social institutions (mass media, parties, economic organizations, and so forth) on it.

Lawrence, David. "Procedural Norms and Tolerance: A Reassessment." *American Political Science Review* 70 (1975):80–108. Lawrence finds more tolerance for "democratic" norms than was true in the 1950s.

Lipset, Seymour Martin. *Political Man.* Garden City, N.Y.: Doubleday, Anchor Books, 1963. This interpretation of American politics by an eminent political sociologist covers a myriad of factors that affect or are affected by the dynamics of political activity. Parts I and III—respectively entitled "The Conditions of the Democratic Order" and "Political Behavior in American Society"—are particularly germane to the discussion in this chapter.

Lipset, Seymour Martin, and Raab, Earl. *The Politics of Unreason.* New York: Harper & Row, 1970. This book is a historical study of right-wing extremism from colonial times to 1970.

Schattschneider, E. E. *The Semisovereign People: A Realistic View of the Democracy in America.* New York: Holt, Rinehart and Winston, 1960. This book discusses the nature of conflict and change in America. Schattschneider argues against the pluralist-group theory bias, which he perceives as the common view of the political system today. He also recognizes the elite-masses dichotomy that exists in the American social and political system. For example, he develops the notion that elites, by virtue of their organizational strengths, can manage conflict within the political system. They can alter it, exploit it, and/or suppress it.

Stouffer, Samuel A. *Communism, Conformity, and Civil Liberties.* New York: Wiley, 1966. This book, originally published in 1955, reports the results of a national survey of six thousand people to "examine in some depth the reactions of Americans to two dangers. One, from the communist conspiracy outside and inside the country. Two, from those who in thwarting the conspiracy would sacrifice some of the very liberties which the enemy would destroy." The study was one of the first systematic attempts to examine the intolerant frame of mind and indicates that a large portion of America's masses would be willing to restrict severely even legitimate activities of unpopular minorities.

Sullivan, John L., James Piereson, and George E. Marcus. "An Alternative Conceptualization of Political Tolerance." *American Political Science Review* 73 (1979):781–794. Sullivan concludes that tolerance has not increased but that new targets of hostility have been found. See also Sullivan, John L., James Piereson, and George E. Marcus. *Political Tolerance and American Democracy* (Chicago: University of Chicago Press, 1982).

6 Elite-Mass Communication: Television, the Press, and the Pollsters

Communication in the American political system flows downward from elites to masses. Television and the press are the means by which elites communicate to the masses not only information but also values, attitudes, and emotions.

For most people most of the time politics is a series of pictures in the mind, placed there by television news, newspapers, magazines, and discussions . . . Politics for most of us is a passing parade of symbols.

—*Murray Edelman,* The Symbolic Uses of Politics, *1967*

Communication in the American political system flows downward from elites to masses. Television and the press are the means by which elites communicate to the masses not only information but also values, attitudes, and emotions. Professional pollsters in turn try to measure mass response to these elite communications. But elite-mass communication often fails. Masses may misinterpret elite messages to them, and elites may not change mass opinion as they intend; frequently, elites, guided by their own biases, misinterpret mass opinion.

The newsmakers

Elites instruct masses about politics and social values chiefly through television, the major source of information for the vast majority of Americans. Those who control this flow of information are among the most powerful people in the nation. In 1972 virtually every family in America (99.8 percent) had a television set, compared with only 19.8 percent in 1952. Thus only in the last twenty years have television newsmakers risen to power. Newspapers have always reported on wars, politics, crime, and scandal, just as they do today; but the American masses could quickly pass over the headlines to the sports and comics, pausing perhaps at the latest scandals and violent crimes. Television is the first true *mass* communication form. Nearly everyone, including children, watches the evening news. Over two-thirds of the public testifies that television provides "most of my views about what is going on in the world." And over two-thirds of the public says that television is its "most trusted" news source.[1]

Television has great impact because it is visual: it can convey emotions as well as information. Police dogs attacking blacks, people loading sacks of dead American soldiers on helicopters, angry crowds burning and looting in cities—all convey emotions as well as information.

141

The power to determine what Americans will see and hear about the world lies with just three private corporations: the American Broadcasting Company (ABC), the Columbia Broadcasting System (CBS), and the National Broadcasting Corporation (NBC), a division of RCA. Local television stations are privately owned and licensed to use broadcast channels by a government regulatory agency, the Federal Communications Commission (FCC). But because of the high cost of producing news and entertainment at the station level, virtually all stations must use news and programming from the three networks. The top officials of these corporate networks are indeed "a tiny, enclosed fraternity of privileged men."*

The top network executives—presidents, vice-presidents, directors, and producers—determine the news and entertainment Americans see. Many people believe that top news anchorpeople like Dan Rather, John Chancellor, David Brinkley, Roger Mudd, and Tom Brokaw select their own material, but for the most part, they simply read what is put in front of them.[2] The leading television reporters—Ted Koppel, Ed Bradley, Harry Reasoner, Mike Wallace, Barbara Walters, and others—occasionally pursue their own story ideas, but the decision to put their stories on the news rests with the news executives. Moreover, network executives exchange views with the editors of the *New York Times*, the *Washington Post*, *Newsweek*, *Time*, and a few of the largest newspaper chains. These television executives and producers and print editors and publishers collectively are the "newsmakers."

The newsmakers frequently make contradictory remarks about their own power. On the one hand, they claim that they do no more than "mirror" reality. The "mirror" myth is nonsense. A mirror makes no choices about what images it reflects, but television executives have the power to create some national issues and ignore others; to elevate obscure people to national prominence; to reward politicians they favor and punish those they disfavor. Indeed at times the newsmakers proudly credit themselves with the success of the civil rights movement, ending the Vietnam war, and forcing two presidents—Johnson and Nixon—out of office. These claims contradict the mirror image theory, but they more accurately reflect the power of the mass media.

The political functions of the mass media

The political power of the mass media arises from several of its vital functions: newsmaking, interpretation, socialization, persuasion, and agenda setting.

---

*So called by former Vice-President Spiro T. Agnew, who also described them more colorfully as "super-sensitive, self-anointed, supercilious electronic barons of opinion." (See *Newsweek*, November 9, 1970, p. 22.)

Newsmaking

Newsmaking is deciding what and who is "newsworthy" and allocating precious television time and newspaper space accordingly. Television producers and newspaper and magazine editors focus attention on certain people, issues, and events, and this attention in turn generates public concern and political action. Without media coverage, the mass public would not know about these personalities, issues, or events. And without public interest, government officials would not consider these topics important.

The media must select from a tremendous oversupply of information and decide what is "news," and this selection process is the root of their power. Television cannot be "a picture on the world" (as some television executives pretend) because the whole world cannot squeeze into the picture (or into the 24 noncommercial minutes of the evening news). Media attention creates events, issues, and personalities; media inattention means obscurity, even nonexistence. Of course, politicians, public relations people, interest group leaders, and aspiring "celebrities" know that the decisions of news executives are vital to their success and even to their existence. So they try, sometimes desperately, to attract the media's attention—to get just thirty seconds on the network news. The result is the "media event"—an activity arranged primarily to stimulate media coverage and attract public attention to an issue or personality. The more bizarre, dramatic, and sensational the event, the more likely it is to attract media attention. It may be a march or demonstration, a dramatic confrontation, an illustration of injustice, a press conference, a visit to a home for the elderly, or a walk down a ghetto street. A media event for television must have good "visuals" (interesting or

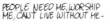

dramatic pictures); television networks are likely to ignore topics or issues without "visuals."

Interpretation

Interpretation of events, issues, and personalities begins when newsmakers search for an "angle" on the story—a way to put it in context and speculate about its meaning and consequences.

Through interpretation, newsmakers provide the masses with explanations and meanings for events and personalities.

Most network news broadcasts now include a "special segment" or "news special"—two or three minutes of "in-depth" coverage of a particular topic, such as the MX missile, gun control, nuclear plant safety, or the war in El Salvador. News staffs prepare these specials well in advance of their showing and use film or videotape and a script with a "lead in," "voice over," and "recapitulation." The interpretive function is clearest in these stories, but interpretation in fact takes place in every news story. Generally, news interpretations have a "liberal" bias (as we will discuss later in the chapter).

Socialization

The media's socialization function is to teach mass audiences preferred political norms and values. Both news and entertainment programming contribute to socialization. Election night coverage shows "how democracy works" and reinforces the values of political participation. Advertising shows Americans how they should live—it illustrates desirable life-styles and encourages viewers to buy such products as automobiles, beer, soap, and perfume.

Entertainment programs also socialize the mass public by introducing social themes and ways of life—for example, racial tolerance (black and white neighbors, situation comedies with cute black children), new sexual mores (sex outside of marriage, unmarried couples living together), divorce and feminism (divorced mothers raising children and living happily outside of marriage; successful, happy, and single professional women), and even homosexuality (well-adjusted, likable, sensitive, humorous homosexuals). Many television executives and producers congratulate themselves on such socially progressive themes.

Persuasion

Persuasion occurs when governments, corporations, unions, political parties, and candidates make deliberate attempts, usually but not always through paid advertising, to affect people's beliefs, attitudes, or behavior. The Defense Department has become a major advertiser in its efforts to recruit for all-volunteer forces—"Be all that you can be!" Corporate advertisers ask Americans not only to buy their products but also to believe that they are concerned with the environment, or with health, or with the economic welfare of the nation. Unions ask television viewers to "Look for the union label."

The most obvious efforts at political persuasion take place during political campaigns. Democratic and Republican party organizations no longer run their own campaigns but instead seek out advertising and public relations specialists to direct sophisticated media campaigns. Candidates can use television to bypass party organizations and go directly to the people. As the image makers have taken over political campaigns, the importance of political parties has declined. When voters can see and hear candidates in their own living rooms, they need not rely so heavily on party leaders to provide them with information and advice. Thus candidate "image" has become a major factor in voters' choices.

Agenda setting

The power of the mass media lies in deciding what will be decided. Defining the issues, identifying alternative policies, focusing on political, economic, or social "crises"—these are critical aspects of national policy making. We can refer to these activities as "agenda setting." Conditions in society that are *not* defined as "crises," or even as "problems," by the mass media never become policy issues. They do not get on political leaders' agendas. Political leaders, anxious to get coverage on the evening news programs, speak out on the issues the mass media have defined as important. These issues are placed on the agenda of decision makers. Governments must then decide what to do about them.

Clearly, then, the power to decide what will be a "crisis," or "problem," or "issue," is critical to the policy-making process.[3] Deciding what will be problems is even more important than deciding what will be the solutions.

Many civics textbooks imply that issues or problems or crises just "happen." Some people argue that in an open plural society such as ours, channels of access and communication to government are open to everyone, so any problem can be discussed and placed on the agenda of decision makers.

But in reality, policy issues do not just "happen." Creating an issue, dramatizing it, calling attention to it, turning it into a "crisis," and pressuring government to do something about it are important political tactics. Influential individuals, organized interest groups, political candidates and officeholders, and, perhaps most important, the mass media all employ these tactics.

The power of television is not in persuading viewers to take one side of an issue or another or to vote for one candidate or another. Instead *the power of television is in setting the agenda for decision making:* deciding which issues and candidates will be given attention and which will be ignored. Systematic research has shown that the issues that receive the greatest attention in the mass media are most likely to be viewed by voters as "important."[4] (In chapter 7, we describe the role of the mass media in defining the "serious" presidential candidates.)

Liberal bias in television news

Television permits far less diversity of views than does the press. Individual publications present conventionally "liberal" or "conservative" views—for example, the *New York Times* versus the *Wall Street Journal*, *Newsweek* versus *U.S. News and World Report*, or *Harper's* magazine versus the *National Review*—and thus balance each other to some degree. But all three major television networks present a conventional liberal point of view. (Only William F. Buckley's "Firing Line"—carried on public, educational television stations—represents the "conservative" viewpoint of network television.)

The liberal bias of the news originates in the values of the newsmakers themselves. The owners (stockholders) of the major corporations that control the television networks, magazines, and newspaper chains usually share the moderate conservatism and Republicanism of the business community; but the producers, directors, and reporters are clearly "left-leaning" and Democratic in their political views. Because newsmakers must rely on their own values in making decisions about what will be "news," the news reflects liberal values: concern for social reform, emphasis on the problems of blacks and the poor, interest in the environment, hostility toward the military, skepticism toward organized religion and the family, and willingness to use government power to "do good."[5] One study of news executives reported that 63 percent described themselves as "left-leaning," and only 27 percent as "middle-of-the-road," and 10 percent as "right-leaning."[6] Newsmakers describe themselves as either "independent" (45%) or Democratic (44%); very few (9%) admit to being Republican. And most are male and upper middle class in origin. (See table 6-1.)

Another study asked members of the Washington press corps if they agreed that the news reflects bias: 51 percent agreed and 49 percent disagreed. Of those who agreed, 96 percent described the bias as "liberal." When asked to describe their own politics, 42 percent of the press corps said "liberal," 39 percent said "middle-of-the-road," and 19 percent said "conservative."[7] However, it should be noted that their views may not appear overtly in news presentations.

Sensational bias in television news

The major bias of the news is toward "hype"—dramatic and sensational presentation of the news designed to capture and hold audience atten-

TABLE 6-1 Social and political characteristics of newsmakers

	Percentage of news executives
Social class	
Father professional or managerial	66
Sex	
Male	91
Education	
College graduate	75
Party	
Independent	45
Democratic	44
Republican	9
Other	3
Ideology	
Left-leaning	63
Middle-of-the-road	27
Right-leaning	10

Source: Derived from data in John Johnstone, Edward Slawski, and William Bowman. *The Newspeople* (Urbana: University of Illinois Press, 1976), pp. 225–226.

tion. Because advertisers pay in proportion to the numbers of viewers, the business of television broadcasting is one of gathering mass audiences to attract advertisers. To attract viewers, the networks bias the news toward violence, confrontation, conflict, scandal, sex, corruption, scares of various sorts, and the personal problems of "celebrities."

Television broadcasters use the term "hard fluff" to describe dramatic or sensational news presentations. Hard fluff is entertainment masquerading as news. The leading illustration of hard fluff is the popular CBS program "60 Minutes." When asked to explain how he selects "news" for this show, the executive producer Don Hewitt responded:

> I don't make decisions intellectually, I make them viscerally. When I get bored, I figure other people get bored. I have the ability to put myself in the place of the viewer because I have the same short attention span he has.[8]

In other words, the criteria for selecting "news" are not intellectual but emotional; the political or social significance of a news story is secondary to its ability to attract audiences; above all, stories must not be boring and must satisfy people who have short attention spans.

The networks select news for its emotional impact. Stories that inspire mass fears (the Tylenol deaths, nuclear power plant accidents, toxic shock syndrome, and so on) are especially favored. Violence, sex, and government corruption are favorite topics because they attract popular interest. When faced with more complex problems—inflation, government deficits, foreign policy—the newsmakers feel they must simplify them, dramatize them, or ignore them altogether.

The television networks' concentration on scandal and corruption in government has not always produced the desired liberal, reformist attitudes in the masses. Contrary to the expectations of the network executives, the emphasis given government scandals—Watergate, CIA investigations, FBI abuses, congressional sex scandals, and others—produces political distrust and cynicism among the masses.

Much of the political apathy among the mass public today stems from "television malaise," a combination of social distrust, political cynicism, feelings of powerlessness, and dissociation from established parties, caused by television's emphasis on the negative aspects of American life.[9] Network executives do not intend to produce television malaise among the masses; but because scandal, sex, violence, and corruption attract large audiences, stories about them receive prominence in the telecast, usually with some vivid visual aids. Negative television journalism in America "is concerned with what is *wrong* with our government structure, our leaders, our prisons, schools, roads, automobiles, race relations, traffic systems, pollution laws, every facet of our society. In Europe there is much less emphasis on exposing what is wrong, much more satisfaction with the status quo."[10] The effect of these unpleasantries on the American public is to produce negative attitudes toward politics and government.

Selective perception: Obstacle to mass indoctrination

Mass attitudes—particularly deeply held hatreds or fears—do not change easily. The liberal-establishment bias of the mass media runs into strong resistance in the masses' *selective perception:* viewers mentally screen out information or images with which they disagree, and they see only what they want to see.

Thus masses do not always respond to the liberal messages of the newsmakers. Consider, for example, the rise of the "law and order" movement of the late 1960s and the election of Richard M. Nixon as president. For several years in the mid-1960s, the networks had provided extensive coverage of urban ghetto riots, campus disruption, and civil disorder in America. The media chiefs believed that this coverage would help bring the civil rights movement to northern urban areas and end U.S. involvement in the Vietnam war. (Until late 1967 media coverage supported the war, but then elite groups deserted the Johnson administration effort.) Televising ghetto riots and campus disorders generally gave them legitimacy; voice-overs cited the social evils of the ghetto and the concern for peace among America's youth. But the strategy backfired. White working-class Americans saw the image of black rioting and campus violence and ignored the words of explanation. The broadcasts reinforced mass hostilities against militant blacks and radical students. This television environment gave rise to a new "law and order" movement, with the principal benefactors in 1968 being George C. Wallace and Richard M. Nixon.[11]

Another example of "selective perception" is the mass response to the popular CBS shows "All in the Family" and, later, "Archie Bunker's

Place." The producer, Norman Lear, and the leadership of CBS believed that the crude, bumbling, working-class, superpatriotic, conservative, racist Archie Bunker would be an effective weapon against prejudice. Bigotry would appear ridiculous. Archie would end each episode a victim of his own bigotry, and the masses would absorb liberal values. But evidence soon developed that many viewers agreed with Archie's bigotry, believing that he was "telling it like it is."[12] The mass audience missed the intended lessons of the show altogether. In fact highly prejudiced people enjoyed and watched the show *more* than less-prejudiced people did.[13] When these trends in public opinion became apparent, the *New York Times* sharply attacked the show.[14] But by that time, "All in the Family" had become one of the top-rated shows on television. CBS executives optimistically predicted that in the long run the humor of the program would help destroy bigotry.[15] Nevertheless, the media elite had misjudged its mass audiences, as it occasionally does. Selective perception had intervened to muddle up elite communication with the masses.

The media and political campaigning

Television has brought about major changes in American political life. It has contributed to the decline of political parties; it has replaced party leaders as "kingmakers"; it has encouraged voting on the basis of candidate "image"; it has fostered the development of media campaigns with professional advertising techniques; and it has significantly increased the costs of running for public office.

The decline of parties

The media have replaced the party organization as the principal link between the candidates and the voters. Candidates can take their campaigns directly to the voters. They can capture party nominations in primary elections dominated by television advertising. Party organizations have little to say about who wins the party's nomination, and next to nothing to say about who wins in the general election. Aspiring candidates no longer begin their quest for public office by calling on party leaders, but instead by hiring professional media advertising firms. Both primary and general elections are now fought largely in the media.

Media as kingmakers

Heavy media coverage creates candidates. The media provides "name recognition," the first requirement for a successful candidate. Indeed, heavy media attention can transform previously unknown figures into "instant" candidates; candidates no longer need to spend long years in political apprenticeship in minor offices to run for Congress or a governorship. The media can also condemn an aspiring candidate to obscurity and defeat simply by failing to report his or her activities. Newsmakers select the "serious" candidates for coverage at the beginning of a race. In primary elections, the media even select "the real winner": if the favorite does not win by as large a margin as the media predicted, the media may declare the runner-up "the real winner" even when his or her vote total is less than the favorite. People who cannot perform well in front of a camera are no longer viable candidates for major public office.

Image elections

In covering elections, television largely ignores policy questions and focuses on candidate image—the personal traits of the candidates. Candidates are not presented on television in terms of their voting records or policy positions, but instead on their ability to project a personal image of charm, warmth, "compassion," youth and vigor, honesty and integrity, and so forth. Elections are presented on television as struggles between competing personalities.

The media cover elections as a political "game," made up of speeches, rallies, press conferences, travels, and perhaps debates. The media report on who is winning or losing, what their strategies are, how much money they are spending, how they look in their public appearances, the response of their audiences, and so on. It is not surprising that policy issues do not play a very large role in voters' decisions, because the media do not pay much attention to policy issues.

The media campaign

Professional media campaigns, usually directed by commercial advertising firms, have replaced traditional party-organized or amateur grass-roots campaigns. Today, professional media people may plan an entire campaign; develop computerized mailing lists for fund raising; select a (simple) campaign theme and desirable candidate image; monitor the progress of the campaign with continuous voter polls; produce television tapes for commercials, as well as signs, bumper stickers, and radio spots; select the candidate's clothing and hair style; write speeches; schedule appearances that will attract news coverage; and even plan the victory party.

Professional campaign management begins with assessing the candidate's public strengths and weaknesses, evaluating those of the opponent, and determining the concerns uppermost in voters' minds. Early polls can test for name recognition, favorable or unfavorable images, and voter concerns; these polls then feed into the campaign strategy— helping to select a theme, choose an image for the candidate, and identify the opponent's weaknesses. Polls during the campaign chart the candidate's progress, assess the theme's effectiveness, and even identify

Drawing by Lorenz; ©1982 The New Yorker Magazine, Inc.

"Senator, you have been described as lazy, humorless, uninformed, unscrupulous, lacking in compassion, and totally unfit for public office. How would you respond to that?"

undecided groups as targets for last-minute campaign efforts. "Negative" campaigns can stress the opponent's weaknesses. Most professional campaigning takes the form of paid television commercials, produced by experienced advertising agencies and shown in specific voter "markets." But a good media campaign manager also knows how to get the candidate "free" time on the evening news. Candidates must attract the media and convey a favorable image: they may visit an old people's home, a coal mine, a black ghetto, or a pig farm to appeal to specific groups of voters. A candidate may work a day digging ditches (particularly if perceived as a playboy millionaire), or walk from city to city (particularly if the opponent flies in a chartered airplane), or participate in a hog-calling contest (particularly if viewed as too intellectual). Such activities are more likely to win a spot on the evening news than is a thoughtful speech on nuclear disarmament.

The cost of campaigning

Media campaigns cost much more than traditional party rallies, speeches to the Chamber of Commerce and League of Women Voters, and handshaking at supermarkets. Today a statewide campaign for governor or U.S. senator in an average-size state costs at least $2 million and could cost as much as $10 million. The high costs primarily reflect the expense of producing and showing quality political advertisements on prime-time television. A quality thirty-second spot commercial may cost $50,000 to produce, plus $1,000 to $5,000 for a single showing on a big-city television station. (In presidential campaigns, a national network thirty-second spot on prime-time television may cost up to $100,000.) A professional campaign may produce three to five commercials and may hold back money for a last-minute television "blitz"—saturation advertising during the last forty-eight hours of the campaign. Clearly, one effect of media campaigning is to greatly increase the costs of running for office.

Elites and public opinion

Opinions flow downward from elites to masses. Public opinion rarely affects elite behavior, but elite behavior shapes public opinion. Elites are relatively unconstrained by public opinion for several reasons. First, few people among the masses have opinions on most policy questions confronting the nation's decision makers. Second, public opinion is very unstable; it can change in a matter of weeks in response to "news" events precipitated by elites. Third, elites do not have a clear perception of mass opinion. Most communications decision makers receive are from other elites—newsmakers, interest-group leaders, influential community leaders—not from ordinary citizens.

Absence of public opinion

Masses do not have opinions on most policy issues. Public opinion polls frequently create opinions by asking questions that respondents never thought about until they were asked.[16] Few respondents are willing to say they have no opinion; they believe they should provide some sort of answer, even if their opinion is weakly held or was nonexistent before the question was asked. Thus they produce "doorstep" opinions. It is unlikely that many Americans have seriously thought about, or gathered much information on, such specific issues as windfall-profits taxes, zero-based budgeting, the B-1 bomber, investment tax credits, municipal bond interest exemption, and similar specific questions.

Instability of public opinion

Public opinion is very unstable and often very weakly held. Asked the same question at a later date, many respondents forget their earlier answers and give the pollster the opposite reply. One study estimates that less than 20 percent of the public holds meaningful, consistent opinions on most issues, even though two-thirds or more will respond to questions asked in a survey.[17]

Opinions also vary according to the wording of questions. One can word almost any public policy question to elicit mass approval or disapproval. Thus differently worded questions on the same issue can produce contradictory results. For example, in a California poll about academic freedom, thirty-nine of fifty-two respondents agreed with the statement: "Professors in state-supported institutions should have freedom to speak and teach the truth as they see it." However, a majority of respondents (by the same ratio) also agreed with the statement: "Professors who advocate controversial ideas or speak out against official policy have no place in a state-supported college or university."[18]

Opinion polls that ask the same question at different times are more reliable indicators of public opinion than are one-time polls, in which respondents may be responding to the wording of the question. If pollsters use the same wording over time, they can more accurately observe changes in opinion.

Bias in communication

Elites can easily misinterpret public opinion because most of the communications they receive have an upper-class bias. Members of the masses seldom call or write their senators or representatives, much less converse with them at dinners, cocktail parties, or other social occasions. Most of the communications decision makers receive are *intraelite* communications—communications from newspeople, organized group leaders, influential constituents, wealthy political contributors, and personal friends—people who for the most part share the same views. Not surprisingly, therefore, legislators say that most of their mail agrees with their position; their world of public opinion is self-reinforcing. Moreover, people who initiate communication with decision makers, by writing or calling or visiting their representatives, are decidedly more educated and affluent than the average citizen.

Elite response to mass opinion

Do elites respond to public opinion, or do they shape public opinion to conform to their own attitudes? When government policy and public opinion are in agreement, is it because the policy adapted to prevailing opinion or because decision makers molded opinion to accept predetermined policy? These questions are difficult to answer, yet so often are policies enacted in the face of widespread public opposition, which eventually melts away into acquiescence, that public opinion seems to follow elite decisions rather than the other way around. Consider national policy on civil rights, one of the few areas in which Americans demonstrably have opinions. Here the decisions of courts, Congress, and executive bureaucracies have consistently run contrary to public opinion.

When the Supreme Court decided in *Brown* v. *Board of Education of Topeka* (1954) that segregation of the races in public schools violated the equal protection clause of the Fourteenth Amendment of the Constitution, a majority of Americans opposed sending their children to integrated schools. Not until several years after this historic decision did a majority of Americans come to favor school integration. In 1967 a public referendum in California resulted in an overwhelming defeat of a "fair housing" proposal, which would have forbidden discrimination in the sale or rental of housing. One year later, Congress passed the Civil Rights Act of 1968, which, among other things, outlawed discrimination in the sale or rental of housing. Several states have held referenda on busing—the assignment and transportation of children to public schools to achieve racial balance in the classroom. Voters have rejected busing in every such referendum, sometimes by margins of 75 to 80 percent; yet the Supreme Court has held that busing may be necessary in schools with a history of racial segregation. The Court's policy answers to the requirements of the Constitution, not to public opinion. In short, elite support for civil rights at the national level is not a response to mass opinion.

When political scientist V. O. Key, Jr., wrestled with the same problem—what impact, if any, does mass opinion have on public policy?—he concluded that the "missing piece of the puzzle" was "that thin stratum of persons referred to variously as the political elite, the political activists, the leadership echelons, or the influentials."[19] In other words, elite opinion, not mass opinion, shapes public policy. Elite preferences are more likely to agree with public policy than are mass preferences. Of course, this fact does not prove that elite preferences determine policies. Policy makers may be acting rationally in response to events and conditions, and well-educated, informed elites understand and approve of government actions more than masses do.

Summary

Communications in the American political system flow downward from elites to masses. Elites are generally isolated from public opinion—not only because the masses do not have opinions on most issues but also because of the many barriers to accurate assessment of public opinion. Our analysis fits the elitist notion that elites are subject to relatively little direct influence from masses. Elites influence mass opinion more than masses influence elite opinion.

1. Television is the principal means by which elites communicate to masses. Control of the flow of information to the masses is highly concentrated. Three television networks and a handful of prestigious news organizations decide what will be the "news."

2. The political functions of the mass media include newsmaking—deciding what to report; interpretation—providing the masses with

explanations of events; socialization—teaching about preferred norms, values, and life-styles; persuasion—making direct efforts to affect behavior; and agenda setting.

3. The most important power of the mass media is agenda setting— deciding what will be decided. The media decide what conditions in society to label "crises" or "problems" or "issues" and thereby place these topics on the agenda of national decision makers.

4. Bias in the news arises from the newsmakers' own liberal-establishment views, plus the need to dramatize and sensationalize the news. However, the newsmakers' concentration on scandal and corruption in government often produces "television malaise"—social distrust, political cynicism, and feelings of powerlessness—instead of reform.

5. "Selective perception" among the masses—the tendency to screen out information with which one disagrees—frequently causes them to resist elite indoctrination through the mass media. In such situations, the masses see violence, disorder, or war on television but ignore the elite messages attached to what they see.

6. Television has brought about major changes in politics. It has contributed to the decline of political parties; it has replaced parties as kingmakers; it has encouraged image voting; it has fostered the use of professional advertising techniques for media campaigns; and it has added to the cost of running for public office.

7. Masses seldom have opinions on specific issues. Pollsters may create "doorstep" opinions by asking questions that respondents had not thought of before the survey. Moreover, public opinion is unstable; it changes over time and may respond to the wording of the question. Elites receive most communications from other elites. This intraelite communication usually reinforces elite views.

8. No evidence suggests that public policy reflects mass opinion. Civil rights laws came about despite majority opposition. Public policy changes with shifts in elite, not mass, opinion.

NOTES

1. *Public Opinion* (August/September, 1979).
2. Edward J. Epstein, *News from Nowhere* (New York: Random House, 1973), pp. 27–28.
3. E. E. Schattschneider, *The Semisovereign People* (New York: Holt, Rinehart and Winston, 1961), p. 61.
4. J. M. McCleod, L. B. Becker, and J. F. Byrne, "Another Look at the Agenda-Setting Function of the Press," *Communications Research* 1 (April 1974):131–66; and "The Political Consequences of Agenda-Setting," *Mass Communications Review* (Spring 1976):8–15; D. L. Shaw and M. E. McCombs, eds., *The Emergence of American Political Issues* (New York: West, 1977).
5. Doris Graber, *Mass Media and American Politics* (Washington, D.C.: Congressional Quarterly, 1980), p. 41.

6. John Johnstone, Edward Slawski, and William Bowman, *The Newspeople* (Urbana: University of Illinois Press, 1976).

7. Stephen Hess, *The Washington Reporters* (Washington, D.C.: Brookings Institution, 1981).

8. Stephen Vito, "Inside 60 Minutes," *American Film* (December/January, 1972):55–57.

9. See Michael J. Robinson, "Public Affairs Television and the Growth of Political Malaise," *American Political Science Review* 70 (June 1976):409–432.

10. Merrill Panitt, "America out of Focus," *TV Guide* (January 15, 1972):6.

11. Byron Shafer and Richard Larson, "Did TV Create the Social Issue?" *Columbia Journalism Review* 11 (September–October 1972):10. See also Richard M. Scammon and Ben J. Wattenberg, *The Real Majority* (New York: Coward-McCann, 1970), p. 162.

12. See Neil Vidmar and Milton Rokeach, "Archie Bunker's Bigotry: A Study in Selective Perception," *Journal of Communications* 24 (Winter 1974):36–47.

13. Ibid.

14. L. Z. Hobson, "As I Listened to Archie Say 'Hebe,' " *New York Times*, September 12, 1972.

15. Norman Lear, "As I Read How Laura Saw Archie," *New York Times*, October 10, 1972.

16. Robert S. Erikson and Norman R. Luttberg, *American Public Opinion: Its Origins, Content and Import* (New York: Wiley, 1973).

17. Philip Converse, "Attitudes and Non-Attitudes," in Edward R. Tufte, ed., *Quantitative Analysis of Social Problems* (Reading, Mass.: Addison-Wesley, 1970), pp. 168–189.

18. Erikson and Luttberg, op cit., p. 38.

19. V. O. Key, Jr., *Public Opinion and American Democracy* (New York: Knopf, 1967), p. 537.

SELECTED READINGS

Barnouw, Erik. *The Image Empire.* New York: Oxford University Press, 1970. This book is a history of broadcasting since 1953, when television swept into America's living rooms. In this historical review, Barnouw shows how news is distorted and even manufactured to hold peak audiences.

Efron, Edith. *The News Twisters.* Los Angeles: Nash Publishing, 1971. Efron's book is a study of television coverage of the 1968 presidential elections and an exposé of liberal bias in the network news that explores the myth of network fairness.

Epstein, Edward J. *News from Nowhere.* New York: Random House, 1973. Epstein discusses the mirror myth of television and discloses in detail how network television executives create news.

Halberstam, David. *The Powers That Be.* New York: Knopf, 1979. This history of the growth of power of the mass media focuses on CBS, the *New York Times*, *Time* magazine, and the *Washington Post*.

Hofstetter, C. Richard. *Bias in the News: Television Network News Coverage of the 1972 Election Campaign.* Columbus: Ohio State University Press, 1976. This discussion of situational bias and ideological bias in television finds neutrality in elections.

Robinson, Michael J. "Public Affairs Television and the Growth of Political Malaise." *American Political Science Review* 70 (1976):409–432. Robinson examines the impact of negative television journalism on mass attitudes, including increases in feelings of distrust, cynicism, and powerlessness.

Robinson, Michael J. "Television and American Politics: 1956–1976." *Public Interest* 52 (Summer 1978):3–39. This thoughtful essay about videopolitics explores the impact of both news and entertainment programming on mass attitudes.

7 Elections: Imperfect Instruments of Accountability

Virtually all modern political systems—authoritarian and democratic, capitalist and communist—hold elections. All political regimes seek to tie the masses to the system by holding symbolic exercises in political participation to give the ruling regime an aura of legitimacy.

Whether elections are only ritualistic as in the Soviet Union, or involve some real choice, their common effort is to bolster the legitimacy of the holders of power.

—*Gerald M. Pomper,* Elections in America, *1970*

Traditional "pluralist" textbooks in American government tell us that elections are a means by which masses can hold elites responsible for their policy decisions. The traditional argument is that elections enable masses to direct future public policy by voting for one candidate or another on election day.

Elections: The myth of the policy mandate

We argue that elections do *not* serve as policy mandates; instead they function as symbolic reassurance to the masses. Enabling the masses to participate in a political activity contributes to the legitimacy of government. Elections allow the masses to help choose personnel for public office, but *not* future public policy.

For elections to serve as policy mandates and for voters to exercise influence over public policy through elections, four conditions would be necessary: (1) competing candidates would offer clear policy alternatives; (2) voters would be concerned with policy questions; (3) election results would clarify majority preferences on these questions; (4) elected officials would be bound by the positions they assume during their campaigns.

In this chapter and the next, we contend that American politics fulfill none of these conditions and that voters consequently cannot directly control public policy for several reasons:

1. The parties do not offer clear policy alternatives. Because both parties agree on the major direction of public policy (see chapter 8), the voters cannot influence it by choosing between the parties.

2. Policy considerations are not the primary motivators of voter decisions. For a mandate to be valid, the electorate must make informed, policy-oriented choices; but traditional party ties and candidate person-

alities influence voters more than policy questions do. Thus party loyalty dilutes the voters' influence over policy.

3. Even if the voters were primarily concerned with policy questions, majority preferences on these questions would not be clear from election results. Victory for a candidate's party need not mean that the voters support its programs. First, voters' policy preferences are inconsistent. Second, voters often misinterpret or pay little attention to a candidate's policy preference. Third, among the voters for a given candidate are opponents (and some who are indifferent to positions) as well as advocates of the candidate's position. Fourth, a popular majority may be composed of many policy minorities. How is a candidate to know which (if any) policy positions brought electoral victory?

4. For voters to exercise control over public officials, elected officials would have to be bound by their campaign pledges. Elected officials frequently ignore their own campaign pledges, however.

Ignorance of the electorate

If elections are to be a means of popular control over public policy, voters must be reasonably well informed about policy issues and must hold opinions on them. Yet large numbers of the electorate are politically uninformed and inarticulate. Some years ago, public opinion analysts reported what is now a typical finding about the low level of political information among adult Americans. Only about one-half the public knew the elementary fact that each state has two U.S. senators; fewer still knew the length of the terms of members of Congress or the number of Supreme Court justices.[1]

Aside from their ability to identify the president, most people can identify only one visible public figure, usually the governor of their state (see table 7-1).

Elites view such political ignorance with astonishment because, to them, the cost of information is cheap. For active and influential elites, the stakes of competition in politics are high; their careers, self-esteem, and prestige are directly and often daily affected by political decisions.

Among the masses, however, political ignorance may be a rational stance—that is, the cost of informing oneself about politics may outweigh the benefits. Most people do not have friends in public office and do not benefit directly from the victory of one candidate or another. Moreover, because one vote in millions is only infinitesimally influential, it must seem quite reasonable to remain ignorant about politics. Thus the average voter systematically tunes out political information.

Those most informed about political issues are usually among the better educated.[2] (See table 7-1.) (Perhaps it is a truism to observe this relationship because the purpose of education is, of course, to increase knowledge.) The more information one already has, the easier it is to

TABLE 7-1. People who correctly identified name and party of their elected leaders (percent)

	Governor		1st Senator		2d Senator		Representative	
	Name	Party	Name	Party	Name	Party	Name	Party
Total	89	77	59	53	39	36	46	41
Characteristics								
Age								
18–29 years	84	68	50	42	30	28	30	25
30–40 years	90	79	62	56	42	40	53	45
50 years and								
over	91	81	63	58	42	40	53	48
Sex								
Men	90	81	64	58	44	41	51	44
Women	87	73	54	48	33	32	42	37
Education								
Eighth grade	76	66	45	42	28	26	35	31
High school	90	76	53	47	32	30	44	37
College	93	83	74	66	52	50	55	49
Income								
Under $5,000	80	68	46	42	29	28	38	34
$5,000–9,999	87	74	55	48	34	32	40	34
$10,000–								
14,999	92	79	61	54	39	36	49	40
$15,000 and								
over	95	87	74	69	53	50	60	55
Party								
Republican	89	80	61	57	39	36	49	46
Democrat	89	79	58	52	39	37	49	42
Independent	90	75	64	57	42	40	45	38

Source: U.S. Senate, Committee on Governmental Operations, *Confidence and Concern: Citizens View American Government* (Washington, D.C.: Government Printing Office, 1973), p. 244.

acquire new information and to sort it into meaningful categories. Informed voters will pay close attention to a surprising statement about the secretary of defense, for example; they relate this information to what they already know about recent defense policy and the relationship between the secretary and the president. Uninformed voters hearing the same statement may not even know who the secretary of defense is and will find the report of little consequence or interest, for they have no way of fitting the information into a larger scheme of understanding. Furthermore, the decisions at issue in the typical presidential election are of little personal significance to the average voter.

As Converse puts it, "For many people, politics does not compete in interest with sports, local gossip, and television dramas." Many people have no opinion about political issues debated vigorously in the mass media. In general, no more than a third of the public recognizes legislative proposals that have been the center of public debate for months, and sometimes years. Even among that third, few would be able to describe the proposal accurately or in detail, and fewer still would successfully describe the intricacies and alternatives available to policy makers.

Contradictions and inconsistencies in voter opinion

Not only are the masses generally ill informed, they also show an inability to sort out and relate the information that they do possess. Frequently people will approve of two candidates with fundamentally different positions. They do so partly because they are poorly informed about the candidates' positions, but also partly, it seems, because broad segments of the public hold opinions that are contradictory.

Except for issues that are unusually visible to large numbers of people (such as civil rights), mass attitudes are very inconsistent. For example, those who support expanding public services do not necessarily support taxes to pay for them; in fact, many who support a tax cut also favor increased federal welfare spending.

People who hold inconsistent positions are most likely to come from the lower social strata. And although they demand expanded federal services and a reduced federal budget, they strongly oppose higher taxes to pay for the services they want. Obviously self-interest makes simultaneous support for tax reduction and expansion of federal welfare quite compatible. However, for the political system as a whole, the combination is irrational. Even if the elite tried, it could not satisfy both demands.

A possible reason for these inconsistencies is the influence of public opinion polls. Because opinion polls ask questions that are meaningless to many people, the answers are often meaningless as well. Many people have never thought about the question before it is asked and will never think about it again. As one moves down the socioeconomic ladder from elites to masses, consistency in political beliefs rapidly fades. At the same time, beliefs shift focus from abstract principles to simple, concrete goals.[3]

To assess the electorate's ability to conceptualize (to think abstractly), the University of Michigan Survey Research Center (SRC) examined the responses of a sample to questions about the good and bad points of the two major parties.[4] Researchers derived the following categories as a result. *Ideologues* are respondents who are either "liberal" or "conservative" and are likely to rely on abstract principles in evaluating candidates and issues. *Near ideologues* are those who mentioned an abstract principle but clearly did not rely on it as much as the ideologues did. Near ideologues used ideology in a way that raised doubts about their understanding of terms. At the next level, the *group benefits* class contained those who did not exhibit any overriding ideology in their thinking but were able to evaluate parties and candidates by expected favorable or unfavorable treatment for social groups. Subjects favored candidates they considered sympathetic to a group with which they identified. A fourth group is respondents who base their judgment on their perception of the *"goodness" or "badness" of the times*. They blame or praise parties and candidates because of their association with conditions of war or peace, prosperity, or depression. The last level includes respondents whose evaluations of the political scene hold *no relationship whatever to policy*, even in the broadest and most symbolic sense. Some of these profess loyalty to one of the two parties but have no understanding of the party's positions.

When social scientists first examined the entire electorate in the 1950s, they found that ideological commitments were significant in the political decisions of only a tiny fraction. (See table 7-2.) Three percent of the total electorate were ideologues, 10 percent were near ideologues, and the remainder displayed no ideological content in their evaluations.

Clearly, then, the majority of the public did not conceptualize politics in the manner of the highly educated. Except for a small, educated portion of the electorate, the ideological debate between the elites has very little meaning. Since the masses lack the interest and level of conceptualization of the educated, they logically do not possess an ideology.

Recent replications of the SRC study show only modest increases in ideological thinking among the masses (table 7-2). By 1972, 7 percent of the population classified as ideologues; 20 percent classified as near ideologues.

At best, one can classify between one-third and 40 percent of today's electorate as having an ideology or near ideology. Figure 7-1 shows that ideology is associated most with education; the increase in the ideological sophistication of those with grade school education was modest and was much greater among the college educated. By the 1970s the electorate's level of ideology stabilized.

TABLE 7-2.   Levels of political conceptualization in the United States: 1956, 1968, 1972

		1956 Percent[a]	*1968 Percent*[b]	*1972 Percent*[c]
A.	Ideology			
	I. Ideology	3	5.9	7
	II. Near ideology	10	17.1	20
B.	Group benefits	15	9.0	—
	I. Perception of conflict single-group interest	18	18.6	—
	II. Shallow group benefit responses	11	5.2	—
C.	Nature of the times	25	24.6	—
D.	No issue content			
	I. Party orientation	4	7.8	—
	II. Candidate orientation	9	6.8	—
	III. No content	5	4.9	—
	Total	100	100.0	—

[a] Survey Research Center coding.

[b] Klingemann-Wright coding.

[c] Arthur Miller coding.

Source: Adapted from Philip Converse, "Public Opinion and Voting Behavior," in Fred I. Greenstein and Nelson W. Polsby, eds., *Handbook of Political Science* (Reading, Mass.: Addison-Wesley, 1975), vol. 4, p. 102; and from Arthur Miller and Warren A. Miller, "Ideology in the 1972 Election: Myth or Reality—A Rejoinder," *American Political Science Review* 70 (September 1976): 844.

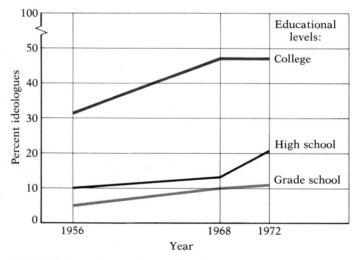

FIGURE 7-1.   Proportions of ideologues at three educational levels, 1956–1972

Note: Combines ideologues and near ideologues.

Source: Data provided through the courtesy of Arthur Miller, University of Michigan, Survey Research Center.

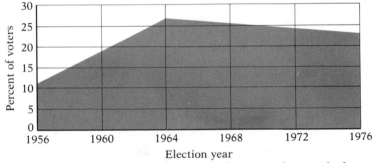

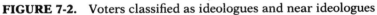

FIGURE 7-2. Voters classified as ideologues and near ideologues

Source: Paul R. Hagner and John C. Pierce. *Conceptualization and Consistency in Political Beliefs.* Paper presented at the annual meeting of the Midwest Political Science Association, Cincinnati, 1981.

Figure 7-2 illustrates this tapering of ideological sophistication from 1956 to 1976. The high point for ideological voting was in 1964 (the Goldwater-Johnson campaign). Combining ideologues and near ideologues still includes no more than one-fourth the electorate. Since 1964, ideological voting has steadily and consistently declined. Notice that in 1972, when Richard Nixon thrashed the decidedly more liberal George McGovern, ideological voting did *not* increase. And in 1976, with Jimmy Carter deliberately obfuscating the issues, issue voting did not *decrease.* Apparently a small core of the electorate will vote ideologically no matter what goes on in the campaign. But what was the pattern in 1980, when conservative Ronald Reagan faced Jimmy Carter, whom the electorate regarded as increasingly liberal despite Carter's attempts to confuse voters? Did this election—something of a repeat of the clear ideological differences in 1964—increase ideological voting?

Unfortunately, no analysis of the 1980 election exactly duplicates the type of analysis begun in 1956. Approximations do exist, however.[5] The original criteria for ideological voting were that the voter had an opinion, knew the government's policy and record on the issue, and believed that the candidates' policies differed. The 1980 approach relied upon answers to "closed" questions (that is, the respondent simply agreed or disagreed with a question and did not need to offer an explanation as in earlier studies. This less strenuous requirement resulted in a somewhat more ideological electorate: 43 percent could place themselves on a variety of "scales" (government spending, tax cuts, relations with Russia, and so on), could place Reagan and Carter on these same scales, and could correctly identify the difference between the candidates. The respondent need not have much sophistication to decide which candidate is more liberal or conservative on such a scale.

For example, for one scale the interviewer says, "Some people feel the government in Washington should see to it that every person has a job and a good standard of living. Suppose these people are at one end of the scale at point number 1. Others believe the government should just let each person get ahead on his own. Suppose these people are at the other end, at point 7. And, of course, some people have opinions somewhere in between at points 2, 3, 4, 5, or 6. Where would you place yourself on this scale, or haven't you thought much about this?" If the respondent provides a scale position, the interviewer asks, "Where would you place (Jimmy Carter, Ronald Reagan)?" The interviewer then gives the respondent a card with a 7-point scale on which to mark Reagan's and Carter's positions along with the respondent's own position.

Figure 7-3 illustrates the card and the average scale scores that resulted on the issue just illustrated. Respondents placed Carter slightly to the left of center and Reagan slightly to the right; they rated their own positions between the two, leaning toward Reagan. The fact that about two in five voters could place the candidates correctly on the scale is hardly strong support for ideological voting, even when they could express an ideological position by picking a point on the scale. On this issue 48 percent of the voters sampled placed themselves, Reagan, and Carter on the scale, and correctly identified Carter as being more liberal. Ideological voters are very unlikely ever to become a majority of the electorate.

Members of the elite frequently make the mistake of confusing the educated minority with the mass of uninformed voters. As Warren Miller concludes, "Levels of conceptualization have not altered much in recent years, but it remains difficult to convey to politically interested and active citizens the lack of complexity or sophistication in the ways most Americans talk and apparently think about politics."[6]

Instability of mass attitudes

The instability of mass opinions also nullifies the masses' influence on public policy. An extended study of public opinion on various issues showed that only about thirteen of twenty people took the same side that they had taken four years earlier on the same issues (ten of twenty would have done so by chance alone). An examination of opinion consistency over time indicates that with the exception of party identifi-

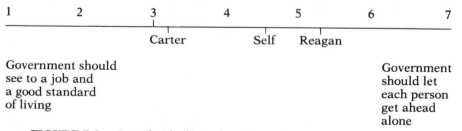

FIGURE 7-3.   Sample ideological voting scale

cation (a .70 correlation over time), remarkable instability exists.[7] This instability suggests once again that issues and ideology are simply not relevant to the mass electorate. The masses hold the most consistent attitudes toward clearly identifiable groups, such as blacks. Attitudes about school desegregation are substantially more stable (.50) than are attitudes toward foreign policy (.35). Evidently the mass electorate thinks about race relations but not about foreign policy, unless someone happens to ask the question. Hence the answers to questions about foreign policy vary randomly through time. Looking at the instability of mass attitudes, Converse concludes that "large portions of the electorate do not have meaningful beliefs, even on those issues that have formed the basis for intense political controversy among elites for substantial periods of time."[8]

Consistency of attitudes—the holding of consistent "liberal" or "conservative" attitudes on a variety of questions—depends upon the willingness of elites to provide appropriate "cues."

If presidential candidates use ideological terms like "liberal" or "conservative" in an election campaign, larger numbers of people become conscious of their meaning (as in the 1964 Goldwater campaign). But when presidential candidates avoid clearly defined labels (as they usually do), then the masses' attitudes slip into inconsistency again.[9]

We have considered three measures of sophistication: information level, ideological conceptualization, and attitude consistency. Information and ideological sophistication are likely to increase slowly as education increases. Attitude consistency will increase if elites conduct ideological elections for which there is no incentive.

Issues and voting behavior

The ideal model of democracy requires that the two major parties offer the voters policy alternatives and compete for votes on the basis of contrasting programs. This competition helps keep the elite responsible. Therefore, the masses, although not necessarily completely informed about the programs advocated by the elites, should at least be aware of their broad outlines.

For this model to work, the voters must perceive alternative policies offered by competing candidates, and they must determine which policies match their own ideological positions most closely. However, evidence suggests that voters do not do this. For example, in *The American Voter* studies, Campbell, Converse, Miller, and Stokes concluded that less than one-third had an opinion, were aware of what the government was doing, and perceived a difference between the parties. This one-third is the *maximum* pool of issue-oriented people. Although the nature of the election to some extent influences the size of the issue-oriented portion of the electorate, it is probable that two-thirds of the electorate make a choice unrelated to any issues raised by the competing candidates or parties.

The behavior of elites may be as responsible for these blurred perceptions as the masses' ignorance, however. If the parties do not, in fact, provide clear alternatives, the voters' failure to perceive alternatives is understandable. Party activists are separated by a wide ideological gulf, but party followers are not. For example, the leaders of the Democratic party are "liberal," and the leaders of the Republican party are "conservative" (when measuring conservatism in economic policy). However, the parties' success in translating these differences into clear statements in election campaigns is questionable. Moreover, most Democratic and Republican voters hold fairly similar opinions on most issues.

Since few voters clearly distinguish between the parties on the issues, American national elections are not high in ideological or issue content. Instead, candidates base their appeals on traditional party loyalties, the "nature of the times," and their own personal characteristics or the personal defects of their opponents.

Case study: 1972—An ideological election?

The George McGovern candidacy in 1972 helped develop a discernible ideological difference between the candidates of the two major parties. McGovern appealed to an ideologically committed core of liberals, leaving the rest of the electorate to Richard Nixon. A landslide for Nixon was the result. In carrying every state except Massachusetts (and Washington, D.C., with its black majority), Nixon gained 61 percent of the vote, roughly equal to the margin by which Lyndon Johnson in 1964 defeated another ideological candidate, Barry Goldwater. McGovern's 38 percent was the lowest proportion received by a major party candidate in recent presidential elections. Not only did Nixon receive 94 percent of the vote among Republicans and 66 percent among independents, he also captured 42 percent of the vote among Democrats.

The American voters obviously found some differences between McGovern and Nixon, regarding McGovern as too far out of the ideological mainstream. It was not so much the *what* of McGovern, but rather the *how* and *when*. On the eve of the election, a Harris poll reported that, by a margin of two to one, the electorate felt McGovern wanted to "change things too much." Actually McGovern and Nixon supporters were in substantial agreement on the issues. Whatever differences occurred did so *within a basic consensus*. Speaking of the electorate, Lipset and Raab conclude:

> What they resist is change that takes place in a nontraditional manner. . . . The basic threat perceived by the electorate in the McGovern candidacy was not so much to existing social arrangements as to the social order itself. And especially to due process. *That* is the "extremism" which the voters finally rejected, not any liberal social or economic policy per se.[10]

Case study *(continued)*

McGovern supporters were appreciably more to the "left" (or liberal) than were Nixon's supporters. However, on those issues that struck at the heart of the counterculture (amnesty for draft resisters, marijuana, busing), a majority of both Nixon and McGovern supporters took a "right" perspective. The majority of McGovern supporters did not want to legalize marijuana, grant amnesty to draft resisters, or bus children out of neighborhoods. Nevertheless, *half* of McGovern's supporters had an ideology stressing social change; *half* of Nixon's supporters opposed social change. Such a split is hardly indicative of the widely protrayed "either-or" election (half of McGovern's supporters did not support social change; half of Nixon's did not oppose it). Actually the Democrats were more divided within their ranks than they were from the Republicans.

Massive defections of Democrats and independents left McGovern with a relatively tight, ideologically intense following. Issues, as distinguished from partisan identification or candidate perception, clearly had an increased impact on the 1972 vote. In some respects, this election was the most ideological in modern history. But still only a small portion of the electorate responded in an ideological manner. We refer here again to the notion of consistency, the ability of an individual to organize "liberal" and "conservative" beliefs and relate these beliefs to voting.

McGovern lost because he was the least popular Democratic candidate in twenty years. Issues were more important than usual, but the most important factor was McGovern himself: his image, his values, his ideology. Nixon, by contrast, was clearly a popular candidate, receiving positive ratings from voters of all ideological leanings.

Party identification is remarkably stable over time, but opinions are quite unstable. Ironically the party is substantially more central to the belief system of mass electorates than are the policies it pursues. Short-term forces, such as a candidate's religion, smile, or television image, can deflect voters from their own party's candidate, but these short-term forces are unrelated to issues.

Of course, *some* voters are issue-oriented and well informed. (Recall that we described about one-third of the electorate as having an opinion, being informed, and perceiving a difference between parties.) Political scientist V. O. Key has characterized the electorate as "responsible," but he bases his conclusion solely upon those who switch from one party to another.[11] However, relatively few voters—one-fifth to one-eighth, depending upon the election—actually switch parties. Nevertheless Key portrays the electorate in more flattering terms than we have. He asserts, for instance, that "from our analyses the voter emerges as a person who appraises the actions of the government, who has policy preferences, and who relates his vote to those appraisals and preferences."[12] Granted that in close elections a few switching voters might be crucial; but to describe "the voter" as Key does ignores that only a tiny fraction of voters can be properly called "responsible."*

Are voters becoming more rational?

Most politicians, elites, and professors want to believe that voters are rational. If most voters are *not* ideological, do *not* understand and evaluate the issues, and *do* make choices based on party identification or candidate image, then another crucial component of the theory of pluralism falls apart.

Pluralist scholars argue that candidates and parties respond to broad mandates from the public, so they must also argue that the public is capable of choosing between candidates and parties on the basis of issues and ideologies. Some pluralist scholars argue that American voters are "changing"—becoming more issue-oriented than they were in the 1950s when *The American Voter* studies began.[13] The pluralists come to this conclusion in part because they more generously define an ideologue as anyone who makes "one implicit or explicit ideological mention" in an interview.[14]

The pluralists' conclusions also reflect different samples of voters at different times. A better technique is to interview the *same* voters at several different times. To show ideological consistency, the voter must respond similarly to a question on more than one occasion. Using this technique, Converse and Markus found that, contrary to the pluralist argument that voters were becoming more consistent, voters were showing virtually *no* change in ideological constraint (consistency). Correlations over time (answering the same question the same way twice, for example) were no higher for the 1970s than for previous decades.[15] Rather than changing and becoming more ideologicaly constrained, the American voter was as rudderless in the 1970s as during the Eisenhower years.

One way to resolve this argument over voter rationality would be to accept more simplistic indications of ideology. Most voters, for example, regard themselves as either "liberal" or "conservative." The Gallup poll generally finds about 75 percent of the voters willing and able to give themselves an ideological label. This approach increases the role of ideology substantially. Rather than citing, at best, one-third, we now can speak of 75 percent of the voters as having an "ideology"—that is, as willing to label themselves. The argument for ideological voters then becomes stronger.

---

*Since Key's book was published after his death, it is doubtful whether he wrote this sentence. Two years before he died, he wrote, "The more I study elections the more disposed I am to believe that they have within themselves more than a trace of the lottery. . . . Even when the public in manifest anger and disillusionment throws an administration from office, it does not express its policy preferences with precision."

Do liberal voters regard themselves as Democrats and conservatives as Republicans, as the popular images of the major parties suggest? In general, yes. Those who identify themselves as Republicans are more conservative than those who regard themselves as Democrats. Furthermore, liberals tend to vote for Democratic presidential candidates, while conservatives tend to vote for Republicans. These patterns persist even when the candidates and issues change from one election to another. This voting behavior also tends to support pluralist political theory.

However, people's images of parties and candidates vary with their self-described ideology.[16] Voters have a strong tendency to perceive a candidate's ideology in terms of their own ideological views. They seek congruence between their own views and the views of the candidates they wish to support. For example, conservative Democrats saw Jimmy Carter as a "conservative," and liberal Democrats saw him as a "liberal." In short, while most voters can label themselves "liberal" or "conservative," they tend to select a candidate independently of these labels and then believe that their candidate agrees with them on the issues.

The notion of ideological or rational voting raises yet another problem. Voters who label themselves "liberal" do not necessarily agree with each other on the issues, and the same is true of "conservatives." *Elites* link attitudes toward various policies with an overreaching liberal or conservative ideology. For elites, ideology is a summary of various specific policy attitudes. But *masses* do not link their policy positions with their "liberalism" or "conservatism."

For example, the proper role of the federal government in guaranteeing jobs and a good standard of living has been the source of enduring partisan debate between party activists and officeholders. Liberal elites, especially liberal Democratic elites, believe that the federal government should take an active role in the economy. Thus a self-described "liberal" *should* know that a liberal position on this issue is to favor governmental guarantees, and a conservative position is to favor individual self-reliance. But the masses do not approach the issue in this way. (See table 7-3.) Only among the college educated and among strong conservatives do more than half know that a liberal policy is one of federal intervention. The masses of non–college-educated voters have very little knowledge of the policy implications of "liberal" or "conservative" labels.

In summary, ideology does not mean very much. Describing oneself as "liberal" or "conservative" does not mean that one advocates or even recognizes policies consistent with one's ideology.[17]

All conclusions are to some extent time bound. In 1976, when Carter's presentation of his positions was very confusing to voters it is understandable that people's individual beliefs strongly influenced their perceptions of him. If, however, people still "project" their own beliefs on to candidates with clearly defined positions, the argument gains credibility. The election of 1980 was a good laboratory for examining voter perceptions (see table 7-4). Whatever else he may have done, Reagan

TABLE 7-3. "Liberals" and "conservatives" who correctly associate liberalism with an active role for federal government in the economy (percent)

Political stance of respondent	College	High school	Grade school
Strong liberal	78	22	0
Liberal	50	35	30
Weak liberal	51	47	0
Centrist	30	28	26
Weak conservative	50	30	0
Conservative	56	42	23
Strong conservative	81	67	54

Note: Entries are the proportion of respondents who associate liberalism with an active role for government and associate conservatism with individual self-help.

Source: Survey Resource Center, University of Michigan.

TABLE 7-4. Percent not aware of candidates' positions on selected issues, 1980

	Carter	Reagan
Inflation/unemployment		
February	38	56
October	47	52
Reducing domestic expenditures		
February	26	46
October	25	35
Reducing defense spending		
February	22	47
October	25	30
Getting along with the Russians		
February	16	42
October	22	31

Source: Survey Research Center, University of Michigan.

stuck to his guns. Throughout the campaign, Reagan's beliefs became clearer as Carter's became increasingly vague and contradictory. Thus 1980 was "half an ideological election."

Carter's efforts to obfuscate issues were thwarted by the fact of his incumbency; an incumbent candidate cannot hide. He did his best to avoid issues, as he had in 1976; but in 1980 he had a four-year record to carry with him. We can nonetheless compare the voters' personal preferences and perceptions of the candidates in 1976 and 1980. In 1980, people who were dissatisfied with Carter's past performance engaged in "negative projection." They decided he did not represent their positions on issues. For example, a person who disliked Carter's performance as president and who believed that getting along with the Russians is very important might believe that Carter did not share this view. On the other hand, Reagan benefited from "positive projection." People who held him in high regard and believed that getting along with the Russians is important were inclined to attribute similar opinions to Reagan. Alternatively, of course, we could argue that a candidate's persuasive ability draws voters closer to his views. Persuasion rarely has such power, however. When a person wants to reconcile personal beliefs with those of a preferred candidate, it is generally "easier to alter one's view of the candidate's issue positions than it is to change one's own position."[18] Reagan was unambiguous but not persuasive. Although his campaign reduced ambiguities about his positions, the polls registered a higher level of voter uncertainty about Reagan's positions than about the positions of the more evasive incumbent.

Because it is difficult to separate personal preference from a candidate's image clear relationships between voter ideology and voting patterns are hard to define. Table 7-5 shows how respondents in the study of ideological voting placed Carter on the issue of federal government involvement in the economic well-being of its constituents. One thing is clear from the overall study results: those who believed that the government should provide jobs, a characteristic Democratic position, voted for Carter. Those who believed that individuals should get along without government help voted for Reagan, whose beliefs mirror those of the Republican party. But, given what we know about the interplay of beliefs and candidate image, we should be suspicious of these findings.

It is possible, even probable, that voters could not place either candidate on these scales, acted more from partisan loyalty, or were attracted or repelled by candidate image. The link between issue preference and candidate preference, as direct as it may seem from media coverage, is an illusion. When we "control" (take into account) other factors, such as beliefs about Carter's integrity and competence or partisan identification, the outcome is quite different: "Political ideology had no net effect whatsoever on the election outcome. Further, Reagan's positions on important domestic and foreign policy matters gained him only one percentage point over Carter, an advantage that was more than countered by the prevailing Democratic bias in the distribution of partisan attachments."[19] In fact, table 7-6 shows that the 1980 voting choice had nothing whatsoever to do with ideological closeness between the voter and the candidate. The most important factor was Carter, as president

TABLE 7-5.   Ratings of Carter on issue of appropriate government role

	Scale position	Percent vote for Carter
Government should see to a job	1	80
and a good standard of living for	2	56
all	3	63
	4	50
	5	40
Government should let each	6	19
person get ahead on own	7	21

Source: Survey Research Center, University of Michigan.

**TABLE 7-6.   The anatomy of a voting decision, 1980
(contribution of factors to Carter's vote)**

Factor	Percent
Incumbent performance dissatisfaction	−6.5
Candidate competence	−2.6
Party identification	+2.0
Policy differences (Carter vs. Reagan)	−1.2
Ideological similarity (voters vs. Carter)	0
Candidate integrity	0

Source: Derived from Gregory B. Markus, "Political Attitudes During an Election Year," *American Political Science Review* 76 (September 1982), p. 559.

and as candidate. Later in this chapter, we will see how 1980 compared to other elections on matters of partisanship, ideology, and candidate image.

Elections as symbolic reassurance

If elections do not enable voters to control public policy directly, what are their purposes? Elections are a symbolic exercise to help tie the masses to the established order by giving them the feeling that they play a role. Political scientist Murray Edelman agrees that voters have little effect on public policy and contends that elections are primarily "symbolic reassurance." According to Edelman, elections serve to "quiet resentments and doubts about particular political acts, reaffirm belief in the fundamental rationality and democratic character of the system, and thus fix conforming habits of future behavior."[20]

Virtually all modern political systems—authoritarian and democratic, capitalist and communist—hold elections. Indeed communist dictatorships take elections very seriously and strive to achieve 90 to 100 percent voter turnout rates, despite the fact that the Communist party offers only one candidate for each office. Why do these nations bother to hold elections when the outcome has already been determined? All political regimes seek to tie the masses to the system by holding symbolic exercises in political participation to give the ruling regime an aura of legitimacy. Of course, democratic governments gain even greater legitimacy from elections; democratically elected officeholders can claim that the voters' participation legitimizes their activities and their laws.

Elections choose personnel, not policy

In democratic nations, elections serve a second function: choosing personnel to hold public office. In 1980 the American voters decided that Ronald Reagan and not Jimmy Carter would occupy "the nation's highest office" for the next four years. (The vast majority of people in the world today have never had the opportunity to participate in such a choice.) However, this choice is one of personnel, not policy: parties do not offer clear policy alternatives in election campaigns; voters do not choose the candidates' policy positions; and candidates are not bound by their campaign pledges anyway.

Elections allow for retrospective judgments

The third function of elections is to give the masses an opportunity to express themselves about the conduct of the public officials who have been in power. Elections do not permit the masses to direct future events, but they do permit the masses to render retrospective judgment about *past* political conduct. For example, in 1968, opposition to the Vietnam war was growing. In the presidential election that year, voters could choose Republican Richard Nixon, Democrat Hubert Humphrey, or Independent George Wallace. All three promised to "end" the war, but none provided a specific program for doing so—whether surrender, all-out bombing, or anything in between. But the voters *were* able to express their discontent with Johnson's handling of the war by voting against a continuation of the Democratic administration.[21]

The voters' retrospective judgment may affect the behavior of current and future elected officials. Political scientist Gerald Pomper contends, rather optimistically, that although the voters have no *power* over government, they nonetheless have *influence* over it. He suggests that because "politicians might be affected by the voters in the next election, they regulate their conduct appropriately."[22] But he fails to say how elected officials can know the sentiments of voters on policy questions in order to "regulate their conduct appropriately." As we have seen, most voters do not have an opinion they can communicate to elected officials; and elected officials have no way to interpret voters' policy preferences from electoral results. By ousting the Democratic administration in 1968, were the voters saying they wanted a military victory in Vietnam? Or that they wanted a negotiated peace and compromise with the Vietcong?

Perhaps the most likely case is that voters' retrospective judgment in an election can help make governing elites more sensitive to mass welfare. Elections do not permit masses to assure political actions in their interests, but they do encourage governing elites to consider the masses' welfare. Knowing that a day of reckoning will come on election day, elected officials strive to make a good impression on the voters in the meantime.

Elections provide protection against official abuse

Some people have argued that elections have a fourth function: to protect individuals and groups from official abuse. John Stuart Mill wrote, "Men, as well as women, do not need political rights in order

Case study: 1976—A return to "normalcy"

Jimmy Carter's narrow victory over Gerald Ford heralded a return to party loyalty. The massive defection of the Democrats in 1972 reversed; 92 percent of those with a strong Democratic identification voted for Carter (as compared to a 73 percent Democratic vote in 1972), and 71 percent of those with a weak Democratic identification voted for Carter (as compared to a 48 percent Democratic vote in 1972). The return of the Democrats was the most important political event of 1976; if they had not returned, Carter would have lost.

From the beginning of his primary campaign to his final victory, Carter sought to solidify his position with the "vital center" of the electorate. Until the final weeks of the primaries, he was not the choice of rank-and-file Democrats (Hubert Humphrey was their choice). Carter's primary victories improved his image, but he was clearly second choice. His strategy was to avoid the bitter polarization of 1972 and, if possible, gain the support of all Democratic factions (right, left, and center). The effect was largely successful. Many Democrats viewed him as left of center, while many others thought he was right of center. Unlike McGovern, whose primary campaign was viewed as a challenge by the left wing of the Democratic party, Carter was himself challenged by the left.

After the nomination, Carter solidified his support with the major urban political machines, organized labor, and blacks. However, despite his best efforts during his campaign, he could not avoid a liberal image. The mass public had acquired a distinctly conservative self-image. Only one-third of the electorate identified themselves as "left," whereas a majority were "middle" or "right." Heeding the lesson of 1972, Carter tried, unsuccessfully, to project himself as a center candidate. Carter's liberalism became more visible to the electorate as the campaign focused increased attention on him. (See table 7-7.) Carter lost his wide, early lead over Ford in the polls. Moreover, he was under constant pressure from media representatives to take a clear liberal position. Finally, the left liberals in the Democratic party were the least enthusiastic Carter supporters during the primaries, and their opinion leaders joined with the liberal columnists in pressuring Carter. Carter's resistance to this pressure contributed to an unflattering portrait—that of a "waffler," one who avoids clarity in public statements.[23]

TABLE 7-7.   Ideological position and choice of candidate, 1976 (percent of electorate)

Perceived ideological position	Perceptions of Carter		Perceptions of Ford		Voters' self-perceptions	
	March	Sept.	March	Sept.	March	Sept.
"Left"	30	48	23	19	31	31
"Middle"	5	7	7	3	10	10
"Right"	30	26	55	59	49	42
Unsure	35	19	15	19	10	17

Source: *Gallup Opinion Index* (December 1976): 41.

Case study *(continued)*

While Carter's image shifted, Ford's remained essentially unchanged; hence Ford sought to make a major theme of Carter's "waffling." Ironically, as Miller suggests, had Carter "waffled" less, he would have lost. Before the campaign, the public's perception of Carter's position matched its self-perception. By September, Carter had moved to the left, while Ford had not moved very much at all.

A more careful analysis reveals how much voters overlooked the disparity between their own conservatism and Carter's liberalism, illustrating again the wisdom of Carter's decision to blur the issues as much as possible. The only voters with whom Carter had any ideological commonality were the Democrats who had voted for McGovern in 1972. Republicans, by contrast, identified ideologically with Ford. Democrats who defected to Nixon in 1972 were substantially closer to Ford ideologically in 1976, yet they voted for Carter.

The entire 1976 campaign appeared to center upon other personal characteristics. Unlike 1972, no single set of polarizing issues emerged. The Vietnam war was over, and protests were a distant memory. While Carter implored voters to trust him, he also projected the image of a person of ability, an intriguing style, and a colorful personality. Thus voters described him using such adjectives as "bright, intelligent" and "colorful, interesting." They described Ford as a "person of average abilities" and as "predictable." Overall candidate ratings thus favored Carter; even though he was regarded as a "waffler," he won as a "personality." Forty-two percent gave him a "highly favorable" rating, compared to 28 percent for Ford. Significantly Ford's rating remained unchanged while Carter's improved substantially (from 20 percent in March). Thus while Ford enjoyed the advantage of being more compatible ideologically with his supporters, and was regarded as equally trustworthy, he was also dull.

Party identification, Carter's major advantage, gave him a final, narrow victory. Democrats returned to their party's nominee. The votes of the party's normal affiliates illustrate the point well: among voters with less than high school education, the Democratic percentage improved from 40 percent in 1972 to 69 percent in 1976; the Democratic black vote improved from 73 to 93 percent; the vote among union members increased from 43 to 64 percent.

Thus Carter, like McGovern, was viewed as liberal; but unlike McGovern, he was not considered an "extremist," and he held the Democratic voters in their party.

that they might govern, but in order that they not be misgoverned."[24] He went on:

> Rulers in ruling classes are under a necessity of considering the interests of those who have the suffrage; but of those who are excluded, it is in their option whether they will do so or not, and however honestly disposed, they are in general too fully occupied with things they must attend to, to have

much room in their thoughts for anything which they can with impunity disregard.[25]

Certainly the long history of efforts to ensure black voting rights in the South suggests that many concerned Americans believed that if blacks could secure access to the polls, they could better protect themselves from official discrimination. Some major steps in the struggle for voting rights were the abolishment of the "white primary" (blacks were not allowed to participate) in 1944; the Civil Rights Acts of 1957, 1960, 1964, and 1965, all of which contained provisions guaranteeing free access to the polls; and the Twenty-fourth Amendment to the Constitution, which eliminated poll taxes. But the high hopes stirred by the development of new law often deteriorated into frustration and disillusionment when blacks realized that the electoral process alone could not solve their problems. Certainly the vote is a symbol of full citizenship and equal rights that can contribute to black self-respect,[26] but questions remain about how much blacks can gain through the exercise of their vote. In the North, blacks have voted freely for decades, but political action has not measurably improved conditions in the urban ghettos. In signing the Voting Rights Act of 1965, President Johnson said:

> The right to vote is the most basic right, without which all others are meaningless. It gives people—people as individuals—control over their own destinies. . . . The vote is the most powerful instrument ever devised by man for breaking down injustice and destroying the terrible walls which imprison men because they are different from other men.

But the black experience in both the North and the South suggests that the ballot cannot eliminate discrimination, much less enable people to "control their own destinies." People probably can *better* protect themselves from government abuse when they possess and exercise their voting rights, but the right to vote is not a guarantee against discrimination.

Electoral participation and nonparticipation

Another problem with the theory of popular control over public policy through elections is the fact that nearly half the adult population fails to vote, even in presidential elections. Since the 1960 Kennedy-Nixon race, voter turnout has steadily slipped from 64 percent of the eligible voters to 63 percent in the 1964 Johnson-Goldwater race, 60 percent in the 1968 Nixon-Humphrey-Wallace race, 56 percent in the 1972 Nixon-McGovern race, 53 percent in the 1976 Carter-Ford race, and about 52 percent in the 1980 Reagan-Carter race. Off-year (nonpresidential) elections bring out fewer than half the eligible voters. Yet in these off-year contests, the nation chooses all its U.S. representatives, one-third its senators, and about one-half its governors. (See figure 7-4.)

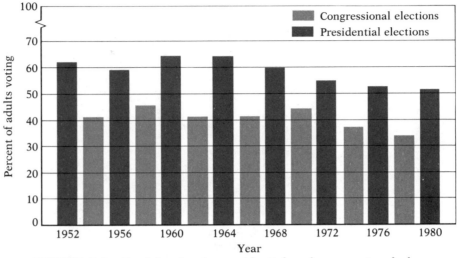

FIGURE 7-4. Participation in presidential and congressional elections, 1952–1980

Source: Data based on annual editions of *Statistical Abstracts of the United States* (Washington, D.C.: GPO).

Lester Milbrath listed six forms of "legitimate" political participation.[27] Individuals may run for public office, become active in party and campaign work, make financial contributions to political candidates or causes, belong to organizations that support or oppose candidates, attempt to influence friends while discussing candidates or issues, and vote in elections. Activities at the top of this list require greater expenditure of time, money, and energy than those at the bottom, and they involve only a tiny minority of the population. Less than 1 percent of American adults ever run for public office. Only about 5 percent are ever active in parties and campaigns, and only about 10 percent make financial contributions. About one-third the population belongs to organizations that could be classified as political interest groups, and only a few more people ever try to persuade their friends to vote a certain way. And finally, only about 50 to 55 percent of the American people will vote in a hard-fought presidential campaign.

Participation is not uniform throughout all segments of the population. Data show the percentages of voter turnout for the 1980 elections. (See table 7-8.) High voter turnout relates to such factors as college education, white-collar occupation, and high income. Although these figures pertain only to voting, other forms of participation follow substantially the same pattern. White, middle-class, college-educated, white-collar Americans participate more in all forms of political activity than do nonwhite, lower-class, grade-school-educated Americans.

Election turnout figures in the United States are lower than those of several other democracies. The turnout in recent elections has been

TABLE 7-8.   Percent turnout in presidential elections by selected groups (1980)

Age		Race	
18–25	36	Whites, non-Hispanics	58
26–40	57	Blacks	45
41–54	68	Hispanics	38
55 + over	64		
Education		*Occupation*	
Eighth grade or less	44	Unskilled	49
Some high school	45	Skilled	53
High school graduate	57	Clerical	60
Some college	59	Self-employed	68
College graduate	76	Professional	69
Income (family)		*Party Identification*	
Less than $5,000	39	Strong Democrats	64
$5,000 to $9,999	44	Weak Democrats	49
$10,000 to $14,999	57	Independent Democrats	56
$15,000 to $19,999	56	Independents	43
$20,000 to $24,999	64	Independent Republicans	62
$25,000 to $29,999	71	Weak Republicans	65
$30,000 to $24,999	65	Strong Republicans	70
$35,000 to $49,999	70		
$50,000 and more	68		

Source: Survey Research Center, University of Michigan.

74 percent in Japan, 77 percent in Great Britain, 83 percent in Israel, 88 percent in West Germany, and 93 percent in Italy. The lower U.S. turnouts may reflect the stricter American residence and registration requirements and greater frequency of elections. But Americans may also be less "political" than citizens of other democracies, less likely to care about the outcome of elections, and less likely to feel that government has much effect on their lives. This lack of interest in politics may be because differences are less significant between opposing parties and candidates, so that the electorate has less invested in which party or candidate wins.[28]

Alienation from the system

The slim majority of Americans who do vote thereby indicate they have an interest in the outcome of elections. However, a sizable number of Americans never vote or participate in politics in any fashion. This nonvoting might reflect "alienation" from the political system: a feeling that voting and other forms of participation are useless, that an election really decides very little, and that the individual cannot personally influence the outcome of political events. The higher frequency of nonvoting among those at the bottom of the income, occupation, education, and status ladder tends to confirm this view, since alienation occurs more

Reprinted by permission: Tribune Company Syndicate, Inc.

frequently in groups who have not shared the general affluence of society. However, this interpretation is discouraging for those who embrace the democratic ideal because it suggests that not all groups in society place a high value on democratic institutions.

To those who value popular participation, the increasing number of alienated people and declining rate of voter participation are cause for concern. As distrust in government soars, alienation tends to spread from its concentration among the traditional have-nots to affect all population groups.

Distrust of government

The growing disillusionment and distrust of government—and attendant feelings of helplessness and lack of influence—began in about 1964 and has continued virtually unabated since then. Americans' alienation from government goes beyond dissatisfaction or opposition to particular politicians or parties. A national survey conducted by pollster Louis Harris in 1976 revealed that a majority of Americans give replies to general questions about American society that reflect their alienation. Few people believe that government improves their lives. The federal government is the worst culprit; a plurality of Americans believe that it

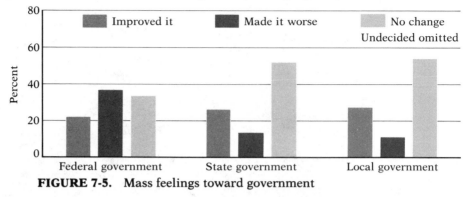

FIGURE 7-5. Mass feelings toward government

Source: Data based on U.S. Senate, Committee on Government Operations, Subcommittee on Intergovernmental Relations, *Confidence and Concern: Citizens View American Government* (Washington, D.C.: GPO, 1973), pp. 42–43.

makes their lives *worse*. State and local governments fare better; most Americans believe they do no great harm. (See figure 7-5.)

Perhaps even more disturbing is the widespread feeling that the quality of life in America is declining. Nearly half (46 percent) of the public believe that the quality of their lives has *declined* in the last decade; 15 percent believe that it has stayed the same; and 35 percent believe that it has improved. (See figure 7-6.) Interestingly, elites think that the quality of life is improving; 61 percent of a national leadership sample believed life had improved over the decade, and only 20 percent believed it had grown worse. Thus elites and masses clearly have different notions of whether life is getting better or worse in this nation.

Mass distrust of a democratic government is an invitation to tyranny. When asked what they thought were the nation's biggest problems, Americans listed inflation, energy shortages, lack of integrity in government, crime, welfare, federal spending, and taxes, well ahead of racial justice, health care, and housing. These responses suggest that the masses do not strongly seek traditional liberal reforms. More ominous, perhaps, is the statement, "It's about time we had a strong federal government to get this country moving again," which elicited agreement from fully 67 percent of the American people (despite the plurality of those who think the federal government has worsened their lives). Some analysts may interpret this reply as a demand for greater integrity or honesty, but a more realistic interpretation is that the nation would welcome a strong leader—perhaps even an authoritarian figure. Democracy is at its weakest when the citizenry loses confidence in its governing elites.

Mass discontent continued to increase from 1964 to 1976, and indeed the spread of distrust accelerated. Political scientist Warren Miller, who

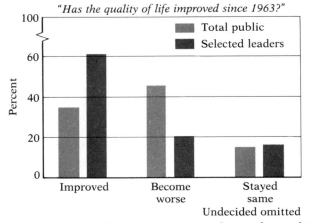

FIGURE 7-6. Elite and mass attitudes on the quality of life

Source: Data based on U.S. Senate, Committee on Government Operations, Subcommittee on Intergovernmental Relations, *Confidence and Concern: Citizens View American Government* (Washington, D.C.: GPO, 1973), p. 231.

used the same questions over the twelve-year span, estimates that 1976 produced the most cynical and distrustful electorate in history. A glance at table 7-9 indicates the massive erosion of trust. In 1964 respondents offered more trusting responses than cynical responses to all five questions; by 1976, they had given more cynical responses than trusting ones, a pattern that continued through 1980. The majority thought the government in Washington was run by incompetent, wasteful crooks who were beholden to powerful interest groups.

As yet no strong counterelites have emerged to channel this surge of discontent. But as issues become more complex and major candidates remain equivocal, the opportunities for the simplistic appeal of the demagogue increase.

TABLE 7-9.   Mass attitudes toward government, 1964–1980

	1964	1972	1976	1980
Trust government in Washington some of the time.	+54	+ 8	−63	−46
Government is run by a few big interests.	+35	−16	−45	−54
Government wastes a lot of money.	+ 5	−33	−73	−60
Quite a few people running the government are crooked.	+38	+23	−30	+ 3
Quite a few people running the government don't know what they are doing.	+41	+15	− 7	−30

Note: Entries are the differences between trusting and cynical responses. In 1964, for example, respondents gave more trusting responses than cynical responses, but in 1976, they gave more cynical responses than trusting ones.

Source: Survey Research Center, University of Michigan.

Case study: 1980—"Conservative revolution" or "Time for a change"?

The 1980 election, in which Ronald Reagan's "landslide" brought in 51 percent of the popular vote, had the lowest turnout since 1948. About 53 percent of eligible voters participated. Clearly, the electorate had little enthusiasm for the candidates, especially for Carter. The landslide was more a rejection of the incumbent than a popular affirmation of Reagan's ideology. Reagan's showing in electoral votes (489) was impressive but represented no mandate for conservatism. Of course, mandates are in the eyes of the beholders. Reagan and his staff frequently spoke of their mandate to increase defense spending, cut domestic spending, and cut taxes. Reagan's New Right supporters interpreted his election as a mandate for an antiabortion amendment, prayers in schools, and other items on its "social agenda."

The 1976 election was a return to "normalcy": Carter won because the Democratic coalition held firm. The 1980 election, on the other hand, was a massive rejection of Carter as president. Except for a trivial gain among Republicans, Carter lost ground across the board: the defections ranged from major to relatively minor, but no group of voters supported him to the degree they had in 1976. (See table 7-10.)

To put this rejection in perspective, consider that in 1980, as the campaign began, 41 percent of the electorate approved of Carter's performance during the preceding four years; in 1976 at a comparable point, 63 percent approved

TABLE 7-10.   Percent decline of Democratic vote by selected groups, 1976–1980

Sex		Age	
Male	− 15%	Under 30	− 10%
Female	− 3%	30–49	− 15%
Female	− 3%	50 years and older	− 16%
Race		**Religion**	
White	− 10%	Protestants	− 14%
Nonwhite	− 2%	Catholics	− 16%
Education		**Politics**	
College	− 7%	Republicans	+ 2%
High school	− 10%	Democrats	− 15%
Grade school	− 8%	Independents	− 8%
Occupation		**Region**	
Professional and business	− 9%	East	− 8%
White collar	− 7%	Midwest	− 7%
Manual	− 12%	South	− 10%
		West	− 16%
		Member of labor union families	− 17%

Source: Survey Research Center, University of Michigan.

Case study (*continued*)

of incumbent Gerald Ford's performance, and in 1972, 71 percent approved of Richard Nixon's first-term performance. Because of his low standing, Carter faced the humiliation of challenge from within his own party. Had the Iranian seizure of U.S. hostages not occurred, he may well have failed to be renominated.

While Carter lost support everywhere, Reagan was not always the major beneficiary. The support that Carter lost among women, college-educated young voters, and independents drifted toward independent candidate John Anderson. But Reagan was the direct beneficiary of Carter's decline among Catholics, older voters, non–college-educated people, manual workers, and union members. Such groups (along with Jews, who also abandoned Carter) have been core supporters of the Democratic coalition since Franklin D. Roosevelt forged the New Deal. The unraveling of this coalition was a direct result of Carter's weakness—an image reinforced by Senator Edward M. Kennedy's challenge of Carter within the Democratic party. As Reagan had done in 1976, Kennedy lost the nomination, but his powerful presence at the convention was impossible to ignore (and the Democratic platform more closely reflected his liberal philosophy than Carter's).

Reagan, viewed correctly as representing the conservative wing of the Republican party, was nevertheless disinclined to emulate the pure right-wing strategy of his most immediate conservative predecessor, Barry Goldwater. Reagan's chief strategist, Richard Wirthlin, wrote in a private memorandum to the candidate: "We can expect Ronald Reagan to be pictured as a simplistic and untried lightweight (dumb), a person who consciously misuses facts to overblow his own record (deceptive), and, if president, one who would be too anxious to engage our country in a nuclear holocaust (dangerous)."[29] Wirthlin's prediction was accurate, for Carter did portray Reagan in these terms, with increasing shrillness as the campaign wore on.

Carter saw a steady deterioration of his early lead, and by midsummer Reagan had passed him. (See figure 7-7.) But the 1980 electorate was unusually volatile. Opinions skyrocketed and declined almost month to month. Unlike most campaigns, in which people make up their minds early and stay on course during the campaign, voter response to this campaign was mercurial. This type of volatility is a natural consequence of media-dominated, image elections in which style replaces substance. Party loyalties weaken, and short-term factors become important. In contrast to 1976, when Carter's early lead narrowed but never disappeared, the lead in 1980 changed hands three times between nomination and election. Many Reagan voters in particular delayed their decision until the final week.

This volatility, recognized by both candidates, led Carter to make harsh attacks on Reagan, causing the media to dub him "Jimmy the Mean." Reagan was an especially apt target when he decided to ad lib. His consultants consistently urged him to stick to the script. (Through long association with General Electric Co.—the sponsors of his "Death Valley Days" television show—and his gubernatorial campaigns, Reagan had developed "the speech," which he could deliver flawlessly and effectively.) In Michigan, angered by a Carter heckler in the crowd, Reagan departed from his speech to criticize the president for opening his campaign in Tuscumbia, Alabama, "a city that

(continued)

Case study (*continued*)

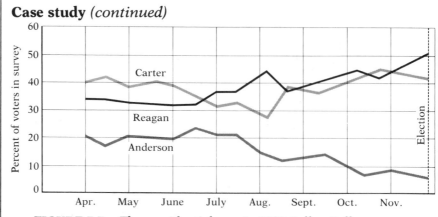

FIGURE 7-7.   The presidential race in 1980 Gallup Polls.

Note: The surveys taken before September 1 reflect the choices of registered voters. The surveys taken after September 1 reflect the choices of likely voters. late October results are based on a partial survey taken before the October 28 debate.

gave birth to and is the parent body of the Ku Klux Klan." Seizing upon the issue to shore up his support in the South, Carter denounced Reagan for resorting to "slurs and innuendos against a whole region of the country based on a false premise. . . ."

This sort of exchange set the tone of the campaign. "Jimmy the Mean" was indeed mean. He disliked Reagan personally and had a long history of personalizing issues. On one occasion he alleged that Reagan was a racist: "You'll determine whether this America will be unified or, if I lose the election, whether Americans might be separated, blacks from whites, Jews from Christians, North from South, rural from urban."

Reagan invariably reacted with sadness rather than anger, creating the image of a "nice guy" without prejudice. But the attacks continued. Carter refused to participate in the first debate in September 1980 on the grounds that John Anderson's participation as a "media candidate" would destroy the legitimacy of the debate.

The polls showed immediate response to each newly created issue. Carter moved ahead in the polls shortly after his "separated blacks from whites" speech. He proceeded to imply that Reagan was a hard-line cold warrior who would be likely to initiate nuclear war: the election would determine "whether this nation will make progress or go backward and *whether we have war or peace.*" Publicly denying any intention to "play dirty," Carter's aides made no secret of what they were up to. Hence the meanness issue ultimately worked to Carter's disadvantage. The media seized the issue and played on it throughout the campaign. Ultimately the president used an October interview with ABC's Barbara Walters to promise that he would quit his mudslinging. His attacks ceased thereafter, but his consultants lamented that "The continuous charges of meanness and pettiness had an effect; people vote on character and that was supposed to be our issue."[30]

Indeed, as in 1976, Carter preferred to concentrate on image rather than substance. Reagan, although benefiting from the backlash against Carter,

Case Study *(continued)*

created his own set of problems by straying from his lines. Dispatching his running mate, George Bush, to the People's Republic of China, Reagan reaffirmed his intention to reestablish diplomatic relations with Taiwan, thus ensuring a hostile reception when Bush arrived. Speaking to the Veterans of Foreign Wars, he briefly referred to the war in Vietnam as "a noble cause." Such gaffes would have passed unnoticed had the media not seized them as Reagan's vulnerable point. The campaign became "Jimmy the Mean" against "Ronnie the Stupid." Reagan could not respond accurately when journalists forced him to speak extemporaneously or when his enthusiasm led him to speak without notes. For example, his answer to those who felt he was too old was that he was younger than "all the heads of state I have to do business with." A safe enough comment when speaking to enthusiastic crowds, it was less so in formal interviews. When NBC's Tom Brokaw told him that the president of France, Giscard d'Estaing, was younger, Reagan replied "Who?" Media interpretation was brutal: either he did not know who d'Estaing was (stupid) or he could not hear (old).

One of his most thoughtful biographers, Lou Cannon of the *Washington Post*, provided the best explanation of Reagan's apparent "stupidity." Cannon called him "the *Reader's Digest* of politics," alluding to his habit of picking up stories at random and using them without checking their accuracy.[31] He believed everything he obtained from such right-wing sources as *Human Events*. Thus he claimed that the Department of Health, Education and Welfare spent $3.00 to deliver $1.00 of services (the actual figure was 12¢); that U.S. oil reserves exceed those of Saudi Arabia; that Mount St. Helens released more sulfur dioxide into the atmosphere in ten days than automobile emissions had in ten years (sulfur dioxide emissions caused by human activities amounted to about 81,000 tons per day; Mount St. Helens released between 500 and 2,000 tons per day).

Believing that continuing errors could make Reagan rather than the unpopular incumbent the major campaign issue, Reagan's advisers began a program of "damage control." They did not allow Reagan close enough to the media to indulge in unrehearsed answers. Although they could not prevent the candidate from telling an audience what it wanted to hear, they did ward off much of the potential damage. Ignorance is an issue only if the media pursue it. Most people who heard Reagan's speeches liked them because they were earthy and reinforced their biases. One reporter noted that "A Reagan gaffe was more like a mistake that came from a family friend. . . ."[32]

Reagan was able to project this comfortable image during the end-of-the-campaign debates with Carter. Although Carter knew more, he looked worse. Generally insisting on knowing his material before he spoke, Carter could still appear nervous and high-strung. During the Democratic convention, rattled by the favorable response to Kennedy and Kennedy's obvious distaste for him, he referred to "Hubert Horatio Hornblower" (meaning, of course, Hubert Humphrey). More important, he was not funny, and Reagan was a good stand-up comedian. Reagan's ability to simplify, a quality Carter did not naturally emulate, proved invaluable. Told by advisers to "stay relaxed," Reagan came across as a serious candidate who nevertheless had a good sense of humor. As the debate wore on, Carter tried to be personable

(continued)

Case study *(continued)*

but did not succeed. In one ill-fated effort to appear as "nice" as Reagan, he spoke of his daughter: "I had a discussion with my daughter Amy the other day before I came here to ask her what the most important issue was. She said she thought nuclear weapons and the control of nuclear arms." The remark became a staple joke for the remainder of the campaign (television football announcer Roger Staubach told viewers that his daughter had advised him about defense against a passing attack; "ask Amy" bumper stickers appeared overnight).

Reagan understood well that television exposes personality. While Carter's attempts to appear "human" appeared ludicrous, Reagan appeared natural, though he rehearsed his appearances carefully. When his advisers tried vainly during rehearsals to explain the complexities of strategic weapons, disarmament, and various domestic policies, Reagan, unconcerned, spent his time planning one liners. One such line, "There you go again"— which Reagan developed during a merciless rehearsal grilling by David Stockman on the issue of nuclear war—served Reagan well in his debates with Carter. When Carter provided a quite accurate description of Reagan's opposition to national health insurance, Reagan used his well-prepared one liner, appearing to be gently scolding an errant child. Combined with Carter's absurd reference to his daughter and Reagan's closing remarks to the television audience ("Are you better off now than you were four years ago?"), this comment sealed Carter's fate. Reagan's "Are you better off?" theme was a simple yet effective way to end the debate. It was a theme anybody could understand, and it worked well against Carter's intense, complex presentation. Indeed, Reagan's level of preparation for the debates was enhanced by his previously-obtained description of the Carter debate plan.

Consequently, a healthy minority of Democrats and majorities of independents and Republicans judged Reagan the winner. (See table 7-11.) (Notice that Carter did not do as well with Democrats as Reagan did with Republicans.) When we link actual vote with the voters' perception of who won the debate, Reagan's performance is even more impressive: 71 percent of the Democrats who thought Reagan won the debates voted for him, while only 37 percent of the Republicans who thought Carter won voted for him. (See table 7-12.)

When challenged with Reagan's question—"Are you better off now than you were four years ago?"—42 percent of survey respondents said "no," compared to 31 percent in 1976 and 23 percent in 1972. Reagan had touched a responsive chord. The debates gave voters an "excuse" for voting for him.

TABLE 7-11. Who won the debate? Voters choosing Reagan or Carter, by party (percent)

	Reagan	Carter
Democrats	27	57
Independents	58	24
Republicans	85	9

Source: Survey Research Center, University of Michigan.

Case study *(continued)*

TABLE 7-12.   Voting choice: Actual vote and perceived winner, by party (percent)

	Thought Reagan won debate, and voted for him	Thought Carter won debate, and voted for him
Democrats	71	95
Independents	85	66
Republicans	93	37

Source: Survey Research Center, University of Michigan.

They did not see him as a warmonger, as Carter had claimed. Since the electorate wanted to punish the incumbent, the debates removed any lingering doubt: the war and peace issue ceased to be a factor. A volatile electorate responds to such nuances more vigorously than an electorate with a strong sense of party loyalty or ideological preference. Last-minute switches cost Carter about 6 percentage points, while Reagan gained 1. This net 7 percent was enough for Reagan to win.

By no means was the election a "shift to the right," however. It was instead a referendum on Carter. The "Are you better off?" theme was an economic one, not an abstract plea to return to conservatism. This theme is virtually identical to voters' claim that "It's time for a change" as their primary reason for voting for Reagan. A voter—whether Democrat, Republican, liberal, conservative, Catholic, or Protestant—who was worse off financially was likely to vote for Reagan. (See table 7-13)

Michael Robinson gives us a good feel for the election through his notion of "medialities." Medialities are "events, developments, or situations to which the media have given importance by emphasizing, expanding, or featuring them in such a way that their real significance has been modified, distorted,

TABLE 7-13   The Carter vote and perceived economic satisfaction (percent)

	Improved economic position	Worsened economic position
Democrats	77	47
Independents	45	21
Republicans	18	6
Liberals	65	44
Moderates	59	26
Conservatives	33	16
Protestants	51	24
Catholics	53	28
Jews	52	30
Union households	65	34
Non-union classroom	48	22

Source: Data taken from CBS News/New York Times Election Day Poll, 1980.

(continued)

Case study *(continued)*

or obscured."[33] Thus they are not "real" events. In 1980 the medialities were Reagan's errors, Carter's "meanness," the "debate" debate (whether Carter would debate Reagan and Anderson), the Carter-Reagan debates, and the Iranian hostages. With these stories dominating the news, it is small wonder that issues seemed trivial. The campaign was a contest of personalities. Most voters agreed that Carter should be thrown out of office but wondered whether Reagan was an acceptable alternative. The debates convinced the voters that he was. The voters selected Reagan not because of his deeply felt conservatism but in spite of it. Few people had enthusiasm for either candidate: about 40 percent would have preferred neither candidate but chose the lesser of two evils. A 1981 survey asked: "Do you agree with people who feel that the Reagan victory was a mandate for more conservative policies in our country, or do you feel it was mostly a rejection of President Carter and his administration?" Two-thirds said the Reagan victory was a rejection of Carter, and 24 percent felt it was a mandate for conservatism.[34] Even Republicans and conservatives agreed with this sentiment.

Focusing cynicism: Whom do you trust the least?

Government is not the only focus of the masses' cynicism and mistrust. Major public and private institutions, such as medicine, organized religion, organized labor, and the military, are also vulnerable to the decline of confidence. Decreased confidence in the major public and private institutions (those listed above plus the press, television, the executive branch, Congress, and major companies), is clear. (See figure 7-8.) In 1966 the average trust in major institutions was 43 percent. This percentage had slipped to 23 percent by 1979. One major exception was television news, the only institution to enjoy an increase in trust and the most trusted major institution in 1979.[35]

The opportunities for the most trusted institution to organize mass opinion are impressive. Research has consistently suggested that attitude change is related to the perception of the source. People are more likely to believe a message coming from a trusted source than the same one coming from a mistrusted source.

Violence as political participation

A strong relationship exists between deprivation and political violence. When conventional political participation loses its meaning, violence may become a device to communicate intense dissatisfaction. The black ghetto rioters of the 1960s were not vagrants or criminals; they were long-time residents of their cities and were, in fact, cited among the more intellectually oriented and politically sophisticated of the black community.[36] Furthermore, the rioters had substantial support among

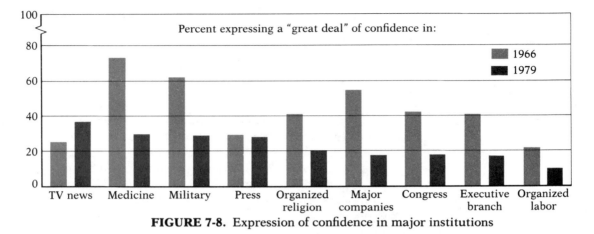

FIGURE 7-8. Expression of confidence in major institutions

blacks who did not participate directly in the riots. Post-riot survey information indicated that roughly 20 percent of the blacks in the Watts area of Los Angeles participated actively in the riot of 1964, and more than half the residents supported the activities of the rioters. Interviewers found that 58 percent of the Watts residents felt that the long-run effects of the riots would be favorable; 84 percent said that the riots made whites more aware of black problems; 62 percent said that the riot was a protest by blacks.

Most political scientists do not consider rioting and political violence political participation, perhaps because we wish to see political violence as an atypical temporary aberration. Actually the American political system is not as stable as we like to assume.[37] Although most whites regard the system as legitimate, a substantial proportion of blacks do not because they believe that it has not provided adequate rewards for their conventional political participation. Middle- and upper-class whites tend to view the American system of government as extremely satisfactory and find it difficult to understand why a minority group communicates its dissatisfaction violently. Milbrath's hierarchy of political involvement excludes violence because the hierarchy of participation does not apply to behavior "designed to disrupt the normal operation of democratic political processes."[38] But violence is a continuing threat to any political system. To be sure, this form of political participation is a criminal one. And it may be irrational and self-defeating, for the great majority of the casualties of the riots in the 1960s—the dead, the injured, and the arrested—were rioters themselves, and much of the property destroyed belonged to ghetto residents. The recurrence of violence in Miami in the summer of 1980 followed the patterns of the 1960s in its origins and resolutions. Although it is comforting to believe that riots were a phenomenon of the 1960s, they are an ongoing form of political participation by the masses. In December 1982 the killing of a black youth by a white police officer touched off a repetition of 1980 in Miami. The precipitating circumstances were identical to those of the riots of the 1960s.

Summary

Elite theory contends that the masses do not participate in policy making and that the elites who do are subject to little direct influence from apathetic masses. But many scholars who acknowledge that even democratic societies are governed by elites seek to reaffirm democratic values by contending that voters can influence elite behavior in elections. In other words, modern pluralists sometimes challenge elitism on the grounds that elections give the masses a voice in policy making by holding governing elites accountable to the people.

Our analysis suggests that elections are imperfect instruments of accountability. Even if the people can hold *government* elites accountable through elections, how can they hold accountable corporate elites, financial elites, union leaders, and other private leadership? The accountability argument usually ignores the realm of *private* decision making to focus exclusively on *public* decision making by elected elites. But certainly our lives are vitally affected by the decisions of private institutions and organizations. So the first problem with the accountability thesis is that, at best, it applies only to elected government elites. However, our analysis of elections also suggests that it is difficult for the voters to hold even *government* elites accountable.

1. Competing candidates in elections do not usually offer clear policy alternatives; hence voters seldom can affect policy by selecting a particular candidate for public office.

2. Voters are not well informed about the policy stands of candidates, and relatively few voters are concerned with policy questions. The masses cast their votes in elections based on traditional party ties, candidates' personalities, group affiliations, and a host of other factors having little relation to public policy.

3. Mass opinion on public policy is inconsistent and unstable. Relatively few voters (generally well-educated, upper-class voters from whom elites are drawn) hold reasonably consistent political ideologies. Mass opinion is unguided by principle, is unstable, and is subject to change.

4. Available evidence suggests that elites influence the opinion of masses more than masses influence the opinion of elites. The masses respond to political symbols manipulated by elites, not to facts or political principles.

5. The only reasonably stable aspect of mass politics is party identification. But party identification in the mass electorate does not allow

for any significant policy choices since Democrats and Republicans hold fairly similar opinions on most issues.

6. Election results do not necessarily reflect majority preferences on policy questions because (a) campaigns generally stress the presentation of political ideologies rather than the content of the ideologies; (b) victory for a party or a candidate may not indicate support for a specific policy position; (c) voters frequently misinterpret candidates' policy preferences; (d) often a candidate's voters include not only advocates of the stated position but some who oppose it and some who vote for the candidate for other reasons; (e) a candidate may take positions on many different issues, so observers cannot know which policy positions resulted in election; (f) for voters to influence policy through elections, winning candidates would be bound to follow their campaign pledges.

7. Elections are primarily a symbolic exercise that helps tie the masses to the established order. Elections offer the masses an opportunity to participate in the political system, but electoral participation does not enable them to determine public policy.

8. Elections are means of selecting personnel, not policy. Voters choose on the basis of a candidate's personal style, filtered through partisan commitment. A candidate's election does not imply a policy choice by the electorate.

9. At best, elections provide the masses with an opportunity to express themselves about the conduct of past administrations, but they do not help them direct the course of future events. Again, a vote against the party or candidate in power does not identify the policy being censured; voters have no guarantee that a newly elected official will pursue any specific policy alternatives.

10. Few individuals participate in any political activity other than voting. Nearly half the adult population fails to vote even in presidential elections.

11. Riots and other forms of political violence are clear signs that some members or groups within the masses no longer consider the system legitimate because they believe it withholds from them the rewards of conventional participation.

NOTES

1. Fred I. Greenstein, *The American Party System and the American People* (Englewood Cliffs, N.J.: Prentice-Hall, 1963), p. 12.
2. A. Campbell, P. Converse, W. Miller, and D. Stokes, *The American Voter* (New York: Wiley, 1960), p. 175.
3. Philip E. Converse, "The Nature of Belief Systems in Mass Publics," in David E. Apter, ed., *Ideology and Discontent* (New York: Free Press, 1964), pp. 213–230.
4. Campbell et al., op cit., p. 227.
5. The following discussion draws from Paul R. Abramson, John H. Aldrich, and

David W. Rohde, *Change and Continuity in the 1980 Election* (Washington, D.C.: Congressional Quarterly Press, 1982), pp. 124–132.

6. Warren E. Miller and Teresa E. Levitin, *Leadership and Change: The New Politics and the American Electorate* (Cambridge, Mass.: Winthrop Publishers, 1976), p. 15.
7. Converse, op cit., p. 240.
8. Ibid., p. 245.
9. Richard Niemi and Herbert Weisberg, eds., *Controversies in American Voting Behavior* (San Francisco: Freeman, 1976), p. 83.
10. Seymour Martin Lipset and Earl Raab, "The Election and the National Mood," *Commentary* 55 (January 1973):44.
11. V. O. Key, Jr., *The Responsible Electorate* (Cambridge, Mass.: Harvard University Press, 1966).
12. Ibid., pp. 58–59.
13. Norman E. Nie, Sidney Verba, and John R. Petrocik, *The Changing American Voter* (Cambridge, Mass.: Harvard University Press, 1976), p. 112.
14. Ibid., p. 375.
15. Philip Converse and Gregory Markus, "Plus Ça Change . . . : The New CPS Election Study Panel," *American Political Science Review* 73 (March 1979):32–49.
16. Teresa Levitin and Warren E. Miller, "Ideological Interpretations of the Presidential Elections," *American Political Science Review* 73 (September 1979):761.
17. Ibid., p. 769.
18. Gregory B. Markus, "Political Attitudes During an Election Year," *American Political Science Review* 76 (September 1982), p. 548.
19. Ibid., p. 538.
20. Murray Edelman, *The Symbolic Uses of Power* (Urbana: University of Illinois Press, 1964), p. 17.
21. Gerald Pomper, *Elections in America: Control and Influence in Democratic Politics* (New York: Dodd, Mead, 1968), pp. 255–56.
22. Ibid., p. 254.
23. *ISR Newsletter* (Winter 1977):4–5.
24. John Stuart Mill, *Considerations on Representative Government* (Chicago: Henry Regnery, Gateway edition, 1962), p. 144.
25. Ibid., pp. 130–131.
26. William R. Keech, *The Impact of Negro Voting: The Role of the Vote in the Quest for Equality* (Chicago: Rand McNally, 1968), p. 3.
27. Lester Milbrath, *Political Participation* (Chicago: Rand McNally, 1965), pp. 23–29.
28. Robert E. Lane, "The Politics of Consensus in an Age of Affluence," *American Political Science Review* 61 (December 1965):880.
29. Albert R. Hunt, "The Campaign and the Issues," in Austin Ranney, ed., *The American Elections of 1980* (Washington, D.C.: American Enterprise Institute, 1981), p. 143.
30. Albert R. Hunt, "The Campaign and the Issues," in Austin Ranney, ed., *The American Election of 1980* (Washington, D.C.: American Enterprise Institute, 1981), p. 156.
31. Lou Cannon, *Reagan* (New York: G. P. Putnam's Sons, 1982), p. 260.
32. Jeff Greenfield, *The Real Campaign* (New York: Summit Books, 1982), p. 93.
33. Michael Robinson, "The Media in 1980," in Ranney, ed., op cit., p. 191.
34. William Schneider, "The November 4 Vote for President: What Did It Mean?" in Ranney, ed., op. cit., p. 235.
35. Louis Harris polls, 1966–1979.
36. *Report of the National Advisory Commission on Civil Disorders* (Washington, D.C., 1968), pp. 111–112, 128–135.
37. See Ted Gurr, "Urban Disorder: Perspectives from the Comparative Study of Civil Strife," *American Behavioral Scientist* 4 (March–April 1968):50–55.
38. Milbrath, *Political Participation*, p. 18.

SELECTED READINGS

Abramson, Paul, Aldrich, John, and Rohde, David. *Change and Continuity in the 1980 Election*. Washington, D.C.: Congressional Quarterly Press, 1982. This book, the best one on this election, is destined to become a classic.

Asher, Herbert. *Presidential Elections and American Politics*. Homewood, Ill.: Dorsey Press, 1976. Asher analyzes presidential elections since 1952.

Burnham, Walter Dean. *Critical Elections and the Mainsprings of American Politics*. New York: Norton, 1970. Burnham argues that a realignment of party loyalties is probable.

Campbell, Angus, Converse, P., Miller, W., and Stokes, D. *The American Voter: An Abridgement*. New York: Wiley, 1964. An abridgement of the classic study of voting behavior in the United States conducted by the Survey Research Center at the University of Michigan.

Congressional Quarterly. *Dollar Politics*. Washington, D.C.: Congressional Quarterly, 1971. This short publication provides an excellent review of campaign fund raising, spending, and costs, as well as a chronological summary of federal legislation regulating campaign finances from 1945 through the 1971 Campaign Spending Act.

Flanigan, William H. *The Political Behavior of the American Electorate*, 2d ed. Boston: Allyn and Bacon, 1972. In this short book, Flanigan draws on a wide range of previous voting studies in explaining American voting behavior. Of particular interest are the discussions in chapters 3 and 4 on social, economic, and psychological correlates of voting.

Koggel, John. *Presidential Campaign Politics*. Homewood, Ill.: The Dorsey Press, 1980. Koggel offers a broad-ranging analysis of the 1960s and 1970s.

Levitin, Teresa, and Miller, Warren E. "Ideological Interpretations of Presidential Elections." *American Political Science Review* 73 (September 1979):751–771. Ideologies such as liberalism and conservatism have little utility in explaining voter choice.

Lipset, Seymour Martin. *Political Man*. Baltimore, Md.: Johns Hopkins University Press, 1981. This interpretation of American politics by an eminent political sociologist covers a myriad of factors that affect or are affected by the dynamics of political activity.

Milbrath, Lester. *Political Participation*. Chicago: Rand McNally, 1965. Milbrath presents a propositional survey of the literature on political participation through the early 1960s.

Miller, Warren E., and Levitin, Teresa E. *Leadership and Change: The New Politics and the American Electorate*. Cambridge, Mass.: Winthrop Publishers, 1976. This book analyzes George McGovern's defeat in 1972.

Nie, Norman H., Verba, Sidney, and Petrocik, John R. *The Changing American Voter*. Cambridge, Mass.: Harvard University Press, 1976. The authors discuss the decline of political parties and the rise of ideology as influences in individual voter choice.

Niemi, Richard, and Weisberg, Herbert, eds. *Controversies in American Voting Behavior*. San Francisco: Freeman, 1976. This book is the best collection of essays on the role of parties, issues, and candidate image.

Pomper, Gerald. *Elections in America: Control and Influence in Democratic Politics*. New York: Dodd, Mead, 1968. This outstanding study of the American electoral process analyzes voting behavior and assesses the impact of that behavior on public policy.

Pomper, Gerald. *Voters' Choice*. New York: Harper & Row, 1975. Pomper argues that elections have become and will continue to become more ideological.

Ranney, Austin, ed. *The American Election of 1980*. Washington, D.C.: American Enterprise Institute, 1982. These essays discuss the campaign, the election, and its meaning.

8 American Political Parties: A System in Decay

It is something of an irony that the parties, as agents of democratic decision making, are not themselves democratic in their structure.

Organization implies the tendency to oligarchy. Every party ... becomes divided into a minority of directors and a majority of directed.

—Roberto Michels, Political Parties, *1915*

The "Tweedledum and Tweedledee" image of American political parties contains a great deal of truth; the Democratic and the Republican parties do in fact share the same fundamental political ideology. Both parties reflect prevailing elite consensus on basic democratic values: the sanctity of private property, a free-enterprise economy, individual liberty, limited government, majority rule, and due process of law. Moreover, since the 1930s both parties have supported the public-oriented, mass-welfare domestic programs of the "liberal establishment": social security, fair labor standards, unemployment compensation, a graduated income tax, a national highway program, a federally aided welfare system, countercyclical fiscal and monetary policies, and government regulation of public utilities. Finally, both parties have supported the basic outlines of American foreign and military policy since World War II: international involvement, anticommunism, the cold war, European recovery, the North Atlantic Treaty Organization, military preparedness, selective service, and even the Korean and Vietnam wars. Rather than promoting competition over national goals and programs, the parties reinforce social consensus and limit the area of legitimate political conflict.[1]

The two parties: nuances within consensus

The major parties are not, of course, identical in ideology; their positions show nuances of difference. For instance, Republican leaders are "conservative" on domestic policy, while Democratic leaders are "liberal." Moreover, the social bases of the parties are slightly different. Both parties draw their support from all social groups in America, but the Democrats draw disproportionately from labor, urban workers, Jews, Catholics, and blacks, and the Republicans draw disproportionately from rural, small-town, and suburban Protestants, business interests, and professionals. (See table 8-1.) To the extent that the aspirations of these two broad groups differ, the thrust of party ideology also differs. This difference, however, is not very great. Democratic identifiers are only slightly more to the "left" than Republicans are. The more active partisans, however, are more ideologically distinct. Active Republicans and Democratic activists are more conservative and more liberal, respectively, than their less active colleagues. Still, all roads lead to the center; active partisans who fail to heed this lesson suffer the electoral consequences. However, since even active partisans cluster toward the center of the political spectrum (figure 8-1), only occasional aberrations, such as Goldwater in 1964 and McGovern in 1972, are likely to occur.

Both party's nominees, then, if they are to succeed, must appeal to the center, with Republicans safely offering somewhat more conservative alternatives on the various issues of the campaign. With only two parties and an overwhelmingly nonideological electorate, "consumer" demand (as perceived by leadership) requires that party ideologies be ambiguous and moderate. Therefore we cannot expect the parties, which seek to attract the maximum number of voters, to take up a cause supported by only a minority of the population.

Since parties seek political office, strong ideology and innovation are virtually out of the question. Firmer, more precise statements of ideology by the political parties would probably create new lines of cleavage and eventually fragment the parties. The development of a clear "liberal" or "conservative" ideology by either party would cost it votes.

Both Goldwater and McGovern in the presidential elections showed that a strong ideological stance will *not* win elections in America. In 1964 the Republicans offered a clear ideological alternative to the majority party that is notable in recent American political history. Goldwater, the Republican presidential candidate, specifically rejected moderation ("moderation in defense of liberty is no virtue") and defended extremism ("extremism in defense of liberty is no vice"). He rejected the "peace" image of Eisenhower in favor of an aggressive, military-oriented stance on foreign policy. The overwhelming 1964 defeat of this conservative position (which drew only 38 percent of the vote) counters the argument

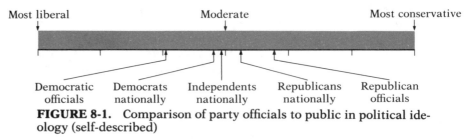

FIGURE 8-1. Comparison of party officials to public in political ideology (self-described)

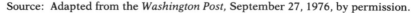

Source: Adapted from the *Washington Post*, September 27, 1976, by permission.

TABLE 8-1 Percent vote by groups in presidential elections, 1960–1980

	1960		1964		1968			1972		1976			1980		
	Kennedy	Nixon	Johnson	Gold-water	Hum-phrey	Nixon	Wallace	Mc-Govern	Nixon	Carter	Ford	Mc-Carthy	Reagan	Carter	Ander-son
National	50.1	49.9	61.3	38.7	43.0	43.4	13.6	38	62	50	48	1	51	41	7
Characteristics															
Sex															
Male	52	48	60	40	41	43	16	37	63	53	45	1	53	38	7
Female	49	51	62	38	45	43	12	38	62	48	51	a	46	45	7
Race															
White	49	51	59	41	38	47	15	32	68	46	52	1	54	36	7
Nonwhite	68	32	94	6	85	12	3	87	13	85	15	a	13	83	4
Education															
College	39	61	52	48	37	54	9	37	63	42	55	2	51	35	11
High school	52	48	62	38	42	43	15	34	66	54	46	a	51	44	3
Grade school	55	45	66	34	52	33	15	49	51	58	41	1	45	50	30
Occupation															
Professional and business	42	58	54	46	34	56	10	31	69	42	56	1	54	33	11
White collar	48	52	57	43	41	47	12	36	64	50	48	2	48	43	7
Manual	60	40	71	29	50	35	15	43	57	58	41	1	47	46	5
Age															
Under 30 years	54	46	64	36	47	38	15	48	52	53	45	1	43	43	11
30–49 years	54	46	63	37	44	41	15	33	67	48	49	2	55	33	11
50 years and older	46	54	59	41	41	47	12	36	64	52	48	a	55	36	5
Religion															
Protestants	38	62	55	45	35	49	16	30	70	46	53	a	62	32	5
Catholics	78	22	76	24	59	33	8	48	52	57	42	1	50	41	7
Politics															
Republicans	5	95	20	80	9	86	5	5	95	9	91	a	84	11	4
Democrats	84	16	87	13	74	12	14	67	33	82	18	a	25	67	6
Independents	43	57	56	44	31	44	25	31	69	38	57	4	54	30	12
Region															
East	53	47	68	32	50	43	7	42	58	51	47	1	47	43	9
Midwest	48	52	61	39	44	47	9	40	60	48	50	1	51	41	7
South	51	49	52	48	31	36	33	29	71	54	45	a	52	44	3
West	49	51	60	40	44	49	7	41	59	46	51	1	54	35	9
Members of labor union families	65	35	73	27	56	29	15	46	54	63	36	1	45	46	7

aLess than 1 percent.

Source: Gallup Opinion Index (December 1976): 16–17. Preliminary 1980 data courtesy of ISR and Congressional Quarterly.

Copyright 1980. United Features Syndicate, Inc. Reprinted by permission.

that the nonideological two-party system suppresses basic ideological cleavages within the masses; in fact in an election offering a clear ideological choice, the masses produced few ideologues to rally to the call.

A party with a "pure" liberal position can suffer disastrous defeat as well. In 1972 McGovern seriously overestimated the liberalism of the electorate. (He won only 38 percent of the vote.)

A superficial interpretation of Ronald Reagan's election in 1980 might conclude that his election ushered in an era of "radical" candidates; indeed his campaign rhetoric was as conservative as was Goldwater's in 1964. Can it be that 1980 marked a "massive shift to the right" (as the media claimed)? Actually, the voters were no more conservative in 1980 than they were in previous years: 31 percent claimed to be conservative, 18 percent liberal, and the rest (51 percent) moderate. So the center was still intact. As we have discussed, a conservative candidate won not because voters responded to his conservatism but because they wanted to make a statement against Carter's incompetence.

In fact the voters' self-proclaimed ideology more closely matched Carter's moderate stance at the beginning of the campaign; Reagan seemed "radical" to many. As the campaign proceeded, neither the voters nor their perception of Reagan changed, but Carter's image became substantially more liberal. Thus the public did not move to the right but simply believed that Carter had moved to the left.

Because the voters passionately wanted to throw out Jimmy Carter, they took Reagan—not necessarily his ideology—as the only alternative. Only 11 percent claimed to have voted for him because he was "a real conservative."[2]

Mass perceptions of the parties

Most voters perceive no difference between the two major parties on most issues. Their failure to discern a difference is not entirely because of voter ignorance, however; the party elites themselves have articulated no clear differences. The elites' strategy is rational, since few voters are issue-oriented and since most lean toward the center of the political spectrum when they do take a stand. Moreover elites see that many voters have no clear opinions on the issues, and therefore have no idea where the parties stand.

One way to discover voters' perceptions of parties is to ask respondents among the masses to volunteer issues that are "on their mind a lot" or cause them "extreme worry." If one asks which party is likely to do what "the people want" on the issue identified as most important by the respondent, the results are hardly encouraging. Since 1963 the largest proportion of voters have seen "no difference" between Democrats and Republicans on their most important problem. Many others are unable to identify a "problem" that the government should take care of. (See table 8-2.) Correctly or incorrectly, most people do not believe the parties offer realistic alternatives and therefore cannot relate policy or issue differences to their vote.

Political parties as organizations

Unlike European mass-membership parties, American parties are not organizations in the normal sense of the term. To be a Democrat or a Republican, a citizen need make no greater commitment to the organization than to occasionally support his or her party's nominees.

American parties do, of course, have an organization, consisting of formally chosen leadership, informal power holders (who do not hold government or party office), and party activists who contribute their time and money and acquire the right to help choose candidates in the party's name. However, neither political party has a hierarchical structure; each is decentralized, with no clear chain of command from national through state to local levels.

TABLE 8-2. Most important problem government should take care of: Which party has best position (percent of respondents)

	1964	1968	1972	1976	1980
Democrats	35	21	23	26	10
Republicans	19	30	24	10	39
No difference	21	35	41	36	41
Don't know	7	10	8	6	7
Wallace	—	2	1	—	—
No problem	18	3	3	22	3

Source: Inter-University Consortium for Political Research: Survey Research Center; CPS American National Election Studies.

Most relevant, however, is the interaction *between* the parties' core activist groups and the overwhelming majority of Democrats and Republicans who do not help formulate party objectives or select candidates (except in primaries). In fact, all but a tiny portion of the participants in the political system are consumers who simply accept or reject the product offered to them by the party activists. Their association with the party is thus entirely passive.

Ironically, then, the parties, as the agents of democratic decision making, are not themselves democratic in their structures. One of the most sweeping indictments of political parties on this count comes from the political philosopher Roberto Michels, whose "iron law of oligarchy" leads him to conclude that "every party . . . becomes divided into a minority of directors and a majority of directed."[3]

American political parties are skeletal organizations, "manned generally by small numbers of activists and involving the great masses of their supporters scarcely at all."[4] In essence, power in American parties rests in the hands of those who have the time and the money to make it a full-time, or nearly full-time, occupation. Party activists—no more than 3 or 4 percent of the adult population—can decide what product is to be offered to political consumers (the party in the electorate). Beyond this link, the party activists and electorate have little interaction.

Who are the party activists? We know, from research cited in previous chapters, that the activists are strongly ideological and committed to the norms of the democratic decision-making process. Since these characteristics describe the upper socioeconomic groups, it is not surprising that party activists are of relatively high socioeconomic status and come from families with a history of party activity. The highest socioeconomic levels are found in the highest echelons of the party organization. As Sorauf notes, "The parties . . . attract men and women with the time and financial resources to be able to afford politics, with the information and knowledge to understand it, and with the skills to be useful in it."[5]

Reflecting the basis of support among the party in the electorate, Democratic activists are of course somewhat lower in socioeconomic status than their Republican counterparts. Nevertheless, the socioeconomic status of both Democratic and Republican activists is above the average for the segment of the electorate they represent. This distinction between elite and mass is especially characteristic of American political parties.

But does it matter whether the parties are democratic in structure? If parties compete much as businesses do, the structural characteristics of each group of producers should not be important. Competitors, democratic or not, have the primary function of satisfying their customers. Yet the political alternatives offered by parties are much more constricted than those offered in business. Voters cannot choose from a number of competing products; they primarily have a choice between two. A voter who finds the product of one competitor unsatisfactory must either accept the single alternative or decline to become a consumer. Given the consensual nature of American parties, the range of alternatives is quite narrow.[6]

Presidential primaries and the deterioration of political parties

The decline in party identification among voters is possibly the most "dramatic change in the American public over the past two decades."[7] For political party organizations, the need to attract independent voters makes candidates with strong partisan "images" unattractive. However, not only have parties lost the loyalty of the masses; they have also lost control over the selection of candidates.

The deterioration of political parties is in part because of the "democraticization" of nominations through the presidential primary system. The growth of presidential primaries is an institutional change as important as the decline in party identification among the masses. In their efforts to make the party organization more responsive, Democratic reformers developed a set of rules for state nominating caucuses and conventions that were so complex that many states chose the primary election for selecting delegates to their national nominating conventions.

Consequently presidential primaries have increased beyond the original reformers' expectations. In 1968 the parties held seventeen presidential primaries. In 1972, the year of the reforms, they held twenty-three. Given the thrashing the Democrats received in 1972, one might have expected the party regulars to try to reverse the reforms. However, the presidential primary was too popular to banish. By 1976 thirty states held presidential primaries, and in 1980 the number had grown to thirty-six. By 1980 over three-fourths of all delegates were chosen by primaries. (See figure 8-2.) Though the Democrats have led the push toward democraticization, the Republicans have moved in the same direction. The

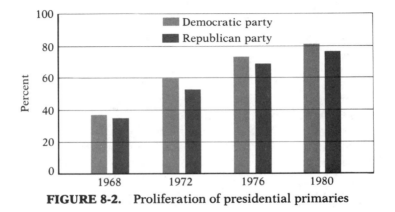

FIGURE 8-2. Proliferation of presidential primaries

increased use of primaries has been written into state law and now generally applies to both parties.

Given the expanded role of primaries, do "the voters" now select the presidential nominees? Actual participation in presidential primaries is far less than in general elections. While voting in general elections hovers around 50 percent, participation in presidential primaries does not exceed 30 percent of eligible voters. Clearly with an average turnout of this size, primaries do not, even in sheer numerical terms, represent the voice of "the people."

In low-turnout elections, the higher social classes are the primary participants. Such is the case in primary elections. Participants come disproportionately from the college-educated, professionally employed, upper-middle classes. In New York, for example, 41 percent of the Democratic primary electorate held professional or managerial jobs, a proportion far in excess of that for all registered Democrats. Conspicuously absent from the primary electorate are working-class voters and ethnic minorities. The primary electorate is "the New Class—the young, college educated, professional, and managerial groups."[8]

The primary season traditionally begins on February 26 in New Hampshire, a tiny state that has jealously guarded its position as the first state to hold a primary in a presidential year. The tradition certainly has nothing to do with the strategic importance of New Hampshire in terms of delegate strength. New Hampshire's voters account for less than 1 percent of all votes cast in Democratic primaries, and they choose less than 1 percent of the delegates to the Democratic convention. Were it not for the fact that New Hampshire kicks off the season, it would be ignored. However, the extensive media coverage in the state might lead one to conclude that New Hampshire is a crucial state in the general election. Thus New Hampshire *is* crucial—as a media event.

Primaries provide an ideal opportunity for the media to separate the serious candidates from the aspirants.[9] While the primary electorate is better educated and more ideologically sensitive than is the electorate in general elections, the issues are rarely well developed by candidates and even more rarely understood by the voters. Not only are early primaries frequently crowded by candidates, but the fact that the candidates are from the same party reduces the opportunity for exploring issues.

Thus candidate "image" becomes crucial. Before the primary season, candidates seek to establish credibility as serious contenders of presidential caliber. They attempt to establish name familiarity, as revealed in public opinion surveys, as serious candidates first, not necessarily as frontrunners. The proliferation of primaries and attendant media attention make it possible for a candidate to become well-known quickly. A reputation can be created by "a strong organization, plenty of funds, shrewd advisors, an appealing campaign style, and a good image on television, even if his position on issues is not well known and

Roy Doty/*Newsweek*

is likely to antagonize many voters once they have become familiar with it."[10]

The absence of party labels and the importance of television are complementary. Television news is more personalized than printed media. Foreign policy can become a test of wills between strong personalities, for example. Candidates are driven to find some device—a slogan, a theme—to make them visible and different. And the media help them in this endeavor: If the media find something dramatic about a candidate, they will magnify it because television journalism thrives on the sensational. Carter in 1976 became the "outsider" who rose from obscurity. Edward Kennedy in 1980 was the "last of a dynasty." In 1980 the public policy positions of Kennedy and Carter were, for all practical purposes, irrelevant. The main issue decided in the New Hampshire primary was one of "leadership." Which of the two candidates would be "steady" under the pressures of the job?

The primary season coincided perfectly with President Carter's rapidly changing political fortunes in 1980. He faced almost certain defeat by Senator Kennedy until the seizure of American hostages in Iran in November 1979. Immediately thereafter, enjoying the "rally 'round the flag" sentiment characteristic of American voters, his popularity improved dramatically. On the day the Iranians seized the hostages, Kennedy was the focus of a CBS special report. He appeared vacuous and confused, with no clear idea of why he wanted to be president. Three days later, he declared his candidacy in a rare instance of bad timing. Not only was Carter on a roll because of Iran, but the Kennedy interview had dredged up once again the personal problems that had plagued the senator for more than a decade: Chappaquiddick, his strained marriage—the "personal factor."

Carter, as was his custom, emphasized issues of leadership and judgment rather than policy. He came in first in New Hampshire, winning 47 percent versus Kennedy's 39 percent. Governor Brown of California, with a dismal 10 percent, withdrew shortly thereafter.

An analysis of the New Hampshire vote illustrates Carter's good fortune: 70 percent of those voters who emphasized personal qualities voted for him, while 65 percent of those who emphasized policy qualities voted for Kennedy.[11] Since the primary coverage completely overshadowed policy issues, the result was inevitable. Even Catholics preferred Carter. However, in focusing on the battle between personalities, the media ignored the fact that the incumbent president had achieved less than a majority, which may have been an early sign of Carter's inherent weakness. Although Carter's popularity once again began to wane, the New Hampshire primary assured his nomination. When he beat Kennedy in Illinois three weeks later, the media declared the contest over.

Reagan also owed much to New Hampshire. Narrowly beaten by George Bush in the earlier Iowa caucuses (not primaries), he could present himself in New Hampshire as the underdog. Bush, Howard Baker, and John Anderson also campaigned hard. By winning half the votes in New Hampshire, Reagan finished off everybody but Bush, who came in second, and Anderson, who, while gaining only 10 percent of the vote, would not quit (he received liberal contributions that normally would have gone to Senator Kennedy). Thus Reagan emerged as the only leader of the conservative Republicans, while the moderates could find no one to give him a serious challenge. (Bush and Anderson continued to compete for the same votes.) The apparent certain victory of the conservative wing of the party led former President Gerald Ford openly to invite a draft. Claiming that Reagan was too conservative to beat Carter, he courted the moderates. Although surveys consistently indicated that Ford would do better against Carter than would Reagan, the primary system prevented him from mounting a serious candidacy. He could not possibly assemble the organization he needed to challenge Reagan's momentum in the primaries.

Because the actual results of the first primary are likely to be ambiguous, the media can declare a victory. Essentially if a candidate does better than public opinion surveys suggest, the media tend to consider the candidate the "winner." A strong showing, not necessarily an actual victory, in this first primary can multiply the votes in primaries occurring shortly thereafter. Thus a "media victory" in New Hampshire can propel a little-known candidate into national prominence. The voters respond to the impression of strength created by the media's focus on the newly created "leading national candidate." In March, a few weeks after the New Hampshire primary, Massachusetts and Florida hold primary elections. If a candidate can achieve similar media victories in one or both of these states, he or she gets a major boost toward the party nomination.

The consequence of the primary system is that political party leaders—governors, senators, the heads of state party organizations, and the like—cannot control the selection of presidential candidates. Without the anchor of party identification, public opinion becomes more volatile, more liable to media manipulation. Presidents and candidates do not develop issues; they respond to events or present themselves in a highly personalized way. Politics without parties becomes even more issueless than it was in the past. The primary system has been a major factor in the demise of parties and the creation of the new media elite: "Because the competing candidates often share most ideological orientations, personal attributes such as appearance, style, and wit attain new importance (presidents today must be fit and not fat, amusing not dull, with cool not hot personalities)."[12]

Convention delegates are *not* representative of "rank-and-file" party voters. First, primary voters attract a disproportionate number of college-educated professionals. Second, party activists are more likely to be "ideologues" than are other voters. Republican convention delegates, for example, are more likely to hold a consistent conservative position on issues than are the mass of Republican voters. And, as shown in table 8-3, Democratic delegates to presidential nominating conventions are significantly more "liberal" in their attitudes than are all Democratic voters.[13]

Rise of the independent voter

Many people on both the left and right in American politics are deserting the Democratic and Republican parties. To be sure, substantial evidence suggests that the poor and the blacks were never wholly within the two-party system in the first place. (Data on nonvoting indicate that a major-

TABLE 8-3.   Convention delegates' opinions compared with voters'

	Democratic delegates	Democratic voters	Republican delegates	Republican voters
No one should live in poverty (percent agreeing)	57	22	10	13
Persons able to work should be required to work (percent agreeing)	69	28	75	79
Most important to protect rights of accused (percent agreeing)	78	36	21	28
Attitude toward military (percent favorable)	42	67	84	71

Average differences:
Democratic delegates/Democratic voters: 39%
Republican delegates/Republican voters: 7%
Republican voters/Democratic voters: 16%
Republican delegates/Democratic delegates: 42%

Source: Survey by NBC News/Associated Press, April 1982. (See *Public Opinion*, December/January, 1982, p. 36.)

ity of blacks and a majority of poor—families of four earning less than $8,500 per year—do not participate in American party politics.)

Several trends indicate that the established parties have decayed, but the chief sign is decline in voter participation. The decline of political parties reflects a continuing deterioration of partisan loyalty—along with trust—which began before Watergate, probably during the turbulent confrontation politics of the 1960s. The percentage of voters who refuse to identify themselves with either party is increasing. (See table 8-4.) By 1976 the proportion of independents had increased to 36 percent; Democratic identifiers had stabilized at 39 percent and Republican identifiers had declined to 24 percent.

One explanation of the growth of independents is the greater proportion of younger, weaker partisans that has occurred primarily because of the low minimum voting age of eighteen. The age composition of

TABLE 8-4.   Changes in voter party identification, 1952–1982

	1952	1982	Percent change
Democrat			
Strong	22	15	− 14
Weak	25	6	− 19
Independent[a]			
Democrat	10	9	− 1
Independent	5	21	+ 16
Republican	7	12	+ 5
Republican			
Strong	15	14	+ 1
Weak	14	13	− 1

[a]These entries indicate the major party with which respondent most identified.

Source: Survey Research Center, University of Michigan.

independents makes this clear. (See figure 8-3.) As for the ultimate, long-term partisan commitment of the independents, each election year, first-time voters have been progressively more independent. But will these younger voters lose their independence as they age? The political parties must face the possibility that their respective strengths may alter significantly, more because the electorate changes in composition than because individuals change partisan identification. As Miller and Levitin observe, "If the young Independents, and the Independents who follow them into the electorate, are never persuaded to establish party ties, the future of the Republican and even the Democratic party may become problematic."[14]

Political campaigns and party voting

If most voters cannot perceive the alternative policy positions of political parties, what do campaigns accomplish? Candidates confer extensively with their advisers, plan elaborate political statements, and make public appearances to discuss the issues they feel are important to the election. The presentation of their ideologies actually produces more voter support than do the ideologies themselves; the candidate's image, not his or her proposed policies, affects voter choice.

Why, then, do candidates travel about the nation speaking mostly to audiences who already support them? They do so to ensure that their supporters turn out to vote on election day. Since more than two-thirds of the potential voters have already made up their minds before the campaign begins, this mobilization of the faithful becomes the most important strategy of the political campaign. To understand why, consider the concept of the *normal vote:* the division of the vote that would occur if party identification were unaffected by such short-term forces as issue orientation and candidate identification.[15] For example, if Democratic and Republican candidates had no "image" impact, if the issues

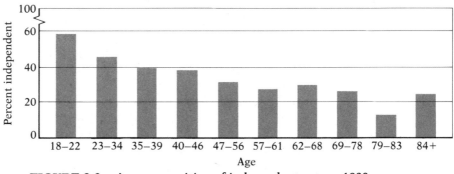

FIGURE 8-3. Age composition of independent voters, 1980

Source: Survey Research Center, University of Michigan.

were of no relevance, and if the turnout for each party matched predictions, the normal vote for the Democrats would be 54 percent of the total. Thus the normal vote is a model, not an actual occurrence, but like any other model, it helps in understanding reality. In this case it is a guideline for assessing the impact of a campaign, specifically for measuring how well the candidates mobilized their supporters. The normal vote model is able to do this because it takes into account predicted voter turnout. Thus the normal vote for any party is not the same as party identification.

For Democratic candidates, the campaign strategy is simply to guarantee that Democratic identifiers maintain their preferences. Since more voters are Democratic identifiers than Republican identifiers, the Democrats will win, barring short-term forces. For Republican candidates, the strategy is to deflect independents and weak Democrats from their partisan affiliation, persuading them to vote more on issues or on perception of candidates. Thus a presidential candidate's strategy can begin with a simple calculation. Approximately 39 percent of the population identify with the Democratic party, 24 percent identify with the Republican party, and 36 percent regard themselves as independents. However, the dominance of Democratic identifiers is complicated by two factors: the question of the stability and reliability of partisan attitudes, and turnout.

Partisan attitudes are generally stable; individual voters rarely change their party affiliation. Although the percentage of independents is increasing and that of party identifiers decreasing, it is because the new, younger voters have poorly developed party affiliations, not because older voters are converting from one party to another. Such conversion is extremely rare.

The increased role of the independent voters adds an element of volatility in presidential elections. During such elections independents, who are not tied to parties and who respond primarily to short-term forces such as candidate image, contribute to the surge and decline in the distribution of votes.

Finally, although an individual's party identification may remain stable, individual Democratic and Republican identifiers increasingly have voted for an opposing party's candidate. Since 1960 the correlation between party identification and party voting has gradually weakened.

Strategic considerations must take into account the second complicating factor of partisan identification: turnout. Despite the preponderance of Democratic identifiers, variations in turnout can favor Republican candidates. Since Republican voters typically are of higher socioeconomic status than are Democratic voters, their turnout rates are substantially higher. Hence, "getting out the vote" is a Democratic strategy, while stimulating short-term defection from party affiliation is a Republican strategy.

Reprinted by permission: Tribune Company Syndicate, Inc.

Creating a favorable image

Candidates seek to create a positive image of themselves or a negative image of their opponents. Hence most campaign energy focuses on image making, not issue making. This choice is further enhanced by the rise of television as the most important source of campaign information—which it is for more than two-thirds of the voters, especially among the less educated, for whom it is the only source of information about candidates. Thus the shift has occurred among passive media users. Voters with more education supplement television viewing by reading newspapers and magazines, which provides more thorough analyses of candidates' positions. Just as candidates favor images rather than issues, so do television newscasters in their competitive bids for higher ratings.

Money and politics

Political campaigns cost money, usually far more than candidates themselves are willing or able to spend. In 1980 Reagan and Carter each spent $30 million on the general election. Earlier each candidate had spent additional millions in the Republican and Democratic primaries. But in 1972 Richard Nixon spent $60 million in his reelection campaign, and his opponent McGovern spent $30 million. Few candidates can even begin a political career for state or local office without first securing financial support from wealthy "angels." The farsighted among the wealthy may choose to back a promising young politician in early career and continue this support for many years.* Few representatives or senators are without wealthy sponsors.

Democrats usually receive less money than Republicans from the corporate world, although about half of Democratic funds come from corporations. Traditionally Democrats have turned to big labor for support, notably to the Committee on Political Education (COPE) of the AFL-CIO and the larger international unions like the United Auto Workers and United Steel Workers. Liberal Democrats have also received support from upper-class liberal philanthropists.

Nevertheless chronic Democratic campaign deficits were a stimulus to campaign "reform," especially when Democrats overwhelmingly controlled both houses of Congress with a close presidential election approaching. In 1974, Congress passed a comprehensive campaign spending law that created a Presidential Election Campaign Fund from voluntary one-dollar-per-person check-offs from individual income taxes, and established the Federal Election Commission (two members selected by the House, two by the Senate, and two by the president) to oversee federal election spending. The election commission distributes campaign monies from the fund (1) to candidates in the primaries (who could raise $5,000 in each of twenty states); (2) to the Democratic and Republican parties for their national conventions; and (3) to the Republican and Democratic candidates in the general election. The law also limits individual contributions in any election to $1,000 and organizational contributions to $5,000. Candidates must report all contributions to the Federal Election Commission.

The Supreme Court modified these provisions by declaring that, as an exercise of First Amendment rights, an individual can spend unlimited personal wealth on his or her own election campaign.[16] Moreover, also as an exercise of First Amendment rights, a person may spend any amount of personal wealth to advertise his or her own political views. As long as these independent expenditures are not tied directly to a political campaign, no legal limits apply. While the campaign spending law, as modified by the Supreme Court, reduces the role of the large financial "angels," it permits wealthy people to spend large amounts on their own campaigns, thus keeping direct exercise of political power, as well as control of the parties, in the hands of the elites.

Although modified several times (most recently in 1979), the campaign finance laws remained unchanged in essentials. But the tax check-

---

*Richard Nixon was long supported by Chicago insurance tycoon W. Clement Stone. George McGovern was backed for many years by Stewart Mott, heir to the General Motors fortune. Jimmy Carter was backed in his early races in Georgia by J. Paul Austin, chairman of the board of Coca-Cola; Charles Kirbo, Atlanta attorney; and Thomas B. (Bert) Lance, former president of the National Bank of Georgia and director of the Office of Management and Budget during part of the Carter administration. For many years the "Ronald Reagan Trust Fund" has been overseen by men like William French Smith of Crocker National Bank and Justin Dart, owner of Rexall Drugs.

off system and public funding guidelines apply *only* to presidential elections. Congressional elections still depend on private funds and are becoming very expensive. This expense, and the provisions of the election finance laws affecting political action committees (PACs), have revolutionized campaign finance. Before the campaign reforms, corporations could not use their funds to form political action committees, though curiously unions could form such committees (one of the most famous is the AFL-CIO's Committee for Political Education).

The campaign reform act lifted the prohibition against corporate spending; amendments in 1974 permitted corporations and unions with government contracts to form political action committees, and 1976 amendments placed modest restraints on PACs. Corporate PACs can seek contributions from stockholders, executives, administrative personnel, and their families. Unions can solicit only from union members or their families. Twice a year, however, the law allows an "open season." Ideological PACs, such as the National Conservative Political Action Committee, are apparently subject to less careful monitoring.

Since congressional elections do not receive public funding and in effect have no ceiling on spending (given liberal interpretation of the law), much PAC money has gone here. However, even though presidential elections operate with some public funds (with special limits) during the primaries (that is, each candidate receives federal funds according to the amount of money raised from individual contributions), and general elections operate with full public funding for major party candidates, these limits are illusory: The law allows unlimited spending on "independent" efforts (those not connected with the candidate's organization). In 1980, each candidate received $29.4 million in federal funds. However, "independent" contributions exceeded $16 million, most of which went to the Reagan campaign.

The spiraling costs of campaigns: Who pays?

In 1982 the cost of congressional campaigns exceeded $300 million, an increase from $40 million in 1972. Of the 1982 total, direct PAC contributions accounted for $70 million. These contributions came from 3300 PACs, an increase from about 600 such organizations a decade ago. Since no limit exists for contributions made outside candidates' organizations, these figures are at best an approximation. The two wealthiest PACs in terms of money raised are the Congressional Club, Senator Jesse Helms' (R–N.C.) personal organization, and the National Conservative Political Action Committee. Neither PAC is in the top ten for contributions to candidates. Ideological groups do spend a great deal of money in massive fund-raising drives, membership recruitment, and handsome salaries for their staffs. Even so, one can assume that they spent much of their money "independently" in support of candidates or, in the case of "negative campaigning," in opposition to them.

Reported PAC contributions amounted to 25 percent of all costs in 1982, up from 16 percent in 1980. While these sums are not staggering, they are substantially greater than the amounts contributed by political party organizations. The Republican National Committee, relying on a well-developed network of direct-mail contributors, spent $169 million in 1982. The Democrats, far less organized, spent only $23 million. The sum of all party contributions was over $100 million less than total PAC contributions. (See table 8-5.)

One-fourth the members of the House of Representatives, including the Speaker of the House and the minority leader, raised more than half their 1982 campaign money from PACs. The chairman of the House Appropriations Committee, Jamie Whitten (D–Miss.) raised 75 percent of his money from PACs, followed by minority leader Robert Michel (R–Ill.), who raised 68 percent. Since PACs like to back winners, they focus upon incumbents, especially those with key assignments. PACs assumed one-third the campaign costs of 1982 winners, for example. Since Democrats have controlled the House in recent years, they benefit from PAC money. In 1982 even corporate PACs favored incumbent Democrats, giving them 44 percent of their contributions, up 10 percent since 1980. Considering that labor's overwhelming preference for Democrats combines with PAC spending, the "party of the little man" has some big spenders. How big is big? Newly elected Senator Pete Wilson (R–Calif.) spent $6.9 million. In the House, Barney Frank (D–Mass.) spent $1.5 million. (See table 8-6.)

Where do the dollars go?

What does all this money buy? It does not necessarily buy victory. Conspicuous examples of expensive defeats include Mark Dayton of Minnesota, who spent $7 million in an unsuccessful Senate campaign, and Adam Levin of New Jersey, who spent $1.5 million yet failed to defeat the Republican House incumbent. Senator William Proxmire (D–Wisc.), on the other hand, reported *no* expenses yet won. Money does not guarantee victory, but it does guarantee the *opportunity* for victory. Politics is a big, expensive business. Increasingly, PACs want to reduce risks by contributing to campaigns with a good chance of success. Candidates therefore end up hiring expensive consultants—media experts, pollsters, direct mail specialists, and advertising consultants—to give their cam-

TABLE 8-5. Congressional campaign costs: 1972–1982 (millions of dollars)

	1972	1974	1976	1978	1980	1982
Senate	26	29	46	87	103	128
House	40	45	79	111	136	172
Total	66	74	125	198	239	300

Source: Federal Election Commission.

TABLE 8-6.   The biggest spenders in the 1982 congressional election

Senate		House	
1. Mark Dayton (D–Minn.)	$7,124,012	1. Adam Levin (D–N.J.)	$1,914,171
2. Pete Wilson (R–Calif.)[a]	$6,910,554	2. Barney Frank (D–Mass.)[a]	$1,478,566
3. Jerry Brown (D–Calif.)	$5,323,627	3. Cissy Baker (R–Tenn.)	$1,195,331
4. Frank Lautenberg (D–N.J.)[a]	$5,211,994	4. Tom Lantos (D–Calif.)[a]	$1,166,358
5. Lloyd Bentsen (D–Tex.)[a]	$4,886,543	5. Johnie Crean (R–Calif.)[a]	$1,139,329
6. James Collins (R–Tex.)	$4,094,876	6. John Rousselot (R–Calif.)	$ 957,570
7. David Durenberger (R–Minn.)[a]	$3,863,462	7. Margaret Heckler (R–Mass.)	$ 954,888
8. Orrin Hatch (R–Utah)[a]	$3,336,509	8. Jim Cooper (D–Tenn.)[a]	$ 883,829
9. Richard Lugar (R–Ind.)[a]	$2,918,333	9. Ronald Dellums (D–Calif.)[a]	$ 834,224
10. Howard Metzenbaum (D–Ohio)[a]	$2,753,970	10. Morris Udall (D–Ariz.)[a]	$ 822,628

[a]Winner.

Note: Figures are expenditures between January 1, 1981, and November 22, 1982.

Source: Federal Election Commission.

paigns appeal. Not only do the consultants charge a lot (perhaps $1,000 per day), but the technology they employ—computers, interviews, and television—is costly. Moreover, surveys, depending on their sophistication, range from a few dollars per person to over $200 per person. In close elections, some candidates have paid for daily surveys, seeking to monitor every nuance of voter reaction. Because consultants need success in order to build their reputations, they too shun struggling candidates and prefer not to worry about money. One student of consulting concludes that "you need $150,000 just to get in the door to see a consultant."[17]

Indeed consultants, fueled by PACs, are far more important to candidates than are political parties. Not only have they usurped the role of parties in the campaign (volunteer doorbell ringers are fast becoming a relic of the past), but they also encourage candidates to deemphasize issues and concentrate on image. The "three p's"—polling, packaging, and promotion—are more important than parties, grass-roots support, and the development of strong positions on the issues. Although consultants do have ideological preferences, and some have strong partisan loyalties, they are, like most professionals, interested more in the results. They have formed a professional association and are somewhat akin to attorneys in their clubby approach to each other. To them, politics is a game to be won.

The return of the "fat cats"

Although the political action committees foot a good part of the bill, wealthy individual candidates, unrestrained by campaign contribution limitations, are still in a strong position after the "reforms." Those who have the $150,000 to get into a consultant's office can be off and running early in a campaign. Wealthy candidates, armed with their consultants, can meet startup costs promptly and attract the attention of the political action committees. Personal expenditures by candidates in 1982 reached almost obscene levels: Mark Dayton spent almost $6.9 million of his own money, and Adam Levin spent $1.7 million. The most conspicuously successful personally financed campaign was that of Frank Lautenberg, who spent $4 million of his own money to defeat Millicent Fenwick in New Jersey in a Senate contest. This level of spending is of course an exception; the average campaign, however, cost $600,000 in 1982.

Whatever the reformers' goals, their work has made the electoral process even more the property of elites—the wealthy candidates, consultants, and political action committees. Party "bosses" are gone, but other elites have replaced them; these new political powers respond to campaigns as high technology business ventures. As a result, elections have become the more trivial, with image overshadowing issues. Parties and candidates trot out a stable of celebrities to trumpet their causes. The Republicans can rely on the Hollywood old timers, such as Bob Hope and the late John Wayne; Democrats can depend upon Robert Redford and Edward Asner. Candidates, once elected, are not necessarily beholden to their benefactors. Before the reform, evidence of vote buying was scant. After the reform, the case for congressional independence from campaign contributors is more difficult to sustain.

Summary

Elitism asserts that elites share a consensus about the fundamental values of the political system. This elite consensus does not mean that elite members never disagree or never compete with each other for preeminence. But elitism implies that competition centers on a narrow range of issues and that elites agree on more matters than they disagree. The single elite model suggests that parties agree about the direction of public policy and disagree only on minor details. Our analysis of the American party system suggests the following propositions:

1. American parties share consensus both on basic democratic values and on major directions of American policy. They believe in the sanctity of private property, the free enterprise economy, individual liberty, and limited government. Moreover, both parties have supported the same general domestic and foreign policies—including social security, a graduated income tax, countercyclical fiscal and monetary policies, anticommunism, the cold war, and the Korean and Vietnam wars.

2. The American parties do not present clear ideological alternatives to the American voter. Both major parties are overwhelmingly mid-

dle class in organization, values, and goals. Deviation from the shared consensus by either party is more likely to lose than attract voters.

3. Both parties draw support from all social groups in America, but the Democrats draw disproportionately from labor, workers, Jews, Catholics, and blacks, and the Republicans draw disproportionate support from rural, small-town, and suburban Protestants, business interests, and professionals.

4. Democratic and Republican party leaders differ over public policy more than do Democratic or Republican mass followers. The consensus about welfare economics extends to Democratic leaders, Democratic followers, and Republican followers; only the Republican leadership is outside this consensus, with a more laissez-faire position. However, all party differences observed fall well within the range of elite consensus on the values of individualism, capitalism, and limited government.

5. American parties are dominated by small groups of activists who formulate party objectives and select candidates for public office. The masses play a passive role in party affairs. They are not really "members" of the party; they are "consumers."

6. Party activists differ from the masses because they have the time and financial resources to be able to "afford" politics, the information and knowledge to understand it, and the organization and public relations skills to be successful in it.

7. The choice of party nominees is a choice of party activists, not a choice of the masses of party members.

8. Political party identification is reasonably stable. However, there has been a rapid growth of independents in recent years, particularly among younger voters.

9. Political campaigns are designed to focus on images of candidates, not issues. They are also designed to increase the turnout of a candidate's supporters.

10. The "normal vote" in America today is Democratic. Republicans must stress image rather than party identification in a campaign. Democrats must stress "getting out the vote" among their more numerous party loyalists.

11. Congress has reduced the role of large campaign contributors in presidential elections through a system of public financing of elections.

NOTES

1. See Walter Dean Burnham, "The Changing Shape of the American Political Universe," *American Political Science Review* 59 (March 1965):28, and Walter Dean Burnham, "Party Systems and the Political Process," in William Nisbet Cham-

bers and Walter Dean Burnham, eds., *The American Party Systems: Stages of Political Development* (New York: Oxford University Press, 1967), pp. 305–307.

2. Walter Dean Burnham, "The 1980 Earthquake: Realignment, Reaction, or What?" in Thomas Ferguson and Joel Rogers, eds., *The Hidden Election* (New York: Pantheon Books, 1981), p. 107.

3. Roberto Michels, *Political Parties: A Sociological Study of the Oligarchical Tendencies of Modern Democracy* (1915; reprint, New York: Dover, 1959), p. 32.

4. Frank J. Sorauf, *Party Politics in America* (Boston: Little, Brown, 1968), pp. 79–80.

5. Ibid., p. 94.

6. See the consideration of the party-voter-as-business-firm–customer relationship in Robert A. Dahl, *Pluralist Democracy in the United States: Conflict and Consent* (Chicago: Rand-McNally, 1967), pp. 247–252.

7. Norman E. Nie, Sidney Verba, and John R. Petrocik, *The Changing American Voter* (Cambridge, Mass.: Harvard University Press, 1976), p. 47.

8. Everett C. Ladd, *Where Have All the Voters Gone?* (New York: Norton, 1978), p. 63.

9. Austin Ranney, *The Federalization of Presidential Primaries* (Washington, D.C.: American Enterprise Institute, 1978), p. 20.

10. Malcolm E. Jewell, "A Caveat on the Expanding Use of Presidential Primaries," *Policy Studies Journal* (Summer 1974):282.

11. Gerald Pomper, *The Election of 1980* (Chatham, N.J.: Chatham House Publishers, 1980), p. 28.

12. Jeane Kirkpatrick, *Dismantling the Parties* (Washington, D.C.: American Enterprise Institute, 1978), p. 7.

13. Denis G. Sullivan, Jeffrey C. Pressman, Benjamin I. Page, and John J. Lyons, *The Politics of Representation: The Democratic Convention of 1972* (New York: St. Martin's Press, 1974), p. 124.

14. Warren E. Miller and Teresa E. Levitin, *Leadership and Change: The New Politics and the American Electorate* (Cambridge, Mass.: Winthrop Publishers, 1976), p. 200.

15. Ibid., p. 37.

16. *Buckley* v. *Valeo*, 424 U.S. 1 (1976).

17. Norman Ornstein, quoted in *Newsweek* (November 8, 1982):31.

SELECTED READINGS

Alexander, Herbert. *Financing Politics*. Washington, D.C.: Congressional Quarterly Press, 1980. This book clearly explains the intricacies of the campaign finance reform legislation.

Crotty, William T. *Political Reform and the American Experiment*. New York: T. Y. Crowell, 1977. This book is a provocative analysis of reform, including reform in political parties, as cyclical, frequently resulting in unanticipated consequences.

Downs, Anthony. *An Economic Theory of Democracy*. New York: Harper & Row, 1959. Downs develops an abstract model of party politics based on traditional democratic political theory. He discusses the relationships among voters, parties, and governmental policy according to the democratic model and deduces empirical propositions.

Eldersveld, Samuel. *Political Parties in American Society* (New York: Basic Books, 1982). Eldersveld discusses parties as organizations, as policy makers, and as competitors for votes, emphasizing changes in their impact on government and elections.

Key, V. O., Jr. *Politics, Parties, and Pressure Groups*. New York: T. Y. Crowell, 1967. This work is a classic discussion of American party politics. Key traces the historical development of our present parties and discusses their role in the political system.

King, Anthony, ed. *The New American Political System*. Washington, D.C.: American Enterprise Institute, 1978. This indispensable collection of original essays is essential to understanding the decline of parties, the impact of primaries, the new intellectuals, and the growth of independence.

Ladd, Everett C., Jr. *American Political Parties*. New York: Norton, 1970. Ladd offers a historical treatment of the consensual nature of American parties.

Ladd, Everett C., Jr. *Where Have All the Voters Gone?* 2nd ed. New York: Norton, 1982. This brief, very readable book highlights recent changes in parties and elections.

Lipset, Seymour Martin, ed. *Party Coalitions in the 1980s* (San Francisco: Institute for Contemporary Studies, 1981). This book contains, among other valuable essays, thoughtful remarks by Reagan's and Carter's principal consultants.

Pomper, Gerald. *Elections in America: Control and Influence in Democratic Politics*. New York: Dodd, Mead, 1968. In focusing on the link between electoral behavior and public policy, Pomper discusses at some length the role of political parties, historically and within the contemporary context. Chapters 5, 7, and 8 are the most useful adjuncts to this chapter of *Irony*.

Ranney, Austin. *Curing the Mischiefs of Faction*. Berkeley: University of California Press, 1975. This book of essays focuses on the role of political parties in maintaining political stability.

Sorauf, Frank J. *Party Politics in America*, 2nd ed. Boston: Little, Brown, 1972. Sorauf employs the organizing concept of the political system in this theoretical work. He focuses on the parties within the American political system—their structure and the functions they perform.

9 Organized Interests: Defenders of the Status Quo

It is widely believed that Americans are joiners, and a majority of the population in fact belongs to at least one formal organization. Yet membership in organized interest groups is clearly linked to socioeconomic status.

There is overwhelming evidence that participation in voluntary organizations is related to upper social and economic status ... The flaw in the pluralist heaven is that the heavenly chorus sings with a strong upper class accent.

—E.E. Schattschneider, The Semi-Sovereign People, *1960*

Organized interest groups, not "the people," have the most direct influence over government. The "public interest" is a fiction, but the organized interests are potent political realities, in Washington, state capitals, and city halls. Interest-group activity, including lobbying, is generally protected by the First Amendment to the U.S. Constitution—"the right of the people peaceably to assemble and to petition the government for redress of grievances." But how democratic is the interest-group system? Do interest groups represent "the people" fairly? Or is the interest-group system a means of elite control over government?

Interest groups: Democratic or elite?

Pluralists contend that interest groups perform several important functions for their members and for a democratic society. First, the organized group links the individual and the government. Political scientists Gabriel Almond and Sidney Verba state:

> Voluntary associations are the prime means by which the function of mediating between the individual and the state is performed. Through them the individual is able to relate himself effectively and meaningfully to the political system.[1]

But is mediation by an organized group any more efficient than direct citizen-government interaction? Why do we need a "middleman"?

Pluralists also argue that interest groups enhance individual well-being. In a complex society, with primary associations (small groups, such as the family) diminishing in importance, secondary associations (less intimate but more goal-oriented) may help people overcome the sense of powerlessness characteristic of mass societies. Groups help integrate the individual with society.

Finally, the pluralists feel that interest groups help reduce potentially divisive conflicts. According to the theory of overlapping group memberships, all citizens are members of groups (unorganized and organized).[2] Each person is a product of group affiliations; a person may be, for example, a lawyer, a southerner, a military veteran, and a Protestant, with each affiliation imposing its own values. No single group affiliation could claim the individual's total, undivided loyalty. Hence multiple group affiliations help modify the demands of any one group and reduce societal conflict. This theory, however, is hard to prove. Because it is difficult to measure affiliation with unorganized groups, the conflict-reducing function of interest groups is also difficult to test.

Thus the theory that interest groups are "bad" because they oppose the "public interest" is no longer in favor. Pluralism now considers groups "good" because (1) they provide a more effective voice for citizens who are competing for resources; (2) they reduce the anxiety produced by feelings of powerlessness; and (3) they provide an element of stability.

But the pluralist theory of interest groups significantly transforms democratic theory. No longer is the emphasis on individual participation; individuals who want something from a government must pool their resources in organized group activity to get it. Indeed thousands of organizations make demands on Congress, administrative agencies, state legislatures, city councils, and even school boards. A glance at the list of registered lobbyists in Washington and in various state capitals gives credence to the argument. Each group, or potential group, is free to organize. Consequently organization produces counterorganization. In the process of resolving group demands, each interest has a voice, and public policy forms in response to these competitive demands. Interest groups, then, serve pluralistic democracy well by ensuring that government decision makers respond to the claims of the various groups. The competition among the groups gives pluralism its most frequently stated defense. Pluralistic interest group theory does not deny the existence of elites but contends that each elite is specialized, representing a set of mass demands and counterbalanced by a set of opposing demands.

However, the pluralist interest-group theory rests on several assumptions that may or may not be correct:

1. Membership in organizations is widespread and thus broadly represents all individual interests.
2. Organized groups efficiently translate members' expectations into political demands; nothing is lost in the translation, and members gain a great deal by presenting demands through a representative association.
3. Although interest groups are not always and uniformly successfully (some win and some lose), each group, whatever its demands, has equal access to the political resources necessary for success.
4. Organizations help make individuals politically effective; thus they strengthen the social fabric.

We shall refute the first three of these assumptions; and, although the fourth assumption is true, we will argue that *because* groups strengthen the social fabric, they guide their members toward accepting the status quo. We suggest that interest groups, rather than articulating the demands of masses, protect the values of established elites.

How widespread is interest-group affiliation?

Common wisdom has it that Americans are joiners and that a majority of the population in fact belongs to at least one formal organization. Yet membership in organized interest groups is clearly linked to socioeconomic status. Membership is greatest among the professional and managerial classes, college-educated and high-income persons. The upper-middle and upper classes are the primary joiners of organized groups.[3]

The class bias of organized groups varies according to the organization. Unions (which frequently are not voluntary) and the Ku Klux Klan recruit from the lower strata. Middle-class blacks lead civil rights organizations; the masses of blacks are uninvolved. For example, the National Association for the Advancement of Colored People represents the moderate black establishment, not the blacks in urban ghettos, who are more likely to take direct and unorganized action if they participate. Liberal causes, such as the women's movement and Common Cause, draw disproportionately from the university-educated and academically connected liberal establishment and rarely appeal to the lower classes. The social bias in association membership, whether or not the association is political, is complemented by the high social origins of lobbyists and the predominance of business organizations in *effective* lobbying.

This bias has obvious implications for the functions of interest groups. Their activities are mostly for the upper-middle and upper classes, not for the total population. Even if interest groups are an effective link between the citizen and government, many citizens do not avail themselves of this benefit. Even if the formal organization reduces anxiety or increases feelings of power, it does not serve the poor and the uneducated, whose alienation from the society is the greatest and whose need for such services is most extreme.[4]

Among members of organizations, active participation—and holding formal office—relates directly to social status. Whereas the majority of Americans are members in organizations, only a minority of members are active. Control typically rests with a small elite. The *iron law of oligarchy* states that even the most democratically inclined organizations gradually evolve into oligarchies. The oligarchs, who help shape the goals of the organizations, come disproportionately from the upper social classes.[5]

Participation in organizations also relates to satisfaction with one's life situation. The more satisfying a worker's job, for example, the more likely the worker will participate in union affairs. Hence, those with the least to complain about are most likely to guide the affairs of formal organizations. The higher one's social status, the less one has to complain about.

Thus our first empirical test of contemporary pluralist interest-group theory fails to corroborate one of its basic assumptions. Those who are active in interest groups constitute only a small portion of the populace; moreover, they tend to be of higher socioeconomic status than those who are not active. In short, the elites are the most active in interest groups in America. The single heaviest spending interest group in congressional lobbying is Common Cause. This so-called people's lobby

> is a model of elitism. Its membership . . . comprises one-tenth of one percent of the American public. . . . Less than one-tenth of those members do more than write their annual dues check. . . . Common Cause has largely been an expression of the personal values of its founder and chairman, John Gardner, a classic American aristocrat.[6]

And as E. E. Schattschneider concludes:

> The business or upper-class bias of the pressure system shows up everywhere. . . . The data raise a serious question about the validity of the proposition that special interest groups are a universal form of political organization reflecting all interests.[7]

How well do groups transmit members' demands?

The next test of pluralist group theory is how well—or whether—interest groups translate members' demands into political action.

The size of the group is an important variable in its leadership's political effectiveness. Since elected officials are sensitive to numbers, a large membership enhances a group's access to legislators. However, large groups find it difficult to commit themselves to an explicit position since their membership is so heterogeneous. The policy positions of mass membership organizations must be vague and broad, devoid of specific content—and thus harmless. The U.S. Chamber of Commerce, for example, seeks to represent "businesspeople," without regard for the nature of the business. Since intrabusiness disputes are often as bitter as labor-management disputes, the chamber cannot take a position on many of the legislative and administrative details that affect the economic health of various segments of the business community. The American Petroleum Institute, representing only the oil industry, is far more effective than the broad-based Chamber of Commerce.

Among the groups most active in the legislative process are large, well-organized labor unions. But even their achievements are often symbolic. The same is true of those civil rights organizations that seek political results through established democratic procedures.

In contrast to these large groups, small and highly organized groups have attained very tangible benefits. Small groups with narrow interests can achieve cohesion more readily and can concentrate their resources on a limited, tangible objective.[8] They can act decisively and persistently based on precise information. Such organizations are most frequently business, professional, or industrial; they are the major employers of lobbyists at the state and national level. Many business people organize into trade associations representing many industrial and commercial activities. Because their membership represents a specific form of business activity—for example, insurance—many trade associations are quite small, some with as few as twenty-five members. Their power to advocate specific values is disproportionate, while the business community as a whole fights symbolic battles.

New single-interest-group politics

"Representative government . . . is in the worst shape I have seen it in my sixteen years in the Senate. The heart of the problem is that the Senate and the House are awash in a sea of special-interest campaign contributions and special-interest lobbying."[9] This complaint by Senator Edward Kennedy reflects his belief that "new" groups, unfamiliar with the processes of bargaining, negotiation, and compromise, are competing with "old" groups that are well established, well connected, and sophisticated about the need for compromise.

"Single-issue" or "single-interest" groups are the powers stimulating Senator Kennedy's complaint. Such groups are indeed more prevalent, or at least more visible, than they were in the past. Older, established groups have a variety of interests that concern their staffs and active members. Single-interest groups live, as the name implies, for the defeat or passage of one law, one cause.

Because single-issue groups focus on one narrow concern (abortion or gun control, for example), they do not have much flexibility for bargaining or compromise. Their strength is almost solely the intensity of their beliefs. They offer no benefits to members other than political commitment which ranges from "merely strong to fanatical." Although not writing explicitly about single-issue groups, Jeffrey Berry described well their characteristics: "For the most part, these people are zealots, and they derive a great deal of satisfaction from their jobs. In contrast to the more mildly committed private interest lobbyists, the public interest activists are more likely to seek out the work they are doing, rather than merely 'drift' into it."[10]

This intense commitment has at least two important consequences. First, leaders have far less freedom of action than they would have with a membership recruited for nonpolitical reasons. For example, the Ad

Hoc Committee in Defense of Life, Inc., an antiabortion group, attracts active political participants with a strong belief in their organization's ability to influence public policy. Their leaders therefore cannot afford to misrepresent their constituents and their concern about the single issue that the group espouses. Consider, by comparison, the National Education Association, whose members include most of the precollegiate teachers in the United States. The NEA lobbied vigorously and successfully for a separate Department of Education. But few teachers knew or cared about such a department.

The second consequence is that the clearer link between leaders and followers and the dedication of both to the cause hampers leaders from fully using the traditional processes of political compromise. (Clearly, a person who sees abortion as a form of murder cannot compromise by saying "I'm going to allow 30,000 federally funded abortions and no more.")

Growth of single-interest groups

Why have single-issue groups proliferated in the past decade? Much of the explanation lies in the reforms of political parties and Congress (see chapter 8). As political parties reformed to increase their responsiveness, the strength of party organization declined. More and more states hold open primaries. Candidates rely more on personal organization and media exposure than on party organization support (see chapter 7). As parties weaken, popular attachment to the parties deteriorates such that neither party attracts the loyalty of a majority of voters. In Congress, party influence has diminished with reforms creating a larger role for subcommittees and reducing the importance of seniority (see chapter 12). Candidates turn to single-interest organizations, whose elective influence appears significant in contrast to the decline of parties and the continuing decline of mass participation in elections. Such groups, of course, represent minorities, but so do all other interest groups. The essential difference is that they are *more* representative of the views of their members–because they cannot compromise–than are the established groups. They are not the functional equivalent of political parties, for their causes are limited. They are, however, more responsive to issues than either parties or traditional interest groups.

Case study: NRA–Washington's top gun

"If lobbying power could be defined by a formula, it might be something like this: size plus organization multiplied by passion, divided by scope of interest."[11] The gun lobby, headed by the National Rifle Association, exemplifies the powerful single-interest lobby: it is large, well-organized, passionate, and focused on a single issue. Over two million dues-paying members, together with advertising revenue from weapons manufacturers, provide NRA with a full treasury to carry its message to Congress, the government

Case study *(continued)*

bureaucracy, the courts, and the general public. A national network of state and local chapters gives it voice in the home constituency of nearly every member of Congress.

NRA began after the Civil War to improve marksmanship among "Yankees" (whose skills were decidedly inferior to the "Rebels"); Ulysses S. Grant was an early NRA president. For many years the U.S. Army sold its surplus arms only through the NRA.

NRA members share interests in hunting, marksmanship, and gun collecting. The organization publishes *The American Hunter* and *The American Rifleman* for its members and offers them free insurance against loss or theft of their firearms or injury from hunting and shooting accidents. Gun-control advocates who envision NRA members as right-wing kooks, fanatics, and paranoids seriously misjudge their enemy. NRA members view hunting, shooting, and gun collecting as recreational activities, and they view themselves as responsible law-abiding citizens, which they are. They believe that efforts to reduce crime by taking away their guns are misguided because they do not misuse their firearms. Indeed, they pride themselves on education, training, and responsibility in gun safety. More important, they see gun ownership as a symbol of independence, self-reliance, and freedom in America.

NRA began lobbying in earnest during the congressional debate over the Gun Control Act of 1968, introduced after the assassinations of Senator Robert F. Kennedy and Martin Luther King, Jr. The act banishes mail-order sales of firearms and ammunition; prohibits sale of firearms to convicted felons; establishes licensing of all firearm dealers by the federal Bureau of Alcohol, Tobacco, and Firearms; requires dealers to keep records on all firearm sales; and calls for registration for ownership of automatic weapons. The NRA succeeded in eliminating a federal ban on all handguns and federal registration of all gun owners. Some very militant gun owners found the NRA efforts unsatisfactory, however, and formed another organization, the Citizens Committee for the Right to Keep and Bear Arms. Their uncompromising position was that gun ownership is a constitutional right that no government restriction can infringe upon.

Gun ownership is widespread in the United States; about 150 million firearms are in the hands of the nation's 236 million people. Half of all American families in public opinion surveys admit to owning guns. A majority of gun owners say their guns are for hunting and sports; about one-third say they own guns for self-defense. In opinion polls, a majority of Americans oppose any outright ban on the possession or sale of handguns, yet a majority also favors "stricter" laws governing handguns.[12]

The NRA argues that any restriction on owning a gun is a step toward the prohibition and confiscation of all guns. Following every highly publicized gun incident—attempted assassinations of presidents Gerald Ford and Ronald Reagan, the shooting of John Lennon, and so on—gun-control advocates have urged a ban on handguns. But the NRA has successfully fought off national legislation to ban handguns, to register them, or to license owners. At the state level, however, NRA has been less successful: as of 1982, twenty-

(continued)

Case study *(continued)*

four states required that all gun purchasers submit a record of sale to police; fourteen states required application and a waiting period to purchase a handgun; ten states required a license to purchase a handgun; and thirty-two states required a license to carry a "concealed" weapon. Four states (Illinois, Massachusetts, New Jersey, and New York) prohibit handgun ownership by anyone other than licensed law enforcement officials.

NRA's success in Congress is generally attributed to its organizational skills and the intensity of feelings of its members on the single issue of gun control. A member of the House Judiciary Committee explains: "This issue is of the highest intensity. Those people who care about guns, care very strongly, almost to the exclusion of other issues."[13] Gun-control advocates contend that members of Congress overestimate NRA's power at the polls but admit that no prudent politician wants to test NRA power.

The NRA directs its legislative efforts primarily toward halting proposed restrictive legislation. Its legislative strategy is to direct antigun sentiments toward increasing the penalties for using a gun to commit a crime. Thus the NRA supports federal and state laws imposing such penalties.

The NRA also supplies technical information and research findings to Congress. For example, the group distributed studies showing that violent crime rates in states with very restrictive gun laws (New York, Massachusetts, New Jersey, and Illinois) are just as high as violent crime rates in states without restrictive gun laws. The NRA focuses on studies showing that gun laws have no effect on violent crime rates, or crimes committed with guns, or even on gun ownership. NRA acknowledges FBI figures showing that 62 percent of all murders are committed with guns. (The NRA supplies accurate information to Congress, even when the data may appear to undermine the group's position, in order to maintain its reputation as a reliable information source.) But the NRA contends that "guns do not kill people, people kill people," and that banning guns only deprives law-abiding citizens of their constitutional right while doing nothing to prevent criminals from using guns.

Finally, NRA also monitors the enforcement activities of the Bureau of Alcohol, Tobacco, and Firearms (BATF) in enforcing the Gun Control Act of 1968. Congress has repeatedly called BATF before its committees to answer NRA charges that it harasses innocent gun dealers and collectors. When BATF tried to establish a centralized national record system of gun sales, NRA vigorously opposed their effort. As a result of NRA's efforts, Congress prohibited the BATF scheme and slashed the BATF budget as a warning against other administrative gun-control efforts.

Lobbying: How organized interests influence government

Lobbying is any communication directed at a government decision maker with the hope of influencing decisions. For organized interests, lobbying is a continuous activity—in congressional committees, in congressional staff offices, at the White House, at executive agencies, at Washington cocktail parties. If a group loses a round in Congress, it continues the fight in the agency in charge of executing the policy, or it challenges the policy in the courts. The following year it resumes the struggle in Congress: it fights for repeal of the offending legislation, for weakening amendments, or for budget reductions that would cripple enforcement efforts. The process can continue indefinitely.

What are the techniques of lobbying? We can classify lobbying techniques in four categories: (1) access, (2) information, (3) grass-roots mobilization, and (4) campaign support. In the real world of Washington power struggles, all of these techniques may be applied simultaneously, or new innovative techniques may be discovered and applied at any time.

One technique that most experienced lobbyists shun is the *threat*. Amateur lobbyists may threaten legislators by vowing to defeat them at

"Could you hurry and find a cure for cancer?
That would be so much easier than prevention."
From *Herblock on All Fronts* (New American Library, 1980)

the next election, a tactic guaranteed to produce a defensive reaction among members of Congress. Out of self-respect, legislators are likely to respond to crude pressures by demonstrating their independence and voting against the threatening lobbyist. Moreover, experienced members of Congress know that such threats are empty; lobbyists can seldom deliver enough votes to influence an election outcome.

Access

To communicate with decision makers, an organized interest first needs access to them. As a prominent Washington lobbyist explained: "Number 1 is the access—to get them in the door and get a hearing for your case . . . knowing the individuals personally, knowing their staffs and how they operate and the kind of information they want . . . that kind of personal knowledge can help you maximize the client's hearing."[14]

"Opening doors" is a major business in Washington. Individuals who have personal contacts with decision makers (or who say they do) sell their services at high prices. Washington law firms, public relations agencies, and "consultants" all offer their insider connections, and their advice, to potential clients. Many professional lobbyists are former members of Congress, former White House aides, or former congressional staff personnel who "know their way around." The personal prestige of the lobbyist, together with the group's perceived political influence, helps open doors in Washington. Occasionally the social skills of a lobbyist are useful in gaining access: the South Korean lobbyist Tongsun Park gained notoriety with his lavish dinners and cocktail parties. But legislators and top White House officials generally tire of parties; party going becomes more a chore than a delight.

Information

Once lobbyists gain access to the seats of power, their knowledge and information become their most valuable resources. A lobbyist may bring such information as: (1) knowledge of the legislative process, (2) expertise on the issue under debate, and (3) information about the group's position on the issue. Because legislators and their aides value all three types of knowledge, lobbyists can often trade their knowledge for congressional support.

Lobbyists must spend considerable time and effort keeping informed about bills affecting their interests. They must be thoroughly familiar with the "ins and outs" of the legislative process—the relevant committees and subcommittees, their schedules of meetings and hearings, their key staff members, the best moments to act, the precise language for proposed bills and amendments, the witnesses for hearings, and the political strengths and weaknesses of the legislators themselves.

The lobbyist's policy information must be accurate as well as timely. A successful lobbyist never supplies faulty or inaccurate information; his or her success depends on maintaining the trust and confidence of the decision makers. A reputation for honesty is as important as a reputation for influence. Lobbyists provide the information and argumentation that Congress members use in legislative debate and in speeches back home. In this role, the lobbyist complements the functions of congressional staff. Testimony at legislative hearings is a common form of information exchange between lobbyists and legislators. Lobbyists also provide the technical reports and analyses used by congressional staffs in their legislative research.

Lobbyists also assist decision makers by communicating their organization's position on policy questions. Legislators want to know how various groups stand on the issues, and it is the job of the professional lobbyist to let them know.

Grass-roots mobilization

Many organized interests also lobby Congress by mobilizing constituents to apply pressure on their behalf. Many lobbyists believe that legislators, especially insecure ones, pay close attention to letters, telegrams, and calls from "the folks back home." The larger organized interests often have local chapters throughout the nation and can mobilize these local affiliates to apply pressure when necessary. Lobbyists encourage influential local elites to personally visit a Congress member's office, or to make a personal phone call, on behalf of the group's positions.

Of course, experienced lawmakers recognize attempts by lobby groups to orchestrate "spontaneous" grass-roots outpourings of cards and letters. Pressure mail is often identical in wording and content. Nevertheless, members of Congress dare not ignore a flood of letters and telegrams from home, for the mail shows that constituents are aware of the issue and care enough to sign their names. Sophisticated lobbyists, such as Richard A. Viguerie, a widely recognized conservative and expert on mass mailings, have refined modern computerized mail techniques.

Another grass-roots tactic is to mobilize the press in a Congress member's home district. Lobbyists may provide news, analyses, and editorials to local newspapers and then clip favorable articles to send to lawmakers. Lobby groups may also buy advertisements in hometown newspapers; and nearly every *Washington Post* carries full- or half-page ads placed by lobby groups.

Campaign support

Increasingly, the key to success in lobbying is the campaign contribution. Interest-group contributions not only help lobbyists gain access and a favorable hearing, but they also help elect people friendly to the group's goals. As the costs of campaigning increase, especially the costs of professional mass media campaigning, legislators must depend more heavily on the contributions of organized interests.

It is very bad taste for a lobbyist to extract a specific vote pledge from a legislator in exchange for a campaign contribution. Crude "vote buying" is usually (but not always) avoided. Instead, organized interests contribute to an incumbent Congress member over a long period of time, and leave it to the lawmaker to figure out how to retain their support. When a legislator consistently votes against an organized interest, that interest may then contribute to the opposition candidate in the next election.

Regulation of lobbies

Although the First Amendment protects lobbying, government can regulate lobbying activities. The principal method is disclosure: the law requires lobbyists to register as lobbyists and to report how much they spend. But definitions of lobbying are unclear and enforcement is weak. Many of the larger lobby groups—for example, the National Association of Manufacturers, the National Bankers Association, and Americans for Constitutional Action—have never registered as lobbyists. These organizations claim that because lobbying is not their "principal" activity, they need not register under the law. Financial reports of lobbyists grossly underestimate the extent of lobbying in Congress because the law requires reports on only money spent on direct lobbying before Congress, not money spent for public relations or for campaign contributions. Another weakness in the law is that it applies only to attempts to influence Congress and does not regulate lobbying activities in administrative agencies or the executive branch. However, restrictive legislation might violate the First Amendment freedom to "petition the government for a redress of grievances."

PACs: The new political parties

Political parties are large, disorganized, and largely devoid of ideology. A contributor wishing to support a specific political cause gets more for his or her money by contributing to a PAC. A PAC, or political action committee, is a non-party organization which solicits voluntary contributions to disburse to political candidates. PACs have been organized by labor unions, trade associations, and liberal and conservative groups. Environmental groups, among others, all have organized PACs, but the large number of PACs are corporate. Contributions to PACs must be voluntary; corporations and labor unions cannot legally use corporate or union treasuries for political campaigns.

The PACs have become a major force in Washington politics in recent years; an estimated one-third of all campaign contributions now originate from them. The increasing costs of television campaigning makes many legislators dependent on PAC contributions to run their campaigns.

The PACs give most of their money to *incumbent* members of Congress. Not only does this practice strengthen incumbents against their opponents, but it also makes incumbents less likely to change the law governing PAC contributions. The PACs hope that their contributions buy access for their lobbyists and support for their legislative positions.

Most PACs know who their friends are in Congress and reward them with contributions. Occasionally, however, PACs make contributions to influential legislators whose friendship they seek. Rarely do PACs try to strike a bargain on specific legislation—that is, to "buy votes." But some PACs are more vengeful than others and may give money to the opponents of unfriendly legislators. NCPAC, the National Conservative Political Action Committee, conducted a controversial "negative" campaign in 1980 to help defeat four liberal senators—McGovern of South Dakota, Church of Idaho, Culver of Iowa, and Bayh of Indiana.

The PACs invest in access and influence. (See table 9-1.) In the past, Democrats enjoyed a financial edge in PAC contributions because Congress had more Democratic incumbents, and the Democratic majority placed its members in committee chairmanships. But since 1980 Republican control of the Senate and the conservative tilt of corporate PACs have brought more PAC contributions to the Republicans.

Although the original intention of the campaign finance laws was to limit the influence of the "special interests," the PACs nonetheless focus the attention of Congress on specific group interests and away from broad consensus issues—the "public interest." Efforts to curb PAC contributions run into an insurmountable obstacle since incumbents are the major beneficiaries of PAC money.

TABLE 9-1. The leading PACs
(The top twenty contributors to 1982 federal elections)

1. Realtors PAC	$2,045,092
2. American Medical PAC	1,638,795
3. United Automobile Workers PAC	1,470,354
4. Machinists Non-Partisan Political League	1,252,209
5. National Education Association PAC	1,073,896
6. American Bankers Association PAC	870,110
7. National Association of Home Builders PAC	852,745
8. Associated Milk Producers PAC	842,450
9. Automobile and Truck Dealers Election Action Committee	829,945
10. A.F.L.-C.I.O. C.O.P.E. Political Contributions Committee	823,125
11. Seafarers Political Activity Donation	802,261
12. Engineers Political Education Committee (Operating Engineers)	651,535
13. Associated General Contractors PAC	651,125
14. Active Ballot Club (Food & Commercial Workers)	634,357
15. National Rifle Association Political Victory Fund	612,137
16. United Steelworkers of America PAC	609,449
17. American Dental PAC	578,950
18. Communications Workers of America-C.O.P.E. Political Contributions Committee	545,278
19. International Ladies Garment Workers Union Campaign Committee	541,918
20. Sheetmetal Workers' International Association Political Action League	527,666

Note: These figures represent the period from January 1, 1981, to October 13, 1982.

Source: Federal Election Commission.

Unlike political parties, the goal of special interests is policy rather than personnel. Political parties seek electoral success, while PACs view electoral success as a means to achieve favorable policy. Political parties seek to build coalitions among competing factions that lead to a working consensus. PACs have a much narrower focus. The demise of parties and the rise of PACs are clearly linked. The dominance of the PAC network by corporations and business organizations solidifies the class bias of the interest-group system.

Conservative influence of organizations

Organizations perform a conservative, stabilizing function for the society. Formal organizations seldom cause social change. Of course, the goals of associations vary, some being more radical than others. But in general, organizations gradually become more moderate as the goal of perpetuating themselves takes priority over the original goal:

> . . . the running of an organization creates problems not related to original goals. These goals of internal relevance assume an increasing proportion of time and may gradually be substituted for externally directed goals. The day-to-day behavior of the permanent staff and active participants (a minority of the membership) becomes centered around proximate goals of primary internal importance, modifying or "displacing" the stated goals of the organization.[15]

In other words, as organizations grow older, they shift from trying to implement their original values to maintaining their structure, even if they thereby sacrifice the organization's central mission.[16] The people who have the greatest stake in the existing social system thus come to dominate the organization. Of course, organizations do not stop seeking change, but the extent of change they seek is minimal. Once they achieve even a few of their goals, they then have a stake in the ongoing system and a rational basis for moderate politics. Social stability is apparently a product of this organization system—not necessarily because of overlapping affiliations but because of the intrinsic nature of organizations. Associations that begin with a radical ideology must modify their views to attract the sustained membership necessary for organizational health.

Since groups serve society by cementing their members to the established social system, those who seek to alter this system find organizations an unsatisfactory mechanism. True, some groups develop with radical change in mind, but the process of bureaucratization and the evolution of the membership from "have-nots" to "haves" gradually reduces any organization's commitment to substantial change. Impoverished people and blacks have gained little from groups because the group structure is dominated by people with a favored position in society. For segments of society effectively barred from other forms of participation, violent protest is the most effective method of entry into the political process. Ironically if deprived peoples succeed in organizing and achieving a more equitable distribution of rewards, violence will probably decline, to be replaced by organizational activity. In time, the new organizations will develop their own commitment to the status quo, thus leaving an opening for more radical groups to fill.

As agents of stability, then, groups function quite effectively. Not only do group members tend to feel effective, but they are also more active and interested in political affairs, are more satisfied with the political system, and identify more readily with the community. Because they contribute to the social integration of their members, organized interest groups have a conservative, stabilizing influence on society.

Summary

Pluralism asserts that organized interest groups provide the individual with an effective way to participate in the political system. It contends that individuals can make their voices heard through membership in the organized groups that reflect their views on public affairs. Pluralists further believe that competition among organized interests provides a balance of power that protects the individual's interests. Interest groups divide power among themselves and hence protect the individual from rule by a single oppressive elite.

Earlier we pointed out that pluralism diverges from classical democratic theory. Even if the plural elite model accurately portrays the reality of American politics, it does not guarantee the implementation of democratic values. Our analysis of interest groups produced the following propositions:

1. Interest groups draw disproportionately from middle- and upper-class segments of the population. The pressure-group system is not representative of the entire community.

2. Leadership of interest groups is recruited from the middle- and upper-class population.

3. Business and professional organizations predominate among organized interest groups.

4. Generally mass membership groups achieve only symbolic success, and smaller, more cohesive groups are able to achieve more tangible results.

5. Considerable inequality exists among organized interest groups. Business and producer groups with narrow membership but cohesive organization achieve their tangible goals at the expense of broad, unorganized groups seeking less tangible goals.

6. Organized interest groups are governed by small elites whose values do not necessarily reflect the values of most members.

7. Business groups and associations are the most highly organized and active lobbyists in Washington and in the state capitals. This influence is especially evident in the growth of political action committees.

8. Organizations tend to become conservative as they acquire a stake in the existing social order. Therefore, pressures for substantial social change must generally come from forces outside the structure of organized interest groups.

NOTES

1. Gabriel A. Almond and Sidney Verba, *The Civic Culture: Political Attitudes and Democracy in Five Nations* (Boston: Little, Brown, 1965), p. 245.
2. David B. Truman, *The Governmental Process* (New York: Knopf, 1951).
3. Almond and Verba, op. cit., p. 249.
4. Sidney Verba and Norman H. Nie, *Participation in America* (New York: Harper & Row, 1972), p. 208.
5. Roberto Michels, *Political Parties: A Sociological Study of the Oligarchical Tendencies of Modern Democracy* (1915; reprint, New York: Dover, 1959), esp. p. 248.
6. *Boston Globe*, April 24, 1977, p. A7.
7. E. E. Schattschneider, *The Semisovereign People: A Realist's View of Democracy in America* (New York: Holt, Rinehart and Winston, 1960), pp. 31–34.
8. Murray Edelman, *The Symbolic Uses of Politics* (Urbana: University of Illinois Press, 1964), pp. 24–26.
9. *Newsweek*, November 6, 1979, p. 50.
10. Jeffrey M. Berry, *Lobbying for the People* (Princeton, N.J.: Princeton University Press, 1977), pp. 100, 109.
11. Congressional Quarterly, *The Washington Lobby*, 4th ed. (Washington, D.C.: Congressional Quarterly Press, 1982), p. 131.
12. *Gallup Report* (July 1981):26–31.
13. Congressional Quarterly, op. cit., p. 133.
14. Ibid., p. 5.
15. Harmon Zeigler, *Interest Groups in American Society*, 2d ed. (Englewood Cliffs, N.J.: Prentice-Hall, 1972), p. 81.
16. Sheldon L. Messinger, "Organizational Transformation: A Case Study of a Declining Social Movement," *American Sociological Review* 20 (February 1955):10.

SELECTED READINGS

Bayes, Jane H. *Ideologies and Interest Group Politics*. Novato, Ca.: Chandler and Sharp Publisher, 1982. Bayes argues that the United States is a special interest group in the world economy.

Berry, Jeffrey. *Lobbying for the People*. Princeton, N.J.: Princeton University Press, 1977. Berry describes the activities of organizations whose efforts do not provide a selective advantage to their members (such as environmental groups and Common Cause).

Boles, Janet K. *The Politics of the Equal Rights Amendment*. New York: Longman, 1979. This case study describes the campaigns for and against the equal rights amendment in various states.

Edelman, Murray. *The Symbolic Uses of Politics*. Chicago: University of Illinois Press, 1967. Edelman discusses the general uses of symbols in society and then the specific uses of political phenomena as symbols. He points out that myth and symbolic reassurance have become key elements in the governmental process. Edelman argues that the masses are generally uninterested in and inattentive to political phenomena as symbols. Only when the masses perceive symbolic or real threats or reassurances do they notice things political. Masses react to stimuli. Therefore, political actions "shape men's political wants and 'knowledge,' not the other way around" (p. 172). Edelman also argues that mass demands, when they are articulated, are most often met with "symbolic" rather than "tangible" rewards.

Engler, Robert. *The Politics of Oil*. Chicago: University of Chicago Press, Phoenix Books, 1961. Although somewhat dated, this book provides important historical background on the power of the American oil industry and its relationships to government, both at home and abroad. Particularly useful to the argument made in this chapter of *Irony* are the sections on the oil lobby, the use of public relations, and the entry of oil corporation officials into appointive government positions.

Garson, G. David. *Group Theories of Politics*. Beverly Hills: Sage Publications, 1978. This book critically evaluates the history and development of group theories, with special attention to the pluralist-elitist dispute.

Gelb, Joyce, and Marian Palley. "Women and Interest Group Politics." *Journal of Politics* 41 (1979):362–392. The authors analyze lobbying efforts for policies that affect women directly.

Greenwald, Carol S. *Group Power*. New York: Praeger, 1977. This book is the current basic text on the subject. It contains a fine analysis of interest groups and pluralism.

Key, V. O., Jr. *Politics, Parties, and Pressure Groups*. New York: T. Y. Crowell, 1967. A classic in the area of American party politics, this book traces the historical development of our present parties and discusses their role in the political system.

Malbin, Michael J. "Campaign Finance Reform and the 'Special Interests.' " *Public Interest* 56 (Summer 1979):21–42. This article is a history and analysis of the growth of political action committees.

Moe, Terry M. *The Organization of Interests*. Chicago: University of Chicago Press, 1980. Moe concentrates solely on interest groups as organizations, with special attention to group formation, membership maintenance, and the development of political goals.

Olson, Mancur, Jr. *The Logic of Collective Action: Public Goods and the Theory of Groups*. New York: Schocken Books, 1968. This well-written work outlines the rational basis for interest-group activity. Individuals are the units of analysis, and Olson constructs a model of individual motivation for collective behavior given an assumption of rationality.

Ornstein, Norman, and Elder, Shirley. *Interest Groups, Lobbying, and Policymaking*. Washington: Congressional Quarterly Press, 1978. This book cites good case studies of the impact of groups on legislation.

Schattschneider, E. E. *The Semisovereign People: A Realist's View of Democracy in America*. New York: Holt, Rinehart and Winston, 1960. This book analyzes the nature of conflict and change in America. Schattschneider argues against the pluralist-group bias, which he perceives as the common view of the political system today. He also recognizes the elite-masses dichotomy that exists in the American social and political system. For example, he develops the notion that elites, by virtue of their organizational strengths, can manage conflict within the political system. They can alter it, exploit it, and/or suppress it.

Verba, Sidney, and Nie, Norman H. *Participation in America*. New York: Harper & Row, 1972. The authors examine the causes and effects of political participation, including participation in organizations.

Zeigler, Harmon, and Peak, Wayne. *Interest Groups in American Society*, 2d ed. Englewood Cliffs, N.J.: Prentice-Hall, 1972. This comprehensive study of the composition and roles of interest groups in the U.S. political system discusses the development of interest-group theory, the relationship of such theory to broader aspects of democratic political thought, and the empirical data available on group phenomena.

10 The Presidency in Crisis

More than any other political figure, the president attracts the attention and emotion of the masses of Americans. The people look to the presidency for leadership and reassurance.

The Presidency is the focus of the most intense and persistent emotions ... The President is ... the one figure who draws together the people's hopes and fears for the political future.

—*James David Barber,* The Presidential Character, *1973*

Government elites in America do not command; they seek consensus with other elites. Decision making by government elites is a process of bargaining, accommodation, and compromise among the dominant interests in American society. Government elites act essentially as go-betweens and mediators, seeking policies that are mutually beneficial to the major interests—industrial, financial, labor, farm, military, bureaucratic, and so on.

The presidency stands at the center of elite interaction in the American political system. For the *elite* itself, the president proposes policy initiatives, mobilizes influence within the political system, and supervises the management of government and the economy. For the *masses*, the president is a symbol of national unity, an outlet to express their emotions toward government, and a vicarious means of taking political action. For *both* elites and masses, the presidency provides a means of handling national crises—taking whatever actions are necessary in an emergency to stabilize the nation, protect its security, and calm its citizens.

The president as symbolic leader

Leadership and reassurance

More than any other political figure, the president attracts the attention and emotion of the American masses. The people look to the presidency for leadership and reassurance. They want a president who will personalize government, simplify political issues, and symbolize the "compassionate" and protective role of the state. They want someone who seems concerned with them.

The people also look for toughness, competence, and decisiveness in the presidency. They are prepared to support a president who is willing to DO SOMETHING, whether "something" is a good idea or not. Presidential popularity goes *up* when the president takes dramatic action or when the nation faces an external crisis or threat. (National surveys regularly gauge presidential popularity by asking, "Do you approve or disapprove of the way [Reagan, or Carter, or Ford, etc.] is handling his job as president?" See figure 10-1.)

The people *want* to support the president. All presidents begin their terms with broad public support. Over time, however, this support wanes as troubles pile up and the president is unable to cope with them. Indeed the popular expectations of a president far exceed his powers to meet these expectations. The result is an inevitable decline in public support until a new crisis occurs or dramatic action is necessary.

A brief overview of presidential popularity ratings over time confirms these notions: that a president takes office with broad public support, that this support tends to decline over time, and that renewal of this support can occur with dramatic action or crisis. Figure 10-1 compares approval ratings for five presidents. Each took office, whether through election or assassination or resignation, with broad popular support. Over time this support declined. But dramatic action—peace in Vietnam for Nixon, the *Mayaguez* affair for Ford, the Iranian crisis for Carter, the assassination attempt on Reagan (see figure 10-2)—produced dramatic increases in presidential support.

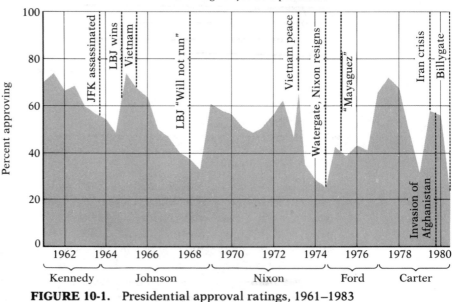

"Do you approve or disapprove of the way _____ is handling his job as a president?"

FIGURE 10-1. Presidential approval ratings, 1961–1983
Source: Data based on *Gallup Opinion Index*.

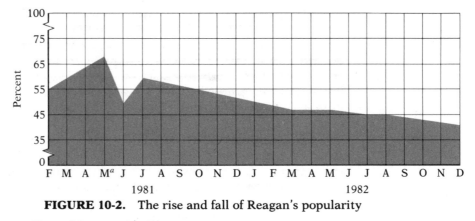

FIGURE 10-2. The rise and fall of Reagan's popularity

^aDate of the assassination attempt.

Source: *Gallup Opinion Index.*

Focus on personality

As the focus of public attention, the president is the nation's leading celebrity. His wife is the nation's "First Lady."* Commentators and scholars dissect the president's personality and compare him to other presidents. When the president chooses to address the entire nation, the television networks cancel their regular programming and provide free television time.

The presidency possesses enormous symbolic significance. The president affects popular images of authority, legitimacy, and confidence in the American political system. He can arouse feelings of patriotism or cynicism, hope or despair, horror or dishonor. Political scientist James David Barber writes:

> The Presidency is the focus for the most intense and persistent emotions. . . . The President is . . . the one figure who draws together the people's hopes and fears for the political future. On top of all of his routine duties, he has to carry that off—or fail.[1]

Effects of power

Presidents themselves are aware of their power as symbolic leader. Abraham Lincoln once declared, "Public sentiment is everything. With public sentiment nothing can fail, without it nothing can succeed."

Presidents' public popularity in part determines their power in interactions with other elites. A president with high ratings in the polls for any reason can get better cooperation from other elites than when

---

*The election of a female president, if she is married, will create some interesting problems for the media. "First Gentleman" just does not have the same ring as "First Lady."

low in the polls. For example, Congress is more likely to sponsor legislation by the president when the president's popularity is high. Political scientist George C. Edwards reports that the overall correlation between presidential popularity and support in Congress is .50 for the House and .40 for the Senate. These correlations are not perfect (1.00), which suggests that Congress frequently ignores the president's popularity. But popularity with the masses is certainly one basic component of presidential power.

Presidents' popularity has little to do with their position on the issues. In recent years, Republican and Democratic, and liberal and conservative, presidents have all both enjoyed high ratings and suffered low ratings in the polls. As Richard Neustadt has written, "Presidential standing outside of Washington is actually a jumble of imprecise impressions held by relatively inattentive men."[2]

The president's formal powers

The president has many sources of formal power (see table 10-1) as chief administrator, chief legislator, party leader, chief diplomat, commander-in-chief, and chief of state and crisis manager. But despite the great powers of the office, no president can monopolize policy making. The president functions within an established elite system and can exercise power only within the framework of that system. The choices available to the president are only those alternatives for which elite support can be mobilized. The president cannot act outside existing elite consensus—outside the "rules of the game"—and must be sensitive to the interests of major elites—business, agriculture, military, education, bureaucratic, and so on.

Presidential powers of persuasion

The presidency's real power depends not on formal authority but on the president's abilities at persuasion. The president does not command American elites, but stands in a central position in the elite structure. Responsibility for initiating public policy falls principally on the president and the presidential staff and executive departments. The president has a strong incentive to fulfill this responsibility, for a large segment of the American public holds the president responsible for everything that happens in the nation during that term of office, whether or not the president has the authority or capacity to do anything about it.

Through the power to initiate policy alone, the president's impact on the nation is considerable. The president sets the agenda for public decision making. The president presents programs to Congress in var-

TABLE 10-1. Formal presidential powers

Chief administrator
  Implement policy—"Take care that laws be faithfully executed" (Art. II, Sec. 2).
  Supervise executive branch of government.
  Appoint and remove policy officials.
  Prepare executive budget.
Chief legislator
  Initiate policy—"Give to the Congress information of the State of the Union and recommend to their consideration such measures as he shall judge necessary and expedient" (Art. II, Sec. 3).
  Vote legislation passed by Congress.
  Convene special session of Congress "on extraordinary occasions" (Art. II, Sec. 3).
Party leader
  Control national party organization.
  Control federal patronage.
  Influence (not control) state and local parties through prestige.
Chief diplomat
  Make treaties ("with the advice and consent of Senate") (Art. II, Sec. 2).
  Make executive agreements.
  Exercise power of diplomatic recognition—"to send and receive ambassadors" (Art. II, Sec. 2).
Commander-in-chief
  Command U.S. armed forces—"The President shall be Commander-in-chief of the army and the navy" (Art. II, Sec. 2).
  Appoint military officials.
  Initiate war.
  Exercise broad war powers.
Crisis manager and chief of state
  Oversee formal national action—"The executive Power shall be vested in a President" (Art. II, Sec. 1).
  Represent the nation as chief of state.

ious presidential messages and in the budget, and thereby largely determines the business of Congress in any session. Few major undertakings ever get off the ground without presidential initiation; the president frames the issues, determines their context, and decides their timing.

Presidents: weak and strong

The powers of the presidency and the importance of this office in the American political system vary with political circumstances and with the personalities of those who occupy the office. The contrasting views of presidents William Howard Taft and Theodore Roosevelt often come up in debates about the true nature of executive power. Taft said:

> The true view of the executive function is, as I conceive it, that the president can exercise no power which cannot be fairly and reasonably traced to some specific grant of power or justly implied and included within such express grant as proper and necessary to its exercise. Such specific grants must be either in the federal constitution or in the pursuance thereof. There is no undefined residuum of power which can be exercised which seems to him to be in the public interest.[3]

Theodore Roosevelt offered an alternative view:

> I decline to adopt the view that what was imperatively necessary for the nation could not be done by the president unless he could find some specific authorization to do it. My belief was that it was not only his right but his duty to do anything that the needs of the nation demanded, unless such action was forbidden by the Constitution or by the laws.[4]

Most evaluations of presidential performance favor the more activist approach to the office. Political analysts usually downgrade Taft, Herbert Hoover, and Dwight Eisenhower, who took more restricted views of the presidency, in comparison with Woodrow Wilson, Theodore and Franklin Roosevelt, and Harry Truman, who were much more active presidents (see "Rating the Presidents" page 245.)

Growth of presidential power

Yet on the whole, presidents of the twentieth century have exercised greater power and initiative than those of the nineteenth century. First, America has assumed greater involvement in world affairs, with a resulting *increase in the importance of military and foreign policy*. In foreign and military affairs, the Constitution gives the president unmistakable and far-reaching powers: to send and receive ambassadors, to make treaties (with the advice and consent of the Senate), and to direct the armed forces as commander-in-chief. In effect, these powers give the president almost exclusive authority over the nation's foreign and military policy.

A second contributor has been *the growth of the executive branch*. The federal bureaucracy has grown into a giant elite structure, and the Constitution places the chief executive at the top of this structure. The Constitution gives the president broad, albeit vague, powers to "take care that the laws be faithfully executed" and to "require the opinion in writing of the principal officer of each of the executive departments upon any subject relating to the duties of their respective offices." This clause gives the president general executive authority over the three million civilian employees of the federal bureaucracy. Moreover, the president has the right to appoint (and the right to remove) the principal officers of the executive branch. The Senate must consent to appointments, but not removals. A major addition to the president's constitutional authority over the executive branch came in the Budget and Accounting Act of 1921, in which Congress vested in the president the power to initiate and execute the federal budget. Budgetary control is a major presidential weapon, for it can mean the life or death of an administrative agency. While Congress still must appropriate all monies spent by executive departments, the president nonetheless has responsibility for formulating the budget. Congress may cut a presidential budget request and even appropriate more than the president asks for a particular agency

Rating the Presidents

The 10 "Best" Presidents	The 10 "Worst" Presidents
1. Abraham Lincoln	1. Warren G. Harding
2. George Washington	2. Richard M. Nixon
3. Franklin D. Roosevelt	3. James Buchanan
4. Theodore Roosevelt	4. Franklin Pierce
5. Thomas Jefferson	5. Ulysses S. Grant
6. Woodrow Wilson	6. Millard Fillmore
7. Andrew Jackson	7. Andrew Johnson
8. Harry S Truman	8. Calvin Coolidge
9. Dwight D. Eisenhower	9. John Tyler
10. James K. Polk	10. Jimmy Carter

Two of Ronald Reagan's recent predecessors rank among the 10 "worst" Presidents in a new survey of historians and political scientists.

Republican Richard M. Nixon was rated the second-worst Chief Executive, Democrat Jimmy Carter the tenth worst in a poll of 49 leading scholars.

The survey, by the *Chicago Tribune*, resembled polls done in 1948 and 1962 by historian Arthur Schlesinger, Sr., for other publications. In all three surveys, Abraham Lincoln, George Washington and Franklin D. Roosevelt led the list of "best" Presidents while Warren G. Harding was rated the very worst.

The biggest shift was the rating for Dwight Eisenhower, who rose from the tenth-worst position in 1962 to ninth best in the 1982 survey. Ike's stature among scholars is believed to have grown in part because of the troubles of his more activist successors.

Calvin Coolidge, a Chief Executive treated too harshly by historians in Reagan's judgment, was ranked as the eighth-worst President in the latest survey. He also finished in the bottom 10 in the earlier polls.

Nixon's role in the Watergate scandal and his resignation from office, it was clear, led to his next-to-lowest rating. A University of Texas historian claimed Nixon was "the most corrupt President in our history."

Carter received one vote in the 10-best category, but he got many votes for the bottom 10. A professor at the University of Illinois speculated that Carter's low rating occurred because of his "failure as a political leader and because it is so recent."

Atlanta Mayor Andrew Young, a close Carter friend, blasted the scholars for what he termed "insensitive elitism."

Reprinted from *U.S. News & World Report*, January 25, 1982. Copyright 1982, The Gallup Organization, Inc.

or program, but in practice Congress tends to accept the bulk of the president's budget.

The third reason for the importance of the presidency in the twentieth century is technological improvements in the mass media, which have *strengthened the role of the president as party leader and molder of mass opinion.* Television brings the president directly in contact with the masses, and the masses' attachment to the president is unlike their attachment to any other public official or symbol of government. Fred I. Greenstein has classified the "psychological functions of the presidency." The president:

1. "Simplifies perception of government and politics" by serving as "the main cognitive 'handle' for providing busy citizens with some sense of what their government is doing";
2. Provides "an outlet for emotional expression" through public interest in his and his family's private and public life;
3. Is a "symbol of unity" and of nationhood (as the national shock and grief over the death of a president clearly reveal);
4. Provides the masses with a "vicarious means of taking political action" in that the president can act decisively and effectively while they cannot do so;
5. Is a "symbol of social stability" in providing the masses with a feeling of security and guidance. Thus, for the masses, the president is the most visible elite member.[5]

The president's legislative skills

The success that presidents have in carrying out many of their formal powers—obtaining passage of the bills they propose, having their vetoes sustained, gaining Senate confirmation of their appointments, and winning Senate ratification of their treaties—depends upon their relationships with Congress. One general measure of presidential success in Congress is the percentage of presidential victories on votes on which the president took a clear stand. (This measure may overestimate presidential influence because it focuses on bills that actually come up for a vote; some presidential legislation is buried in committees and never reaches a vote.)

One factor influencing presidential-congressional relations is party: Democratic presidents have more success with Democratic Congresses than do Republican presidents.* Three Republican presidents posted lower average success rates (Eisenhower, 72 percent; Nixon, 67 percent; Ford, 58 percent) than did three Democratic presidents (Kennedy, 84

---

*And the last Democratic president to face a Republican Congress, Harry Truman, experienced the worst Congressional relations of any other modern president.

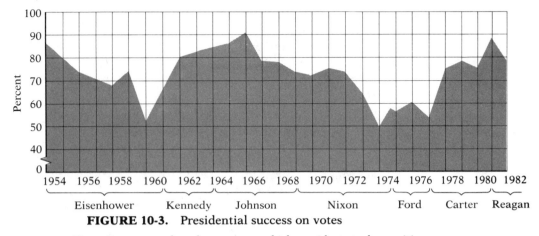

FIGURE 10-3. Presidential success on votes

Note: Percentages based on votes on which presidents took a position.

Source: *Congressional Quarterly.*

percent; Johnson, 83 percent; Carter, 77 percent). However, the Reagan success rate has been higher than other Republican presidents (89 percent in 1981 and 79 percent in 1982).

Issues in presidential power: The war-making controversy

For decades, the liberal intellectuals in America praised the presidency and scorned Congress. Textbooks taught students that the hope of the nation rested with a powerful president; they presented Congress as unprogressive, dilatory, even reactionary. Strong presidents—Lincoln, Roosevelt, Truman—were eulogized; weak presidents—Coolidge, Hoover, Eisenhower—were ridiculed. Leading establishment scholars—for example, Harvard political scientist Richard Neustadt—taught that presidents should conduct themselves so as to maximize their power.[6] These political analysts led Americans to believe that because the president is the only official elected by *all* of the people, the presidential powers would be used to "do good."

But then came two successive presidents—Johnson and Nixon—whom most of the nation's liberal intellectuals distrusted. As a result, establishment views of the presidency did an about-face. The Vietnam war and Watergate convinced liberal intellectuals that the presidency was too powerful and that Congress must more actively check the actions of unruly presidents. Many commentators, journalists, intellectuals, and, of course, senators and House members argued the importance of curtailing the president's war-making powers, overseeing White House activities, and protecting the nation from the abuses of presidential power.

War and the Constitution

Division of powers. The American colonists who declared their independence from Britain in 1776 were deeply suspicious of standing armies and of a king who would send British troops to the colonies. This distrust carried over after independence, causing the Founding Fathers to make military affairs subject to civilian control. The Second Continental Congress had overseen the conduct of the military during the Revolutionary War. It commissioned George Washington to be commander-in-chief but instructed him "punctually to observe and follow such orders and directions . . . from this or a future Congress." But Washington chaired the Constitutional Convention of 1787, and he recognized the need for a strong chief executive who could respond quickly to threats to the nation. Moreover, he was aware of the weaknesses of civilian militia and favored a national army and navy.

The Constitutional Convention of 1787 divided the war power between Congress and the president. Article I, Section 8, says, "The Congress shall have the power to . . . provide for the common defense . . . to declare war . . . to raise and support armies . . . to provide and maintain a navy . . . to make rules for the government and regulation of the land and naval forces." Article II, Section 2, says, "The President shall be Commander-in-Chief of the army and navy of the United States." In defending the newly written Constitution, *The Federalist* papers construed the president's war powers narrowly, implying that the war-making power of the president was little more than the power to defend against imminent invasion when Congress was not in session.

Presidential supremacy in reality. Historically the president has exercised much more than strictly defensive war-making powers. Since 1789 U.S. forces have participated in military actions overseas on more than 150 occasions, but Congress has declared war only five times: the War of 1812, the Mexican War, the Spanish-American War, World War I, and World War II. Supreme Court Justice William H. Rehnquist wrote before he was elevated to the Court:

> It has been recognized from the earliest days of the Republic, by the President, by Congress and by the Supreme Court, that the United States may lawfully engage in armed hostilities with a foreign power without Congressional declaration of war. Our history is replete with instances of "undeclared wars" from the war with France in 1789–1800 to the Vietnamese War.[7]

The Supreme Court has generally refused to take jurisdiction in cases involving the war powers of the president and Congress.

Thus, while Congress retains the formal power to "declare war," in modern times wars are seldom "declared." Instead they begin with direct military actions, and the president, as commander-in-chief of the armed forces, determines what those actions will be. Over the years Congress generally recognized the supremacy of the president in military affairs. Not until the Vietnam war was there serious congressional debate over who shall have the power to commit the nation to war. In the past, Congress tended to accept the fact that under modern conditions of war only the president has the information-gathering facilities, the speed, and the secrecy for reaching quick military decisions during periods of crisis.

The war in Vietnam

The war in Vietnam was not an unprecedented use of the president's war-making powers. John Adams fought a war against the French without a congressional declaration; Thomas Jefferson fought the Barbary pirates; every president in the nineteenth century fought the Indians; Abraham Lincoln carried presidential war-making powers further than any president before or since; Woodrow Wilson sent troops to Mexico and a dozen Latin American nations; Franklin D. Roosevelt sent U.S. destroyers to protect British convoys in the north Atlantic before Pearl Harbor; and Harry Truman committed American forces to a major war in Korea. So when President Johnson ordered bombing attacks on North Vietnam in 1965 and eventually committed more than half a million men to the battle, he was not really assuming any greater powers than those assumed by presidents before him. Perhaps his greatest mistake was his failure to achieve either a military or diplomatic solution to the war.

In the early days of the Vietnam war, the liberal leadership of the nation strongly supported the war effort, and no one questioned the president's power to commit the nation to war. However, by 1969 most liberal congressional leaders who had supported the war in its early stages had rushed to become doves. Indeed senators argued over who had been the first to change his mind about the war. Moreover, with a new *Republican* president and a *Democratic* Congress, congressional attacks on presidential policy became much more partisan. As public opposition to the Vietnam war grew, and with different parties in control of the presidency and Congress, the members of Congress now sought to reassert their role in war-making decisions.

Congress made several attempts to curtail the president's war-making powers by cutting off money for U.S. military activity in Southeast Asia. Most people recognized that Congress did not have the authority to end the Vietnam war by congressional declaration, but it could set a cutoff date for spending government funds in support of U.S. troops in Southeast Asia. Nonetheless, antiwar legislators could not get their colleagues to cut off funds for the war until *after* President Nixon announced a peace agreement in 1973. Congress then cut off funds for Vietnam (an action that former Secretary of State Henry Kissinger says led to the collapse of South Vietnam). But it is important that Congress has never voted to cut off funds to support American armies in the field.

The War Powers Act

In 1973 the Congress passed the War Powers Act, designed to restrict presidential war-making powers. President Nixon vetoed the bill, but the Watergate affair appeared to undermine his support in this struggle with Congress, and Congress overrode his veto. The act is an interesting example of the continuing struggle over checks and balances in the American government. The act has these provisions:

1. In the absence of a congressional declaration of war, the president can commit armed forces to hostilities or to "situations where imminent involvement in hostilities is clearly indicated by the circumstances" only:

   To repel an armed attack on the United States or to forestall the "direct and imminent threat of such an attack."

   To repel an armed attack against U.S. armed forces outside the United States or to forestall the threat of such attack.

   To protect and evacuate U.S. citizens and nationals in another country if their lives were threatened.

   With specific statutory authorization by Congress, not to be inferred from any existing or future law or treaty unless Congress so specifies.

2. The president must report promptly to Congress the commitment of forces for such purposes.
3. Involvement of U.S. forces must be no longer than sixty days unless Congress authorizes their continued use by specific legislation.
4. Congress can end a presidential commitment by a concurrent resolution, an action that does not require the president's signature.

The combination of executive failures in Vietnam and executive abuses in Watergate has encouraged Congress to reassert its powers relative to the executive branch. The War Powers Act may be more symbolic than instrumental in times of real crisis; Congress has supported the president in the initial stages of every U.S. overseas military involvement, including Vietnam. Hence a real constitutional confrontation between the president and Congress over its implementation is unlikely. However, the War Powers Act is a reminder that the president is a member of a larger elite group. Even presidential command of America's military depends on broad elite consensus.

Watergate and the resignation of a president

The president must govern the nation within the boundaries of elite consensus. Mass opinion can be manipulated, but elite opinion is a powerful restraint on executive action. Voters may elect the president, but elites determine what is done in office.

The forced resignation of President Nixon is one of the most dramatic illustrations in American history of the president's dependence on elite support. A president reelected by an overwhelming majority had to resign his office less than two years after his landslide victory. We contend that Nixon's threatened impeachment and subsequent resignation were not entirely because of specific misdeeds or improprieties in office. Instead Nixon's demise was a result of (1) his general isolation from established elites, (2) his failure to adopt an accommodating style of politics, and (3) his frequent disregard of traditional "rules of the game."

Impeachment as a political process

The Constitution defines an impeachable offense as "treason, bribery, or other high crimes and misdemeanors." But impeachment is not really a *legal* process; it is a political process, and Nixon's offenses perhaps were more political than criminal.*

The House Judiciary Committee voted in early August 1974 to recommend to the full House of Representatives "the impeachment and trial and removal from office" of President Richard M. Nixon. The committee charged that the president,

---

*The only precedent for a presidential impeachment—the impeachment and trial of Andrew Johnson in 1868—was also political. No evidence proved President Johnson's personal involvement in a crime for which he could be indicted and found guilty in a court of law. Johnson was a Southern Democrat, a U.S. senator from a seceding state (Tennessee) who had remained loyal to the Union. Lincoln chose him as vice-president in 1864 as a gesture of national unity. When Johnson acceded to the presidency after Lincoln's assassination, he resisted attempts by "radical" Republicans in Congress to restructure Southern society by force. When Johnson dismissed some federal officials who opposed his conciliatory policies, Congress passed the Tenure of Office Act over Johnson's veto, forbidding executive removals without Senate consent. Johnson contended that the act was an unconstitutional infringement of his powers as chief executive. (Years later the Supreme Court agreed, holding that the power of removal is an executive power and specifically declaring that the Tenure of Office Act had been unconstitutional.) When Johnson dismissed his "radical" Republican secretary of war, Edwin M. Stanton, Congress was enraged. The House impeached Johnson on a party line vote, charging that Johnson had violated the Tenure of Office Act. The Civil War had left a legacy of bitterness against Johnson as a Southerner and a Democrat. But following a month-long trial in the Senate, the result was thirty-five "guilty" votes and nineteen "not guilty" votes—one vote short of the necessary two-thirds vote for removal. Seven Republicans joined the twelve Democrats in supporting the president. John F. Kennedy, in his book *Profiles in Courage*, praised the strength and courage of those senators who resisted popular emotions and prevented the president's removal. See Michael Les Benedict, *The Impeachment and Trial of Andrew Johnson* (New York: Norton, 1973).

... using the powers of his high office, engaged personally and through his close subordinates and agents, in a course of conduct or plan designed to delay, impede, and obstruct the investigation of such unlawful entry; to cover up, conceal, and protect those responsible; and to conceal the existence and scope of other unlawful activities.[8]

Isolation from established elites

Nixon's ouster was chiefly a result of his isolation from established elites and the suspicion, distrust, and hostility generated by his isolation. Established eastern elites never fully accepted him. Despite his apprenticeship in a top Wall Street law firm, he was always regarded as opportunistic, uncultured, and middle class by the eastern corporate and financial leaders he served, by influential segments of news media, and by intellectuals in prestigious universities and foundations. Nixon was upwardly mobile, competitive, self-conscious, boorish; he stood in marked contrast to the wealthy, cool, self-assured, aristocratic John F. Kennedy. Nixon fought his way up from rooms over his father's grocery store, through the local, unprestigious Whittier College (California), to Duke Law School (North Carolina), by self-sacrifice and hard work, long hours of studying, and postponement of pleasures and luxuries.

When Nixon came to the presidency, he found a giant Washington bureaucracy, overwhelmingly liberal in its politics and more responsive to the news media, influential interest groups, and key senators and House members than to the chief executive. This is how it has always been in Washington. But Nixon sought to exert power over the bureaucracy by adding to the size and powers of his own White House staff and centralizing decision making. His national security adviser, Henry Kissinger, became more powerful than the secretary of state (which he later became) or the secretary of defense; his domestic affairs adviser, John Ehrlichman, became more powerful than the secretaries who headed the domestic departments; and his chief of staff, H. R. Haldeman, became more powerful than anyone else, determining what information the president received and carrying out presidential orders. This style of administration won the president the lasting enmity of the Washington bureaucracy, and it also contributed to his isolation from other elites.

Nixon's long-standing hostility toward the press, a hostility that was more than reciprocated, contributed immeasurably to his isolation. But it was Nixon himself who, in reaction to a hostile press, cut himself off from the dialogue with influential publics. James David Barber writes, "Progressively, Nixon isolated himself not only from legislative and executive powers that be, but from his own aides, setting his assistant H. R. Haldeman to the task of keeping the horde at a distance."[9]

"Of course, after his political indiscretions he was ousted to this position. . ."
© Len Norris/ROTHCO–Vancouver Sun, Canada

Failure at accommodation

Nixon's personality made it difficult for him to engage in the friendly, hand-shaking, back-slapping politics that his predecessor Lyndon Johnson had developed into a fine art. As a consequence Nixon never fit comfortably into the accommodationist style of elite interaction. Nixon did not enjoy politics; he was by nature a loner. He made his major decisions alone in the presidential retreat at Camp David or at his San Clemente or Key Biscayne homes far from the hubbub of Washington.

Nixon also cut himself off from other elites. House members and senators could not reach him, aides handled his telephone calls, and he seldom, if ever, consulted key influential persons outside the government. Only the "Germans" at the White House—Haldeman, Ehrlichman, Ziegler (the press secretary), and Kissinger—had direct access to him. They stood as a "Berlin Wall," isolating the president from other elites because the president wanted it that way. Those who directed the influential news media (such as CBS News, the *Washington Post*, and the *New York Times*), whom Nixon (correctly) perceived as his enemies, were aggressively shut out; Nixon held fewer press conferences than any other president since Herbert Hoover.

Nixon's style was to confront crisis directly, to avoid surrender, to test his own strength of character against adversity. His instinct in a crisis was to "fight like hell" rather than to bargain, accommodate, and compromise. Nixon viewed "politics" as a burden to be borne rather than an art to enjoy. James David Barber believes that such political figures eventually become rigid.[10]

As the Watergate affair broadened and intensified, Nixon increasingly viewed it as a test of his strength and character. He perceived a conspiracy of liberal opponents in Congress and the news media to reverse the 1972 election outcome. He became unyielding in his stance on executive privilege, withholding tapes and documents. He came to believe that he was defending the presidency itself.

Violating rules of the game

The Watergate bugging and burglary of Democratic national headquarters violated established "rules of the game." Elites and masses in America have generally condoned repressive acts against communists, subversives, and "radicals." But turning these tactics against established political opposition—Democrats, liberals, and assorted presidential critics—clearly violates elite consensus.

Yet despite all the media's revelations, Nixon would *not* have had to resign if he had publicly repented and cooperated with Congress, the news media, and representatives of the eastern establishment in cleansing his administration.

Nixon's final line of defense was legal and technical: a feeble plea to abide by the constitutional definition of impeachment, "high crimes and misdemeanors." But the president was really forced to resign because of political acts: his isolation from establishment elites, his failures in accommodationist politics, and his misunderstanding of the rules of elite interaction.

The irony of Richard Nixon

It is ironic that Richard Nixon saw himself as a tribune of the people—"the great silent majority," as he identified them—pitting himself against a liberal establishment that was not popularly elected and did not reflect grass-roots sentiments. Nixon believed he understood "Middle America," and he probably did, since he was Middle American himself. But in the end, established elites turned Middle America against him. Public opinion is unstable, changeable, and susceptible to manipulation by the mass media. In six months in 1973, Nixon suffered the steepest plunge in public opinion approval ratings ever recorded.

Richard Nixon failed to understand that without elite support, even landslide victories at the polls are meaningless. Popular majorities elect a president, but a president can govern only with the support of the nation's elite. Nixon learned this costly lesson in his "final crisis."[11]

Jimmy Carter: A smile on the face of the establishment

James Earl Carter, Jr., was a political outsider who catapulted in less than two years from a Plains, Georgia, peanut farmer to president of the United States. At first glance, Carter's meteoric rise from rustic obscurity to the nation's most powerful office would seem to demolish the elitist notion that America selects its leaders from upper-class backgrounds or from the ranks of seasoned officeholders. But a closer examination of elite concerns in 1976—especially concern over declining public confidence in established elites themselves, together with Carter's reassuring, smiling style of politics—provides a better understanding of how and when an "outsider" can rise to national leadership. Specifically we argue that (1) established elites in 1976 were concerned with declining public trust in national institutions and national leaders; (2) established elites realized the need to replace many old faces in order to give a "new look" to the national leadership structure; and (3) the "new look" would be cosmetic only, including no fundamental changes in policies, programs, or values.

Building an image: The honest "outsider"

One year before his election, Jimmy Carter was unknown to three-quarters of the American people. He had served only one lackluster term as governor of Georgia. He had never served in Congress, and except for seven years in the navy, he had never worked for the federal government. He was not even a lawyer. His family's $4 million holdings in Sumter County, Georgia, gave them *local* influence, but few *national* leaders had ever heard of Sumter County. Carter, however, judged correctly in early 1974 that these political disadvantages could work in his favor given popular discontent with national leadership over Watergate and defeat and humiliation in Vietnam.

Developing an image.   In his campaign, Carter was careful not to offend the established liberal leadership. He supported standard liberal policies, avoided specifics on issues, and campaigned on charm, decency, and brotherly love. He described himself as "a farmer, an engineer, a businessman, a planner, a scientist, a governor, and a Christian." No one campaigned harder, worked more zealously, or hungered more obsessively for the presidency than did Jimmy Carter. He was a conservative before conservative groups, a liberal before liberal groups, a farmer in the farm belt, a businessman before the local chamber of commerce, a born-again Christian, a navy man for the hawks, a friend of prominent blacks, and a "good ole boy" to southern whites. His choice of Mondale as vice-presidential running mate reassured liberals that he was not a southern populist and that his values were consistent with those of the party leadership and the nation.

Elite contacts.   Carter had been introduced to the "political and economic elite" several years before he began his race for the presidency. The Coca-Cola Company is the largest industrial corporation headquartered in Atlanta. J. Paul Austin, its chairman of the board and a friend and supporter of Jimmy Carter, nominated the Georgia governor to serve as a U.S. representative on the international Trilateral Commission. The Trilateral Commission, established in 1972 by David Rockefeller (chairman of the board of Chase Manhattan Bank) with the assistance of the Council on Foreign Relations and the Rockefeller Foundation, is a group of officials of multinational corporations and of the governments of several industrial nations who meet periodically to coordinate economic policy among the United States, Western Europe, and Japan.* Rockefeller himself appointed Carter, with support from Coca-Cola and Lockheed, both Atlanta-based multinational corporations. The executive director of the commission was Columbia University professor Zbigniew Brzezinski, later Carter's national security adviser. The commission's membership is a compendium of power and prestige; it included the president of California Institute of Technology, Harold Brown (later secretary of defense); Coca-Cola's J. Paul Austin; *Time* magazine editor Hedley Donovan; Paul Warnke, senior partner in Averell Harriman's Wall Street investment firm; Alden Clausen, president of the Bank of America, the nation's largest bank; United Auto Workers president Leonard Woodcock; Bendix Corporation president Werner M. Blumenthal (the first secretary of the treasury in the Carter administration); Cyrus Vance, senior Wall Street lawyer (first secretary of state in the Carter administration); and U.S. Senator Walter Mondale (later vice-president of the United States).

Acceptance into the elite.   Thus Carter as an "outsider" provided the new face, the smile, the reassuring manner, that a worried establishment perceived as essential in winning back mass confidence in national leadership. At the same time, Carter reinforced established programs and policies. He personified traditional American values: humble beginnings; hard work; success in business and politics; deep roots in the soil, the family, and the community; and pronounced Christian morals and principles. Top elite circles welcomed him as a man who could restore mass confidence in public institutions and national leadership, and do so without changing things much.

Jimmy Carter's rapid rise to national leadership, and his welcome into top elite circles, represents still another tactic available to an embattled elite: replace the old faces associated with past defeats and

*Or as Jane Fonda's husband, California Assemblyman Tom Hayden, put it, "The Commission is just another form of colonialism. The basic idea is to act in concert to make the underdeveloped nations of the world economically dependent on the West." *San Francisco Examiner* (December 12, 1976), p. 14.

humiliation with smiling new faces promising honesty, compassion, and good times.

How a "media" president governs

Jimmy Carter knew how to run for office but not necessarily how to run a government. The year-long presidential campaign requires candidates to meet high standards in political organizing, campaign effort, and media image making. But these standards may not be the ones required for good performance of presidential duties once in office. During his first three years in office, Carter's popular support dropped dramatically—to the same level as Nixon's just before his resignation. Carter did not maintain consistent or effective policies in the struggle against inflation; his energy programs bogged down in Congress; he canceled defense programs recommended by his predecessors, the military, and Congress; he projected an image of weakness and vacillation in the face of Cuban aggression in Africa and Soviet troops in Cuba. Inflation rose from 6 percent per year to 14 percent per year. Carter obtained Senate approval of the Panama Canal Treaty, returning the Canal Zone to the Republic of Panama. But he lost the battle to win ratification of SALT II (the second strategic arms limitation treaty with the Soviets) even before the Soviets invaded Afghanistan. Only after the Afghanistan invasion did Carter give serious consideration to restoring the strength of U.S. defense forces.

Carter had less success with Congress than did his two Democratic predecessors. During John F. Kennedy's tenure, Congress supported about 85 percent of the legislation upon which the president took a clear position; during Lyndon B. Johnson's tenure, Congress supported the president on 84 percent of his legislative requests. But Carter, even with Democratic Congresses, won approval for only about 75 percent of his legislative proposals.

More important, Carter did not project *an image of presidential leadership*. Gradually the media began to portray Carter as weak, indecisive, and unable to control people or events. The media's early demands for "honesty" gave way to demands for "leadership." Carter responded predictably in the summer of 1979: he delivered a nationally televised speech in which he talked of a "national malaise" that was destroying his leadership efforts, especially in the energy field. He spoke of a "crisis of confidence" and tried to project a new image of leadership. But his approval ratings in the polls remained low; the new Carter image failed to take hold; and Senator Edward M. Kennedy announced that he would pick up the fallen banner of national leadership.

With Carter's approval ratings at an all-time low, and the last remaining bearer of the Kennedy "Camelot" legend challenging his leadership, most political commentators predicted Carter's defeat. But then the crisis occurred that caused popular opinion to rally around the president: Iranian terrorists, with the approval of political and religious leaders of that nation, kidnapped and held hostage fifty American diplomats and employees in the American embassy in Tehran. Shortly thereafter Soviet troops invaded neighboring Afghanistan.

Americans tend to equate support for the president with support for America in a period of crisis. Carter's approval ratings leaped upward, even though the president failed to obtain the early release of the hostages or the withdrawal of Soviet troops from Afghanistan. These events brought only an initial burst of support, however, in a "rally around the flag" effect. As no immediate solution emerged, Carter's popularity began to plummet again. His popularity had increased dramatically from the seizure of the hostages until the beginning of 1980. From then, the percentage of Americans approving Carter's performance began as dramatic a decline as the earlier increase in approval. An unsuccessful attempt at rescue of the hostages in the spring of 1980 did nothing to halt the erosion of support; by summer Carter's popularity was as low as it had been before the international crises beginning in November (32 percent approved of his performance in November 1979; 58 percent approved in January 1980; but only 33 percent approved by June).

Ronald Reagan: The "Great Communicator" as president

Ronald Wilson Reagan has never been the right-wing extremist portrayed by his political opponents. His ties to the nation's corporate and financial establishment are long-standing. When his Hollywood acting career nose-dived in the 1950s, Ralph J. Cordiner, chairman of the board of General Electric, selected Reagan not only to host the "G.E. Theater" on television but also to give lectures throughout the country on the merits of the free enterprise system. When Reagan lost viewer ratings to one of his own favorite programs, "Bonanza," he turned more and more to the business-lecture circuit as a source of income. Reagan had always been a Democrat and (as he so often reminds us) a six-time elected president of his union, the Screen Actors Guild. But in 1964 he delivered an impressive television appeal for Republican presidential candidate Barry Goldwater. A group of prominent businessmen decided that Reagan had political potential; William French Smith (a wealthy Los Angeles attorney and director of Crocker National Bank and Pacific Telephone), Justin Dart (chairman of Dart Industries, which owns Rexall drugs and Kraft Foods), the late A. C. Rubel (chairman of Union Oil Company), and others agreed to establish a "Ronald Reagan trust fund" to help guide his financial and political future. Two years later, in 1966, Reagan defeated Edmund G. "Pat" Brown (Jerry Brown's father) to become governor of California.

Reagan served two terms as governor of the nation's largest state, waiting impatiently for the opening that would lead him to the Oval Office. As governor, Reagan was closer to the center of the political spectrum, and more willing to bargain and compromise with a Democratic legislature, than his earlier conservative speech making suggested. In 1976 Reagan almost succeeded in taking away the Republican presidential nomination from Gerald Ford. Reagan posed as the conservative and Ford as the moderate within the Republican party. But in 1980, when it was clear that Reagan was the front-runner for the GOP nomination, he began to portray himself as a moderate. His "aw shucks" mannerisms and "nice guy" image sheltered him from accusations that he was a fanatic of the radical Right.

Reagan's cabinet appointments reaffirmed the establishment character of his administration: Alexander M. Haig, secretary of state (former NATO commander, president of United Technologies Corp.); George Schultz, secretary of state (president of the Bechtel Corporation and former secretary of the treasury); Caspar Weinberger, secretary of defense (vice-president of the Bechtel Corporation and former secretary of health, education and welfare); and Donald T. Regan, secretary of the treasury (chairman of the Wall Street investment firm of Merrill Lynch & Co.).

Thus the name and party of the president may change, but governing elites are drawn from the same pool of established leaders.

The contradictions of the "Great Communicator"

The media portrayed Reagan's 1980 victory as a "popular landslide"; yet he actually won a scant 51 percent of the vote (Carter won 41 percent and independent John Anderson got 7.9 percent of the vote). The turnout in 1980 was the lowest in thirty-two years.

Widely regarded as a president of extraordinary popularity, Reagan began his administration with an approval rating of only 55 percent, substantially below that of the disgraced Carter (75 percent) and Ford (71 percent). Treated by the media as a master of public relations—they dubbed him the "Great Communicator"—his highest approval rating, 68 percent in May 1981, was only slightly better than Richard Nixon's highest rating. Though biographers described Reagan as a somewhat "passive" president, his success rate with Congress in his first year was 81.9 percent, the best since Lyndon Johnson. Portrayed by his enemies as stubborn and inflexible, he enraged his New Right supporters by relegating their "social agenda" to low priority. Accused by Democrats of unwillingness to compromise on economic issues, he astonished his budget director, David Stockman, by giving up numerous pork barrel projects (favored special-interest programs) in order to secure the necessary votes for his budget and taxation proposals. Labeled an old-fashioned anticommunist hawk by the left wing of his party, Reagan continued the United States' long-term commitment to the People's Republic of China.

Beneath these contradictions lies the true Reagan, a media president. Carter used the media to get elected but could not use it to govern. Reagan is a media professional in the governmental process. His presidency is an image presidency, and it is a delegated presidency. Bored by details, Reagan allows his staff great latitude in decision making. One of his major advisers, Edwin Meese, developed the delegating style of administration for Reagan in California and simply moved it to Washington, along with much of the California staff. Counselor to the President, Meese, along with White House Chief of Staff James A. Baker, Deputy Chief Michael Deaver and National Security Adviser William Clark, form a tight circle of trusted confidants. The president also relies heavily on the small group of California businessmen who rescued him from bankruptcy during his years as an actor.

The delegated presidency works reasonably well in persuading a reluctant Congress to approve general budget and tax programs. But it is not necessarily an effective way to keep the president well informed about public policy. Reagan maintains good humor, and does not lose his composure in public, as did Carter. But Reagan occasionally appears shockingly ill informed. A campaigner is "human" when he appears uninformed; a president must know what he is doing. As a performer, Reagan understands image, but he is less interested in the complexities of issues. Members of the Washington press corps found out quickly that they could embarrass him, and they occasionally do. (Reagan and his staff view press conferences as performances, but they disagree about the amount of necessary preparation. Reagan uses a seating chart during his press conferences as an aid in addressing reporters by their first names. He can also use it to single out sympathetic reporters when the going gets rough.) Lacking information, Reagan occasionally slips into (sometimes fictitious) anecdotes as well.

Yet Reagan clearly has a vision of his presidency: his charter, as he views it, is to reduce the role of government in Americans' everyday affairs, to establish and maintain a strong military force, and to lighten the tax burden. Like Franklin Roosevelt, to whom he likes to be compared, Reagan entered the White House committed to reversing an established pattern of policy. Roosevelt intended to reduce the commitment to laissez faire economics and increase the role of the government in the economic life of the country. Reagan was committed to a reduction of the role of government in economic life. Both proposed seemingly radical changes (although they were far less radical than the media claimed). However, unlike Roosevelt, who had no clearly thought out ideology, Reagan had, if not a blueprint, at least a strong personal commitment to rugged individualism. Thus he may believe that burdening himself with detail (as did Carter) is unproductive and of secondary importance to shaping his overall program.

Like Roosevelt, Reagan appreciates the value of conflicting points of view. Presidents sometimes become victims of "group think," punishing or ostracizing those whose views do not mesh with those of their inner circle. Reagan has not fallen victim to this practice, however; staff and cabinet members not only argue within the executive office but also occasionally go public with their disagreement. The resulting image may be one of disarray within the presidency.

Reagan and Congress: Pragmatism and pork

Reagan seeks to avoid the Jimmy Carter image of inconsistency and unclear direction; hence his rhetoric is ideologically consistent. However, Reagan's politics are more pragmatic than his public statements would suggest. Consider his first-year record in Congress, for example. His first goal was to reduce federal domestic spending and increase military spending. Reagan backed his proposals for budget reductions with an intensive lobbying campaign. White House lobbyists met regularly with business organizations to guide the program through the Democratic-controlled house. Speaker of the House "Tip" O'Neill, a symbol of old-style mainstream liberal Democratic ideology, announced that he would fight all the way. The battle centered on the "boll weevils"— southern Democratic congressmen sympathetic to Reagan's goals. Both sides lobbied heavily, with O'Neill pleading for party loyalty and the president's lobbying team urging House members to vote their conviction rather than party loyalty.

As the tug-of-war continued, Reagan met personally with the conservative southerners, often giving them the pet projects they demanded in exchange for votes. The process reached its climax with the president's appearance on television. Unlike his predecessor, Reagan views television as a medium of influence within governmental elites. At his best when he can simplify the issues, Reagan presented the nation with a clear choice: continued excessive government spending, and hence inflation; or budget reduction, and hence reduced inflation. While Democrats criticized his presentation as simplistic, as indeed it was, they conceded that it was effective. Most House members were deluged by letters from constituents. The technologically sophisticated business lobbyists engineered much of the letter writing using computerized mailing lists, but the tactic was clearly effective. On May 7, 1981, sixty-three Democrats, most of them "boll weevils," rejected O'Neill's plea and voted with the president. *All* Republicans supported the president. Thus the first part of the president's program for economic recovery was in place, humiliating the Democratic House leadership in the process.

The confrontation was a classic one between new media politics and the old constituency group politics as practiced by Speaker O'Neill. Every day, especially on Sunday morning talk shows, the most photogenic members of the executive branch argued their case; O'Neill declined invitations to respond.

The next phase, the tax cut (considered more important than budget reductions by Reagan's supply-side advisers) repeated the techniques of the first. An executive-led business coalition mobilized a coordinated lobbying effort; Reagan met personally with the southern conservatives; and another address to the nation climaxed the lobbying effort. Reagan again offered clear, simple choices: economic recovery or economic decline. And again Congress responded, with Reagan picking up forty-eight Democratic votes and losing only one Republican vote. He owed his victory to the "boll weevils" and to the loyalty of his party. He also owed it to his extraordinary ability to use the media.

When Reagan's promised economic recovery failed to materialize, the president and his advisers entered a period of agony. The administration was in the embarrassing position of asking for a tax *increase* to help reduce the deficit created by earlier tax reductions. This reversal required even more skillful negotiations. Reagan had angered and humiliated Speaker O'Neill during the first votes. Now he needed O'Neill's support because Republican conservatives and the southern Democrats did not take kindly to tax increases. At this point, previous concessions to individual legislators became valuable because numerous House members who had benefited from presidential promises were still in debt to the president.

But the president needed O'Neill, and eventually he got him. "The President is right," said the Speaker. Many conservatives, especially the unrepentant supply-siders such as Congressman Jack Kemp and the American Conservative Union resisted to the end. However, such influential business organizations as the National Association of Manufacturers, the American Business Conference, and most important, the Business Roundtable declared their support for the increase. This time Speaker O'Neill led a bare majority in support of the president.

The end of the honeymoon

Reagan's first-year record was brilliant by any standards. Though unwilling to master details, he won major victories in the House by forging first a conservative coalition against the liberal Democrats and then a liberal coalition against the conservatives in his own party.

In foreign policy, an area in which Reagan professes no expertise and in which he entertains a strong anti-Soviet bias, his inclination to leave decision-making details to others was especially strong. The administration's lobbying proved less skillful on foreign policy issues.

Reagan narrowly won his first major foreign policy test when the Senate rejected a resolution to disapprove the sale of AWACS radar planes to Saudi Arabia. Reagan's dissatisfaction with the lobbying efforts of Richard Allen (later dismissed for a trivial violation of personal ethics) was apparent. Careful cultivation of individual Congressmen, so apparent in the economic victories, was absent here. A potent lobby, the American Jewish community, was active and making headway in favor of the resolution. In the end, the president resorted to appeals to preserve the prestige of the presidency. His victory proved costly, for it revealed greater presidential vulnerability than had been evident before.

In 1982, Reagan suffered his first major loss in Congress when the legislators overrode his veto of a supplemental appropriation bill. In foreign and defense policy, Congress rejected his proposal for a "dense pack" deployment of MX missiles (although not rejecting the missile system itself). These defeats triggered an uncharacteristically hostile response from the president, and his 1982 budget negotiations showed far less flexibility than those of 1981. Because of Reagan's intransigence, Senate and House Republican leaders took over the 1982 budget process, and Reagan virtually withdrew. His 1982 "batting average" with Congress dropped 10 points, lower than Carter's in his last year. (See figure 10-4.)

Thus, after a superb first year, Reagan began to falter. The media renewed their attack. The *New York Times* and *Washington Post* pub-

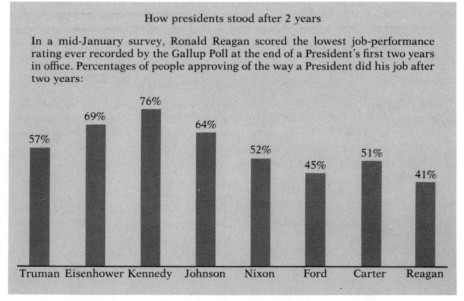

How presidents stood after 2 years

In a mid-January survey, Ronald Reagan scored the lowest job-performance rating ever recorded by the Gallup Poll at the end of a President's first two years in office. Percentages of people approving of the way a President did his job after two years:

Truman 57% | Eisenhower 69% | Kennedy 76% | Johnson 64% | Nixon 52% | Ford 45% | Carter 51% | Reagan 41%

FIGURE 10-4.   Presidential performance: The first two years

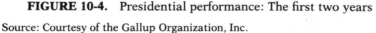

Source: Courtesy of the Gallup Organization, Inc.

The White House Bureaucracy

The White House is a big operation—over 350 people on the President's immediate staff; more than four times that number in his extended family—the Executive Office of the President.

When President Franklin Roosevelt first established a blue-ribbon panel to advise him on the creation of a Presidential staff, they suggested six senior assistants—"men with high competence, great physical vigor and a passion for anonymity." Over the years since that modest beginning, the White House staff has grown enormously. This growth has been due—in large part—to the desire of each incoming President to get control of the massive Federal bureaucracy beyond the White House. Ironically, the principal effect has been to create within the President's own office a large, unwieldy and unresponsive bureaucracy. . . .

The frustrations don't end with the personal distance from the President of the paper flow, however. There are also the meetings. The incredible, interminable, boring, ever-multiplying meetings. There are staff meetings, trip meetings and general-scheduling meetings, meetings to make decisions and unmake them and to plan future meetings where decisions will be made. . . .

What this problem calls for is a much maligned but very effective management tool—the meat axe. The White House staff should be cut in half—for openers. With half as many position papers on half as many issues. Good.

The President is the leader of the nation. He doesn't need to be, and he shouldn't be, involved in every issue, major and minor, that is raised by the Congress, the special interests, the press or the public. With half the staff there would be only half as many people to comment on and water down the decisions that did receive Presidential attention. There might even be only half as many meetings.

With half the staff, the White House would probably be unable to "liaison" with everything that moves in the outer world. Some of the nicest and most competent people in the White House are "liaison" to blacks or Jews or women or old people or young people or Hispanics or whatever—I've lost track of them all. They should all be let go or transferred to real jobs. The concept of liaisoning is inherently misleading and insulting. . . .

Finally, with the White House staff cut in half, those who remained might be a happier and more productive lot. The remaining staff could focus on a few truly Presidential issues, attend only those meetings which are necessary and important and spend the rest of their time actually producing something that has a chance of reaching the President reasonably intact. The quality of advice to the President would improve greatly. The White House product—which is to say, national policy—would benefit.*

lished editorials alleging that Reagan had lost control of his administration; that his momentary lapses revealed more than bad homework habits; that he was indeed no more than a symbolic president unable to prevent his staff from going their separate ways. So alarmed was the president that he called a news conference early in 1983 specifically to deny these claims. At one point he exclaimed, "I make the decisions." In 1983, polls indicated that Reagan trailed the presumed Democratic contenders, Walter Mondale and John Glenn in popularity. This midterm drop was lower than that of any of his predecessors at the same point in their first terms.

Other executive elites

The president is not one person but more than five thousand permanent employees in the executive office of the president, which includes the White House Office, the Office of Management and Budget, the Council of Economic Advisers, the National Security Council, the National Aeronautics and Space Council, the Office of Emergency Planning, and the Office of Science and Technology. In addition is the presidential cabinet, consisting of heads of thirteen major executive departments. Finally more than forty independent agencies function outside the regular departmental organization of the executive branch, including the Interstate Commerce Commission, the Federal Reserve Board, the Federal Trade Commission, the Federal Power Commission, the Federal Communications Commission, the Securities and Exchange Commission, the National Labor Relations Board, the Civil Aeronautics Board, and the Atomic Energy Commission. (See chapter 11.)

Closest to the president is a group of aides and assistants who work with the chief executive in the White House Office, which the president can organize as he sees fit. These aides and assistants perform whatever duties the president assigns them. They usually include a chief of staff, a press secretary, an appointment secretary, and one or more special assistants for liaison with Congress. Some of the president's assistants have ad hoc assignments, while others have a specialty. Theodore Sorensen, special assistant to President Kennedy, defined the role of the White House staff as the auxiliary eyes and ears of the president, with responsibilities as broad as those of the president.[12] See *Newsweek*'s view of White House bureaucracy on page 264.

Increasingly White House staff members have come to exercise great power in the name of the president. They frequently direct affairs in the name of the president ("The president has asked me to tell you . . ."), but the president may have little direct oversight of their activities. Even more serious is the fact that staff members may come into power with little preparation or experience for elite membership. Often their training consists of nothing more than serving as "advance guard" in presidential election campaigns: scheduling presidential appearances, handling campaign advertising, and fetching coffee and doughnuts. These staff are valued not for their independent contributions to policy but rather for their personal loyalty to the president.

Frequently in recent presidential administrations, staff members have embarrassed the president: Truman's personal secretary went to jail for fixing a tax case; Eisenhower's assistant to the president, Sherman Adams, retired in disgrace for accepting expensive gifts; Johnson's White House adviser, Walter Jenkins, was convicted of a homosexual assault; almost all of Nixon's original White House staff were indicted in the Watergate scandal; Carter's director of the Office of Management and Budget, Bert Lance, was forced to resign after disclosures of irregularities in his banking business.

Summary

The president is the popular symbol of governmental authority. In fact, however, presidents are substantially less able to control decisions than they would like to be.

1. Government elites in America do not command; they seek consensus. Government decision making involves bargaining, accommodation, and compromise among government and nongovernment elites. Our examination of the presidency provides clear evidence of the consensual nature of elite interaction and the heavy price a president must pay for failure to pursue accommodationist policies.

2. The president is the first among equals of America's elites. Presidential power depends not on formal authority but on personal abilities of persuasion. Moreover, the president must still function within the established elite system. The choices available to presidents are limited to alternatives for which they can mobilize elite support. Despite access to mass opinion, the president can be effectively checked by other public and private elites.

3. In the twentieth century, presidential power has increased as a result of the growing importance of military and foreign policy in national life, areas in which the president has greatest constitutional powers. The growth of the executive branch of government and the increased visibility of the president in the mass media also contribute to the growth of presidential power.

4. Controversies over presidential power are always linked to their political context. While liberal writers generally praise strong pres-

idents in history, they turn against the presidency under Johnson and Nixon. Congress passed the War Powers Act to try to restore control over armed interventions such as Vietnam.

5. The forced resignation of President Nixon was a dramatic illustration of the president's dependence on elite support. A president must govern within the boundaries of elite consensus or face removal from office. The president can be removed not only for "high crimes and misdemeanors" but also for *political* offenses—violating elite consensus.

6. The resignation of Nixon was a product not only of specific improprieties in office but also of his isolation from established elites, his failure to adopt an accommodationist style of politics, and his disregard of traditional rules of the game.

7. Established elites who are concerned with declining public trust and confidence frequently turn to "new faces" to provide the appearance of change. But the change is cosmetic only and does not include fundamental change in programs, policies, or values. Jimmy Carter's rapid rise to the presidency probably resulted from this need to find a "new face" to reassure the masses.

8. Carter's first term was unsuccessful in that he lost public approval and had relatively low congressional support scores. However, international crises in Iran and Afghanistan caused voters to rally around the president as a display of patriotism.

9. Reagan's presidency allows a second look at media presidents. His rapid decline in popularity and influence may illustrate the problems encountered by relatively inexperienced presidents who surge to victory on the strength of image but find it impossible to build successful governing coalitions.

NOTES

1. James David Barber, *The Presidential Character*, 2d ed. (Englewood Cliffs, N.J.: Prentice-Hall, 1977), p. 4.
2. Richard Neustadt, *Presidential Power* (New York: New American Library, 1960), pp. 88–89.
3. William Howard Taft, *Our Chief Magistrate and His Powers* (New York: Columbia University Press, 1938), p. 138. Reprinted in John P. Roche and L. W. Levy, eds., *The Presidency* (New York: Harcourt Brace Jovanovich, 1964), p. 23.
4. From Arthur B. Tourtellot, *President on the Presidency* (Garden City, N.Y.: Doubleday, 1964), pp. 55–56.
5. Fred I. Greenstein, "The Psychological Functions of the Presidency for Citizens," in Elmer E. Cornwell, ed., *The American Presidency: Vital Center* (Chicago: Scott, Foresman, 1966), pp. 30–36.
6. See Note 2 above.
7. Congressional Quarterly, *The Power of the Pentagon* (Washington, D.C.: Congressional Quarterly Press, 1972), p. 42.

8. U. S. House, Committee on the Judiciary, "Bill of Impeachment Against Richard M. Nixon," reprinted in *Newsweek*, August 5, 1974.
9. James David Barber, *The Presidential Character* (Englewood Cliffs, N.J.: Prentice-Hall, 1972), pp. 423–424.
10. James David Barber, "Tone-Deaf in the Oval Office," *Saturday Review*, January 12, 1974, p. 14.
11. For further information on Richard M. Nixon's career, see his political autobiography, *Six Crises* (Garden City, N.Y.: Doubleday, 1962).
12. *Playboy* (July 1976).

SELECTED READINGS

Barber, James David. *The Presidential Character: Predicting Performance in the White House*, 2nd ed. Englewood Cliffs, N.J.: Prentice-Hall, 1977. This extremely readable book seeks to classify presidents along two continua: an "active-passive" baseline, according to the amount of energy and enthusiasm displayed in the exercise of presidential duties, and a "positive-negative" baseline, dealing with the degree of happiness or "fun" each president displays in manipulating presidential power. Using these two baselines, Barber classifies the modern presidents into four types: active-positive (F.D.R., Truman, Kennedy), active-negative (Wilson, Hoover, Johnson), passive-positive (Taft, Harding), and passive-negative (Coolidge, Eisenhower). President Nixon was analyzed while in office to demonstrate the predictive capacity of these concepts.

Canton, Lou. *Reagan.* New York: Putnam, 1982. This *Washington Post* White House correspondent provides a balanced account of Reagan's career.

Edwards III, George C. *Presidential Influence in Congress.* San Francisco: Freeman, 1980. A systematic analysis of the factors that affect a president's success in Congress, including party, popularity in the polls, and legislative skills.

Gold, Gerald, ed. *The White House Transcripts.* New York: Bantam Books, 1974. One of several publications that reproduce in its entirety the "Submission of Recorded Presidential Conversations to the Committee on the Judiciary of the House of Representatives by President Richard Nixon." Later versions of the recordings (including the House Judiciary Committee's version) contain some important variations from the material reported in this version.

Halberstam, David. *The Best and the Brightest.* New York: Random House, 1972. Deals with the men who advised presidents Kennedy and Johnson with regard to the conduct of the war in Vietnam. Based on interviews of former *New York Times* Vietnam correspondent, David Halberstam, this book reveals an excellent view of the men and processes responsible for decision making at the highest levels of the federal executive.

Neustadt, Richard. *Presidential Power.* New York: Wiley, 1960. Neustadt focuses on the attributes of the individuals who occupy the office of the president rather than the attributes of the office itself. Instead of a discussion of the roles and formal powers attached to the presidential office, this book examines the ability of the president to use his personality, persuasive abilities, professional reputation, public prestige, and other qualities to increase his power and influence.

Rossiter, Clinton. *The American Presidency*, 2d ed. New York: New American Library, 1964. This classic traditional work on the roles and powers of the president was originally published in 1956. It discusses the several roles of the president (chief of state, chief executive, commander-in-chief, chief diplomat, chief legislator, chief of party, chief manager of prosperity, and so on). In addition, Rossiter discusses the several limitations of the president's powers, the historical and modern presidency, and the "hiring, firing, retiring, and expiring of presidents."

Schlesinger, Arthur, Jr. *A Thousand Days.* Boston: Houghton Mifflin, 1965. *The Imperial Presidency.* Boston: Houghton Mifflin, 1973. *A Thousand Days* is an entertaining and instructive chronicle of the Kennedy administration, devoted mostly to historical accounts of executive decision making, primarily in the area of foreign policy. In *The Imperial Presidency,* Schlesinger describes the changes in the modern presidency under Richard Nixon, which he believes have resulted in an alarming concentration of power in just one man: Nixon. The argument runs directly counter to an earlier liberal point of view that held that the presidency, especially in the hands of Democrats, was not sufficiently powerful to push public-regarding public policy through a conservative, obstructionist Congress.

11 The Bureaucratic Elite and Public Policy

The Washington bureaucracy has become a major base of power in American society—independent of the Congress, the President, the Courts, or the people.

The problem is not conspiracy or corruption, but unchecked rule. And being unchecked, the rule reflects not the national need but the bureaucratic need.

—*John K. Galbraith,* The New Industrial State, *1967*

The Washington bureaucracy is a negative phrase. People generally view bureaucracy as red tape, paper shuffling, duplication of effort, waste and inefficiency, impersonality, insensitivity, unresponsiveness, and overregulation. We have no quarrel with this description of the Washington bureaucracy. We would add, however, that the *Washington bureaucracy has become a major base of power in American society—independent of Congress, the president, the courts, or the people.*

Power in America is gradually shifting from those who control economic and political resources to those who control technology and organized expertise. We should *not* conclude that because large government bureaucracies are wasteful, inefficient, incompetent, and impersonal that they are hopeless giants with little effective control over our lives. On the contrary, government bureaucracies invade every aspect of modern life: in the home, in communications, in transportation, in the environment, in the work place, in schools, on the streets.

The "faceless bureaucrats" are not really accountable to anyone. The president, Congress, and courts can place only the broadest restrictions on bureaucratic power. And certainly "the people" have no direct means of altering bureaucratic decisions. Even the president, the White House staff, and cabinet officials have great difficulty establishing control over the bureaucracy. The bureaucrats control information and technology, and they almost invariably outlast their political superiors in office. Indeed very often the bureaucrats feel "a certain contempt for their superiors" because political leaders do not share the information, technical expertise, or experience of the bureaucrats.

Bureaucratic power

Public policy is whatever governments choose to do or not to do. Public policies are the activities of government agencies and bureaucrats, acting within their official capacities. By far the overwhelming majority of these activities are initiated by bureaucrats themselves, not by any elected officials and certainly not by "the people."

The power of bureaucracies grows with advances in technology and increases in the size and complexity of society. Large, complex, technological societies cannot be governed by a single president and 535 Congress members who lack the expertise, time, and energy to look after the myriad details involved in nuclear power, or environmental protection, or occupational safety, or communications, or aviation, or trucking, or fair employment, or hundreds of other aspects of American life. So the president and Congress create bureaucracies, appropriate money for them, and authorize them to draw up detailed rules, regulations, and "guidelines" to govern us. These bureaucracies receive only vague and general directions from the president and Congress. Actual governance is in the hands of the Nuclear Regulatory Commission, the Environmental Protection Agency, the Occupational Health and Safety Administration, the Federal Communications Commission, the Federal Aviation Administration, the Interstate Commerce Commission, the Equal Employment Opportunity Commission, and hundreds of similar bureaucratic agencies. (There are approximately two thousand federal government agencies with rule-making powers.) One estimate suggests that the bureaucracies announce *twenty* rules or regulations for every *one* law of Congress. In this way, the power to make policy has passed from the president and Congress to the bureaucratic elite.

Why is policy making shifted to the bureaucracy?

1. The standard explanation is that Congress and the president do not have the time, energy, or expertise to handle the details of policy making. A related explanation is that the increasing complexity and sophistication of technology require that technical experts ("technocrats") actually carry out the intent of Congress and the president.

No single bureaucrat can master the complex activities of even a single large government agency—from budgeting, purchasing, personnel, accounting, planning, communication, and organization, to the complexities of nuclear plants, energy transmission, the internal revenue (tax) code, or the computerized social security files. Each bureaucrat has relatively little knowledge of overall policy. But that person's narrow expertise, when combined with the narrow expertise of thousands of other bureaucrats, creates an organized base of power that political leaders find difficult to control.

A few years ago, economist John K. Galbraith wrote about the "technocrats" who increasingly dominate decision making in large private corporations. The same commentary applies to government "technocrats":

> It is a common public impression, not discouraged by scientists, engineers and industrialists, that modern scientific, engineering and industrial achievements are the work of a new and quite remarkable race of men. This

is pure vanity. The real accomplishment of modern science and technology consists in taking ordinary men, informing them narrowly and deeply and then, through appropriate organization, arranging to have their knowledge combined with that of other specialized but equally ordinary men. This dispenses with the need for genius.[1]

2. Another reason is that Congress and the president deliberately pass vague and ambiguous laws, largely for *symbolic reasons*—to ensure nuclear safety, protect the environment, ensure occupational safety, allocate broadcasting channels, guarantee flight safety, prevent unfair interstate charges, guarantee "equal employment opportunity," and so on. Bureaucrats' role is to use "authority" of these symbolic laws to decide what actually will be done. Thus bureaucrats must give meaning to these symbolic measures. Frequently Congress and the president do not want to take public responsibility for unpopular policies; they find it easier to blame the bureaucrats and pretend that unpopular policies are a product of an ungovernable Washington bureaucracy. This explanation allows an elected president and an elected Congress to impose regulations without accepting responsibility for them.

3. Finally, the bureaucracy itself is now sufficiently powerful to have its own laws passed—laws that allow agencies to expand in size, acquire more authority, and obtain more money. Bureaucracy has become its own cause. Political scientist James Q. Wilson comments on "the great, almost overpowering, importance of the existing government and professional groups in shaping policy":

> I am impressed by the extent to which policy making is dominated by the representatives of those bureaucracies and professions having a material stake in the management and funding of the intended policy and by those political staffs who see in a new program a chance for publicity, advancement, and a good reputation for their superiors.[2]

Organization of the Washington bureaucracy

How big is big government? The United States now has eighty thousand separate governments, including federal, state, and local governments, as well as public school districts. These governments collectively spend about 35 percent of the gross national product (GNP), the sum of all goods and services produced in the nation. The federal government alone accounts for 22 percent of the GNP, and other governments account for 14 percent. The "private sector" accounts for the remaining 65 percent of the GNP; however, most, if not all, of the private sector comes under government regulation.

The executive branch of the U.S. government includes thirteen departments, forty independent executive agencies operating outside of these departments, and the large Executive Office of the President. (See figure 11-1.)

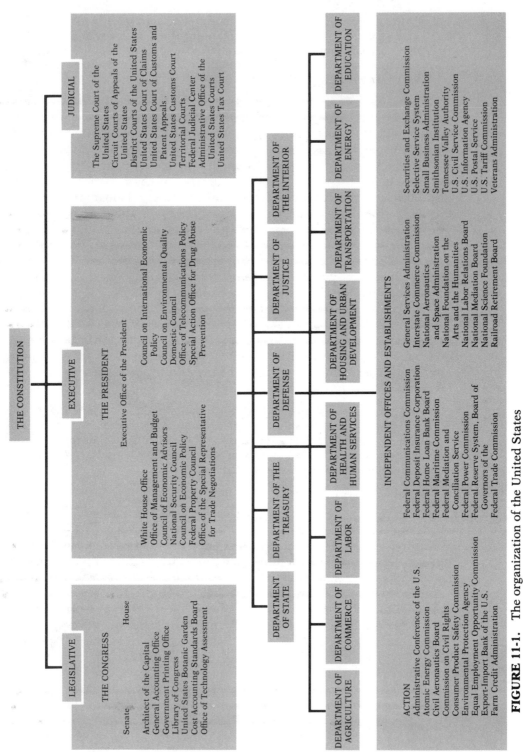

FIGURE 11-1. The organization of the United States

Source: *The United States Government Manual 1982–1983* (Washington, D.C.: Government Printing Office, 1982), p. 22.

Cabinet.   The cabinet rarely functions as a group. It consists of the secretaries of the thirteen executive departments, the vice-president, the UN ambassador, the CIA director, and the special trade representative, with the president as its head. Cabinet officers in the United States are powerful because they head giant administrative organizations. The secretary of state, the secretary of defense, the secretary of the treasury, the attorney general, and to a lesser extent, the other departmental secretaries are all people of power and prestige in America. But the cabinet, as a council, rarely makes policy.[3] Seldom does a strong president hold a cabinet meeting to decide important policy questions. More frequently, the president knows what he wants and holds cabinet meetings only to help him sell his views.

NSC.   The National Security Council (NSC) resembles a cabinet; the president is chairman and the vice-president, secretary of state, secretary of defense, and director of the Office of Emergency Planning (a minor unit in the executive office) are participating members. The chairman of the Joint Chiefs of Staff and the director of the Central Intelligence Agency are advisers to the Security Council. A special assistant to the president for national security affairs heads the NSC staff. The purposes of the council are to advise the president on security policy and to coordinate foreign, military, and domestic policies. However, presidents do not rely exclusively on the National Security Council for direction in major foreign and military decisions.

OMB.   The Office of Management and Budget (OMB) is the largest agency in the Executive Office of the President. Its function is to prepare the budget of the United States for the president to submit to Congress. The federal government cannot spend money without appropriations by Congress, and all requests for congressional appropriations must clear the OMB first, a requirement that gives OMB great power over the executive branch. Since all agencies request more money than they can receive, OMB has primary responsibility for reviewing, reducing, and approving estimates submitted by departments and agencies (subject, of course, to appeal to the president); it also continuously scrutinizes the organization and operations of executive agencies in order to recommend changes promoting efficiency and economy. Like members of the White House staff, the top officials of OMB are solely responsible to the president; thus they must reflect the president's goals and priorities in their decision making.

CEA.   The president, with Senate consent, appoints three professional economists of high standing to the Council of Economic Advisers. Created by the Employment Act of 1946, the council analyzes trends in the economy and recommends to the president the fiscal and monetary policies necessary to avoid depression and inflation. In addition, the council prepares the economic report that the act requires the president to submit to Congress each year. The economic report, together with the annual budget message to Congress, gives the president the opportunity to outline the administration's major policies.

Bureaucratic maneuvers

How can bureaucrats outmaneuver the president? One illustration of bureaucratic leeway and discretion in implementing presidential decisions has been widely quoted:

> Half of a President's suggestions, which theoretically carry the weight of orders, can be safely forgotten by a cabinet member. And if the President asks about a suggestion the second time, he can be told that it is being investigated. If he asks a third time, the wise cabinet officer will give him at least part of what he suggests. But only occasionally do Presidents ever get around to asking three times.[4]

Bureaucratic maneuvers can become even more complex. Morton Halperin, former staff member of the National Security Council under Henry Kissinger (Halperin later charged Kissinger and others with bugging his telephone), describes "ten commandments" of bureaucratic infighting.[5] These suggest the power of the bureaucracy and the frequently bitter nature of bureaucratic welfare:

1. Never play "politics" with security. But use your own notions of politics to screen out information from the president that conflicts with your own objectives.
2. Tell the president only what is necessary to persuade him of the correctness of your own position. Avoid giving him "confusing" information. Isolate the opposition by excluding them from deliberations.
3. Present your own policy option in the middle of two other obviously unworkable alternatives to give the president the illusion of choice.
4. If the president selects the "wrong" policy anyhow, demand "full authority" to deal with the undesirable consequences, which you say are sure to arise.
5. Always predict the consequences of not adopting your policy in terms of worst cases, making predictions of dire consequences that will follow.
6. If the president chooses your own policy, urge immediate action; if he selects another policy, you may agree in principle but argue that "now is not the time."
7. If the opposition view looks very strong, "leak" damaging information to your supporters in the press or Congress and count on "public opposition" to build.

8. Fully implement orders that result from the selection of your own policy recommendation; circumvent or delay those that do not.

9. Limit the issues that go to the president. Bring up only those favorable to your position or that he is likely to favor.

10. Never oppose the president's policy in such extreme terms that you lose his trust. Temper your disagreements so that you can live to argue another day.

Bureaucrats do not really consider these "commandments" cynical. Indeed they may not realize when they are following them. They often sincerely believe that their own policies and projects are in the nation's best interest.

Presidential control

Constitutionally the president has direct control over the bureaucracy. The president has the formal power to appoint all secretaries, under secretaries, and deputy secretaries and most bureau chiefs in the federal government. The president also has the power to reorganize the federal bureaucracy, subject to congressional veto. And, of course, the president exercises formal control over the budget. OMB works directly under presidential supervision. The Budget and Impoundment Act of 1974 recognized the long-standing practice of presidents' withholding funds from programs and projects, even if Congress has already appropriated funds. However, Congress must now approve presidential impoundment of funds.

Limitations on presidential power

The president's formal powers over the bureaucracy center on appointments, reorganization, and the budget. We should, however, consider the *real* limitations on these three powers.

Appointments.   Although the federal bureaucracy consists of three million employees, the president actually appoints only twenty-five hundred people. Only about six hundred of these appointments are policy-making positions; the rest are subordinate positions often used for patronage. Many patronage positions go to professional bureaucrats by default because a president cannot find qualified political appointees. Many political appointees are baffled by the career bureaucrats in the agencies. The bureaucrats have the knowledge, skills, and experience to continue existing programs with little or no supervision from their nominal political chiefs. Many political heads "go native": they yield to the pressures of the career bureaucrats. The president's appointee whose charter is to control a bureau ends up the bureau's captive instead.

Since a majority of career bureaucrats are Democrats, exercising policy control over the bureaucracy is particularly difficult for a Republican president. Richard Nixon attempted to deal with this problem by increasing the power of his immediate White House staff; he placed control of major programs in the White House staff at the expense of the cabinet departments. The unhappy result was that the White House staff itself became a powerful bureaucracy, frequently locked in conflict with executive departments, and duplicating much of the departments' research and development activities. More seriously for Nixon and the country, White House staff, speaking "in the name of the president," developed power bases independent of the president.

Ronald Reagan's approach has been to appoint conservatives and Republicans to head many key agencies. But the bureaucracy has fought back by isolating and undermining Reagan's appointees within the agencies. Lower-level bureaucrats have supplied damaging information to the press and to Congress, claiming that Reagan appointees are not enforcing the laws properly.

Reorganization. The president can choose to reorganize the bureaucracy to reflect his priorities. However, most presidents limit this practice to one or two key presidential programs; and presidential reorganizations are subject to legislative veto. For example, to emphasize his commitment to cancer research, President Nixon created the National Cancer Institute and gave it substantial independence from its parent organization, the U.S. Public Health Service. In the 1960s President Kennedy created the National Aeronautics and Space Administration as an

Reprinted by permission: Tribune Company Syndicate, Inc.

independent agency to carry out his commitment to a national space program. President Carter created the new Department of Education to fulfill his campaign pledge to emphasize educational matters, even though the new department's parent organization, the Department of Health, Education and Welfare, bitterly opposed it. President Reagan promised in his campaign to eliminate the Department of Education and the Department of Energy. But reorganization is a difficult task. Nothing arouses the fighting instincts of bureaucrats as much as the rumor of reorganization. Presidents usually resort to reorganization only for their priority programs.

The budget.   The president must exercise budgetary power over the bureaucracy through OMB. Thus the OMB director must be a trusted ally of the president, and OMB must support the president's programs and priorities if presidential control over the bureaucracy is to be effective. But even OMB must accept the budgetary base (the previous year's budget, adjusted for inflation) and engage in "incremental" budgeting. Despite its own expertise, OMB must acknowledge the budgetary base of most agencies and concentrate its attention on requested increases.

Any agency that feels shortchanged in the president's budget can leak the fact to its supporting interest groups and congressional subcommittee. Any resulting "public outcry" may force the president to restore the agency's funds. Or Congress itself can appropriate money not requested by the president. The president may go along with the increased expenditures simply to avoid another confrontation with Congress. If the president chooses not to spend the funds appropriated by Congress (impoundment), the Budget and Impoundment Act of 1974 requires him to report this fact to the Congress. Congress must approve the impoundment, or else the president will be legally obliged to spend the money.

Incrementalism and public policy

Ideally, governments should decide policy questions by identifying society's goals, examining all possible policies to achieve these goals, researching the benefits and costs of each policy alternative, calculating the benefits and costs of each policy alternative, and then selecting the policy that maximizes benefits and minimizes costs. In other words, policy making should be *rational.* In fact it is not. Instead, policy makers, in both Congress and the White House, tend to continue past governmental programs, policies, and expenditure levels with only incremental changes each year. This practice is *incrementalism.*

Why is decision making incremental rather than rational? Why do presidents, members of Congress, and especially bureaucrats generally agree to continue the policies of the past, accept existing budget levels, and avoid annual reexamination of all previous decisions?

First, policy makers do not have the time, intelligence, or money to investigate all possible alternatives to existing policy. The cost of collecting the necessary information is too great. And policy makers do not have the predictive capabilities, even in an age of computers, to accurately forecast the consequences of each policy alternative; nor can they accurately calculate all benefits and costs when many diverse and noncomparable political, social, economic and cultural values are at stake.

Second, policy makers accept previous policies and decisions because of the inherent uncertainty of a completely new or different approach. They find it safer to stick with known programs.

Third, heavy investments in existing programs ("sunk costs") may preclude really fundamental changes. Investments may be in money, buildings, or other hard items, or they may be in popular expectations, perceived "entitlements," administrative practices, or organizational structures. Accepted wisdom holds, for example, that bureaucracies tend to persist long after their usefulness is over. People develop routines that are difficult to unlearn, and groups acquire a stake in organizations and practices. Change is very difficult.

Fourth, incrementalism is politically expedient. Agreement is easier when disputed items are only increases, decreases, or modifications in existing programs. Political conflict lessens with continuity of policies. It would "overload the system" with political tension to reconsider every policy or decision every year. Incrementalism reduces conflict, maintains stability, and helps preserve the political system.

Fifth, policy makers cannot always agree on society's goals and values, or on "benefits" and "costs." One group's benefits may be another group's costs, and vice versa. Since no rational comprehensive understanding of goals or values is possible, each administration finds it easier to continue past policies into the future.

Finally, policy makers, like most of us, do not always act to "maximize" all desirable values. Instead, they try to satisfy particular demands. Rather than search for "one best way," they end their search when they find "a way that works." This search usually begins with the familiar—that is, policy alternative close to current policies. Only if minor modifications appear unsatisfactory will policy makers venture out toward more radical policy innovations.

Incrementalism is particularly apparent in government spending. Today over three-quarters of the federal budget is "uncontrollable"—that is, bound by previous congressional decisions and not easily changed in annual budget making.

One source of uncontrollable spending is interest on the federal debt. Interest payments have grown rapidly as a percentage of all federal spending; today they are 15 percent of the total. The federal government must make these payments to maintain its credit and the nation's banking system. These interest payments are a product of a long history of federal deficits. The federal government has failed to balance its budget for the past twenty-five years; the result is a national debt of over $1 *trillion.* As the deficit increases each year, interest payments go up.

"Entitlement programs" are the largest source of uncontrollable spending. These programs provide classes of people with a legally enforceable right to benefits. Entitlement programs account for *two-thirds* of all federal spending, including social security, welfare payments, Medicaid, and Medicare. Though these entitlements are benefits that past Congresses have pledged the federal government to pay, they are not really uncontrollable: Congress could amend or repeal the laws that established them. But such actions are difficult politically and make legislators vulnerable to charges of breach of faith or failure of trust by those who have come to depend on the benefits.

Case study: Incrementalism and Reagan's budget "cuts"

Even the Reagan budget "revolution" has been more incremental than revolutionary. A careful comparison of Carter and Reagan budgets shows that Reagan's budget "cuts" have been largely reductions in growth rate, not reductions in aggregate spending. On January 15, 1981, the outgoing Carter administration presented the 1982 budget to Congress. When the Reagan administration took over on January 20, the Office of Management and Budget, under its new director, David Stockman, revised the Carter 1982 budget. Reagan's requests were lower than the earlier Carter requests for everything except defense spending. The mass media referred to these lower requests as "cuts," but in most categories, including health and welfare, the new Reagan requests were still higher than the 1981 spending figures.

The Reagan administration successfully reduced the growth of total federal outlays from what it would have been under Carter. Carter proposed a 19.5 percent increase in total federal spending for 1982 over the 1981 base. Reagan proposed a 17.7 percent increase. For 1983, Reagan proposed only a 4.4 percent increase, lower than any Carter budget but still an increase over the previous year (see table 11-1).

TABLE 11-1. **Incrementalism: Comparing presidential budgets**

Billions of dollars (percent increase)	1981 Base	1982 Carter	1982 Reagan	1983 Reagan
Total outlay	615.8	739.3 (19.5)	725.3 (17.7)	757.6 (4.4)
Defense	146.2	184.4 (26.1)	187.5 (28.2)	221.7 (17.9)
Income security	220.0	255.0 (15.9)	250.9 (14.0)	261.7 (4.3)
Health	62.4	74.6 (19.5)	73.4 (17.6)	78.1 (6.4)
Receipts	600.0	711.8 (18.6)	626.8 (4.5)	666.1 (6.2)
Deficit	15.8	27.5	98.5	91.5

Source: *Budget of the United States Government,* 1981, 1982, 1983.

(continued)

Case study *(continued)*

The media characterized Reagan's budget requests for welfare and health as "slashes," "attacks," "cutbacks," and "assaults." Scholars wrote about a "new class war" against the poor and aged.[6] Yet total spending for income security (social security and public assistance) *increased* in Reagan's 1982 budget by 14.0 percent and rose again in 1983 by an additional 4.3 percent. Likewise, total spending for health (Medicare and Medicaid) increased in Reagan's 1982 budget by 17.6 percent and rose again in 1983 by an additional 6.4 percent. Of course, funding for specific programs did drop below 1981 base levels (such as child nutrition, aid to families with dependent children, home heating assistance, and legal services). But the major programs—social security, supplemental security income, Medicaid, Medicare—all continued to increase under the Reagan administration. Defense spending under Reagan has been only slightly higher than it would have been under Carter. Both Carter and Reagan recognized the need to rebuild the nation's defenses.

Incrementalism, then, ensures continued expansion of government spending, even when a Republican president committed to budgetary restraint replaces a Democratic president.

Inside Washington: The iron triangles

Traditionally it was assumed that when Congress passed a law and then created a bureaucracy and appropriated money to carry out the intent of the law, this was the end of the political process. Traditionally it was assumed that the intent of Congress would be carried out, the political battle had ended, and now government would get on with the job of "administering" the law.

It turns out, however, that political battles do not end with victory or defeat in Congress. Organized interests do not abandon the fight and return home simply because the site of the battle shifts from the "political" arena to an "administrative" one. We tend to think that "political" questions are the province of the president and Congress, and "administrative" questions the province of the bureaucracy. Actually "political" and "administrative" questions do not differ in content; they differ only in who decides them.

Once the bureaucracy takes over an issue, three major power bases— the "iron triangles"—come together to decide its outcome: the executive agency administering the program, the congressional subcommittee charged with its oversight, and the most interested groups, generally those directly affected by the agency. These interest groups develop close relationships with the bureaucratic policy makers. And both the interest groups and the bureaucrats develop close relationships with the congressional subcommittees that oversee their activities. Agency-sub-committee-interest-group relationships become established; even the individuals involved remain the same over fairly long periods of time, as senior members of Congress retain their subcommittee memberships.

As political scientist Kenneth J. Meier observes:

> Together Congress, interest groups, and bureaus all have the necessary resources to satisfy each other's needs. Bureaus supply services or goods to organized groups but need resources to do so. Congressional committees supply the bureaus with resources but need electoral support to remain in office and political support to win policy disputes in Congress. The interest group provides the political support that the member of Congress needs, but the interest group needs government goods and services to satisfy members' demands. The result is a tripartite relationship that has *all of the resources necessary to operate in isolation from politics* if no great crisis occurs.[7]

Note that the parts of this triumvirate do *not* compete (as pluralist ideology suggests). Instead bureaucratic agency, congressional subcommittee, and organized interest come together and cooperate in bureaucratic policy making.

The bureaucracy does more than fill in the details of congressional policies, although, of course, this function is one source of its power. Bureaucracies make important policies of their own (1) by proposing legislation for Congress to pass; (2) by writing rules, regulations, and guidelines to implement laws passed by Congress (the *rule-making* function); and (3) by deciding specific cases in applying laws or rules (the *adjudicating* function). Bureaucracies have decided such important questions as the safety of nuclear power plants; the degree of coal rather than oil use for energy; the extent to which affirmative action programs will favor blacks, women, and minorities; whether to allow opposition political parties and candidates on television to challenge a presidential speech or press conference; how much airlines can compete through increased flights and reduced costs; and whether welfare agencies can search social security files to locate nonsupporting fathers to enforce payment orders.

Controlling the bureaucracy: Congress and courts

Congress or the courts can overturn the decisions of bureaucracies if sufficient opposition develops to bureaucratic policies. But such opposition is unlikely if bureaucracies work closely with their congressional subcommittees and their interested groups.

Congressional constraints

Congress can restrain the bureaucracy by:

1. Passing direct legislation changing rules or regulations or limiting bureaucratic activity;

2. Altering or threatening to alter the bureau's budget;
3. Retaining specific veto powers over certain bureaucratic actions (agencies must submit some proposed rules to Congress; if Congress does not act within a specified time, the rules take effect);
4. Conducting investigations, usually during legislative or appropriations hearings, that publicize unpopular decisions, rules, or expenditures by bureaus;
5. Making direct complaints to the bureaucracy through formal contacts.

Yet it is difficult for Congress to use these powers as a truly effective check on the bureaucracy.

Direct legislation.   Consider the use of direct legislation to affect tax policy. The U.S. tax code enacted by Congress fills eleven hundred pages with tax legislation, but the U.S. Internal Revenue Service (IRS) issues an additional six thousand pages interpreting the tax code. Nonetheless occasionally even the IRS is thwarted by Congress. In 1979 the IRS ruled that private schools that did not enroll specified numbers of blacks and minorities would no longer qualify as educational institutions and therefore could not accept tax-free donations. Congress acted to overturn the IRS. However, when the Federal Trade Commission ordered an end to all cigarette advertising on television, congressional efforts to overturn this order were unsuccessful. In general, Congress rarely overturns a bureaucratic decision.

Budgetary changes.   Congressional control of the budget is not as potent a weapon as it appears to be given the number of "uncontrollable" expenditures and incremental budgeting practices. Congress looks at proposed *increases* in agency budgets each year, but it rarely looks at the agency's base—that is, the previous year's appropriation. Thus even agencies that have seriously offended Congress can expect that the legislators will at most penalize them by reducing or eliminating their requested budget increases.

Veto powers.   Legislative veto provisions apply to only a limited number of bureaucratic regulations. And because Congress is so busy with new legislation each year, only rarely does it take the time to act on a regulation sent to it for review. Indeed Congress seldom uses the legislative veto.

Investigations.   Certainly bureaucrats do not like to be embarrassed in congressional hearings. No one really wants to be the recipient of Senator William Proxmire's "Golden Fleece" award, which he regu-

larly announces to the press for what he considers an excessively wasteful program or project. But it is unclear how much effect Congress's
formal investigation and oversight function has on bureaucratic policy.
The best studies contend that congressional oversight has relatively little influence over bureaucratic policies.[8]

Complaints.   Most agencies handle congressional complaints, usually passed on from constituents, with speed. However, the agencies
handle these complaints through existing rules and regulations; they do
not *change* their rules and regulations to accommodate Congress members or their constituents. Thus the only advantage in having a Congress
member complain to an agency on one's behalf is to speed up consideration of the case. But congressional intervention in individual cases
does not allow control of bureaucratic policy.

Judicial constraints

The federal courts exercise more direct control over the bureaucracy
than does Congress. Decisions by executive agencies can usually be
appealed to federal courts. Moreover, federal courts can issue injunc-
tions (orders) to executive agencies before they institute their rules, regulations, projects, or programs.

Judicial control of the bureaucracy has its limitations, however:

1. Judicial oversight usually emphasizes *procedural* fairness rather
   than policy content.
2. Bureaucracies themselves have set up elaborate administrative
   processes to protect their decisions from challenge on procedural
   grounds.
3. Lawsuits against bureaucracies are very expensive; the bureaucracies have armies of attorneys paid for out of tax monies to
   oppose anyone who attempts to challenge them in court.
4. Excessive delays in federal courts add to the time and expense
   of challenging bureaucratic decisions.

In fact, citizens have not had much success in court cases against bureaucracies. Political scientists Bradley Cannon and Michael Giles report
that the courts rarely reverse the decisions of federal regulatory commissions. For example, the Federal Power Commission and the Federal
Trade Commission win 91 percent of the cases they argue before the
Supreme Court; the National Labor Relations Board wins 75 percent;
and the Internal Revenue Service wins 73 percent. Only the Immigration
and Naturalization Service has a mediocre record of 56 percent.[9]

The bureaucratic elite

What kind of person inhabits the Washington bureaucracy? In a study of over a thousand people who occupied top federal positions during five presidential administrations, the prestigious Brookings Institution reports that 36 percent rose through the ranks of government itself, 26 percent came from law firms, 24 percent from business, and 7 percent from a variety of other fields.[10] A plurality of top federal executives are career bureaucrats. Most (63 percent) top federal executives were federal bureaucrats at the time of their appointment to a top post; only 37 percent had no prior experience as federal bureaucrats. Thus the federal bureaucracy is producing its own leadership, with some limited recruitment from business and law.

Like other sectors of the society, the bureaucracy recruits its top federal executives primarily from the middle- and upper-middle-class segments of the population. Over 99 percent of top federal executives are college educated, and 68 percent have advanced degrees (44 percent in law, 17 percent with earned master's degrees, and 11 percent with earned doctorates). The Brookings Institution reports that the Ivy League schools plus Stanford, Chicago, Michigan, and Berkeley educated over 40 percent of the top federal executives, with Yale, Harvard, and Princeton leading the list.[11]

Little difference exists between Republican and Democratic administrators. Of course, Democratic presidents tend to appoint Democrats to top posts while Republican presidents tend to appoint Republicans. However, few discernible differences are evident in the class backgrounds, educational levels, occupational experiences, or previous public service of Democratic or Republican appointees.

One troublesome problem at the top of the federal bureaucracy is federal executives' short tenures. The median tenure in office of top federal executives is only two years. Only the regulatory commissions have significantly longer tenure. Such a short tenure at the top has obvious disadvantages. The head of a large department or agency needs a year or more to become fully productive by learning the issues, programs, procedures, technical problems, and personalities involved in the work. If such a person resigns after two years, the federal bureaucracy is not getting continuous, knowledgeable direction from its top officials.

The regulatory quagmire

The Washington bureaucracy has become the regulator of the national economy, the protector of business against its rivals, and the guardian of the American people against everything from tainted foods to rickety stepladders. Federal regulatory bureaucracies began in 1889 with the creation of the Interstate Commerce Commission to regulate railroad rates. Since then thousands of laws, amendments, court rulings, and executive orders have expanded the powers of the regulatory commissions over every aspect of our lives. (See table 11-2 for a list of the major regulatory laws and agencies.) Not until 1978 in the Airline Deregulation Act was there a major step in the opposite direction of deregulation.

Federal regulatory bureaucracies are legislatures, investigators, prosecutors, judges, and juries—all wrapped into one. They issue thousands of pages of rules and regulations each year; they investigate thousands of complaints and conduct thousands of inspections; they require businesses to submit hundreds of thousands of forms each year; they hold hearings, determine "compliance" and "noncompliance," issue corrective orders, and levy fines and penalties. Most economists agree that overregulation adds greatly to the cost of living (perhaps $100 billion to $200 billion per year), that it is an obstacle to innovation and productivity, and that it hinders economic competition. Most regulatory commissions are *independent:* they are not under an executive department, and their members are appointed for long terms by a president who has little control over their activities.

The "captured" regulators

Over the years, the reform movements which led to the establishment of the older regulatory agencies have diminished in influence. Many regulatory agencies have become closely identified with regulated industry. The "capture" theory of regulation describes how regulated industries come to benefit from government regulation, and how regulatory commissions come to represent the industries they are supposed to regulate rather than "the people."

Historically regulatory commissions have acted only against the most wayward members of an industry. By attacking the businesses giving the industry bad publicity, the commissions actually helped improve the public's opinion of the industry as a whole. Regulatory commissions provided symbolic reassurance to the public that the behavior of the industry was proper.

By limiting entry into an industry by smaller firms (either directly by denying them routes or broadcast channels, for example, or indirectly by making the requirements for entry very costly), the regulatory commissions reduce competition. This is an important asset to larger established businesses; they no longer fear new "cut rate" competitors.

The close relationships between the regulatory bureaucracies and their client industries stem from a common resource: expertise. Not only do the regulatory commissions frequently turn to the regulated industries for information, but they also recruit bureaucrats from industry leaders. Commission members usually come from the industry they are

TABLE 11-2.   The regulatory bureaucracy

Date of legislation	Agency	Power granted
1887	Interstate Commerce Commission (ICC)	Regulate water and routes of railroads, water carriers, and trucks.
1913	Federal Reserve Board (FRB)	Regulate activities of banks that are members of federal reserve system; set money and credit policy.
1914	Federal Trade Commission (FTC)	Carry out broad powers to curb "unfair" trade practices, protect consumers, and maintain competition.
1931	Food and Drug Administration (FDA)	Originally, regulate prescription drugs; later, determine if all prescription and nonprescription drugs are "safe and effective."
1932	Federal Home Loan Bank Board	Regulate savings and loan associations.
1933	Federal Deposit Insurance Corporation (FDIC)	Regulate banks not in the federal reserve system; insure small deposits.
1934	Federal Communications Commission (FCC)	Regulate radio and television broadcasting and interstate telephones and telegraph.
1934	Securities and Exchange Commission (SEC)	Regulate all publicly traded securities (stocks, bonds, etc.) and the markets on which they are traded. Require public disclosure and police securities fraud.
1935	Federal Power Commission (FPC)	Regulate interstate natural gas prices.
1935	National Labor Relations Board (NLRB)	Regulate labor-management relations; define and punish "unfair labor practices" by business and labor.
1938	Food and Drug Administration	Require preclearance of new drugs before marketing.
1938	Department of Agriculture (DOA)	Establish price supports for agricultural products and regulate land and markets.
1938	Civil Aeronautics Board (CAB)	Regulate airline fares and routes.
1947	National Labor Relations Board	Extend powers to regulate union activities.
1958	Food and Drug Administration	Extend preclearance requirement to foods as well as drugs.
1962	Food and Drug Administration	Require proof of "effectiveness" as well as "safety" for drugs.
1962	Office of Federal Contract Compliance	Administer prohibitions against discrimination by race or sex by government contractors.
1964	Equal Employment Opportunity Commission (EEOC)	Administer prohibitions against discrimination by race or sex by private employers.
1970	Environmental Protection Agency (EPA)	Regulate clear air, water quality, waste disposal, and toxic and hazardous material, among others.
1970	National Highway Traffic and Safety Administration (NHTSA)	Regulate manufacturing of autos, buses, tires, and so forth.

TABLE 11-2.   *(continued)*

Date of legislation	Agency	Power granted
1971	Occupational Safety and Health Administration (OSHA)	Regulate safety and health practices in work places.
1972	Consumer Product Safety Commission (CPSC)	Establish standards for all consumer products for safety, labeling, and construction.
1973	Nuclear Regulatory Commission (NRC)	Regulate civilian nuclear safety and license nuclear plants.
1974	Pension Benefit Guarantee Corporation	Regulate private pension plans.
1975	Federal Trade Commission	Extend powers to order refunds and "corrective advertising"; regulate intrastate as well as interstate commerce.
1978	Civil Aeronautics Board (CAB)	Airline deregulation: reduce control over airline routes and rates.
1980	Interstate Commerce Commission (ICC)	Partially deregulate railroad shipping rates.
1981	Department of Energy (DOE)	Oil price deregulation: end oil-price controls.

supposed to regulate.[12] And after a few years in government, the "regulators" return to high-paying jobs in the industry. This practice is known as the "revolving door" problem of federal regulators.

Many regulatory commissions attract young attorneys, fresh from law schools, to the staffs. When these attorneys are successful, they frequently receive offers for much higher-paying jobs in the industries they are regulating. So industry siphons off the "best and the brightest" to become defenders against government regulation. And, of course, these people have already learned the intricacies of government regulation, with taxpayers paying for their training. People see jobs in federal regulatory agencies as stepping stones to lucrative careers in private (regulated) industry.

Over the years, then, industry came to *support* the regulatory bureaucracies. Industry often strongly opposes proposals to reduce government control—deregulation. Proposals to deregulate railroads, interstate trucking, and airlines have met with substantial opposition from both the regulating bureaucracies and the regulated industries, working together. Thus industry views most regulation favorably.

The new bureaucracies

Recently, however, Congress has created or expanded several bureaucracies to cover areas in which they have little or no expertise. To make matters worse, their jurisdiction extends to all industries rather than specific ones. Prime examples are the Equal Employment Opportunity Commission (EEOC), the Occupational Safety and Health Administration (OSHA), and the Environmental Protection Agency (EPA). The business community widely resents regulations by these agencies. Rules developed by EEOC to prevent discrimination in employment and promotion *(affirmative action guidelines)* have been awkward, and EEOC enforcement of these rules has been nearly chaotic. Many businesses do not believe EEOC has the expertise to understand their industry or their labor market. The same is true of the much-despised OSHA, which has issued thousands of safety regulations that appear costly and ridiculous to those in the industry. The complaint about EPA is that it seldom considers the *costs* of its rulings to business or the consumer. Industry representatives contend that EPA should weigh the costs of their regulations against the benefits to the environment.

Note that the EEOC, OSHA, and EPA have general responsibilities across all business and industry. Thus these agencies are unlikely to develop "expertise" in the fashion of the FCC, ICC, CAB, or other single-industry regulators. On the other hand, after a few years of interaction between business and these new regulators, conflict may diminish and cooperation may become the prevailing style of interaction.

Deregulation: Reversing historical trends

The demand for "deregulation" has echoed in Washington for many years. Complaints about excessive regulation include the following:

1. The increased costs to businesses and consumers of complying with many separate regulations, issued by separate regulatory agencies, are excessive. Environmental regulation alone may be costing Americans $100 billion a year, but these costs never appear in a federal budget because businesses and consumers absorb them.

2. Overregulation hampers innovation and productivity. (New drug research has decreased over 75 percent in the past decade because of lengthy FDA testing. Most observers feel that FDA would not approve aspirin if it were proposed for marketing today.) The costs and delays in winning permission for a new product tend to discourage invention.

3. Regulatory bureaucracies' involvement in licensing and entry into a field reduces competition. The cost of complying with federal reporting requirements *(red tape)* is itself an obstacle to small businesses.

4. Industries eventually tend to "capture" the agencies that are supposed to regulate them. Certainly the older regulatory agencies responsible for only one industry are easier to "capture" than are the newer regulatory agencies with supervisory powers over many industries.

5. Regulatory agencies do not weigh the costs of complying with

their regulations against the benefits to society. Regulators generally introduce controls with no regard for the cost-benefit trade-offs.

Not until 1978 did Congress act for the first time to significantly reduce the burden of regulation. Acting against the objections of the airline industry itself, which wanted continued regulation, Congress stripped the CAB of its power to allocate airline routes to various companies and to set rates. The airlines were "set free" (against their will) to choose where to fly and what to charge, and to openly compete with each other. Competition on heavily traveled routes reduced fares dramatically, and one major airline (Braniff) went bankrupt as airline profits declined.

The Reagan administration ended long-standing oil-price controls in 1981, completing a decontrol effort that began in the Carter years. Reagan ordered immediate decontrol upon taking office, calling price controls "a cumbersome and inefficient system of regulations that served to stifle domestic oil production, increase our dependence on foreign oil, and discourage conservation."[13] Gasoline prices at first increased following price decontrol. But after a few months, the effects of conservation spread worldwide; prices leveled off, and the industry faced a "glut" of oil.

Deregulation is a stated goal of the Reagan administration. Upon taking office, Reagan ordered all executive agencies to consider the costs to society of every new regulation. He established a Task Force on Regulatory Relief, chaired by Vice-President George Bush. He abolished the Council on Wage and Price Stability (which had regulated wages and prices in an effort to halt inflation), postponed automobile airbags, blocked new antinoise regulations, and generally tried to curtail regulatory expansion. Nonetheless, reversing the historical trend toward greater government regulation will be difficult.

Case study: Affirmative action

Affirmative action programs illustrate how the president and Congress frequently pass *symbolic* policies while the bureaucracy decides on their *substance*. Though Congress supposedly authorized these programs in the Civil Rights Act of 1964, we contend that as important as they are in the struggle over equality of opportunity in America, these programs were begun by *bureaucrats* without specific congressional, presidential, or judicial approval.

The Civil Rights Act of 1964, Title VI, states that each federal department and agency shall take action to end discrimination and segregation in any program or activity receiving federal financial assistance in any form. The act authorizes federal bureaucracies to establish rules, regulations, and

(*continued*)

Case study *(continued)*

"guidelines" to achieve desegregation and to terminate federal aid to any program that fails to meet these guidelines. Title VII of the same act makes it unlawful for any private employer to discriminate or segregate individuals in any fashion in employment and authorizes the Equal Employment Opportunity Commission to establish rules, regulations, and guidelines to investigate violations, and to enforce nondiscrimination by civil action in federal court.

What *specific* policies should government pursue to eliminate discrimination in federally financed programs and in private employment? Is it sufficient that government eliminate direct discrimination, guarantee "equality of opportunity" for blacks and whites, and apply "colorblind" standards to both groups? Or should government take "affirmative action" to overcome past unequal treatment of minorities, such as providing preferential or compensatory treatment that favors minority applicants for university admissions and scholarships, job hiring and promotions, and other opportunities for advancement in life?

The federal bureaucracy's first response to the Civil Rights Act was to concentrate on nondiscrimination. Governments and corporations advertised themselves as "equal opportunity employers." The U.S. Civil Service Commission stated that equal opportunity employment "was not a program to offer special privilege to any one group of persons because of their particular race, religion, sex, or national origin."[14] This rule appeared to conform to the original nondiscrimination approach found in the act itself. There were no quota systems for black applicants that might result in lower-qualified blacks being selected over higher-qualified whites for schools, jobs, or promotions.

In the late 1960s, however, federal bureaucracies began to shift from the traditional aim of equal opportunity through nondiscrimination to affirmative action through "goals and timetables" to achieve specific percentages of blacks in schools and jobs.* While carefully avoiding the word *quota*, the bureaucracy advanced the notion that affirmative action is a means of testing the success of equal employment opportunity by observing whether minorities achieve admissions, jobs, and promotions in proportion to their numbers in the population. One of the first applications of affirmative action occurred in 1967 when the U.S. Office of Federal Contract Compliance issued its "Philadelphia Plan," requiring contractors bidding on federal projects to submit affirmative action plans that included specific percentage goals for the employment of minorities. At first the U.S. Civil Service Commission resisted "goals" in federal employment, equating "goals" with "quotas" and holding that quotas are inconsistent with the merit system. But pressure developed within the bureaucracy itself to require greater minority representation. Eventually the Civil Service Commission relented: "While quotas are not permissible, federal agencies may use numerical guidelines to assess progress toward equal employment opportunity." The U.S. Office of Education proposed affirmative action requirements for the nation's colleges and universities. In 1972 it issued guidelines that mandated "goals" for

Case study *(continued)*

university admissions and faculty hiring of blacks and women. At the same time the EEOC was shifting its campaign from "equal employment opportunity" to "affirmative action." Some employers simply adopted the double phrases—"an equal employment opportunity/affirmative action employer"—to make sure that they were abiding by all of the changing regulations.

The shift in policy to affirmative action "goals and timetables" was a bureaucratic decision. Congress did not amend the Civil Rights Act to require affirmative action. Nor did the courts interpret the act to require affirmative action. On the contrary, the major threat to bureaucratic power in this field came *from* the courts.

In 1978 in *Regents of the University of California* v. *Bakke*, the U.S. Supreme Court struck down a special affirmative action admissions program for minorities at a state medical school, on the grounds that it excluded a white applicant because of his race and violated his constitutional rights under the Fourteenth Amendment's equal protection clause. Allan Bakke applied to the medical school of the University of California at Davis two consecutive years and was rejected; in both years black applicants with significantly lower grade point averages and medical aptitude test scores obtained admission through a special program that reserved sixteen minority places in a class of one hundred. The University of California acted under the guidance of the U.S. Office of Education in implementing its affirmative action guidelines. The university argued that its racial classification was "benign" rather than "discriminatory"—that is, it was designed to assist disadvantaged groups, not hinder them. The Supreme Court held that this objective was legitimate and that a state school *may* consider race in reviewing applications without violating the equal protection clause. However, the Court also held that a separate admissions program for minorities with a specified quota of openings unavailable to white applicants violates the equal protection clause. The Court ordered Bakke admitted to medical school and required the school to eliminate its special admissions program. However, it recommended that the university consider an affirmative action program that recognized racial or ethnic background as a "plus" in an *overall* evaluation of all applicants, as long as it did not set numerical quotas or exclude any person from competing for all positions.

Reaction to the decision was predictable: supporters of affirmative action, particularly government officials running affirmative action programs, emphasized the Supreme Court's willingness to allow consideration of minority status as a positive factor; opponents emphasized the Supreme Court's unwillingness to allow quotas that exclude whites from competing for a certain number of positions. Since Bakke had won the case, most observers felt that the Supreme Court would prevent government bureaucracies from imposing racial quota systems.

But the routines of government bureaucracies, especially affirmative action programs and the EEOC, did not change significantly after the decision. And in 1979, in *United Steelworkers of America* v. *Weber*, the U.S. Supreme Court approved a plan developed under pressure from federal affirmative

(continued)

Case study *(continued)*

action officials in which a private employer and a union agreed to reserve 50 percent of higher paying skilled jobs for minorities. Kaiser Aluminum Corporation and the United Steelworkers union had agreed to establish this racial quota in training programs in order to get more blacks into skilled technical jobs. When Weber, a white employee, was excluded from the training program and blacks with less seniority and fewer qualifications were accepted, he filed suit in federal court claiming discrimination in violation of the Civil Rights Act of 1964. Title VII of that act prevents all discrimination in employment on the basis of race; it does not specify race. But the Supreme Court held that the Civil Rights Acts of 1964 "left employers and unions in the private sector free to take such race-conscious steps to eliminate manifest racial imbalances in traditionally segregated job categories. . . . We hold that Title VII does not prohibit such . . . affirmative action plans."

The *Bakke* and *Weber* decisions are difficult to reconcile; apparently a divided court will examine each affirmative action program on its own merits. In the absence of any clear restraint, the federal bureaucracy is likely to continue its affirmative action programs.

Clearly, this major thrust in public policy, affecting the lives of many Americans, began and grew within the federal bureaucracy itself. Neither Congress nor the Supreme Court, and certainly not "the people," was responsible for "affirmative action."

*President Johnson's executive order of September 1965, legitimized the language of affirmative action.

Summary

The federal bureaucracy is a major base of power in America, largely independent of the other government branches and not very responsive to "the people." Government bureaucracies invade every aspect of modern life, and their power is growing each year. A bureaucratic elite that both formulates and implements public policy is emerging. Elitism in bureaucracy takes several forms:

1. Bureaucratic power increases with the size and technological complexity of modern society. Official lawmaking bodies—Congress and the president—set forth only general policy statement. Bureaucracies write tens of thousands of rules and regulations and actually undertake the tasks of government.

2. Bureaucratic power increases because (1) Congress and the president do not have the time or expertise to master policy details; (2) Congress and the president deliberately pass vague laws for sym-

bolic reasons and then turn over actual governance to bureaucracies; and (3) the bureaucracy has now amassed sufficient power to influence the president and Congress.

3. The federal government alone employs three million people and spends 22 percent of the gross national product. State and local governments hire millions more and bring the total governmental portion of the GNP to approximately 35 percent.

4. Although the president is officially in charge of the executive branch of government, his control is limited by (1) the relatively small number of patronage positions and large numbers of professional civil service bureaucrats, (2) the difficulty of achieving meaningful reorganization, and (3) the large number of "uncontrollable" items in the budget.

5. Once a political question shifts to the bureaucracy, a "triumvirate" of power bases come together to decide its outcome: the executive bureaucracy, the congressional subcommittee, and the organized interest groups.

6. In theory, Congress restrains the bureaucracy directly by ordering changes in rules, altering the budget, retaining veto powers over bureaucratic action, conducting investigations, and registering complaints. In practice, however, Congress rarely reverses bureaucratic decisions and seldom tampers with "uncontrollable" budget items.

7. In theory, the courts can also restrain the bureaucracy. But rarely do they actually reverse administrative decisions.

8. The federal regulatory commissions are investigators, prosecutors, judges, and juries—all wrapped into one. Members of these commissions serve long, overlapping terms, and they do not report to executive departments. They are relatively free from mass influence.

NOTES

1. John K. Galbraith, *The New Industrial State* (Boston: Houghton Mifflin, 1967), p. 73.
2. James Q. Wilson, "Social Science: The Public Disenchantment, A Symposium," *American Scholar* (Summer 1976):358; also cited by Aaron Wildavsky, *Speaking Truth to Power* (Boston: Little, Brown, 1979), p. 69.
3. See Richard F. Fenno, Jr., *The President's Cabinet* (Cambridge, Mass.: Harvard University Press, 1959).
4. Graham T. Allison, *Essence of Decision* (Boston: Little, Brown, 1971), p. 172.
5. Leslie H. Gelb and Morton H. Halperin, "The Ten Commandments of the Foreign Policy Bureaucracy," *Harper's* (June 1972):28–36.
6. Francis Fox Piven and Richard A. Cloward, *The New Class War* (New York: Pantheon Press, 1982).
7. Kenneth J. Meier, *Politics and the Bureaucracy* (North Scituate, Mass.: Duxbury Press, 1979), p. 51.

8. Randall P. Ripley and Grace A. Franklin, *Congress, the Bureaucracy and Public Policy* (Homewood, Ill.: Dorsey Press, 1976); Francis Rourke, *Bureaucracy, Politics, and Public Policy* (Boston: Little, Brown, 1976).

9. Bradley Cannon and Michael Giles, "Recurring Litigants: Federal Agencies before the Supreme Court," *Western Political Quarterly* 15 (September 1972):183–191.

10. David T. Stanley, Dean E. Mann, and Jameson W. Doig, *Men Who Govern* (Washington, D.C.: Brookings Institution, 1967).

11. Ibid., p. 21.

12. Marver H. Bernstein, *Regulating Business by Independent Commissions* (Princeton, N.J.: Princeton University Press, 1965), p. 118.

13. Office of the President, *A Program for Economic Recovery* (Washington, D.C.: Government Printing Office, February 18, 1981), p. 18.

14. See David H. Rosenbloom, "The Civil Service Commission's Decision to Authorize the Use of Goals and Timetables in Federal Equal Opportunity Programs," *Western Political Quarterly* 26 (June 1973):236–251.

SELECTED READINGS

Lindbloom, Charles E. *The Intelligence of Democracy.* New York: Free Press, 1965. Lindbloom analyzes democratic decision-making processes and offers a prescription for the best way to make collective decisions. The book discusses in depth the implications of incremental decision making.

Wildavsky, Aaron. *The Politics of the Budgetary Process.* Boston: Little, Brown, 1964. This book is the classic introduction to budgetary decision making and the folkways of bureaucracies. Wildavsky concludes that "budgeting turns out to be an incremental process, proceeding from a historical base, guided by accepted notions of fair shares, in which decisions are fragmented, made in sequence by specialized bodies, and coordinated through multiple feedback mechanism." The importance of this book lies in its argument against policy formation based strictly on rational considerations.

Wildavsky, Aaron. *Speaking Truth to Power: The Art and Craft of Policy Analysis.* Boston: Little, Brown, 1979. An important essay on why policies do not always work as intended, this book examines how and why bureaucracies substitute their own purposes for their original goals, how past policies create new problems, and how national planning conflicts with good politics.

12 Congress: The Legislative Elite

It seems clear that there are elites within elites. There are elites within the House, the Senate, and the executive branch who exercise disproportionate control over government and who are not representative even of the majority of government elites.

The heart of the trouble is power exercised by minority, not majority, rule.

—*Joseph S. Clark,* The Senate Establishment, *1963*

The Founding Fathers established Congress to represent the people in policy making. But how does Congress "represent" the people, and who are "the people"? Because of the way its members are elected, Congress tends to represent local elites in America and thereby injects a strong parochial influence into national decision making. Representatives are part of local elite structures; they retain their local businesses, club memberships, and religious affiliations. They are also recruited by local rather than national elites. They are not responsible to national political leaders but rather to leaders within their home constituencies. Thus congressional members represent many small segments of the nation rather than the nation as a whole.

Social backgrounds of Congress: The class bias

The "representational bias" of Congress begins with recruitment. Senators and House members are seldom recruited from the masses; they mostly hail from the well-educated, prestigiously employed, affluent upper and upper-middle classes.[1] Only a small minority come from families of wage earners or salaried workers. (See table 12-1.)

Occupation

Professional and business occupations dominate the halls of Congress, meaning that congressional members are generally of higher social standing than their constituents. One reason is that candidates for Congress have a better chance at election if their occupations are socially "respectable" and provide opportunities for extensive public contacts. Lawyers, insurance brokers, farm implement dealers, and realtors establish in their businesses the wide circle of friends necessary for political success. A more subtle reason is that successful candidates must have

TABLE 12-1.   Profile of the 98th Congress

	House[a]	Senate
Party		
Democrats	267	54
Republicans	165	46
Average age		
97th Congress	48.0	52.3
98th Congress	48.6	53.6
Sex		
Men	411	98
Women	21	2
Religion		
Protestants	258	70
Roman Catholics	123	17
Jews	29	8
Others	22	5
Profession		
Lawyers	173	55
Business executives	107	25
Public officials	63	4
Educators	31	4
Farmers, ranchers	17	5
Journalists	12	1
Congressional aides	9	0
Dentists, doctors	4	0
Clergymen	2	0
Judge	1	1
Pro athlete	1	1
Airline pilot, astronaut	0	2
Navy admiral	0	1
Others	12	1
Race		
Whites	400	98
Blacks	20	0
Hispanics	9	0
Orientals	2	2
Polynesian	1	0

[a]Three vacancies.

occupations with flexible work responsibilities. Lawyers, landowners, and business owners can adjust work responsibilities to campaign and legislative schedules, but office managers cannot.

The overrepresentation of lawyers in Congress and other public offices is particularly marked, since lawyers constitute no more than two-tenths of 1 percent of the labor force.[2] Lawyers have always played a prominent role in the American political system. Twenty-five of the fifty-two signers of the Declaration of Independence and thirty-one of the fifty-five members of the Continental Congress were lawyers. The legal profession has also provided 70 percent of the presidents, vice-presidents, and cabinet officers of the United States, and over 50 percent of the U.S. senators and House members. Lawyers are in a reasonably high-prestige occupation, but so are physicians, business executives, and scientists. Why, then, do lawyers dominate Congress?

Some people argue that lawyers bring a special kind of skill to Congress. They represent clients in their work; therefore they can use the same skill to represent constituents in Congress. Also lawyers deal with public policy as it is reflected in the statute books, so they may be reasonably familiar with public policy before entering Congress. But professional skills alone cannot explain the dominance of lawyers in public office. Of all the high-prestige occupations, only lawyers can really afford to neglect their careers for political activities. Physicians, corporate managers, and scientists pay a high cost if they neglect their vocations for political activity. But political activity can help boost lawyers' careers; free public advertising and contacts with potential clients are two important benefits. Moreover, lawyers have a natural monopoly on public offices in the law and the court system, and the offices of judge or prosecuting attorney often provide lawyers with stepping-stones to higher public office, including Congress.

Thus information on the occupational background of congressional members indicates that more than high social status is necessary for election to Congress. Experience in personal relations and public contacts, easy access to politics, and a great deal of free time to devote to political activity are also helpful.[3]

Education

Congressional members are among the most-educated occupational groups in the United States. Their educational level is considerably higher than that of the populations they represent. Their education reflects their occupational background and their middle- and upper-class origins. White Anglo-Saxon Protestants are substantially overrepresented in Congress. About two-thirds of the House and three-fourths of the Senate are Protestant. The main minority groups—blacks, Catholics, Jews, and foreign born—have disproportionately fewer seats in Congress.

Religion

Religious denominations of high social status, such as Episcopalians and Presbyterians, are regularly overrepresented in Congress. About one-third of the U.S. senators and House members are affiliated with the Congregational, Presbyterian, Episcopalian, or Unitarian churches. Although the representation of Catholics and Jews has increased in recent years, evidence indicates that these minorities can win representation in Congress only in districts in which they are a majority or near majority. Nearly all Catholic and Jewish members come from northern and industrial states, notably from major cities; Mississippi, Georgia, and South Carolina send congressional delegations composed largely of Baptists and Methodists; whereas New York City sends delegations almost solidly Catholic and Jewish. Apparently local electorates prefer their representatives to reflect the dominant religious and ethnic backgrounds in their districts.

Race

If blacks had representation in Congress equal to their proportion of the population, forty-three blacks would serve in the House of Representatives and ten in the Senate. However, not until 1966 was the first black, Republican Edward Brooke of Massachusetts, popularly elected to the Senate; he served until 1977. The House contained twenty black representatives in 1982, whose districts were chiefly the black ghetto areas of large cities: Chicago, New York, Philadelphia, Los Angeles, Cleveland, and Baltimore. All were Democrats.

Case study: Women in Congress

In recent years, women have been competing for public office at a substantially increased rate. The number of women holding state and local elected offices has increased sharply. Chicago and San Francisco, along with several other medium and large cities, have elected women mayors. Women have also increased their membership on city councils and school boards. And the number of women state legislators has more than doubled from 344 in 1970 to 908 in 1982. Yet the number of women in Congress stays between 10 and 21 out of the 535 members of the House and Senate, almost exactly the same as in 1950. One might suppose that the increase in women in state and local government would eventually produce more female Congress members, but this upward mobility has not taken place. In 1982, the U.S. Senate had only 2 women members: Nancy Landon Kassebaum (R–Kansas) and Paula Hawkins (R–Fla.).

Perhaps the most significant reason women do not move up to national office is that they do not attract money from political action committees, which now play a major role in campaign finance. Without adequate financing, women's campaigns frequently appear poorly organized, perpetuating the notion that they cannot win. Also, with so few women running, women candidates come under intense scrutiny: "When there are so few women in office or running, if one or two screw up it's a lot more noticeable than when men do stupid things."[4]

In primary elections, in which candidates must build up personal organizations with little help from the existing party mechanism, the relative inexperience of women has proved more of a handicap than it has for men. Traditionally women have not played policy roles in campaigns and consequently do not have the expertise required to mount a successful campaign. Media politics exaggerate the problem. Theoretically the absence of party organizations and the reliance upon personal effort should help outsiders. So far women have not benefited.

Elite-mass interaction: Legislators and the folks back home

Larger constituencies give legislators more freedom

Congressional members must represent the interests of local elites; they are not as free as the president or the executive elites to direct themselves to national problems or concerns. Moreover, congressional members represent a more homogeneous constituency than does the president; a congressional constituency is usually well defined—rural or urban, mining or manufacturing or agricultural, defense oriented or cotton producing or citrus growing. A president, on the other hand, must please a much wider and more heterogeneous constituency. No single interest need dominate his judgment; he is freer to focus on the general welfare, and he can take a more cosmopolitan view of national affairs. Similarly senators, who represent larger constituencies than do House members, are somewhat less parochial and are freer to attend to the general public welfare.[5]

Elites: The relevant constituents

A congressional member's relevant political constituency is the elite of the district rather than the general district population. In reality, a constituency is not an aggregate body of people but a relatively small group of political activists with the time, interest, and skill to communicate about political events. Consequently their social status is usually disproportionately high for their districts, as high as (or higher than) their representatives.

Constituents' ignorance.   For the great mass of people, Congress is an institution with very low visibility. A study commissioned by the Senate Subcommittee on Intergovernment Relations discovered some grim facts about the public's awareness of Congress. Only 59 percent of a national sample of Americans could identify one senator from their state, and barely half could name that person's party. Only a paltry 39 percent could name both senators. Members of the House of Representatives, allegedly closer to their constituents, fared even worse. Only 46 percent could identify their representatives and only 41 percent their political affiliation. Further, many people were ignorant of even the most rudimentary institutional arrangements. For example, 20 percent thought that Congress included the Supreme Court.[6] People so confused cannot assess performance, even in the most general terms.

Even when constituents know a congressional member's name, few know the member's specific policy positions or, for that matter, overall political position. Hence, Miller and Stokes found that among those who offered a reason for candidate choice, only 7 percent indicated that their choice had any "discernible issue content."

If one measures political awareness by the ability to define general issue content (for example, to identify one's representative as "for the working person"), only a tiny fraction of the population qualifies as an attentive public. If one asks for detailed information about policy stands, only a "chemical trace" of the population qualifies as attentive. Legislators are not completely insulated from their districts. Approximately 15 percent of the population has *ever* written a letter to their senators or House representative, and 3 percent of the population accounts for over two-thirds of congressional mail. During periods of turmoil the flow of letters becomes more urgent. However, even in critical national situations, the flow of communication is unrepresentative.[7]

Political activists of the district.   A legislator's relevant constituents, then, are the home district's active, interested, and resourceful elites. In an agricultural district, they are the leaders of the American Farm Bureau Federation and the major agricultural producers—cotton producers, wheat growers, and so on; in the Southwest, oil producers or ranchers; in the mountain states, the copper, lead, and silver mining interests; in upper New England, the lumber, granite, and fishing interests; in central Pennsylvania and West Virginia, the coal interests and leaders of the United Mine Workers. More heterogeneous urban constituencies may contain a variety of influential constituents—bankers and financial leaders, real estate owners and developers, owners and managers of large industrial and commercial enterprises, top labor leaders, and the owners and editors of newspapers and radio and television facilities. In certain big city districts with strong, disciplined party organizations, the key congressional constituents may be the city's political and government elites—the city or county party chairpersons or the mayor. And, of course, anyone who makes major financial contributions to a congressional candidate's campaign becomes an important constituent, for such money is hard to come by.

Sending the message to legislators

The elite of a constituency tends to transmit messages to its representatives that are in *agreement* with the representative's known policy preferences.[8] Representatives, like most other people, tend to associate with people with whom they agree. Thus they will maintain contact with the constituency largely through existing acquaintances. Representatives gain two-thirds of their information about constituency preferences through such personal contact, and another 25 percent through mail. Representatives hear what they want to hear. Perhaps this selective perception helps explain why conflicting reports of public opinion are so common.

© 1979 Engelhardt in the St. Louis Post-Dispatch/
Reprinted by permission

'Now Here's The Cornerstone We Want To Replace.'

As we have seen, legislators' communication with local *elites* is relatively intense. Since elites and masses do not share the same opinion, it is not surprising that legislators' actions do not necessarily fit what the masses want. On particularly visible issues, those that invite clear communication, the agreement between legislative performance and constituency demand can be relatively high. On civil rights issues, for instance, the correlation between congressional voting and constituency opinion is high. On most other issues, however, the correlation is low. If the constituents knew what their representative was doing, they would not be particularly happy (or unhappy, since Congress is of such low salience). Except for the few major issues—such as civil rights—the "average" constituent would say of the representative's behavior "I don't like it; I don't dislike it; I just don't think about it very much."

While we cannot say with assurance what the representative process *is*, we certainly know what it is *not*. It is not the representation of the will of the people. At best, representation is intraelite communication.

Reelection of incumbents

The ultimate reprisal for congressional members who fail to keep their ears to the ground is to be sent home. Legislators, of course, subscribe to the popular theory of representative government, summarized by Charles O. Jones: "[Election time] is the period of accounting; either the representative is instructed further, or he is defeated for malrepresentation, or he is warned, or he is encouraged."[9]

Actually very little such accounting takes place; incumbents rarely lose. Indeed if we accept the standard theory of election, Americans are ecstatic over the performance of Congress. Roughly 81 percent of the senators who seek reelection win, and a whopping 93 percent of House members who seek reelection win.

Table 12-2 looks at Congress and its constituents from another perspective. Popular support for Congress is diminishing; criticism is increasing. But do the voters want to throw out rascals: Clearly not. Not only does the electorate routinely return incumbents to their seats; the general postwar trend is toward even greater safety for incumbents.

TABLE 12-2.   Popular support for Congress and reelection of incumbents

Year	Percent of public rating Congress positively	Percent of senatorial incumbents reelected	Percent of House incumbents reelected
1948	—	65	—
1950	—	80	—
1952	—	74	—
1954	—	85	95
1956	—	86	96
1958	—	65	91
1960	—	96	94
1962	—	90	96
1964	—	93	88
1965	64	—	—
1966	49	96	90
1967	38	—	—
1968	46	83	96
1969	34	—	—
1970	34	88	95
1971	26	—	—
1972	24	84	93
1974	29	92	90
1976	33	61	96
1978	34	68	95
1980	18	59	92
1982	16	93	92

Source: Gallup Opinion Index

These findings should not be surprising. We know that the electorate has a marked inability to identify its representatives in Congress. We can imagine how many voters can identify the challenger. Name familiarity—in the absence of any knowledge of issues—can be a powerful advantage. The average voters, even if only vaguely aware of the incumbents, are likely to perceive them favorably and vote for them.

Additionally incumbents are more likely to have an effective political organization and a stable network of communication with local elites. Assiduous incumbents can use their franking privilege for mailing newsletters, polls, and other information; they can appear at various public events, call news conferences, address organizational meetings, and, in general, make themselves as visible as possible at minimum expense.

By developing such ties with local elites, and because the "smart money" backs a winner, incumbents have more to spend and can maximize exposure. Incumbents generally can raise almost twice as much money as challengers.

Thus the cue for voters is incumbency (name familiarity) rather than issue position or even party affiliation (as the role of incumbency grows, the role of party identification weakens). Clearly, then, Congress is an

© Szep, *The Boston Globe*

"I always promise them the good life. They always re-elect me and that's exactly what I get—the good life."

institution that can generally operate free of mass reprisals: "We have neither a Democratic nor a Republican party. Rather, we have an incumbency party which operates a monopoly."[10]

Congress and the president: An unstable balance of power

How do the roles of Congress and the other governmental elites differ? Policy proposals begin outside Congress; Congress's role is to respond to proposals from the president, executive and military elites, and interested nongovernment elites. Congress does not merely ratify or rubber stamp decisions; it plays an independent role in the policy-making process. But this role is essentially deliberative; Congress accepts, modifies, or rejects the policies initiated by others. For example, the national budget, perhaps the most important policy document, is written by executive and military elites and modified by the president before Congress receives it. Congress may modify it further but does not formulate the budget. Of course, Congress is a critical conduit through which appropriations and revenue measures must pass. But sophisticated lawmakers are aware that they function as arbiters rather than initiators of public policy.

The relationship between Congress and other policy-making elites is not necessarily stable. Whether Congress operates merely to ratify the decisions of others or to assert its voice independently depends on many factors, such as the aggressiveness and skill of the president and the strength of congressional leadership. Congress may be tenacious in *rejecting* policy, but it rarely *initiates* policy.

The potential constitutional power in Congress is very great. Article I empowers Congress to levy taxes, borrow and spend money, regulate interstate and foreign commerce, coin money, declare war, maintain armies and navies, and to perform other important functions, including passing all laws "necessary and proper" to carry out these powers.

The pendulum of power swings between Congress and the executive branch, but the general trend since Franklin D. Roosevelt has been toward the president. A key event in the power struggle between Congress and the president was the depression of the 1930s and the creation of the massive New Deal federal programs. In economic crisis, Congress, with its cumbersome decision-making process, simply gave up. Roosevelt's first act was to close all banks by executive order, explaining that he intended to use executive power to wage war against depression just as he would in the event of foreign invasion. In the early days of the New Deal, senators and House members voted for bills they had never even read.

Granted that these events were exceptional, Roosevelt's "revolution" nonetheless remained intact. Although Congress has recovered a more active role in domestic affairs (confined, however, to modifying executive-sponsored legislation), its role in foreign affairs remains minimal. Under the pressure of cold war ideology, the president frequently has withheld information on the grounds that "national security" made it imperative to minimize congressional participation. Huge military appropriations bills routinely passed both houses with only one day of debate and usually without amendment. The president decided to commit troops to Korea with only the most cursory communication to Congress; the decision to escalate in Vietnam—the famous Tonkin Resolution of 1965—received technical approval from Congress after only two days of debate and with only two dissenting votes.

Elaborate procedures of legislative elites

The rules and procedures of Congress are elaborate but important to the functioning of legislative elites. Much legislative debate concerns rules and procedures, and many policy questions turn on the question of proper procedure. Legislative procedures and rules make the legislative process fair and orderly; without established customs, rules, and procedures, 535 men and women could not arrive at collective decisions about the thousands of items submitted to them during a congressional session. Yet the same rules also delay or obstruct proposed changes in the status quo; they strengthen Congress's conservative role in policy making. In congressional procedures, legislation faces many opportunities for defeat and many obstacles to passage. Of course, it is not surprising that an elite that functions as an arbiter of public policy operates under rules and procedures that maximize deliberation and grant advantages to those who oppose change.

Law-making process

Congress follows a fairly standard pattern in the formal process of making laws; figure 12-1 describes briefly some of the more important procedural steps. Bills generally originate in the president's office, in executive departments, or in the offices of interested elites, but a member of the House or Senate must formally introduce them into Congress. Except for bills raising revenue, which must begin in the House according to the Constitution, bills can be introduced in either house. Upon introduction, a bill moves to one of the standing committees of the House or Senate, which may: (1) recommend it for adoption with only minor changes; (2) virtually rewrite it into a new policy proposal; (3) ignore it and prevent its passage through inaction; (4) kill it by majority vote. The full House or Senate *may* overrule a committee decision but does so rarely. Most members of Congress are reluctant to upset the prerogatives of the committees and the desires of recognized leaders. Therefore committees have virtual power of life or death over every legislative measure.

FIGURE 12-1. How a bill becomes law

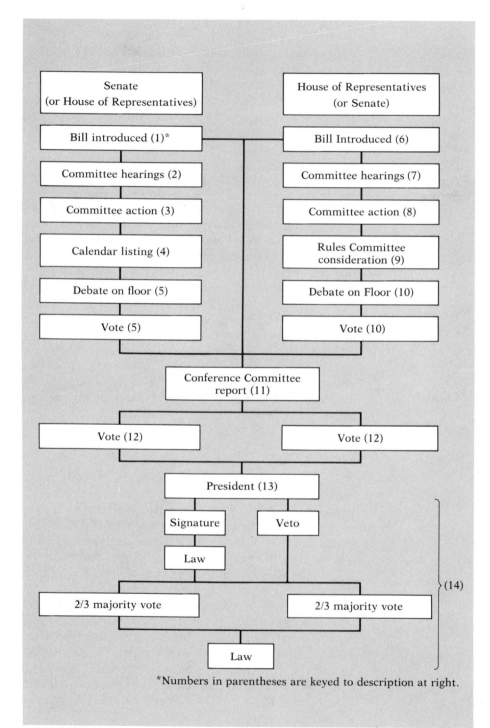

*Numbers in parentheses are keyed to description at right.

FIGURE 12-1. *continued*

1. *Introduction.* Most bills can be introduced in either house. (In this example, the bill is first introduced in the Senate.) It is given a number and referred to the proper committee.

2. *Hearings.* The committee may hold public hearings on the bill.

3. *Committee action.* The full committee meets in executive (closed) session. It may kill the bill, approve it with or without amendments, or draft a new bill.

4. *Calendar.* If the committee recommends the bill for passage, it is listed on the calendar.

5. *Debate, amendment, vote.* The bill goes to the floor for debate. Amendments may be added. The bill is voted on.

6. *Introduction to the second house.* If the bill passes, it goes to the House of Representatives, where it is referred to the proper committee.

7. *Hearings.* Hearings may be held again.

8. *Committee action.* The committee rejects the bill, prepares a new one, or accepts the bill with or without amendments.

9. *Rules Committee consideration.* If the committee recommends the bill, it is listed on the calendar and sent to the Rules Committee. The Rules Committee can block a bill or clear it for debate before the entire House.

10. *Debate, amendment, vote.* The bill goes before the entire body, is debated and voted upon.

11. *Conference Committee.* If the bill as passed by the second house contains major changes, either house may request a conference committee. The conference—several persons from each house, representing both parties—meet and try to resolve their differences.

12. *Vote on conference report.* When they reach an agreement, they report back to their respective houses. Their report is either accepted or rejected.

13. *Submission to the president.* If the report is accepted by both houses, the bill is signed by the speaker of the House and the president of the Senate and is sent to the president of the United States.

14. *Presidential action.* The president may sign or veto the bill within ten days. If he does not sign and Congress is still in session, the bill automatically becomes law. If Congress adjourns before the ten days have elapsed, it does not become law. (This is called the "pocket veto.") If the president returns the bill with a veto message, it may still become a law if passed by a two-thirds majority in each house.

Standing congressional committees and subcommittees

Committee work is essential to the legislative process; Congress as a body could never hope to review all the measures put before it. As early as 1885 Woodrow Wilson described the American political process as "government by the standing committees of Congress."[11] But while reducing legislative work to manageable proportions, the committees exercise considerable influence over the outcome of legislation. A minority of the legislators, sometimes a single committee chairman, can delay and obstruct the legislative process.

In the Senate, the most prestigious committees are Foreign Relations, Appropriations, and Finance; in the House, the most powerful are the Rules Committee, Appropriations, and Ways and Means. (Table 12-3 lists the twenty-two standing committees of the House and the sixteen of the Senate.) To expedite business, most standing committees create subcommittees to handle particular matters falling within their jurisdiction. This practice further concentrates power over particular subject matter in the hands of a very few congressional members. Considerable power lies in the hands of subcommittee members, especially the chairpersons; interested elites cultivate the favor of powerful subcommittee and committee chairpersons.

Public hearings.   In examining legislation, a committee or subcommittee generally holds public hearings on bills deemed worthy by the

TABLE 12-3.   The standing committees of Congress, 1983

Senate committees	House committees
Foreign Relations	Appropriations
Appropriations	Ways and Means
Finance	Armed Services
Budget	Banking, Finance and Urban Affairs
Agriculture, Nutrition and Forestry	Agriculture
Armed Services	Education and Labor
Judiciary	Government Operations
Commerce, Science and Transportation	Judiciary
Banking, Housing and Urban Affairs	Budget
Rules and Administration	Foreign Affairs
Governmental Affairs	Science and Technology
Veterans' Affairs	Post Office and Civil Service
Environment and Public Works	Standards of Official Conduct
Energy and Natural Resources	Small Business
Labor and Human Resources	House Administration
Small Business	Merchant Marine and Fisheries
	Veterans' Affairs
	District of Columbia
	Rules
	Interior and Insular Affairs
	Public Works and Transportation
	Energy and Commerce

chairperson or, in some cases, by the majority of the committee. Influenced by the legal profession, represented by a majority of legislators, the committees tend to look upon public hearings as trials in which contestants present their side of the argument to the committee members, the judges. Presumably, during this trial the skillful judges will sift facts on which to base their decisions. In practice, however, committees use public hearings primarily to influence public opinion or executive action or, occasionally, to discover the position of major elite groups on the measure under consideration.

Committee membership.   The membership of the standing committees on agriculture, labor, interior and insular affairs, and judiciary generally reflects the interest of particular elite groups in the nation. Legislators representing farm interests sit on the agricultural committees; representatives of land, water, and natural resource interests serve on interior and insular affairs committees; members of Congress with labor ties and urban industrial constituencies gravitate toward the labor committee; and lawyers dominate the judicial committees of both houses.

Given the power of congressional committees, the assignment of members to committees is one of the most significant activities of Congress. In the House of Representatives, the Republicans assign their members to committees through the Committee on Committees, which consists of one representative from each state that sends a Republican to Congress. Each representative votes with the strength of his or her state delegation. But the real business of this committee is conducted by a subcommittee appointed by the Republican party leader. The subcommittee fills committee vacancies with freshman members and those who request transfer from other committees. The Committee on Committees considers the career backgrounds of members, their seniority, and their reputation for soundness, which usually means adherence to conservative policy positions. Often the chairperson of a standing committee tells the Committee on Committees his or her preferences for committee members. Democrats in the House make committee assignments through the Steering and Policy Committee. Created in 1973, this committee is comprised of the party leadership; the caucus elects twelve members to represent geographic regions, and the Speaker appoints the additional nine members.

In the Senate, the Committee on Committees fills Republican committee positions, and a steering committee appointed by the Democratic floor leader selects Democratic committee members. Usually only senators with seniority are eligible for major committee positions in the Senate, such as Foreign Relations, Armed Services, and Appropriations.

Power of the chair.   Committee and subcommittee chairpersons are very powerful. They usually determine the bills the committee will consider, select issues for public hearings, and establish the agenda of the committee. Government and nongovernment interests officially must consult the chairperson on all questions relating to his or her committee; this procedure confers status on the committee with the executive branch and with interested nongovernment elites. Only occasionally does a majority within the committee-subcommittee "baronage" overrule a chairperson's decision on a committee matter.

Growing power of subcommittees

The chairperson's power has eroded somewhat due to successful House Democratic caucus challenges of the seniority system and the growth in the power of subcommittees. Indeed the move to strengthen the autonomy of subcommittees may be the most significant structural change in Congress in the last decade, eclipsing the more publicized seniority issue. Many subcommittee chairpersons have eclipsed full committee chairpersons in influence and autonomy. Those leading the drive to establish subcommittee autonomy were the younger Democrats, who gained more influence than they would have had without reforms. Today no House member can be chairperson of more than one subcommittee, so younger members can gain access to these key positions. A subcommittee "bill of rights" gives the Democrats on each committee (rather than the committee chairperson) the authority to select subcommittee chairpersons, guarantees all members sufficient assignments, and provides adequate subcommittee budgets. Finally all committees with more than twenty members must have at least four subcommittees.

Thus subcommittee chairpersons assume influence almost equal to their committee counterparts. The growth of subcommittees, and the attendant fragmentation of authority, is at odds with the centralizing impact of budget reform and the increasing influence of the Democratic caucus and leadership. Once acquired, however, power is not readily relinquished.

Seniority system

Guarantee of conservatism.   The practice of appointing chairpersons according to seniority also guarantees conservatism in the legislative process. The member of the majority party with the longest continuous service on the committee becomes chairperson; the member of the minority party with the longest continuous service on the committee is the ranking minority member. Therefore chairpersons are not chosen by their own committees, by their own party, or by the House and Senate as a whole. They are chosen by the voters of noncompetitive congressional districts, whose representatives are likely to stay in office the longest. The major decisions in Congress rest with those members from areas where party competition and voter participation are low; in the past, these areas have been southern and rural or big-city machine constituencies. In both houses, the seniority system works against the competitive urban and suburban districts. In 1971 both parties modified seniority to allow review and ratification by the party caucus. However, though the Democratic caucus will occasionally displace a committee chairperson, most senior members remain at the top of the Capitol hierarchy.

In recent years, the strengthening of the national Democratic party and the growth of the Republican party in the South have weakened southerners' position in Congress; about half the Democrats in Congress were once southerners, whereas now only one-fourth are. As young southerners replace old and as Democrats from other regions build seniority, Democratic southern domination of committee chairs has diminished.

Conspicuous by their absence in key committee assignments are legislators from the most populous states in the country: New York, California, and Illinois. Also notably absent are senators whose public visibility far exceeds their influence: Goldwater, Kennedy, and Moynihan. In the world of the Senate, their power is considerably less than that of, say, Senator Byrd of West Virginia.

Growth of influence. As their influence within Congress grows, high-seniority legislators tend to identify with Congress as an institution, to the detriment of possible constituency influence. Two factors are at work here. Legislators get to know each other well (they see each other more regularly than they see constituents); and older legislators probably have learned from experience that a perceived unpopular vote will not bring the vigorous constituency response they once thought was inevitable. Thus the experienced legislator tends to develop a more realistic view of the electorate, expressed well in one senator's remarks: "After several terms, I don't give a damn any more. I'm pretty safe now and I don't have to worry about reaction in the district."[12] Legislators also specialize in certain kinds of legislation, thus developing expertise that draws their colleagues to them as credible sources of information. As one put it, "That's the beauty of the seniority system—there are informed, experienced people on each Committee you can consult."[13] When congressional members need advice, they usually turn to someone of higher seniority.

Initial committee assignments do not depend strictly on seniority. But once assigned, the legislator can remain, building up seniority. First, though, each party must make its selection. Since control of Congress depends upon reelection, the party leadership tried to place party members where they can do the most good for their constituents. As we noted, this practice assures representation of the major interests in a constituency on the appropriate committee.

The seniority system has both critics and defenders. Its most active critics are: (1) those with low seniority, (2) those without formal leadership positions, (3) those from urban districts, and (4) those with a more liberal voting record.[14] Supporters of seniority (with characteristics in direct contrast to those reformers listed above) talk more of the rewards of experience, the development of expertise, and the nurturing of stability in relationships. Seniority helps maintain the "subsystem": without it, the established network of relationships among interests groups, executive agencies, and committees would flounder.

Lobbyists, committees, and committee reform

Lobbyists try to focus their activities as narrowly as possible, thus enabling them to develop strong ties with relevant congressional committees and administrative agencies. Such a "subsystem" can develop to the benefit of all participants. Legislators benefit from campaign contributions by interest groups; lobbyists benefit from personal working relationships with committees and their staffs; administrative agencies benefit from interest groups' and congressional committees' support of their budget requests.

Legislative procedure

House Rules Committee.   After a standing committee reports a bill in the House (step 8 in figure 12-1), the Rules Committee must issue a special rule or order before the bill can go before the House membership for consideration. Consequently each bill must go through two committees. (The only exceptions are bills reported by the House Appropriations and the Ways and Means committees; the House may consider their bills at any time as privileged motions.) The Rules Committee can kill a bill by shelving it indefinitely. It can insist that the bill be amended as the price of permitting it on the floor and can even substitute a new bill for the one framed by another committee. The Rules Committee determines how much debate will be permitted on any bill, and the number and kind of amendments that may be offered from the floor. The only formal limits on Rules Committee authority are the *discharge petition* (which is rarely used and hardly ever successful) and *calendar Wednesday,* a cumbersome procedure that permits standing committees to call up bills the Rules Committee has blocked. The Rules Committee, clearly the most powerful committee in Congress, is dominated by senior members elected from noncompetitive districts.

Senate filibusters.   In the Senate, control of floor debate rests with the majority leader. But the majority leader does not have the power to limit debate; a senator who has the floor may talk without limit and may choose to whom he or she yields the floor. If enough senators wish to talk a bill to death *(filibuster)*, they may do so. This device permits a small minority to tie up the business of the Senate and prevent it from voting on a bill. Under rule 22 of the Senate, debate can be limited only by a process called *cloture*. Sixteen member signatures on a petition will bring cloture to a vote; a three-fifths vote of the full Senate ends the filibuster: but cloture has been successful only fifty-four times in the history of the Senate. It has been a major weapon in civil rights legislation; the Civil Rights Act of 1964 passed the Senate through a cloture petition. But generally senators agree to protect each other's right of unlimited debate. Like the Rules Committee in the House, the filibuster is a means by which a small elite can defend itself against majority preferences.

Final vote.   Of the ten thousand bills introduced into Congress every year, only about a thousand, or one in ten, become law. After approval of a bill by the standing committee in the Senate or by the standing committee and the Rules Committee in the House, the bill moves to the floor for a vote. Usually the most crucial votes come on the amendments to the bill that are offered to the floor (however, the Rules Committee may prevent amendments in the House). Once the membership defeats major amendments or incorporates them into the bill, the bill usually picks up broad support, and the final vote is usually heavily in favor of it.

Conference committees.   One of the most conservative features of American government is its *bicameralism;* after following a complicated path in one house, a bill must repeat the process in the other. A bill must pass both branches of Congress in identical form before it goes to the president for his signature. However, the Senate often amends a House bill, and the House usually amends Senate bills; and every time a house amends a bill, it must resubmit it to the originating house for concurrence with the changes. If either house declines to accept changes in the bill, an ad hoc joint committee, called a *conference committee,* must iron out specific differences. Disagreements between the houses are so frequent that from one-third to one-half of all public bills, including virtually all important ones, must go to conference committees after passage by both houses.

Conference committee members, appointed by the presiding officers of each house, usually come from the two standing committees that handled the bills in each house. Since the final bill produced by the conference committee is generally accepted by both houses, these committees have tremendous power in determining the final form of legislation. Both houses must accept or reject conference committee reports as a whole; they cannot further amend them. Most conference committees are now open, but still with unrecorded records; outside testimony is rare. The bill that emerges from their deliberations may not represent the view of either house and may even contain items never considered by either one. Some people have dubbed conference committees a "third house" of Congress, whose members are not elected by the people, keep no record of their work, and usually operate behind closed doors—with no debate of their product allowed.

Elites within elites: The congressional establishment

A power hierarchy exists among federal government elites that is supported by protocol, by the distribution of formal constitutional powers, by the powers associated with party office, by the committee and seniority systems of Congress, and by the "informal folkways" of Washington. According to the protocol of Washington society, the president holds the highest social rank, followed by former presidents and their widows, the vice-president, the Speaker of the House, members of the Supreme Court, foreign ambassadors and ministers, cabinet members, U.S. senators, governors of states, former vice-presidents, and, finally, House members.

Senatorial power

The Constitution grants greater formal powers to senators than to House members. With only one hundred senators, individual senators are more visible than House members in the social and political life of Washington, as well as in their home states. Also senators have special authority in foreign affairs not accorded to House members, for the Senate must advise and consent by a two-thirds vote to all treaties entered into by the United States. The threat of Senate repudiation of a treaty makes it desirable for the president to solicit Senate views on foreign affairs; generally the secretary of state works closely with the Foreign Relations Committee of the Senate on such matters. Influential senators undertake personal missions abroad and serve on delegations to international bodies. Another constitutional power afforded senators is to advise and consent on executive appointments, including Supreme Court justices, cabinet members, federal judges, ambassadors, and other high executive officials. Although the Senate generally approves the presidential nominations, the added potential for power contributes to the difference between the influence of senators and of House members. Finally, senators serve a six-year term and represent a broader and more heterogeneous constituency. Thus they have a longer guaranteed tenure in Washington, more prestige, and greater freedom from minor shifts in opinion among nongovernment elites in their home states.

Senators can enhance their power through their political roles; they often wield great power in state parties and can usually control federal patronage dispensed in their state. The power of the Senate to confirm nominations has given rise to the important political custom of "senatorial courtesy": senators of the same party as the president have virtual veto power over major appointments—federal judges, postmasters, customs collectors, and so on—in their state. Presidential nominations that go to the Senate are referred to the senator or senators from the state involved. If the senator declares the nominee personally obnoxious to him or her, the Senate usually respects this declaration and rejects the appointment. Thus before the president submits a nomination to the Senate, he usually makes sure that the nominee will be acceptable to his party's senator or senators from the state involved.

Party leadership

Party leadership roles in the House and the Senate are major sources of power in Washington. (See table 12-4 for a list of Senate and House leaders for the 98th Congress.)

Speaker of the House. The Speaker of the House of Representatives, elected by the majority party of the House, exercises more power over public policy than any other member of either house. Before 1910 the Speaker appointed all standing committees and their chairmen, possessed unlimited discretion to recognize members on the floor, and served as chairman of the Rules Committee. But in 1910, progressives severely curtailed the Speaker's authority. Today the Speaker shares power over the committee appointments with the Committee on Committees; committee chairpersons are selected by seniority, not by the Speaker; and the Speaker no longer serves as chairman of the Rules Committee. However, the Speaker retains considerable authority: referring bills to committees, appointing all conference committees, ruling on all matters of House procedure, recognizing those who wish to speak, and generally

TABLE 12-4. Party leadership in the 98th Congress

	Senator	State
President Pro Tempore	Thurmond	S.C.
Majority Leader	Baker	Tenn.
Majority Whip	Stevens	Alaska
Democratic Conference Secretary	Inouye	Hawaii
Minority Leader	Byrd	W. Va.
Minority Whip	Cranston	Calif.
Republican Policy Comm. Chair	Tower	Texas
Republican Conference Chairman	Heinz	Pa.

	Representative	State
Speaker	O'Neill	Mass.
Majority Leader	Wright	Texas
Majority Whip	Foley	Wash.
Minority Leader	Michel	Ill.
Minority Whip	Lott	Miss.
Democratic Caucus Chairman	Long	La.
Republican Conference Chairman	Kemp	N.Y.

directing the business of the floor. More importantly, the Speaker is the principal figure in House policy formulation, leadership, and responsibility; although sharing these tasks with standing committee chairpersons, he is generally "first among equals" in his relationship with them.

Floor leaders and whips.   Next to the Speaker, the most influential party leaders in the House are the majority and minority floor leaders and the party whips. These party leaders are chosen by their respective party caucuses, which take place at the beginning of each congressional session. The party caucus, composed of all the party's members in the House, usually does little more than elect these officers; it makes no major policy decisions. The floor leaders and whips have little formal authority; their role is to influence legislation through persuasion. Party floor leaders must combine parliamentary skill with persuasion, maintain good personal relationships with party members, and cultivate close ties with the president and administration. They cannot deny party renomination to members who are disloyal to the party, but because they can control committee assignments and many small favors in Washington, they can prevent a maverick from becoming an effective legislator.

The whips, or assistant floor leaders, keep members informed about legislative business, see that members are present for important floor votes, and communicate party strategy and position on particular issues. They also serve as the eyes and ears of the leadership, counting noses before important votes. Party whips should know how many votes a particular measure has, and they should be able to get the votes to the floor when the roll is called.

Vice-president.   The vice-president of the United States, who serves as president of the Senate, has less control over Senate affairs than the Speaker of the House has over House affairs. The vice-president votes only in case of a tie and must recognize senators in the order in which they rise. The majority party in the Senate also elects from its membership a president pro tempore who presides in the absence of the vice-president.

Majority and minority leaders.   The key power figures in the Senate are the majority and minority leaders, who are chosen by their respective parties. The majority leader usually has great personal influence within the Senate and is a powerful figure in national affairs. The majority leader, when of the same party as the president, is in charge of getting the president's legislative program through the Senate. Although having somewhat less formal authority than the Speaker of the House, the majority leader has the right to be the first senator to be heard on the floor and, with the minority floor leader, determines the Senate's agenda. He or she can greatly influence committee assignments for party members. But on the whole the majority leader's influence rests on powers of persuasion. Many people consider Lyndon Johnson the most persuasive, and therefore most effective, majority leader in recent times (1953–1960).

Committee chairpersons.   The committee system and the seniority rule also create powerful congressional figures: the chairpersons of the most powerful standing committees, particularly the Senate Foreign Relations, Appropriations, and Finance committees, and the House Rules, Appropriations, and Ways and Means committees. Chairpersons of the standing committees in both houses have become powerful through members' respect for the authority of their committees. The standing committee system is self-sustaining because an attack on the authority of one committee or committee chairperson is much like a threat to all; members know that if they allow one committee or committee chairperson to be bypassed on a particular measure, they open the door to similar infringements of power. Hence committee chairpersons and ranking committee members tend to stand by each other and support each other's authority over legislation assigned to their respective committees. Committee chairpersons or ranking committee members also earn respect because of their seniority and experience in the legislative process. They are often experts in parliamentary process as well as in the substantive area covered by their committees. Finally, and perhaps most importantly, committee chairpersons and ranking committee members acquire power through their relationships with executive and private elites who influence policy within the committee's jurisdiction.

Policy clusters.   "Policy clusters"—alliances of leaders from executive agencies, congressional committees, and private business and industry—tend to emerge in Washington. Through their control over legislation in Congress, committee chairpersons are key members of these policy clusters. One policy cluster might include the chairpersons of the House and Senate committees on agriculture, the secretary of agriculture and other key officials of the Department of Agriculture, and the leaders of the American Farm Bureau Federation. Another vital policy cluster would include the chairperson of the House and Senate Armed Services committees; the secretary and under secretaries of defense; key military leaders, including the Joint Chiefs of Staff; and the leadership of defense industries such as Lockheed and General Dynamics. These alliances of congressional, executive, and private elites determine most public policy within their area of concern.

Key members of Congress.   Power also accrues to key senators and representatives by virtue of custom and informal folkways. Professor David B. Truman writes that Congress "has its standards and conventions, its largely unwritten system of obligations and privileges. . . . The neophyte must conform, at least in some measure, if he hopes to make effective use of his position."[15] A new member of Congress who wishes to "get along" should expect to "go along" with its customs. These informal folkways appear more important in the Senate, which has fewer formal controls over members than in the House. Donald Matthews has described some of the folkways of the Senate as respect for the seniority system; good behavior in floor debate; humility in freshman senators; a willingness to perform cheerfully many thankless tasks, such as presiding over floor debate; deference to senior members; making speeches only on subjects on which one is an expert or that concern one's committee assignment or state; doing favors for other senators; keeping one's word when making an agreement; remaining friendly toward colleagues, whether one is in political agreement with them or not; and speaking well of the Senate as an institution.[16]

Ralph K. Huitt describes the Senate type as:

> . . . a prudent man, who serves a long apprenticeship before trying to assert himself, and talks infrequently even then. He is courteous to a fault in his relations with his colleagues, not allowing political disagreements to affect his personal feelings. He is always ready to help another Senator when he can, and he expects to be repaid in kind. More than anything else he is a Senate man, proud of the institution and ready to defend its traditions and perquisites against all outsiders. He is a legislative workhorse who specializes in one or two policy areas. . . . He is a man of accommodation who knows that "You have to go along to get along"; he is a conservative, institutional man, slow to change what he has mastered at the expense of so much time and patience.[17]

Clearly, Congress has elites within elites. Within the House, the Senate, and the executive branch are elites who exercise disproportionate control over government and who are not representative even of the majority of government elites. Power within the House and Senate appears to flow downward from senior party leaders and influential committee chairpersons, whose dominance in congressional affairs is seldom challenged by the rank and file. Senator Joseph Clark has written, "The trouble with Congress today is that it exercises negative and unjust powers to which the governed, the people of the United States, have never consented. . . . The heart of the trouble is that power is exercised by minority, not majority, rule."[18]

Conflict and consensus: Voting in Congress

Party voting

Studies of roll-call voting in Congress show that the role of party influence in legislative conflict varies according to the issue.[19]

Cohesion.   *Party* votes, those roll-call votes in which a majority of voting Democrats oppose a majority of voting Republicans, occur on less than *half* the roll-call votes in Congress. Roll-call voting follows party lines more often than it follows sectional, urban-rural, or any other divisions that have been studied. How much cohesion exists within the parties? Table 12-5 shows the number of party votes in Congress in recent years and the average support Democratic and Republican mem-

TABLE 12-5.   **Party voting in Congress**

	Party votes as percent of total votes	Party support, Democrats[a]	Party support, Republicans[a]
1970			
Senate	35	58	56
House	27	55	60
1971			
Senate	42	64	63
House	38	61	67
1972			
Senate	36	57	64
House	27	58	61
1973			
Senate	40	69	64
House	42	68	68
1974			
Senate	44	63	59
House	29	62	63
1975			
Senate	48	68	64
House	48	69	72
1976			
Senate	37	62	61
House	36	66	67
1977			
Senate	42	63	66
House	42	68	71
1978			
Senate	45	66	59
House	33	63	69
1979			
Senate	47	69	72
House	47	66	70
1980			
Sente	46	64	65
House	38	69	71
1981			
Senate	48	71	81
House	37	69	74
1982			
Senate	43	72	76
House	36	72	69

[a]Party support: Average percentage of times a member voted with majority of own party against the other party's majority.

Source: Compiled from *Congressional Quarterly.*

bers of Congress have given to their parties. Democrats and Republicans appear equally cohesive, with members of both parties voting with their party majority more than two-thirds of the time. Party voting appears more frequent in the House than in the Senate.

Conflict. *Bipartisan* votes, those roll calls in which divisions do not fall along party lines, occur most frequently on foreign policy and defense issues. Bipartisan agreement is also likely on appropriation bills and roll calls on low-conflict issues. Recently bipartisan voting has settled issues of federal aid to education, highway beautification, water pollution, voting rights, presidential continuity, and increases in federal employees' pay and veterans' benefits.

Conflict between parties occurs most frequently over social welfare programs, housing and urban development, economic opportunity, medical care, antipoverty programs, health and welfare, and the regulation of business and labor. Party conflict is particularly apparent in the budget, the most important policy document of the national government. The budget is the president's product and carries the label of his party. On some issues, such as civil rights and appropriations, voting generally follows party lines during roll calls on preliminary motions, amendments, and other preliminary matters but swings to a bipartisan vote on the final legislation. In such situations the parties disagree on certain aspects of the bill but compromise on its final passage.

Influence of the issue. Many issues that cause conflict between the Democratic and Republican parties relate to the conflict between government and private initiative. In general, Democrats have favored federal subsidies for agriculture; federal action to assist labor and low-income groups through social security, relief, housing, and wage-hour regulation; and generally a larger role for the federal government in launching new projects to remedy domestic problems. Republicans, on the other hand, have favored free competition in agriculture, less government involvement in labor and welfare matters, and reliance on private action.

Each party supports the president to a different degree. The president generally receives greater support from his own party than from the opposition party in Congress, although party lines are hazy on issues involving veterans, civil service, public works, and states' rights; and partisan differences on foreign policy are practically nonexistent. Before World War II, Democrats tended to support U.S. international involvement, while the Republicans strongly advocated neutrality and "isolationism." Now only the question of foreign aid divides the parties significantly in foreign affairs: Democrats generally support it more than do Republicans.

To some extent, party influences counter the decentralization inherent in the committee system; yet party votes are *not* common on *most* issues voted on in a given session. The probability that a legislator will vote in accordance with the party leadership is only slightly better than chance. The feeling of party identification is apparently more significant to legislators than actual party voting.

Early in his term President Reagan attracted the votes of many southern Democrats in Congress—the "boll weevils"—who supported him against the wishes of their party leadership. (Seeking to reestablish party discipline, the House Democrats removed Texas boll weevil Phil Gram from his position on the budget committee; however, Gram was the only boll weevil they punished.) Among Republicans, a few moderate to liberal "gypsy moths" from the Northeast and Midwest resisted the conservative president. Yet party voting increased in both parties. Party voting was especially apparent in the Senate, where Republicans, enjoying majority status for the first time in years, achieved the highest party unity yet recorded. Even in the House, where the Democratic party was supposedly in disarray because of Reagan's successful wooing of the southerners, the record of party loyalty remained stable and improved in 1982. The actual number of party votes did not increase, however. Examples of consistent differences between the parties remained nonetheless. In the 1982 session, House Republicans voted to reduce domestic spending 77 percent of the time; House Democrats voted for spending reductions only 22 percent of the time.

Conservative coalition

Although party voting appears more important than regional alignments, one regional voting bloc holds firm on a significant number of issues in Congress. As David Truman explains:

> The evidence is clear that there [is] a solid and sharply identifiable die-hard element among the Southern Democrats, whose opposition extend[s] well beyond the issues of intense regional loyalty to almost a whole range of questions growing out of the strains and stresses to which the American society has been subjected in the mid-twentieth century.[20]

On civil rights votes, this block of southern Democrats votes in opposition to a majority of both northern Democrats and Republicans.

More significant, however, is the conservative coalition of southern Democrats and Republicans who oppose the northern Democrats. In recent years this coalition has been evident in about 20 percent of all congressional roll calls. (See table 12-6.) The coalition votes together on such issues as aid to depressed areas, minimum wage laws, federal aid to education, public housing, urban renewal, medical care for the aged, taxation, and other domestic welfare questions. Not all southern Democrats or Republicans vote with the coalition; a roll-call coalition is any roll call in which a majority of voting southern Democrats and a majority of voting Republicans oppose a majority of northern Democrats. The

TABLE 12-6. The conservative coalition in Congress, 1970–1982

	Percent of coalition roll calls to total	Percent of coalition victories on coalition roll calls
1970		
Senate	26	64
House	20	70
1971		
Senate	28	86
House	31	79
1972		
Senate	25	63
House	29	79
1973		
Senate	23	54
House	21	67
1974		
Senate	21	54
House	26	67
1975		
Senate	28	48
House	28	52
1976		
Senate	26	58
House	22	59
1977		
Senate	28	74
House	24	60
1978		
Senate	22	46
House	19	57
1979		
Senate	22	65
House	19	73
1980		
Senate	20	75
House	16	67
1981		
Senate	20	95
House	22	88
1982		
Senate	17	90
House	19	78

Source: Compiled from *Congressional Quarterly*.

coalition generally has resisted expanded federal power and increases in federal spending programs. The conservative coalition has had varying success over the years.

However, the 1980 elections reinvigorated the conservative coalition. The Republicans gained control of the Senate for the first time in twenty-eight years, and the Democratic margin in the House dropped to 51. Most Democratic losses were not from the conservative coalition; hence the coalition was in a position to increase its influence. The 1980 campaign, dominated by Reagan-style traditional conservatism, placed reelected liberals in a more defensive posture. In 1980 and beyond, the conservative coalition could count on between 30 and 40 votes in the House and between 15 and 20 in the Senate. Formally established caucuses—the Conservative Democratic Forum in the House and an unnamed caucus in the Senate—institutionalized the coalition, and the media attached the "boll weevil" label to the southern contingent.

The result of this resurgence was the greatest success ratio for the conservative coalition since congressional record keeping began. Although evidence of coalition voting was not appreciably higher, victories were impressive. The coalition won 95 percent of the time in the Senate and 88 percent of the time in the House. A glance at table 12-6 indicates, however, that the coalition had been on the upswing since 1978. Indeed, many boll weevil stalwarts assumed office in 1978. In the 1982 elections, the Democrats gained 26 seats in the House but none in the Senate. No boll weevils met defeat. However, very few of the 1982 class from the South appeared sympathetic to coalition goals, thereby diluting the coalition's strength and reducing its ability to operate as a balance of power.

Conservative coalition support was nevertheless essential to President Reagan's 1981 budget and tax victories. Assured of success in the Republican Senate, the Reagan budget and tax program relied upon the coalition for victory in the House. The coalition did indeed provide the margin of victory for the president's proposed budget reduction schemes: thirty coalition members, all Democrats, stuck with Reagan in every vote; when Reagan turned his attention to reducing taxes, he attracted an even larger number, forty-four. But the coalition did not consistently support the president. His inability to persuade Congress to fund the "dense pack" mode of basing MX missiles was partly because of the coalition's reluctance to buy his plan. As Reagan's influence declined in 1982, so did the coalition's.

Summary

This analysis of Congress proposes several ways to refine elite theory and apply it to a specific institution:

1. Congress tends to represent locally organized elites, who inject a strong parochial influence in national decision making. Congressional members are responsible to national interests that have a strong base of support in their home constituencies.

2. A member's relevant political constituency is not the general population of the home district but its elite. Less than half the general population of a district knows its legislator's name; fewer still have any idea of how their representative voted on any major issue. Only a tiny fraction ever express their views to their legislators.

3. With the possible exception of civil rights questions, most congressional members are free from the influence of popular preferences in their legislative voting. However, a member's voting record generally reflects the socioeconomic makeup of the home district. A congressional member is the product of the social system in his or her constituency and shares its dominant goals and values.

4. Congress seldom initiates changes in public policy. Instead it responds to policy proposals initiated by the president, executive and military elites, and interested nongovernment elites. The congressional role in national decision making is usually deliberative: Congress responds to policies initiated by others.

5. Congressional committees are important to communication between government and nongovernment elites. "Policy clusters," consisting of alliances of leaders from executive agencies, congressional committees, and private business and industry, tend to develop in Washington. Committee chairpersons are key members of these policy clusters because of their control over legislation in Congress.

6. The elaborate rules and procedures of Congress delay and obstruct proposed changes in the status quo, thus strengthening its conservative role in policy making. Transforming a bill to law is a difficult process; congressional procedures offer many opportunities for defeat and many obstacles to passage.

7. An elite system within Congress places effective control over legislation in the hands of relatively few members. Most of these congressional "establishment" members are conservatives from both parties who have acquired great seniority and therefore control key committee chairs.

8. Most bills that do not die before the floor vote pass unanimously. The greatest portion of the national budget passes without debate. The conflict that exists in Congress tends to follow party lines more often than any other factional division. Conflict centers on the details of domestic and foreign policy but seldom on its major directions.

NOTES

1. See Donald R. Matthews, *The Social Background of Political Decision-Makers* (New York: Doubleday, 1954).
2. Heinz Eulau and John D. Sprague, *Lawyers in Politics* (Indianapolis, Ind.: Bobbs-Merrill, 1964).
3. See Joseph A. Schlesinger, *Ambition and Politics* (Chicago: Rand McNally, 1966).
4. *Congressional Quarterly* (August 12, 1978):2108.
5. Lewis A. Froman, *Congressmen and Their Constituencies* (Chicago: Rand McNally, 1963).
6. U.S. Senate, Committee on Government Operations, Subcommittee on Intergovernmental Relations, *Confidence and Concern: Citizens View American Government* (Washington, D.C.: Government Printing Office, 1973), pp. 72–77.

7. Warren Miller and Donald Stokes, "Constituency Influence in Congress," *American Political Science Review* 57 (March 1963):55.

8. Raymond A. Bauer, Ithiel De Sola Pool, and Lewis A. Dexter, *American Business and Public Policy* (New York: Atherton Press, 1963), chap. 35.

9. Charles O. Jones, "The Role of the Campaign in Congressional Politics," in M. Kent Jennings and Harmon Zeigler, eds., *The Electoral Process* (Englewood Cliffs, N.J.: Prentice-Hall, 1966), p. 21.

10. Fred Westheimer, quoted in *Congressional Quarterly* (December 1, 1973):3130.

11. Woodrow Wilson, *Congressional Government* (1885; New York: Meridian Books, 1956), p. 178.

12. John W. Kingdon, *Congressmen's Voting Decisions* (New York: Harper & Row, 1973), p. 62.

13. Ibid., p. 88.

14. Roger H. Davidson, David M. Kovenock, and Michael K. O'Leary, *Congress in Crisis: Politics and Congressional Reform* (Belmont, Calif.: Wadsworth, 1966), pp. 67–91.

15. David B. Truman, *The Governmental Process* (New York: Knopf, 1955), p. 344.

16. Donald R. Matthews, "The Folkways of the United States Senate: Conformity to Group Norms and Legislative Effectiveness," *American Political Science Review* 53 (December 1959):1064–1089.

17. William S. White, *The Citadel: The Story of the U.S. Senate* (New York: Harper & Row, 1956), chap. 7.

18. Joseph S. Clark, *Congress: The Sapless Branch* (New York: Harper & Row, 1964), pp. 22–23.

19. See Malcolm E. Jewell and Samuel C. Patterson, *The Legislative Process in the United States* (New York: Random House, 1966); William J. Keefe and Morris Ogul, *The American Legislative Process* (Englewood Cliffs, N.J.: Prentice-Hall, 1964).

20. Truman, op. cit., p. 344.

SELECTED READINGS

Clark, Joseph S., et al. *The Senate Establishment*. New York: Hill and Wang, 1963. This book contains speeches made on the Senate floor that deal with power relationships in the Senate, especially the disproportionate power of the conservative coalition.

Davidson, Roger H. *The Role of the Congressman*. New York: Pegasus, 1969. Davidson's focus is the legislator's image of his or her job.

Fenno, Richard. *The Power of the Purse*. Boston: Little, Brown, 1966. Fenno provides an exhaustive analysis of the budgetary process.

Fenno, Richard. *Congressmen in Committee*. Boston: Little, Brown, 1973. This book outlines the strengths and weaknesses of the committee system.

Fenno, Richard. *Home-Style*. Boston: Little, Brown, 1978. This book is Fenno's impressionistic account of how Congress members communicate with constituents.

Huitt, Ralph K., and Peabody, Robert L. *Congress: Two Decades of Analysis*. New York: Harper & Row, 1969. This volume collects seven authoritative essays—Huitt's major contributions on the U.S. Senate and the executive-legislative process and Peabody's critical review of scholarship and trends in legislative research during the 1950s and 1960s.

Jones, Charles O. *The United States Congress*. Homewood, Ill.: Dorsey Press, 1982. This book is the best text on Congress.

Kingdon, John W. *Congressmen's Voting Decisions*. New York: Harper & Row, 1973. This book is the result of an intensive issue-by-issue examination of how individual House members made decisions in 1969. Focusing on one issue at a time,

Kingdon uses interviews with selected congressmen to determine how they came to vote the way they did. The result is a highly informative and readable text reflecting the complex relationships among the actors—the individual Congress members, his or her constituents, fellow Congress members, party leaders in and out of Congress, interest-group lobbyists, the executive branch, the legislative staff, and the media—and the decision-making process—structural influences, information problems, and decision norms.

Mann, Thomas E., and Ornstein, Norman. *The New Congress.* Washington, D.C.: American Enterprise Institute, 1981. The authors frankly assess the myths and realities of the "reformed" Congress.

Nathan, James A., and Oliver, James K. *United States Foreign Policy and World Order.* Boston: Little, Brown, 1976. Chapter 13 analyzes congressional-executive relations and foreign policy.

Rieselbach, LeRoy N. *Congressional Reform in the Seventies.* Morristown, N.J.: General Learning Press, 1977. Using responsiveness as an organizing concept, Rieselbach evaluates the reform efforts.

Ripley, Randall B. *Congress: Process and Policy.* New York: Norton, 1975. Ripley offers a comprehensive, historical analysis of the institutional development of Congress.

White, William S. *The Citadel: The Story of the U.S. Senate.* New York: Harper & Row, 1956. Although White's attitude toward the Senate is reverential when compared to Joseph Clark's critical view, *The Citadel* collects much information in an easy, enjoyable, if somewhat dated book.

13 Courts: Elites in Black Robes

Nine justices—none of whom are elected and all of whom serve for life—possess ultimate authority over all of the other institutions of American government.

Scarcely any political question arises in the United States that is not resolved, sooner or later, into a judicial question.

—*Alexis de Tocqueville,* Democracy in America, *1835*

The Supreme Court of the United States and the federal court system comprise the most elitist institution in American government. Nine justices—none of whom are elected and all of whom serve for life—possess ultimate authority over all other institutions of American government. These people have the power to declare void the acts of popularly elected presidents, Congresses, governors, state legislators, school boards, and city councils. No appeal is possible of their determination of the "supreme law of the land," except perhaps to undertake the difficult task of amending the Constitution itself.

The Supreme Court, rather than the president or Congress, has made many of the nation's most important domestic policy decisions. The Supreme Court took the lead in eliminating segregation from public life, ensuring separation of church and state, defining rights of criminal defendants and the powers of law enforcement officials, ensuring voters equality in representation, defining the limits of free speech and free press, and declaring abortion a fundamental right of women. Courts, then, are deeply involved in policy making on such diverse issues as school segregation, busing, public school prayers, federal aid to church-supported schools, capital punishment, police brutality, crime and law enforcement, malapportionment of representation, pornography, censorship, and abortion. Sooner or later in American politics, most important policy questions come before judges—who are not elected to office and cannot be removed for anything other than "treason, bribery, or high crimes and misdemeanors." As de Tocqueville observed as early as 1835, "Scarcely any political question arises in the United States that is not resolved, sooner or later, into a judicial question."[1]

Judicial review as an elitist principle

Recognition of the undemocratic character of judicial power in America is not new. The Founding Fathers viewed the federal courts as the final bulwark against mass threats to principle and property.[2]

In *Marbury* v. *Madison*, the historic decision establishing the power of judicial review, John Marshall argued persuasively that (1) the Constitution is "the supreme law of the land," and that U.S. and state laws must be congruent with it; (2) Article III of the Constitution gives to the Supreme Court the judicial power, which includes the power to interpret the meaning of laws and, in case of conflict between laws, to decide which law shall prevail; and (3) the courts are sworn to uphold the Constitution, so they must declare void a law that conflicts with the Constitution.

Since 1803 the federal courts have struck down more than eighty laws of Congress and uncounted state laws that they believed conflicted with the Constitution. Judicial review and the power to interpret the meaning and decide the application of law are judges' major sources of power.

The Founding Fathers' decision to grant federal courts the power of judicial review of *state* decisions is easy to understand. Article VI states that the Constitution and national laws and treaties are the supreme law of the land, "anything in the Constitution or laws of any state to the contrary notwithstanding." Federal court power over state decisions is probably essential in maintaining national unity, for fifty different state interpretations of the meaning of the Constitution or of the laws and treaties of Congress would create unimaginable confusion. Thus few people question the power of federal judicial review over state constitutions, laws, and court decisions.

However, at the national level, why should an appointed court's interpretation of the Constitution prevail over the views of an elected Congress and an elected president? Members of Congress and presidents swear to uphold the Constitution, and we can assume that they do not pass laws they believe to be unconstitutional. Since both houses of Congress and the president must approve laws before they become effective, why did the Founding Fathers establish that federal courts could set aside these decisions?

Apparently the Founding Fathers distrusted popular majorities and the elected officials subject to their influence. They believed that limitations on government would prevent it from attacking principle and property, whether to do so was the will of the majority or not. So the government's founders deliberately insulated the courts from popular majorities; by appointing judges for life terms, they sought to ensure their independence. The Founding Fathers originally intended that a president, not even directly elected himself, would appoint judges and that a Senate, also not directly elected, would confirm the president's appointments. Only in this way, the writers of the Constitution believed, would judges be sufficiently protected from the masses to permit them to judge courageously and responsibly.

Do the courts rule the nation?

George C. Wallace once put the argument bluntly: "Thugs and federal judges have just about taken charge of this country."[3] Others have also worried about the increasing role of the judiciary—the ability of courts to intrude into people's lives in ways unprecedented in history. One need not be a "conservative" in politics to be concerned about the extent to which we now rely upon a nonelected judiciary to solve our problems rather than upon democratically elected executives and legislators.

Growing reliance on the courts

Harvard Law School professor Archibald Cox, who became famous as the first Watergate prosecutor, warned that "excessive reliance upon courts instead of self-government through democratic processes, may deaden the people's sense of moral and political responsibility for their own future, especially in matters of liberty, and may stunt the growth of political capacity that results from the exercise of the ultimate powers of decision."[4]

For good or for ill, Americans have come to rely on courts to solve problems once handled by legislatures, local officials, school boards, teachers, parents, or other social organizations. Consider the following examples:

In 1975 after the kind of brawl on the ice that has become commonplace in professional hockey, a player for the Boston Bruins was indicted and tried by a Minneapolis court. He was accused of using his hockey stick in an aggravated assault against a player for the Minnesota North Stars. The case ended in a hung jury. But the courts for the first time had reviewed the conduct and rules of a game.

In 1977 a federal district court found that an elementary school pupil had been unconstitutionally denied promotion to the next grade. The court held that the pupil had been denied due process because the reasons for his failure had never been adequately explained.

In 1977 actor Lee Marvin was sued in California court for half of his earnings during the time that he and his girlfriend lived together. The court did not grant the full amount demanded but required Marvin to pay a smaller amount to assist his ex-girlfriend in readjusting to a new life, a payment quickly dubbed "palimony."

If these items were trivial or typical examples of the extension of court power into sports, education, and personal relations, few people would worry about judicial elitism. But the trend is toward increased judicial intervention in every aspect of our lives.

Court congestion

Each year American courts try over ten million cases, most of them in state and local courts. Nearly two hundred thousand cases begin in federal courts each year. Most of these cases will be settled before trial, but about twenty thousand (10 percent) go to trial. People appeal over twenty thousand cases to U.S. courts of appeal each year. And the U.S. Supreme Court receives over five thousand cases each year, although it can give serious attention to only about two hundred of these.

About one-half million lawyers practice in the United States. The federal government, through its Legal Services Corporation, operates its own law firm for the poor, with over thirty-five hundred lawyers in three hundred programs throughout the country.

The growing number of legal cases not only raises questions about the increasing power of a nonelected, lifetime, judicial elite, but it also overburdens the court system and creates many injustices. As more and more cases get into the judicial system, congestion and costs mount. Cases may be backed up on court dockets for years. As a result, injured parties in civil cases must suffer long delays before receiving compensation. Defendants in criminal cases who are free on bail may deliberately delay the trial, hoping that witnesses will move away or forget important details, or that victims will grow frustrated and give up trying to prosecute. Most lawsuits require attorneys on both sides, and attorneys are expensive. The longer a case drags on, the more expensive it is likely to be.

Congestion forces prosecuting attorneys in criminal cases to *plea bargain* with defendants—that is, to make special arrangements for criminal defendants to plead guilty in exchange for reduced charges. For example, a prosecutor may reduce the charge of rape to sexual assault, which usually carries a lighter penalty. The prosecutor enters into such a bargain in order to avoid the delays and costs of a trial; the defendant makes such a bargain to escape serious penalty for the crime. Estimates suggest that 90 percent of all criminal cases are now plea bargained.

Proposed judicial reforms

People concerned about judicial power have suggested changes in the law that might reduce the role of courts in our daily lives. One possible set of changes centers on "decriminalizing" some offenses that clog criminal courts. One frequent argument is that courts could function better if states would decriminalize possession of small amounts of marijuana, sexual activities among consenting adults, private gambling, and public drunkenness. "Decriminalizing" these behaviors does not mean government approval of them; it simply means that the criminal justice system is too overburdened to handle them. However, elected officials are reluctant to vote for "decriminalizing" these activities because they do not want to appear to endorse them.

Legal reformers also urge wider acceptance of "no-fault" concepts in civil disputes. Most states have now adopted some form of "no-fault" divorce, which allows the court to grant divorces without assigning fault to one or another spouse. But "no fault" can also extend to negligence (accident) cases, particularly automobile accidents. If such reform came about insurance companies would be obliged to make prompt payment for real, out-of-pocket losses due to accidents but not for "pain and suffering." Opposition to the "no-fault" notion arises from the nation's trial lawyers, many of whom depend for their livelihood on costly divorce and negligence cases. Since attorneys are prevalent in the nation's governing elite, these simple reforms have made slow progress.

Federal courts are so insulated from popular pressure and from congressional and presidential pressures that we will probably have to wait for them to "reform" themselves. If federal judges are slow in handling cases, if their decisions are arbitrary, if congestion and confusion reign in their courtrooms, if they bog themselves down in details of managing school districts or prisons or hospitals, if they are lazy or poorly trained in the law, if they are in poor health or senile, no one can do much about it. Only four federal court judges have *ever* been impeached and convicted by Congress, none since 1936. Federal Judge Otto Kerner (former governor of Illinois) resigned his judicial post only five days before he was scheduled to enter prison for income tax evasion, perjury, bribery, and mail fraud.[5] In short, the American citizenry has little control over the judiciary, despite the control it exercises over all of us.

The making of a judge

Judges' social backgrounds reflect close ties with the upper social strata. Over 90 percent of the Supreme Court justices serving on the Court between 1789 and 1962 were from socially prominent, politically influential, upper-class families.[6] Over two-thirds of the justices ever serving on the Court attended Ivy League or other prestigious law schools. No blacks served on the Supreme Court until the appointment of Associate Justice Thurgood Marshall in 1967; and no women served on the Court until the appointment of Sandra Day O'Connor in 1981. The typical Supreme Court justice is: "white, generally Protestant. . . ; fifty to fifty-five years of age at the time of his appointment; Anglo-Saxon ethnic stock. . . ; high social status; reared in an urban environment; member of a civic-minded, politically active, economically comfortable family; legal training; some type of public office; generally well educated."[7]

Of course, social background does not necessarily determine judicial philosophy. But "if . . . the Supreme Court is the keeper of the American conscience, it is essentially the conscience of the American upper-middle class, sharpened by the imperative of individual social responsibility and political activism, and conditioned by the conservative impact of legal training and professional legal attitudes and associations."[8]

Appointment process

Nomination.   All federal judges are appointed by the president and confirmed by a majority vote of the Senate. The recruitment process is highly political. Herbert Jacob reports that 80 percent of federal judges held political office some time before their appointment.[9] (See table 13-1.) Less than one-third of the nation's Supreme Court justices have had prior experience as judges. Few Supreme Court justices rise through the federal court system; political support and friendship with the president are more promising avenues toward high judicial appointment. Agreement with the political philosophy of the president is generally necessary for consideration. Of course, once appointed, a Supreme Court justice can pursue a course at variance with the president, and many have done so. The attorney general's office assists the president in screening candidates for all federal judgeships; the president usually requests the American Bar Association to comment on the qualifications of the proposed nominees.

Confirmation.   Until recently the Senate Judiciary Committee, which holds hearings and recommends confirmation to the full Senate, has accepted nominations by the president with a minimum of dissent. (The Senate has rejected only 28 of the 130 Supreme Court nominations ever sent to it.) The prevailing ethos is that a popularly elected president deserves the opportunity to appoint his own judges; that the opposition party in Congress will have its own opportunity to appoint judges when it captures the presidency; and that partisan bickering over judicial appointments is undesirable.

TABLE 13-1.   Position of Supreme Court Justice at time of appointment

Justice	Position
Chief Justice:	
Warren Burger	Judge, U.S. Court of Appeals
Associate Justices:	
Thurgood Marshall	U.S. Solicitor General
William J. Brennan, Jr.	Justice, Supreme Court of New Jersey
Sandra Day O'Connor	Judge, Arizona Court of Appeals
Byron R. White	U.S. Deputy Attorney General
Harry A. Blackmun	Judge, U.S. Court of Appeals
Lewis F. Powell, Jr.	Private practice
William H. Rehnquist	Assistant Attorney General
John Paul Stevens	Judge, U.S. Court of Appeals

Changes in political philosophy

Presidents usually nominate judges who share their political philosophy. One might assume that this practice is a democratizing influence on the Court, assuming that the people elect a president because they agree with *his* political philosophy. But Supreme Court justices frequently become independent once they reach the Court. Former Chief Justice Earl Warren, as Republican governor of California, had swung critical delegate votes to Eisenhower in the 1952 Republican convention. When the grateful president rewarded him with the chief justiceship, little in Warren's background suggested that he would lead the most liberal era in the Court's history. Later Eisenhower complained that the Warren appointment was "the biggest damn mistake I ever made."[10]

Special style of judicial policy making

An *appearance of objectivity* cloaks the power of the courts to shape American life. Because judges serve for life and are legally accountable to no one, they maintain the fiction that they are not engaged in policy making but merely "applying" the law to specific cases.[11] To admit otherwise would spotlight the conflict between judicial power and the democratic myth of policy making by elected representatives.

Many of the nation's best judicial thinkers question this mechanistic theory of judicial objectivity, however. For example, former Justice Felix Frankfurter once observed:

> The meaning of "due process" and the content of terms like "liberty" are not revealed by the Constitution. It is the Justices who make the meaning. They read into the neutral language of the Constitution their own economic and social views. . . . Let us face the fact that five Justices of the Supreme Court are the molders of policy rather than the impersonal vehicles of revealed truth.[12]

The courts also maintain the *fiction of nonpartisanship*. Judges must not appear as if political considerations affect their decisions. Once appointed to the federal bench, they are expected to have fewer direct ties to political organizations than do members of Congress. They must not appear to base their decisions on partisan considerations or party platforms or to bargain in the fashion of legislators. Perhaps as a result of their nonpartisan appearance, courts enjoy a measure of prestige that other government institutions lack. Court decisions are more acceptable to the public if the public believes that the courts dispense unbiased justice.

Courts function under *special rules of access*. For example, they seldom initiate policies or programs as does Congress or the executive branch. Instead they wait until a case involving a policy question comes before them. The Constitution gives jurisdiction to federal courts only in "cases and controversies." Courts do not issue policy pronounce-ments, rules, or orders on their own initiative. For example, courts do not declare a law of Congress or an action of the president unconstitu-tional immediately upon its passage or occurrence. Nor do the federal courts render advisory opinions prior to congressional or executive action. The courts assume a passive role and wait until a case comes before them that directly challenges a law of Congress or an action of the president.

To gain access to the federal courts, one must present a *case* in which the federal courts have *jurisdication.* A case must involve two disputing parties, one of which must have incurred some real damages as a result of the action or inaction of the other. The federal courts will accept jurisdiction based on (1) the nature of the parties—a case in which the U.S. government is a party; or a controversy between two or more states, or between a state and a citizen of another state, or between citizens of different states; or a case involving a foreign nation or citizen; or (2) the nature of the controversy—a case that arises under the Constitution (a "constitutional question") or under the laws and treaties of the United States. Congress has further limited the jurisdiction of federal courts in cases between citizens of different states by requiring that the dispute involve over $10,000. State courts hear all other cases.

Judicial policy making follows a *legalistic style.* Plaintiffs and defen-dants present facts and arguments to the courts in formal testimony, cross-examination, legal briefs, and oral arguments, all of them highly ritualized. Legal skills are generally necessary to make presentations that meet the technical specifications of the courts. Decorum in court proceedings is highly valued because it conveys a sense of dignity; leg-islative or executive offices rarely function with as much decorum.

These distinctive features of judicial policy making—the appear-ance of objectivity, the fiction of nonpartisanship, special rules of access, limited jurisdiction, and legalistic style—all contribute to the power of the courts. These features help to legitimize court decisions, to win essential support for them, and thus to contribute to the influence of judges in the political system.

Structure of the federal court system

The federal court system consists of three levels of courts with general jurisdiction, together with various special courts (the Court of Claims, Customs Court, Patent Court, and Court of Military Appeals). The Con-stitution establishes only the Supreme Court although Congress deter-mines the number of Supreme Court justices—traditionally nine. Article III authorizes Congress to establish "such inferior courts" as it deems appropriate. Congress has designed a hierarchical court system consisting of nearly one hundred U.S. federal district courts and eleven U.S. circuit courts of appeals, in addition to the Supreme Court of the United States. (See figure 13-1.)

Federal district courts

Federal district courts are the trial courts of the federal system. Each state has at least one district court, and larger states have more. (New York, for example, has four.) Over five hundred judges, appointed for life by the president and confirmed by the Senate, preside over these courts. The president also appoints a U.S. marshal for each district court to carry out orders of the court and maintain order in the courtroom. Federal district courts hear criminal cases prosecuted by the U.S. Department of Justice, as well as civil cases. As trial courts, the district courts use both grand juries (juries composed to hear evidence and, if warranted, to indict a defendant by bringing formal criminal charges against that person) and petit, or regular, juries (juries that determine guilt or innocence). District courts may hear as many as three hundred thousand cases in a year.

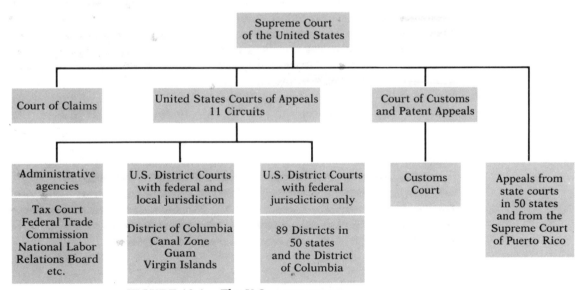

FIGURE 13-1.   The U.S. court system

Source: U.S. House of Representatives, Committee on the Judiciary, *The United States Courts: Their Jurisdiction and Work* (Washington, D.C.: Government Printing Office, 1969), p. 3.

Circuit courts of appeals

Circuit courts of appeals are *appellate courts*. They do not hold trials or accept new evidence but consider only the record of the trial courts and oral or written arguments (briefs) submitted by attorneys. Federal law provides that every individual has a right to appeal his or her case, so courts of appeals have little discretion in hearing appeals. Appellate judges themselves estimate that over 80 percent of all appeals are "frivolous"—that is, they are without any real basis at all. These courts require over one hundred circuit court judges, appointed for life by the president and confirmed by the Senate. Normally three judges serve together on a panel to hear appeals. Over 90 percent of the cases decided by circuit courts of appeals end at this level. Further appeal to the Supreme Court is not automatic; the Supreme Court itself decides what appeals it will consider. Hence, for most cases, the decision of the circuit court of appeals is final.

U.S. Supreme Court

The Supreme Court of the United States is the final interpreter of all matters involving the U.S. Constitution and federal laws and treaties, whether the case began in a federal district court or in a state court. In some cases the Supreme Court has original jurisdiction (authority to serve as a trial court), but it seldom uses this jurisdiction. Appellate jurisdiction is the Supreme Court's major function. Appeals may come from a state court of last resort (usually a state supreme court) or from lower federal courts. The Supreme Court determines for itself whether to accept an appeal and consider a case. It may do so if a "substantial federal question" is at issue in the case, or if "special and important reasons" apply. Any four justices can grant an appeal. However, the Supreme Court denies most cases submitted to it on *writs of appeal* and *writs of certiorari*; and the Court need not give any reason for denying appeal or certiorari.*

In the early days of the republic, the size of the U.S. Supreme Court fluctuated, but since 1869 its membership has remained at nine: the chief justice and eight associate justices. The Supreme Court is in session each year from October through June, hearing oral arguments, accepting written briefs, conferring, and rendering opinions.

---

*The Court technically must hear writs of appeal, but only a few matters qualify; among them are those involving clear constitutional issues (for example, a finding that a federal law is unconstitutional, that a state law is in conflict with federal law, or that a state law is in violation of the U.S. Constitution). Writs of certiorari are granted when four members agree that an issue involves a "substantial federal question" (as decided by the Supreme Court).

Jurisdiction of the federal court system

In the American federal system, each state maintains its own court system. The federal courts are not necessarily superior to state courts; both state and federal courts operate independently. But since the U.S. Supreme Court has appellate jurisdiction over state supreme courts, as well as over lower federal courts, the Supreme Court oversees the nation's entire judicial system.

State courts have general jurisdiction in all criminal and civil cases. According to Article III of the U.S. Constitution, federal court jurisdiction extends to:

1. Cases arising under the Constitution, federal laws, or treaties;
2. Cases involving ambassadors, public ministers or counsels, or maritime and admiralty laws;
3. Cases in which the U.S. government is a party;
4. Cases between two or more states;
5. Cases between a state and a citizen or another state;
6. Cases between citizens of different states;
7. Cases between a state or a citizen and a foreign government or citizen of another nation.

Obviously, it is not difficult "to make a federal case out of it," regardless of what "it" might be. The Constitution contains many vaguely worded guarantees—"due process of law," "equal protection of the laws," protection from "cruel and unusual punishment" and "unreasonable searches and seizures," and so forth—which allow nearly every party to any case to claim that a federal question is involved and that a federal court is the proper forum.

The great bulk of cases begins and ends in state court systems, however. The federal courts do not intervene once a state court has started hearing a case, except in very rare circumstances. And Congress has stipulated that legal disputes between citizens of different states must involve $10,000 or more in order to be heard in federal court. Moreover, parties to cases in state courts must "exhaust their remedies"—that is, appeal their case all the way through the state courts—before the federal courts will hear their appeal. Appeals from state supreme courts go directly to the U.S. Supreme Court and not to federal district or circuit courts. Usually appeals from state supreme courts to the U.S. Supreme Court are on the grounds that the case raises "a federal question"—that is, a question on the application of the U.S. Constitution or federal law. The U.S. Supreme Court reviews only a very small fraction of appeals from state court decisions.

Of the 10 million civil and criminal cases begun in the nation's courts each year, only about 2 percent are in federal courts. The U.S.

Supreme Court will receive about five thousand appeals each year but will hear only about two hundred of them. So state and local courts hear the great bulk of legal cases. The U.S. Constitution "reserves" general police powers to the states so that crimes and civil disputes are generally matters of state and local concern. Murder, robbery, assault, and rape are normally state offenses rather than federal crimes. Federal crimes generally center on offenses (1) against the U.S. government or its property; (2) against U.S. government officials or employees while they are on duty; (3) that involve crossing state lines (such as nationally organized crime, unlawful escape across state lines, taking kidnapping victims across state lines); (4) that interfere with interstate commerce; and (5) that occur on federal territories or on the seas.

Majority opinions of the Supreme Court are usually written by a single justice who summarizes majority sentiment. Concurring opinions are written by justices who vote with the majority but who feel the majority opinion does not fully explain their reasons. A dissenting opinion is written by a justice who is in the minority; such opinions have no impact on the outcome of the case. Written opinions are printed, distributed to the press, and published in *U.S. Reports* and other legal reporting services.

Activism versus self-restraint in judicial policy making

Great legal scholars have argued the merits of activism versus self-restraint in judicial decision making for more than a century.[13] The view for self-restraint argues that since justices are not popularly elected, the Supreme Court should move cautiously and avoid direct confrontation with legislative and executive authority. Justice Felix Frankfurter wrote, "The only check upon our own exercise of power is our own sense of self-restraint. For the removal of unwise laws from the statute books, appeal lies not to the courts but to the ballot and to the processes of democratic government."[14] But Frankfurter was arguing a minority position on the Court. The dominant philosophy of the Warren Court (1953–1969) was one of judicial activism. The Warren Court believed it should shape constitutional meaning to fit its estimate of the needs of contemporary society. By viewing the Constitution as a deliberately broad and flexible document, one can avoid dozens of new constitutional amendments to accommodate a changing society. The strength of the American Constitution lies in its flexibility—its relevance to contemporary society.[15]

Court's interpretive philosophy

Nonetheless the notion of self-restraint appears in a number of self-imposed maxims of interpretive philosophy, maxims that the Supreme Court generally, but not always, follows:

1. The Court will not pass upon the constitutionality of legislation in a nonadversary proceeding but only in an actual case. Thus the Court will not advise the president or Congress on constitutional questions.

2. The Court will not anticipate a question on constitutional law; it does not decide hypothetical cases.

3. The Court will not formulate a rule of constitutional law broader than required by the precise facts to which it must be applied.

4. The Court will not pass upon a constitutional question if some other ground exists upon which it may dispose of the case.

5. The Court will not pass upon the validity of a law if the complainant fails to show that he or she has been injured by the law, or if the complainant has availed himself or herself of the benefits of the law.

6. When doubt exists about the constitutionality of a law, the Court will try to interpret the meaning of a law so as to give it a constitutional meaning and avoid the necessity of declaring it unconstitutional.

7. A complainant must have exhausted all remedies available in lower federal courts or state courts if the Supreme Court is to accept review.

8. The constitutional issue must be crucial to the case, and it must be substantial rather than trivial, before the Court will invalidate a law.

9. Occasionally the Court defers to Congress and the president and classifies an issue as a political question, and refuses to decide it. The Court has stayed out of foreign and military policy areas.

10. If the court holds a law unconstitutional, it will confine its decision only to the particular section of the law that is unconstitutional; the rest of the statute stays intact.[16]

Courts are also limited by the principle of *stare decisis*, which means that the issue has already been decided in earlier cases. Reliance upon precedent is a fundamental notion in law. Indeed the underlying common law of England and the United States is composed simply of past decisions. Students of the law learn through the case-study method: the study of previous decisions. Reliance on precedent gives stability to the law; if every decision is new law, then no one would know what the law would be from day to day. Yet the Supreme Court frequently discards precedent. Former Justice William O. Douglas, who seldom felt restrained by legal precedent, justified disregard of precedent as follows:

The decisions of yesterday or of the last century are only the starting points. . . . A judge looking at a constitutional decision may have compulsions to revere the past history and accept what was once written. But he remembers above all else that it is the Constitution which he swore to support and defend, not the gloss which his predecessors may have put on it. So he comes to

© 1976 Punch/Rothco.

*"I realise you committed the crime
because of your background, and you,
no doubt, will also realise that I'm
sentencing you to five years
imprisonment because of my background!"*

formulate his own laws, rejecting some earlier ones as false and embracing others. He cannot do otherwise unless he lets men long dead and unaware of the problems of the age in which he lives do his thinking for him.[17]

Issue of constitutionality

Distinguished jurists have long urged the Supreme Court to exercise self-restraint. A law may be unwise, unjust, unfair, or even stupid and yet still be constitutional. One cannot equate the wisdom of a law with its constitutionality, and the Court should decide only the constitutionality and not the wisdom of a law. Justice Oliver Wendell Holmes once lectured his colleague, sixty-one-year-old Justice Stone, on this point:

> Young man, about 75 years ago I learned that I was not God. And so, when the people . . . want to do something I can't find anything in the Constitution expressly forbidding them to do, I say, whether I like it or not, "Goddamn it, let 'em do it."[18]

However, the actual role of the Supreme Court in America's power struggles suggests that the Court indeed equates wisdom with constitutionality. People frequently cite broad phrases in the Fifth and Fourteenth amendments establishing constitutional standards of "due process of law" and "equal protection of the laws" when attacking laws they believe are unfair or unjust. Most Americans have come to believe that unwise laws must be unconstitutional and that the courts have become the final arbiter of fairness and justice.

Supreme Court in elitist perspective

We can best understand the Supreme Court as an elitist institution rather than as a conservative or liberal institution in American government. During the 1930s, the Supreme Court was a bastion of conservatism; it attacked the economic programs of the New Deal and clung to the earlier elite philosophy of rugged individualism. Yet many people criticized the Warren Court later as too liberal in its views of equality of the law, church-state relations, and individual rights before the law. This apparent paradox is understandable if we view the Court as an exponent of the dominant elite philosophy rather than as a constant liberal or conservative element in national politics. When the dominant elite philosophy was rugged individualism, the Court reflected this fact, just as it reflects a liberal philosophy today. Of course, owing to the insulation of the Court even from other elites, through life terms and independence from the executive and legislative branches, a time lag exists between changes in elite philosophy and the Court decisions reflecting these changes.

The New Deal period

The Supreme Court's greatest crisis occurred when it failed to respond swiftly to changes in elite philosophy. When Franklin D. Roosevelt became president in 1933, the Supreme Court acted on the philosophy of rugged individualism. In a four-year period (1933–1937), the Court made the most active use of its power of judicial review over congressional legislation in its history in a vain attempt to curtail the economic recovery programs of the New Deal. It invalidated the National Industrial Recovery Administration, nullified the Railroad Retirement Act, invalidated the National Farm Mortgage Act, and threw out the Agricultural Adjustment Act. Having denied the federal government the power to regulate manufacturing, petroleum, mining, agriculture, and labor conditions, the Court reaffirmed the notion that the states could not regulate hours and wages. By 1936 it appeared certain that the Court would declare the Social Security Act and the National Labor Relations Act unconstitutional.

The failure of the Court to adapt itself quickly to the new liberalism of the national elite led to its greatest crisis. Roosevelt proposed to "pack" the Court by expanding its size and adding new liberal members. But the nation's leadership itself was divided over such a drastic remedy; so well had the Court served the interests of the established order over its history that Congress was reluctant to accept Roosevelt's plan. Moreover, at a critical point in the debate, the Court changed its attitude, with Chief Justice Hughes and Justice Roberts making timely changes in their position. In *National Labor Relations Board* v. *Jones & Laughlin Steel Corporation*, the Court expanded the definition of interstate commerce to remove constitutional barriers to government regulation of the economy.[19] It also upheld the power of the federal government to establish a social security system in a series of decisions that struck down due-process objections to social and economic legislation. And it reinterpreted the contract clause to permit Congress and the states to regulate wages, hours, and work conditions.

The Warren Court

A liberal concern for the underprivileged in America characterized the Supreme Court under the leadership of Chief Justice Earl Warren. The Court firmly insisted that no person in America should be denied equal protection of the law. It defended the right of blacks to vote, to attend integrated schools, and to receive equal justice in the courts; it upheld the power of Congress to protect blacks from discrimination in public accommodations, employment, voting, and housing. It ruled that discrimination against any group of voters by state legislatures in the apportioning of election districts was unconstitutional. It protected religious minorities (and the nonreligious) from laws establishing official prayers and religious ceremonies in public schools. The Court also protected defendants in criminal cases from self-incrimination through ignorance of their rights, confessions extracted unethically by law enforcement officials, or lack of legal counsel.

The Court, however, was noticeably less concerned with civil liberty when it involved the liberal establishment's cold war ideology. In *Dennis* v. *United States* the Court permitted the prosecution of communists for merely "advocating" the overthrow of the government, and in *Communist Party, U.S.A.* v. *Subversive Activities Control Board* it upheld the right of government to require registration of "subversive" organizations.[20] It permitted congressional committees to interrogate citizens about their political views and upheld loyalty oaths and loyalty-security programs. But by the late 1960s, after a decline of cold war ideology among the nation's elite, the Court began to protect "communists" and "subversives" from some of the harsher provisions of federal law.

The Burger Court

Popular predictions that the Burger Court, with four Nixon appointees including Chief Justice Warren Burger, would reverse the liberal decisions of the Warren Court did not take into account the elitist character of the Court. Supreme Court efforts to end racial segregation under law, ensure equality in representation, and maintain separation of church and state are fundamental commitments of the national elite. Hence the Burger Court was unlikely to reverse the landmark decisions of the Warren Court in these areas. The Burger Court extended the doctrine of *Brown* v. *Board of Education of Topeka* to uphold court-ordered busing of children to end racial imbalance in public schools with a history of segregation under law (southern school districts).[21] However, the Court refused to extend the busing requirement to force independent suburban school districts to bus students into central cities to achieve racial balance in predominantly black city schools. The Burger Court also struck down state payments to church schools for nonreligious instruction.[22] Only in the area of criminal defendants' rights has the Burger Court altered the direction of Warren Court holdings; even here, the Burger Court has not reversed any earlier holdings but has merely resisted extending them further.

Liberals hoped that the Burger Court would continue to expand the meaning of the equal protection clause of the Fourteenth Amendment by ordering state funding of local schools to compensate for financial inequalities in the property tax bases of local school districts. But the Court declined to do so, refusing to overrule the judgment of state and local authorities about how schools should be financed.[23] Many civil rights groups also hoped the Burger Court would use the Eighth Amendment prohibition against "cruel and unusual punishment" to strike down the death penalty. But the Court, while insisting on fairness and uniformity in application, upheld the death penalty itself.[24] Again, the Court declined to substitute its own notions about "cruel and unusual punishment" for the judgment of the many state legislatures that had voted to retain the death penalty.[25]

The Burger Court, however, issued one of the most sweeping declarations of individual liberty in the Supreme Court's history: the assertion of the constitutional right of women to have abortions.[26] The ultimate social impact of this decision—on population growth, the environment, and the role of women in society—may be as far-reaching as any other decision ever rendered by the Court. Certainly this decision clearly indicates that the Supreme Court continues to be a powerful institution capable of affecting the lives of virtually all Americans.

Case study: Life or death decisions

It is ironic indeed that a nation that thinks of itself as a democracy must call upon a nonelective, lifetime elite of nine people to decide a question as fundamental as life or death. It is even more ironic when Americans attack the Supreme Court as "conservative" because it tries to return this difficult decision to the states for the people to decide it.

(continued)

Case study *(continued)*

Prior to 1972, thirty-five states officially sanctioned the death penalty; only fifteen states had abolished capital punishment. Federal law also retained the death penalty. However, no one had actually suffered the death penalty since 1967 because of numerous legal tangles and direct challenges to the constitutionality of capital punishment. (See table 13-2.)

TABLE 13-2.   Persons executed, by race, 1930–1980

	Total	*White*	*Black*
All years	3,862	1,753	2,067
1930–1939	1,667	827	816
1940–1949	1,284	490	781
1950–1959	717	336	376
1960–1967	191	98	93
1968–1976	0	0	0
1977	1	1	0
1978	0	0	0
1979	1	1	0
1980	0	0	0
1981	1	1	0
1982	1	0	1

Several constitutional arguments are possible against the death penalty, aside from whatever moral, ethical, or religious objections one might raise. The first is that the death penalty is "cruel and unusual punishment," prohibited by the Eighth Amendment to the U.S. Constitution. The problem with this argument is that the early Jeffersonians who wrote the amendment, and the other sections of the Bill of Rights, themselves employed the death penalty. Indeed the Fifth Amendment mentions the death penalty, specifically indicating that this penalty was acceptable at the time. For nearly two hundred years the general agreement was that death was not "cruel" or "unusual" unless carried out in a particularly bizarre or painful fashion. Most executions were by hanging; the electric chair was introduced in the 1920s as a "humane" alternative, and the gas chamber followed in some states. Nonetheless one can still argue that by today's standards the death penalty is "cruel and unusual," recognizing that moral standards change over time.

Another constitutional argument against the death penalty is that courts apply it in a discriminating fashion, violating the equal protection clause of the Fourteenth Amendment. While blacks comprise only 12 percent of the population, over half the people executed have been black. (See table 13-2.) Moreover, among both blacks and whites, the less educated and less affluent individuals tend to be the ones executed. Finally, some people argue that imposition of the death penalty is arbitrary—that no clear, consistent criteria exist for deciding who should be executed and who should be spared.

The primary advocate of abolishing the death penalty on the Supreme Court has been Justice Thurgood Marshall, who believes that the death

Case study *(continued)*

penalty is the ultimate form of racial discrimination. Marshall wants to see the death penalty struck down once and for all. When a series of cases, including *Furman* v. *Georgia*, came to the Court in 1972,[27] over seven hundred people throughout the nation waited under sentence of death. But Marshall was unable to convince his colleagues on the Court that the death penalty was always "cruel and unusual." Of the other liberals on the Court, only Justice William J. Brennan seemed to agree that death itself was a cruel and unusual punishment. But Justice William O. Douglas, together with Potter Stewart and Byron White, believed that application of the death penalty was arbitrary, random, unfair, and discriminatory. Some individuals, usually poor, black, and uneducated, were sentenced to die for crimes for which other individuals, usually affluent, white, and educated, were sentenced to only a few years in jail. Justice Douglas wrote, "A penalty should be considered 'unusually' imposed if it is administered arbitrarily or discriminatorily." So Justice Marshall lined up five votes in 1972 to strike down the death penalty *as it was then imposed*. But Marshall was not able to convince a majority of the justices to abolish the death penalty altogether.

The minority view in 1972, which upheld the death penalty, was led by Chief Justice Warren Burger. Burger argued that the courts of the United States had always permitted the death penalty and had never held it to be cruel and unusual. Indeed as an indicator of contemporary standards, Burger observed that most states and the federal government itself retained the death penalty. The federal government had recently enacted death penalty laws for airplane hijacking where death resulted and for assassination of the president or vice-president. "The word cruel," said Burger, "can mean grossly out of proportion to the severity of the crime; but certainly when the crime is murder, the death penalty is not out of proportion to the crime." Chief Justice Burger reminded the states that the majority had not abolished the death penalty itself but had merely struck down its arbitrary use. He invited the states to reconsider and rewrite their death penalty laws. In private conversation, however, neither Burger nor Marshall believed that the states would reenact death penalty laws. Both men believed that "there will never be another execution in this country."[28]

Thus by a five-to-four vote, the Supreme Court struck down all capital punishment laws as they were written and administered in 1972. (See table 13-3.) The seven hundred people on death row received a permanent reprieve. But the Court was badly divided. The justices wrote nine separate opinions, totaling fifty thousand words on 243 pages—the longest Supreme Court decision in history.

To the surprise of many who hoped to abolish the death penalty, the *Furman* v. *Georgia* case in 1972 stimulated thirty-five states to reenact the death penalty with specific guidelines to avoid arbitrary or discriminatory use. By 1976 another six hundred people waited on death row for the Supreme Court to examine these new state laws.

The Supreme Court finally considered these new state laws in a series of death penalty cases in 1976.[29] Only Marshall and Brennan believed that

(continued)

Case study *(continued)*

TABLE 13-3.   Voting on the Supreme Court: The death penalty cases

	Strike down death sentence	Uphold death sentence
1972 *Furman* v. *Georgia*	Marshall Brennan Douglas Stewart White — 5	Burger Rehnquist Blackmun Powell — 4
1976 *Gregg* v. *Georgia*	Marshall Brennan — 2	Burger Rehnquist Blackmun Powell Stewart White Stevens — 7

capital punishment always violates the "cruel and unusual" punishment clause of the Eighth Amendment. Justice John Paul Stevens had replaced the aging liberal, William O. Douglas, on the Court. Stevens, together with Burger, Blackmun, Powell, and Rehnquist, provided five votes to uphold the death penalty. And Justices White and Stewart would uphold the death penalty if it was shown not to be arbitrarily imposed or discriminatory.

Georgia, Florida, and Texas, as well as several other states, had enacted very carefully designed capital punishment laws after the 1972 *Furman* v. *Georgia* decision. The objective was to ensure fairness and uniformity of application. Most of these laws provided for two trials: one to determine guilt or innocence and another to determine whether to impose the death sentence. The second trial called for evidence of "aggravating" and "mitigating" factors; if only aggravating factors were evident, the death penalty would be mandatory.

Justices Stewart, Powell, and Stevens together wrote the majority opinion in all of the death penalty cases in 1976. They ruled on behalf of the court that "the punishment of death does *not* invariably violate the Constitution." They upheld the death penalty with the following rationale: the men who drafted the Bill of Rights, including the Eighth Amendment, accepted death as a common sanction for crime. Clearly, one must interpret the Eighth Amendment prohibition against "cruel and unusual" punishment in a dynamic fashion, reflecting changing moral values. But the decisions of more than half the nation's state legislatures to reenact the death penalty since 1972 and the decisions of juries to impose the death penalty on hundreds of people under these laws are evidence that "a large proportion of American society continues to regard it as an appropriate and necessary criminal sanction." Moreover, said the Court majority, the social purposes of retri-

Case study *(continued)*

bution and deterrence justify the use of the death penalty. This ultimate sanction is "an expression of society's moral outrage at particularly offensive conduct." The Court reaffirmed that *Furman* struck down the death penalty only when inflicted in "an arbitrary and capricious manner." The Court approved the consideration of "aggravating and mitigating circumstance." The Court also approved of automatic review of all death sentences by state supreme courts to ensure that the sentence did not reveal the influence of passion or prejudice, that evidence supported aggravating circumstances, and that the sentence was proportionate to the crime. However, the Court disapproved of state laws making the death penalty mandatory in all first-degree murder cases, holding that such laws were "unduly harsh and unworkably rigid."

Marshall wrote a very emotional opinion dissenting from the majority view. And Brennan too was very upset over the changing attitude of the Court. "Justice of this kind is obviously no less shocking than the crime itself," he wrote, "and a new 'official' murder, far from offering redress for the offense committed against society, adds instead a second defilement to the first." But these dissents had no effect on the outcome of the case.

Summary

The Supreme Court determines many of the nation's most important policies. Indeed most political questions sooner or later end up in the courts. Any fair examination of the court system in America will reveal the elitist character of judicial decision making.

1. The Supreme Court is the most elitist branch of the national government. Nine justices—none of whom are elected and all of whom serve for life—can void the acts of popularly elected presidents, Congresses, governors, legislatures, school boards, and city councils.

2. The principle of judicial review of congressional acts grew out of the Founding Fathers' distrust of popularly elected officials subject to influence by popular majorities. Judicial review enables the courts to protect constitutional principles against attacks by elected bodies.

3. The social backgrounds of judges reflect close ties to upper-class segments of society. Presidents may attempt to influence court decisions through their selection of judges, but life terms make judges independent of presidential or congressional influence once they are appointed.

4. Judicial decision making takes on an appearance of objectivity, maintains the fiction of nonpartisanship, employs special rules of access,

and reflects a legalistic style. These features help legitimize the decisions of people who have no electoral mandate.

5. Since justices are not popularly elected, some scholars and jurists have urged self-restraint in judicial policy making. They argue that the Court should decide only the constitutionality of a law, not its wisdom; the Court should not substitute its own judgment for the judgment of elected representatives. But over the years judicial activism has augmented the power of judges. Justices have used broad phrases in the Constitution such as "due process of law" and "equal protection of the law" to strike down laws they believe are unfair or unjust.

6. Over its history the Supreme Court has not been consistently liberal or conservative but rather has reflected dominant elite philosophy. The greatest crisis in the Court's history occurred in the 1930s when dominant elites accepted New Deal "liberalism," but the Court continued to reflect the "rugged individualism" of an earlier era. Contrary to popular beliefs, the Burger Court has not reversed any of the landmark decisions of the Warren Court. Instead it has continued to reflect prevailing liberal establishment concerns for civil rights, equality in representation, and separation of church and state. The Burger Court's assertion of the constitutional right to have abortions may be one of the most important decisions in the Court's history.

NOTES

1. Alexis de Tocqueville, *Democracy in America* (New York: Mentor Books, 1956), p. 73.
2. James Madison, Alexander Hamilton, and John Jay, *The Federalist* (New York: Modern Library, 1937), p. 505.
3. *Newsweek* (January 10, 1977):42.
4. Archibald Cox, *The Role of the Supreme Court in American Government* (New York: Oxford University Press, 1976), p. 103.
5. *Time* (August 20, 1979):54.
6. John R. Schmidhauser, *The Supreme Court* (New York: Holt, Rinehart and Winston, 1960), p. 59.
7. Henry Abraham, *The Judicial Process* (New York: Oxford University Press, 1968), p. 58.
8. Schmidhauser, op. cit., p. 59.
9. Herbert Jacob, *Justice in America* (Boston: Little, Brown, 1965), p. 95.
10. Joseph W. Bishop, "The Warren Court Is Not Likely to Be Overruled," *New York Times Magazine* (September 7, 1969):31.
11. *U.S. v. Butler,* 297 U.S. 1 (1936); Carl Brent Swisher, "The Supreme Court and the Moment of Truth," *American Political Science Review* 54 (December 1960):879.
12. Felix Frankfurter, "The Supreme Court and the Public," *Forum* 83 (June 1930):332–334.
13. Frank Jerone, *Law and the Modern Mind* (New York: Coward-McCann, 1930); Benjamin N. Cardozo, *The Nature of the Judicial Process* (New Haven, Conn.: Yale University Press, 1921); Roscoe Pound, *Justice According to Law* (New Haven, Conn.: Yale University Press, 1951).
14. *West Virginia State Board of Education* v. *Barnette,* 319 U.S. 624 (1943).

15. Archibald Cox, *The Warren Court* (Cambridge, Mass.: Harvard University Press, 1968), p. 2.
16. See Abraham, op. cit., pp. 310–326.
17. Justice William O. Douglas, "Stare Decisis," *Record* (April 1947).
18. Quoted by Charles P. Curtis, *Lions Under the Throne* (Boston: Houghton Mifflin, 1947), p. 281.
19. *National Labor Relations Board* v. *Jones & Laughlin Steel Corporation*, 301 U.S. 1 (1937).
20. *Dennis* v. *U.S.*, 341 U.S. 494 (1951); *Communist Party, U.S.A.* v. *Subversive Activities Control Board*, 367 U.S. 1 (1961).
21. *Swann* v. *Charlotte-Mecklenburg Board of Education*, 39 L.W. 4437 (1971).
22. *Lemon* v. *Kurtzman*, 403 U.S. 602 (1971).
23. *Rodriguez* v. *San Antonio Independent School Board*, 411 U.S. 1 (1973).
24. *Furman* v. *Georgia*, 408 U.S. 238 (1972).
25. *Gregg* v. *Georgia, Profitt* v. *Florida, Jurek* v. *Texas*, 428 U.S. 242 (1976).
26. *Roe* v. *Wade*, 410 U.S. 113 (1973); *Doe* v. *Bolton*, 410 U.S. 179 (1973).
27. *Furman* v. *Georgia*, 408 U.S. 400 (1972).
28. Bob Woodward and Scott Armstrong, *The Brethren: Inside the Supreme Court* (New York: Simon and Schuster, 1979), p. 219.
29. *Gregg* v. *Georgia, Profitt* v. *Florida, Jurek* v. *Texas*.

SELECTED READINGS

Abraham, Henry J. *The Judicial Process.* New York: Oxford University Press, 1968. This book is one of the most comprehensive introductions to the basics of the judicial process. It provides both a sound theoretical introduction to the nature, sources, and types of law and a thorough nuts-and-bolts knowledge of the staffing, organization, and technical processes involved in the judicial process. The book provides four extensive bibliographies dealing with American constitutional law, biographies and autobiographies of and by justices of the Supreme Court, a discussion of comparative constitutional law, and analysis of civil liberties.

Jacob, Herbert. *Justice in America,* 2d ed. Boston: Little, Brown, 1972. Jacob assesses how well American courts administer civil and criminal justice. He views the courts as political, policy-making institutions and examines their participants, procedures, and restraints. The book gives special attention to out-of-court settlements, plea bargaining, and political justice and injustice.

Schmidhauser, John R. *The Supreme Court.* New York: Holt, Rinehart and Winston, 1960. Although somewhat dated, *The Supreme Court* is still one of the best historical treatments of the development of the Court as an institution. It examines changes in the organization, procedures, and personnel of the Court over time.

Schubert, Glendon. *Judicial Policy-Making.* Glenview, Ill.: Scott, Foresman, 1965. This book by a judicial behavioralist views the judicial process as an integral part of the political system. After examining the relationship of the courts to other structural elements in the political system, Schubert focuses upon the judicial process itself as a policy-making system. He offers a systemic model of judicial policy making and discusses it in terms of its "policy inputs, conversion, and outputs." Also included in the book is an evaluation of several approaches to the study of judicial policy making, including the traditional, conventional, and behavioral.

Woodward, Bob, and Armstrong, Scott. *The Brethren: Inside the Supreme Court.* New York: Simon and Schuster, 1979. This sensationalized behind-the-scenes account of decision making by the Supreme Court supposedly exposes the fact that members of the Court maneuver, argue, politick, and compromise over major issues confronting the Court and the nation.

14 American Federalism: Elites in States and Communities

Decentralization—decision making by subelites—reduces strain on the national political system and on national elites by keeping many issues out of the national arena.

The importance of denationalizing conflicts can hardly be over-estimated, particularly in a large country like the United States where there is great diversity in resources and local problems.

—Robert A. Dahl, Pluralist Democracy in the United States, *1967*

In the United States are nearly eighty thousand separate governments, over sixty thousand of which have the power to levy their own taxes; these governments include states, counties, cities, towns, boroughs, villages, special districts, school districts, and public authorities. Legally states are important units of government in America. The U.S. Constitution endows them with all government powers not vested specifically in the national government or reserved to the people. All other government jurisdictions are subdivisions of states. States may create, alter, or abolish these other units of government by amending state laws or constitutions. Over time, the number of local governments in America has been decreasing, mostly because of the consolidation of small school districts. Even so the multiplicity of governments in America is still impressive.[1]

Decentralization—decision making by subelites—reduces strain on the national political system and on national elites by keeping many issues out of the national arena. This system avoids conflict among subelites by allowing each to pursue its own policies within the separate states and communities; they need not battle for a single national policy to be applied uniformly throughout the land. For example, subelites who wish to raise taxes and spend more money for public schools can do so in their own states and communities, and those who wish to reduce taxes and eliminate what some consider to be educational "frills" can also do so within their own states and communities.

The masses play an even smaller role in state and local politics than they do in national politics. The news media emphasize national politics rather than state or community politics. Very few citizens know who their state senator or state representative is or who their council members or county commissioners are. We can expect 50 to 55 percent of the nation's eligible voters to cast ballots in presidential elections, but turnout in state gubernatorial elections in nonpresidential years is generally less than 50 percent. Municipal elections often attract fewer than 20 or 30 percent of the eligible voters.

Federalism: The division of power between nation and states

The Constitution divides power between two separate authorities, the nation and the states, each of which can directly enforce its own laws on individuals through its own courts. American federalism differs from a "unitary" political system in that the central government has no legal authority to determine, alter, or abolish the power of the states. At the same time, American federalism differs from a confederation of states, in which the national government depends on its states for power. The American system shares authority and power constitutionally and practically. Some people view national and state power as the opposite ends of a seesaw; if national powers increase, then state power must decline. But in fact both national and state powers have expanded over the years; states and communities now perform more services, employ more people, spend more money, and have a greater impact on the lives of their citizens than they have ever had in the past.

The U.S. Constitution originally defined federalism in terms of (1) the powers exercised by the national government (delegated powers) and the national supremacy clause; (2) the powers reserved to the states; (3) the powers denied by the Constitution to both the national government and the states; (4) the constitutional provisions giving the states a role in the composition of the national government; and (5) the authority of the U.S. Supreme Court to settle disputes between the nation and the states.

Delegated powers

The U.S. Constitution lists eighteen grants of power to Congress, including authority over war and foreign affairs; authority over the economy—"interstate commerce"; control over the money supply; and power to tax and spend "to pay the debts and provide for the common defense and general welfare." Finally, after seventeen specific grants of power comes the power "to make all laws which shall be necessary and proper for carrying into execution the foregoing powers and all other powers voted by this Constitution in the government of the United States or in any department or offices thereof." This statement is generally known as the "necessary and proper clause."

These delegated powers, when coupled with the assertion of "national supremacy" (in Article VI), ensure a powerful national government. The national supremacy clause is very specific in asserting the supremacy of federal laws over state and local laws:

> This Constitution, and the laws of the United States which shall be made in pursuance thereof; and all treaties made or which shall be made under the authority of the United States, shall be the supreme law of the land; and the judges in every state shall be bound thereby, anything in the constitution or laws of any state to the contrary notwithstanding.

Reserved powers

Despite these broad grants of power to the national government, the states retained considerable governing power from the beginning of the republic. The Tenth Amendment reassured the states that "the powers not delegated to the United States . . . are reserved to the states respectively, or to the people." The states generally retain control over property and contract law, criminal law, marriage and divorce, the provision of education, highways, and social welfare activities. The states control the organization and powers of their own local governments. Finally, the states, like the federal government, retain the power to tax and spend for the general welfare.

Powers denied to the states

The Constitution denies some powers to both national and state government, namely the powers to abridge individual rights. The first eight amendments to the U.S. Constitution, the Bill of Rights, originally applied only to the national government; but the Fourteenth Amendment, passed by Congress in 1866, provided that the states must also adhere to fundamental guarantees of individual liberty.

The Constitution denies the states some powers in order to safeguard national unity: the powers to coin money, enter into treaties with foreign nations, interfere with the "obligations of contracts," levy taxes on imports or exports, engage in war, and some others.

State role in national government

The states are also basic units in the organization scheme of the national government. The House of Representatives apportions members to the states by population, and state legislatures draw up their districts. Every state has one House representative regardless of population. Each state elects two U.S. senators regardless of population. The president is chosen by the electoral votes of the states; each state has as many electoral votes as it has senators and House representatives. Finally, three-fourths of the states must ratify amendments to the U.S. Constitution.

Growth of power in Washington

Over time governmental power has centralized in Washington. While the formal constitutional arrangements of federalism remain in place, power has flowed relentlessly toward the national government since the earliest days of the nation. Perhaps the most important developments over time have been (1) the broad interpretation of the necessary and proper clause to obscure the notion of "delegated powers" and allow the national government to do anything not specifically prohibited by the Constitution; (2) the victory of the national government in the Civil War, demonstrating that states could not successfully resist federal power by force of arms; (3) the establishment of a national system of civil rights based upon the Fourteenth Amendment, which brought federal government into the definition and enforcement of civil rights; (4) the growth of federal power under the interstate commerce clause as a national industrial economy emerged; and (5) the growth of federal grants-in-aid to state and local governments as a major source of revenues for these governments and a major source of federal intervention into state and local affairs.

Necessary and proper clause

Chief Justice John Marshall added immeasurably to national power in *McCulloch* v. *Maryland* (1819) when he broadly interpreted the necessary and proper clause of Article I, Section 8, of the Constitution. In approving the establishment of a national bank (a power not specifically delegated to the national government in the Constitution), Marshall wrote:

Let the end be legitimate, let it be within the scope of the Constitution, and all means which are appropriate, which are plainly adopted to that end, which are not prohibited but consistent with the letter and the spirit of the Constitution, are constitutional.

Since then, the "necessary and proper clause" has been called the "implied powers" clause or even the "elastic" clause, suggesting that the national government can do anything not specifically prohibited by the Constitution. Given this tradition, the courts are unlikely to hold an act of Congress unconstitutional simply because no formal constitutional grant of power gives Congress the power to act.

The Civil War

The Civil War was the nation's greatest crisis in federalism. Did a state have the right to oppose federal action by force of arms? This issue was decided in the nation's bloodiest war. (Combined casualties in the Civil War, military and civilian, exceeded U.S. casualties in World War II, even though the U.S. population in 1860 was only one-quarter of the population in 1940.) The same issue was at stake when the federal government sent troops to Little Rock, Arkansas, in 1957 and Oxford, Mississippi, in 1962 to enforce desegregation; however, in these confrontations it was clear which side held the military advantage.

Civil rights

Over the years, the U.S. Supreme Court has built a national system of civil rights based on the Fourteenth Amendment. This amendment rose out of the Civil War: "No *state* shall . . . deprive any person of life, liberty, or property, without due process of law; nor deny any person within its jurisdiction the equal protection of the laws." In early cases, the Supreme Court held that the general guarantee of "liberty" in the first phrase (the due process clause) prevents states from interfering with free speech, press, religion, and other personal liberties. Later, particularly after *Brown* v. *Board of Education of Topeka* in 1954, the Supreme Court also used the equal protection clause to ensure fairness and equality of opportunity throughout the nation.

Interstate commerce clause

The growth of national power under the interstate commerce clause is also an important development in American federalism. The industrial revolution created a national economy governable only by a national government. Yet until the 1930s the Supreme Court placed many obstacles in the way of government regulation of the economy. Finally in *National Labor Relations Board* v. *Jones & Laughlin Steel Corporation* (1937), the Supreme Court recognized the principle that Congress could regulate production and distribution of goods and services for a national market under the interstate commerce clause. As a result, the national government gained control over wages, prices, production, marketing, labor relations, and all other important aspects of the national economy.

Money and power and federal guidelines

Money and power go together. When the national government acquired the power to tax incomes in the Sixteenth Amendment in 1913, financial power shifted from the states to Washington. The income tax gave the federal government the authority to raise large sums of money, which it spent for the "general welfare," as well as for defense. Of course, federal land grants to the states began as far back as the famous Northwest Ordinance in 1787, giving federal land to the states to assist in building public schools. But the first major federal money grants to the states began shortly after enactment of the federal income tax. Grant programs began in agricultural extension (1914), highways (1916), vocational education (1917), and public health (1918).

Grants-in-aid

Gradually the federal government expanded its power in states and communities by use of grants-in-aid. During the Great Depression of the 1930s, the national government used its taxing and spending powers in a number of areas formerly reserved to states and communities. Congress began grants-in-aid programs to states and communities for public assistance, unemployment compensation, employment services, child welfare, public housing, urban renewal, highway construction, and vocational education and rehabilitation. The inadequacy of state and local revenue systems contributed significantly to the increase of national power in states and communities. Federal grants-in-aid to state and local governments have expanded rapidly in recent years in both dollar amounts and the percentage of the total revenue of states and communities that comes from the federal government.

Congressional guidelines

Whenever the national government contributes financially to state or local programs, the state or local officials have less discretion in using the funds than they would have otherwise. Federal grants-in-aid invariably come with congressional standards or "guidelines" to which states and communities must adhere to receive their federal money. Often Congress delegates to federal agencies the power to establish the conditions attached to grants. Federal standards are designed to ensure compliance with national minimum standards, but they are bound to annoy state and local leaders; protests from local constituencies are sometimes loud enough to induce Congress to yield to the views of subelites.

States or communities can reject federal grants-in-aid if they do not wish to meet federal standards, and some have done so; however, most find it difficult to do. The temptation of much-needed federal money can be a form of "bribery"; and the thought that other states and communities will get the federal money if they do not (although the money comes in part from federal taxes paid by their own citizens) can seem like "blackmail." Thus through the power to tax and spend for the general welfare and through the conditions attached to federal grants-in-aid, the national government can exercise important powers in areas originally "reserved" to the states. Of course, federal grants-in-aid have enabled many states and communities to provide necessary and desirable services that they could not have afforded without federal aid, and federal guidelines have often improved standards of administration, personnel policies, and fiscal practices in states and communities. Federal guidelines have also helped ensure that states and communities do not engage in racial discrimination in federally aided programs.

Many commentators genuinely fear that states and communities have surrendered many of their powers to the national government in return for federal money. They argue that federal grant-in-aid programs and federally established conditions have weakened the role of states and communities by centralizing power in Washington and diminishing the individuality of state and local elites.

Revenue sharing

Because of their many dissatisfactions with conditional grants-in-aid, governors and mayors lobbied vigorously in Washington for unconditional money grants from the federal treasury. Their efforts were partially successful with the passage of the state and local Fiscal Assistance Act of 1972, better known as "revenue sharing," which provided for direct awards of federal tax dollars to state and local governments to do with as they see fit.* The idea of revenue sharing assumes that the federal government is better at *collecting* revenue than are state or local governments but that state and local governments are better at *spending* it. Revenue sharing did not replace any of the existing five hundred or more conditional grant-in-aid programs. A state or city need not formally apply to receive its revenue-sharing funds; the U.S. Department of Treasury sends these funds to states and communities based on a formula that includes population, income, and local tax effort. Governments receiving these funds must not practice racial discrimination, must hold public hearings on their use to encourage popular participation, must observe federal labor laws, and must file reports on how the money is spent. But these restrictions are minor compared to the maze of restrictions surrounding other grant-in-aid programs.

The New Federalism

President Reagan's approach to federal-state relations has been consistent with his desire to diminish the influence of the federal government in the lives of its citizens. He calls his program "the New Federalism" (a phrase borrowed directly from Richard Nixon; revenue sharing was part of Nixon's new federalism, as was greater reliance on block grants— grants with far broader guidelines than categorical grants).

Reagan's New Federalism envisions a clear division of responsibility between the states and the federal government. For Reagan, revenue sharing and block grants are merely the first steps in a program to restructure federalism—to return to the states more power than they have enjoyed since the New Deal. In his 1982 State of the Union message, he proposed "with a single stroke" to return authority to states, which he feels are "more responsive to the people." Indeed opinion surveys indicate that large majorities believe that states are more responsive, more efficient, and less corrupt than the federal government. These attitudes may partially result from the anti–federal government rhetoric that pervaded Reagan's campaign. In 1978 surveys indicated that a plurality of people believed that the national government gave them the most for their money. In 1980 respondents saw the national government as less responsive and less efficient than state and local governments. (See figure 14-1.)

The New Federalism leans toward more state and local government rather than less. But urban and minority groups have traditionally expressed dissatisfaction with these governments. Much of the federal legislation developed since the 1960s has benefited minorities, who do

*The state portion was eliminated in 1981.

"From which level of government do you feel you get the most for your money—federal, state, or local?"

	1972	1973	1974	1975	1976	1977	1978
Federal	39%	35%	29%	38%	36%	36%	35%
State	18	18	24	20	20	20	20
Local	26	25	28	25	25	26	26
Don't know	17	22	19	17	19	18	19

SOURCE: Advisory Commission on Intergovernmental Relations, *Changing Public Attitudes on Government and Taxes* (Washington, D.C.: Government Printing Office, 1978), p. 4.

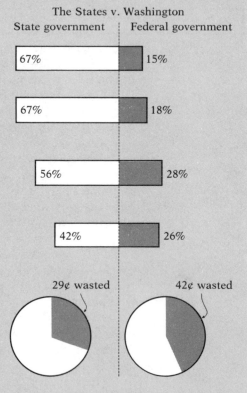

The States v. Washington

State government   Federal government

Which do you think is more understanding of the real needs of the people of this community?   67%   15%

Which do you think is more likely to administer social programs efficiently?   67%   18%

Which theory of government do you favor—concentration of power in the federal government or concentration of power in the state governments?   56%   28%

Which do you think is more likely to make decisions free of political corruption?   42%   26%

Of every tax dollar that goes to the federal government in Washington how many cents of each dollar do you think are wasted?   29¢ wasted   42¢ wasted

And how many cents of each tax dollar that goes to the government of this state do you think are wasted?

SOURCE: The Gallup Poll, conducted Sept. 18–21, 1981; reprinted from *Opinion Outlook*, Feb. 12, 1982

FIGURE 14-1. Public images of the federal system

not share the consensus that state governments are more reliable than the federal government. Indeed, the "categorical grant" (with explicit and detailed federal guidelines) was a response to minority interest groups' allegations that they could not get a fair shake from many state governments. In opposing the New Federalism, these groups were not as concerned about the governments of large, industrial states (although they had reason to be) as they were about the rurally dominated state legislatures in the South (although reapportionment had made such legislatures more urban). They saw the federal government as the key to equality of opportunity (as enforced by "conditional grants-in-aid") and felt that the new administration's commitment to local responsiveness would be at the expense of continued gains for minorities. Minority groups had long ago learned that their best chance to influence policy was in Washington, so they promptly began serious lobbying against Reagan's New Federalism. State and local officials, their bureaucracies, and their lobbyists were alarmed as well. For years they had asked for flexibility and money. Now they saw the New Federalism offering them more flexibility but substantially less money.

Reagan's New Federalism proposed first to consolidate eighty-four health, education, and social service categorical grant programs into six "no strings" block grants. But the federal government would reduce its contribution to these block grants to about 15 percent below the level in Carter's last year. Additionally Reagan proposed trading federal and state responsibilities: the federal government would assume full responsibility for Medicaid, while the states would take full responsibility for food stamps and aid to families with dependent children. To aid in the transition, Reagan wanted to establish a trust fund (derived from excise and windfall-profits taxes on oil) until 1990, when all responsibility for funding would pass to the states.

The block-grant phase got off to a shaky start. Beneficiaries of specific programs successfully lobbied to preserve their categorical status (the handicapped "saved" their special education program, for example). At the end of Reagan's first budget tussle with Congress, the new block grants accounted for about 8 percent of the $89 billion for federal grants. Nonetheless the president won some highly visible victories: one was replacement of the much-maligned Comprehensive Education and Training Act (CETA), which expired in 1982, with block grants to the states.

The states themselves have not been enthusiastic partners in Reagan's experiment. Most states operate under constitutional requirements to balance their budgets (unlike the federal government). In hard times, they also face tax limitation schemes, making their job even more difficult. Moreover, some states are richer than others—Alaska's per capita income is twice that of Mississippi—and they vary in political culture, tradition, and patterns of influence. Less professional than Congress, many state legislatures are more beholden to interest groups.

© 1982, Dana Summers in the *Journal Herald*, Dayton, Ohio.

"It's from the White House . . . They've run out of room!"

(Groups powerful in national politics are frequently less so in state legislatures. For example, business interest groups are most powerful at the state level, while minorities have difficulty competing politically.) Governors are less able to control the agenda of state legislatures than the president is able to control the congressional agenda. As a result, they anticipated bitter struggles over control of the programs "turned back" to their states. Thus some states are more able than others to assume responsibility for programs, even if they are willing. The powerful constituency and administrative-professional lobbies that have formed around categorical aid programs also worried about loss of access under the New Federalism: would they be as successful in Texas as they had been in Washington?

In essence the New Federalism threatened the established distribution of power among elites, and Reagan had to modify his plans somewhat to avoid alienating subelites. Sustained opposition from urban mayors (who do not trust state legislatures) forced the administration to retain certain programs it had planned to "turn back" to the cities. In the face of successful professional- and constituency-group lobbying in Congress, Reagan withdrew plans to turn over to the states the food-stamp program and aid to families with dependent children. Even so, big-city mayors charged that, while the rhetoric of the revised package was less inflammatory, the substance was the same.

Thus the New Federalism is a struggle within a bewildering array of elites: the professional and constituency groups dependent on categorical grants share opposition with the urban mayors; state governors worry about finding the money they need and lend credence to minority groups' fear that the New Federalism is a form of "benign neglect." By 1983, Reagan's New Federalism, unable to overcome this opposition, had shrunk to a modest block-grant proposal.

Elite structures in the states

Elite structures vary among the fifty states.[2] To understand elite patterns in state politics, we can identify several categories of elite systems.

Unified elite system

In states with nondiversified economies and weak, noncompetitive parties, a cohesive group of economic interests generally dominates state politics. Maine is a good example of this type of elite system: "In few American states are the reins of government more openly, more completely in the hands of a few leaders of economic interest groups than in Maine."[3] Power, timber, and manufacturing interests (the "big three") have formed a cohesive economic elite because of their key position in the state's economy. Over three-fourths of the state is woodland, most of it owned by a handful of timber and paper companies. The timber interests, combined with power companies and textile and shoe manufacturers, control Maine politics to protect their own economic well-being. Challenges to the predominance of the big three are rarely well-organized or sustained efforts.

The Deep South states also display the cultural homogeneity and unified elites characteristic of nondiversified or agricultural economies. Occasionally "populist" candidates have briefly challenged the dominance of the planting, landowning, and financial elites in southern states. But once in power, the demagogues have seldom implemented populist programs; more frequently they have become instruments of the established elites whom they castigated in campaign oratory.

Dominant elites among lesser elites

The second type of elite structure also develops in states with a nondiversified economy, although the states may display a reasonably competitive party system, with moderate party cohesion in the legislature. This structure features a dominant elite with several lesser elites; its primary characteristic is the prevailing influence of a single industry.

Political histories abound of the power of Anaconda in Montana, duPont in Delaware, the oil companies in Texas and Louisiana, the coal companies in West Virginia, and so on. Doubtless their reputations for absolute control of a state far exceed their actual control over public policy. In Delaware, for instance, the duPont Corporation and the duPont family do not become actively involved in many issues. Yet it is unlikely that the state of Delaware would ever enact legislation adversely affecting the duPont Corporation. Similarly the oil industry's reputation for control of Texas politics is exaggerated. The chairman of the Texas Democratic Executive Committee once said, "It may not be a wholesome thing to say, but the oil industry today is in complete control of state politics and state government."[4] This type of overstatement is common in political circles; in fact, many issues in state politics are of little concern to the oil interests. However, Texas politicians are unlikely to oppose the oil depletion allowance in the federal tax structure due to its direct and vital impact on the oil producers. The same is true of the dominant interests in other states: although they may not control all aspects of state politics, they control those matters that directly affect them.

Bipolar elite structure

The bipolar structure is most likely in an industrial, urban, competitive state with strong, cohesive political parties. Michigan is the prototype of this form. The state's economy is industrial rather than agricultural, but it is nondiversified and heavily dependent on the automotive industry, the largest single employer. But automobile manufacturers do not dominate Michigan politics because organized labor has emerged as an effective counterbalance to the manufacturers. Joseph La Palombara concludes that "no major issues of policy (taxation, social legislation, labor legislation, etc.) are likely to be decided in Michigan without the intervention, within their respective parties and before agencies of government, of automotive labor and automotive management."[5] Labor and management elites in Michigan each have "their own" political party, and polarization in the elite system accompanies strong competition between well-organized, cohesive, and disciplined Democratic (labor) and Republican (management) party organizations.

Plural elite structure

A state with a highly diversified economy is likely to produce a plural elite structure. California may have the most diversified economy of any state in the nation, with thriving agricultural interests, timber and mining resources, and manufacturing enterprises that run the gamut from cement to motion pictures. Railroads, brewers, racetracks, motion pictures, citrus growers, airplane manufacturers, insurance companies, utilities, defense contractors, and a host of other economic interests coexist in this state. No one economic interest or combination of interests dominates California politics. Instead a variety of elites govern within specific issue areas; each elite concentrates its attention on matters directly affecting its own economic interest. Occasionally the economic interests of elites may clash, but on the whole elites coexist rather than compete. Political parties are somewhat less cohesive and disciplined in the plural elite system. Economic elites, hesitating to identify too closely with a single party, even make financial contributions to opposing candidates to ensure protection of their interests no matter which party or candidate wins.

Single elites in American communities

One of the earliest studies of community elites was the classic study of Middletown by Robert Lynd and Helen Lynd in the mid-1920s and again in the mid-1930s.[6] In Muncie, Indiana ("Middletown"), the Lynds found a monolithic power structure dominated by the X family, owners of the town's largest industry. Community power was firmly in the hands of the business class, which controlled the economic life of the city, particularly through its ability to control the extension of credit. The city was run by a "small top group" of "wealthy local manufacturers, bankers, the local head managers of . . . national corporations with units in Middletown, and . . . one or two outstanding lawyers." Democratic procedures and government institutions were window dressing for business control. The Lynds described the typical city official as a "man of meager caliber" and as a "man whom the inner business control group ignores economically and socially and uses politically." Perhaps the most famous passage from the Lynds' study was a comment by a Middletown man made in 1935:

> If I'm out of work, I go to the X plant; if I need money I go to the X bank, and if they don't like me I don't get it; my children go to the X college; when I get sick I go to the X hospital; I buy a building lot or house in the X subdivision; my wife goes downtown to buy X milk; I drink X beer, vote for X political parties, and get help from X charities; my boy goes to the X YMCA and my girl to their YWCA; I listen to the word of God in a X subsidized church; if I'm a Mason, I go to the X Masonic temple; I read the news from the X morning paper; and, if I'm rich enough, I travel via the X airport.[7]

W. Lloyd Warner, who studied Morris, Illinois, in the 1940s, describes a power structure somewhat similar to Muncie's. About one-third of the city's workers had jobs in "the Mill," which Warner says dominated the town:

> The economic and social force of the mill affects every part of the life of the community. Everyone recognizes its power. Politicians, hat in hand, wait upon Mr. Waddell, manager of The Mill, to find out what he thinks on such important questions as "Shall the tax rate be increased to improve the

education our young people are getting?"—"Should the city support various civic and world enterprises?"—"Should new industries enter the town and possibly compete with The Mill for the town's available labor supply?" They want to know what Mr. Waddell thinks. Mr. Waddell usually lets them know.[8]

Hollingshead studied the same town (sociologists seem to prefer to disguise the names of towns they are studying: Warner called the town Jonesville; Hollingshead called it Elmtown), and his findings substantially confirmed Warner's.[9] And in sociologist Floyd Hunter's influential study of Atlanta, Georgia, he found that community policy originated in a group composed primarily of business, financial, religious, and education leaders rather than from the people of the community.[10]

According to Hunter, only those holding the right positions in the business and financial community were admitted to the circle of influential persons in Atlanta. Hunter explained that the top power structure concerned itself only with major policy decisions, from which the leaders of certain substructures—economic, government, religious, educational, professional, civic, and cultural—then took their cues, communicating and implementing the policies decided at the top level.

> [The substructures] are subordinate . . . to the interests of the policy makers who operate in the economic sphere of community life in the regional city. The institutions of the family, church, state, education, and the like draw sustenance from economic institutional sources and are thereby subordinate to this particular institution more than any other. . . . Within the policy-forming groups the economic interests are dominant.[11]

The top power holders seldom operate openly: "Most of the top personnel in the power group are rarely seen in the meetings attended by associational understructure personnel in Regional City [Atlanta]."[12] Hunter describes the process of community action as follows:

> If a project of major proportions were before the community for consideration—let us say a project aimed at building a new municipal auditorium—a policy committee would be formed. . . . Such a policy committee would more than likely grow out of a series of informal meetings, and it might be related to a project that has associations for months or even years. But the time has arrived for action. Money must be raised through private subscription or taxation, a site selected, and contracts let. The time for a policy committee is propitious. The selection of the policy committee will fall largely to the men of power in the community. They will likely be businessmen in one or more of the large business establishments. Mutual choices will be agreed upon for committee membership. In the early stages of policy formulation there will be a few men who make basic decisions. . . . Top ranking organizational and institutional personnel will then be selected by the original members to augment their numbers; i.e., the committee will be expanded. Civil associations and the formalized institutions will next be drawn into certain phases of planning and initiation of the projects on a community-wide basis. The newspapers will finally carry stories, the min-

isters will preach sermons, the associations will hear speeches regarding plans. This rather simply is the process, familiar to many, that goes on in getting any community project underway.[13]

Note that in Hunter's description of community decision making, decisions tend to flow down from top policy makers (composed primarily of business and financial leaders) to the civic, professional, and cultural association leaders, the religious and educational leaders, and the government officials who carry out the program. The masses of people have little direct or indirect participation in the whole process. Policy does not go *up* from associational groupings or from the people themselves:

> The top group of the power hierarchy has been isolated and defined as comprised of policy makers. These men are drawn largely from the businessmen's class in Regional City. They form cliques or crowds, as the term is more often used in the community, which formulate policy. Committees for the formulation of policy are commonplace; and on community-wide issues, policy is channeled by a "fluid committee structure" down to institutional, associational groupings through a lower-level bureaucracy which executes policy.[14]

According to Hunter, elected public officials are clearly part of the lower-level institutional substructure that executes rather than formulates policy. Finally, Hunter found that this whole power structure is held together by "common interests, mutual obligations, money, habit, delegated responsibilities, and in some cases by coercion and force."[15]

Hunter's findings in Atlanta reinforce the elite model and are a source of discomfort to those who wish to see America governed in a truly democratic fashion. Hunter's research challenges the notion of popular participation in decision making or grass-roots democracy; it raises doubts as to whether cherished democratic values are being realized in American community life.[16]

Plural elites in American communities

Pluralist models of community power stress the fragmentation of authority, the influence of elected public officials, the importance of organized group activity, and the roles of public opinion and elections in determining public policy. Who, then, rules in the pluralist community? "Different small groups of interested and active citizens [rule] in different issue areas with some overlap, if any, by public officials, and occasional intervention by a larger number of people at the polls."[17] Citizens' influence is felt not only through organized group activity but also through elites' anticipating their reactions and endeavoring to satisfy their demands. Not only elected public officials exercise leadership in community affairs but also interested individuals and groups who confine their participation to one or two issues. The pluralist model regards interest and activity, rather than economic resources, as the key to elite membership. Competition, fluidity, access, and equality characterize community policies.

In his significant study of power in New Haven, political scientist Robert A. Dahl admits that "tiny minorities," whose social class is not representative of the community as a whole, make most community decisions.[18] However, Dahl challenges the notion that the elite system in American community life is pyramidal and cohesive and unresponsive to popular demands. Dahl studied major decisions in urban redevelopment and public education in New Haven, as well as the nominations for mayor in both political parties. In contrast to Hunter's highly monolithic and centralized power structure in Atlanta, Dahl found a polycentric and dispersed system of elites in New Haven. Many elites exercised influence from time to time, each exercising some power over some issues but not over others. One set of leaders was influential in urban renewal matters; another was powerful in public education.

Business and financial elites, who dominate Atlanta according to Hunter's study, are only two of many influential elites in New Haven. According to Dahl:

> The economic notables, far from being a ruling group, are simply one of many groups out of which individuals sporadically emerge to influence the politics and acts of city officials. Almost anything one might say about the influence of the economic notables could be said with equal justice about a half dozen other groups in the New Haven community.[19]

Yet Dahl also finds that the people involved in community decisions in New Haven add up to only a tiny minority of the community. For example, Dahl writes:

> It is not too much to say that urban redevelopment has been the direct product of a small handful of leaders.[20]
> The bulk of the voters had virtually no direct influence on the process of nomination.[21]
> The number of citizens who participated directly in important decisions bearing on the public schools is small.[22]

Moreover, Dahl notes that people exercising leadership for each issue have higher social status than the rest of the community and that these middle- and upper-class elite members possess more of the skills and qualities required of leaders in a democratic system.

Dahl's New Haven obviously parallels the pluralist model. However, New Haven is clearly not a democracy in the sense that we defined that term earlier. Not all citizens of New Haven participated in the decisions that affected their lives, and not all had an equal opportunity to influence public policy.

Aaron Wildavsky's study of Oberlin, Ohio, revealed an even more pluralistic structure of decision making than Dahl found in New Haven. Oberlin was a reaffirmation of small-town democracy, where "the roads to influence . . . are more than one; elites and non-elites can travel them, and the toll can be paid with energy and initiative as well as wealth."[23]

Wildavsky studied eleven community decisions in Oberlin, including the determination of municipal water rates, the passage of the fair housing ordinance, the allocation of United Appeals funds, and a municipal election. He found "that the number of citizens and outside participants who exercise leadership in most cases is an infinitesimal part of the community," but that no person or group exerted leadership on all issue areas.[24] The overlap that did exist among leaders in issue areas involved public officials—the city manager, the mayor, and city council members—who owed their position directly or indirectly to "expressions of the democratic process through a free ballot with universal suffrage." Leaders often competed among themselves and did not appear united by any common interest. People exercising leadership had somewhat higher social status than the rest of the community, but neither status nor wealth distinguished leaders from nonleaders; their degree of interest and activity in public affairs did.

Edward Banfield's excellent description of decision making in Chicago also fails to reveal a single "ruling elite," although the city has a centralized structure of influence. Banfield found that Mayor Daley's political organization, not a business or financial elite, was the center of Chicago's influence structure. According to Banfield:

> Civic controversies in Chicago are not generated by the efforts of politicians to win votes, by differences about ideology or group interest, or by the behind-the-scenes efforts of a power elite. They arise, instead, out of the maintenance and enhancement needs of large formal organizations. The heads of an organization see some advantage to be gained by changing the situation. They propose changes. Other large organizations are threatened. They oppose, and a civic controversy takes place.[25]

Proposals for change did not generally originate with business organizations in Chicago: "in most of the cases described here the effective organizations are public ones, and their chief executives are career civil servants." Although business and financial leaders played an important role in Chicago politics, they did not constitute a single elite.

After studying seven major decisions in Chicago, Banfield concluded that political heads such as Mayor Daley, public agencies, and civic associations used top business leaders to lend prestige and legitimacy to policy proposals. He criticized the "top leaders" of Chicago—the Fields, McCormacks, Ryersons, Swifts, and Armours—and the large corporations—Inland Steel, Sears Roebuck, Marshall Field's, and the Chicago Title and Trust Company—less for interfering in public affairs than for "failing to assume their civic responsibilities." Few top leaders participated directly in the decisions Banfield studied. Banfield admits that this fact is not proof that the top business leadership did not influence decisions behind the scenes, and he acknowledges the widespread belief in the existence of a ruling elite in Chicago. He quotes the head of a black civil association: "There are a dozen men in this town who could go into City Hall and order an end to racial violence just like you or I could go into a grocery store and order a loaf of bread. All they would have to do is say what they wanted and they would get it."[26] Banfield states that top business leaders in Chicago have great "potential for power": "Indeed, if influence is defined as the *ability* to modify behavior in accordance with one's intentions, there can be little doubt that there exist 'top leaders' with aggregate influence sufficient to run the city."[27] But he maintains that these top leaders do not, in fact, run the city. Business leaders, divided by fundamental conflicts of interest and opinion, do not have sufficient unity of purpose in community politics to decide controversial questions. They have no effective communication system that enables them to act in concert; and they lack the organization to carry out their plans, even if they could agree on what should be done.

The key to understanding community power, then, is relating the types of power structure to local social, economic, and political conditions. For example, we may find that large communities with social and economic diversity, a competitive party system, and a variety of well-organized, competing interest groups have pluralist elite systems. On the other hand, small communities with a homogeneous population, a single dominant industry, nonpartisan elections, and few competing organizations may be governed by a single cohesive elite.

Thus, although descriptions of the power structures in American communities may differ only because social scientists differ in theory and methods of research, more likely community power structures in the United States in fact range from monolithic elites to very dispersed pluralistic elites. But we do not yet know enough to estimate the pervasiveness of specific community power structures across the nation.

Summary

The existence of political subelites within the larger American political system permits some decentralization of decision making. Decentralization, or decision making by subelites, reduces potential strain on the consensus of national elites. Each subelite sets its own policies in its own state and community, without battling over a single national policy to be applied uniformly throughout the land. The following propositions summarize our consideration of American federalism and our comparative analysis of elites in states and communities.

1. Debate over state versus national power reflects the power of various interests at the state and national level. Currently the liberal public-regarding elites, dominant at the national level, generally assert the supremacy of the national government. In contrast parochial, conservative, rural interests, dominant in some states and communities but

with less power at the national level, provide the backbone of support for "states' rights."

2. Although national elites now exercise considerable power in states and communities, particularly through federal "grant-in-aid" programs, this growth of national power has not necessarily reduced the power of state and local governments. State and local government activities are growing.

3. Legislators generally rank economic elites in states and communities as the "most powerful groups."

4. States with the most cohesive elite system are likely to be one-party states, not competitive two-party states; states in which political parties show little cohesion and unity; and states that are poor, rural, and agricultural. Wealthy, urban, industrial states have more elite groups, and a single elite cannot easily dominate the political scene.

5. Scholars have described American communities in terms reflecting both single-elite and plural-elite models. Yet even the plural-elite studies conclude that "tiny minorities" make "the key political, economic, and social decisions." They also find that these "tiny minorities" come from the upper- and middle-class community. Few other citizens participate in community decisions that affect their lives.

6. Evidence is conflicting about the extent of competition among community elites, the extent of elite concentration, the fluidity of elites, the ease of access to elite membership, the persistence of elite structures over time, the relative power of economic elites, and the degree of mass influence. Some scholars have reported a polycentric structure of power, with different elite groups active in different issue areas and a great deal of competition, bargaining, and sharing of power among elites.

7. Elite structures in communities are related to the community's size, economic function, and social composition. Small communities with a homogeneous population, a single dominant industry, a weak party structure, and few competing organizations are more likely to be governed by a single cohesive elite. Larger communities with social and economic diversity, a competitive party system, and well-organized competing interest groups are more likely to have plural-elite systems.

8. Monolithic power structures correlate with a lack of political confidence among residents and with a widespread belief that political activity is useless. A plural-elite system correlates with a sense of political effectiveness among citizens and with adherence to the rules of the game by leaders.

NOTES

1. For a comprehensive survey of government and politics in American states and communities, see Thomas R. Dye, *Politics in States and Communities*, 3d ed. (Englewood Cliffs, N.J.: Prentice-Hall, 1977).
2. Harmon Zeigler, "Interest Groups in the States," in Herbert Jacob and Kenneth A. Vines, eds., *Politics in American States* (Boston: Little, Brown, 1965), p. 114.

3. Duane Lockard, *New England State Politics* (Princeton, N.J.: Princeton University Press, 1959), p. 79.
4. Robert Engler, *The Politics of Oil* (New York: Macmillan, 1961), p. 354.
5. Joseph La Palombara, *Guide to Michigan Politics* (East Lansing: Michigan University, Bureau of Social and Political Research, 1960), p. 104.
6. Robert S. Lynd and Helen M. Lynd, *Middletown* (New York: Harcourt, Brace & World, 1929); and *Middletown in Transition* (New York: Harcourt, Brace & World, 1937).
7. Lynd and Lynd, *Middletown in Transition*, p. 74.
8. W. Lloyd Warner, *Democracy in Jonesville* (New York: Harper & Row, 1949), p. 10.
9. August B. Hollingshead, *Elmtown's Youth* (New York: Wiley, 1949).
10. Floyd Hunter, *Community Power Structure* (Chapel Hill: University of North Carolina Press, 1953).
11. Ibid., p. 94.
12. Ibid., p. 90.
13. Ibid., pp. 92–93.
14. Ibid., p. 113.
15. Ibid.
16. For a more pluralist view of Atlanta's power structure, see Kent Jennings, *Community Influentials* (New York: Free Press, 1964).
17. Aaron Wildavsky, *Leadership in a Small Town* (Totowa, N.J.: Bedminister Press, 1964), p. 8.
18. Robert Dahl, *Who Governs?* (New Haven, Conn.: Yale University Press, 1961).
19. Ibid., p. 72.
20. Ibid., p. 115.
21. Ibid., p. 106.
22. Ibid., p. 151.
23. Wildavsky, op. cit., p. 214.
24. Ibid., p. 265.
25. Edward Banfield, *Political Influence* (New York: Free Press, 1961), p. 263.
26. Ibid., p. 289.
27. Ibid., p. 290.

SELECTED READINGS

Dahl, Robert A. *Who Governs?* New Haven, Conn.: Yale University Press, 1961. This book is perhaps the most important pluralist community power study. Using a decisional approach, Dahl finds that a number of elites make decisions in different issue areas.

Hunter, Floyd. *Community Power Structure.* Chapel Hill: University of North Carolina Press, 1953. Although classical elitism has its origins in European sociological theory, much of the current American controversy over elitism has resulted from community power research. This book was one of the first community power studies reporting elitist results. Hunter's use of the reputational method in this study of Atlanta set the scene for a heated debate with the pluralists.

Ricci, David M. *Community Power and Democratic Theory: The Logic of Political Analysis.* New York: Random House, 1971. This book is an excellent review of both past and current philosophical, ideological, and methodological differences between elitists and pluralists of each theory, including the contributions of Joseph Schumpeter ("process" theory of democracy), David Truman ("group" theory of democracy), Floyd Hunter ("reputational" theory of elitism), C. Wright Mills ("positional" theory of elitism), and Robert Dahl ("pluralist" theory of democracy). The text also includes an excellent discussion of "the present scholarly impasse" between advocates of each point of view and an annotated bibliography of relevant literature.

Walton, John. "Substance and Artifact: The Current Status of Research on Community Power Structures." *American Journal of Sociology* 72 (1966):430–438. Walton makes an extensive survey of community power literature and finds that use of the reputational method tends to yield elitist results, while use of the decisional method tends to yield pluralist results.

15 Protest Movements: Challenge to Dominant Elites

Protest leaders, irrespective of the movements they represent, do <u>not</u> come from the lower strata of society.

The social origins of protest leaders are rather similar to, instead of strikingly different from, the social origins of leaders of established parties with whom they clash.

—Anthony Oberschall, Social Conflict and Social Movements, *1973*

People without access to the resources of interest-group politics, and people whose values are substantially at odds with the prevailing public policy, occasionally enter mass protest movements. Protests can come from the right and the left, from the rich and the poor. The more visible protests of the last several decades centered on blacks, native Americans, and Mexican-Americans, none of whom had much access to the traditional resources of elite politics. Occasionally such groups consider violence, disruption, demonstrations, and strikes to be rational means of participation.[1] Other groups—such as Common Cause, environmental organizations, feminist organizations, the antinuclear movement, and the anti-war movement—consist of upper-middle-class and upper-class members with the skills and resources to penetrate the elite-dominated interest-group structure.[2]

Protest *movements* frequently lead to the establishment of protest *organizations* designed to "represent and shape the broadly held preferences . . . of the social movement."[3] This shaping and organizing is where protest movements and the protest organizations either succeed or fail. Generally protest movements without organizations fail because intermittent violence isolates the movement from established elites.[4] Of course, established elites do not ignore violence. Rather they may (1) make symbolic gestures to pacify the active protesters (co-opting them through programs that bring protest leaders into the "system"), (2) limit protests through repression (by such means as FBI surveillance or increased law enforcement) of followers, or (3) do both simultaneously. Often elite response is a combination of accommodation and repression, with heavier doses of accommodation handed out to movements whose goals are within the general framework of elite consensus.[5]

As organizations arise to direct the aspirations of protest movements, the advantages of accommodation increase.[6] The leaders find that by moderating their demands they can gain a portion of their original goals and also achieve for themselves and the organization a stake in the elite system. Thus protest movements that become protest organizations eventually come to share the elite consensus.

Protest movements tend to be cyclical. Many do not achieve organizational stability and soon fade from memory. Others successfully travel the road from protest to organization to accommodation, but the price is high. Movement toward political success not only requires accommodation to the acceptable norms of established elites; it also requires organizational leadership by people with negotiating skills and willingness to sustain activity for long periods of time. These leaders, regardless of the movements they represent, do *not* come from the lower strata of society.[7]

From the variety of movements that have risen and fallen during the history of the United States, the civil rights movement and the feminist movement offer interesting and contemporary examples for discussion.

The history of black subjugation

Blacks' place in American society has been a central issue of domestic American politics since the first black slaves stepped on these shores in 1619. The American nation as a whole, with its democratic tradition, has felt strong conflicting sentiments about slavery, segregation, and discrimination. But white America has also harbored an ambivalence toward blacks—a recognition of the evils of inequality but a reluctance to take steps to eliminate it. This "American dilemma" reflects the larger issue of the American masses' attitudes toward democracy: commitment to abstract ideals with substantially less commitment to their practice.[8] To a large extent, we can view blacks' struggle for full citizenship as a dialogue—sometimes violent, sometimes peaceful—between the demands of black counterelites and the response of dominant white elites.

Legacy of slavery

The period of slavery has more than historical interest; Americans still feel the impact of the brutality of this period. The scars of the rigidly enforced obedience system and the matriarchal family structure characteristic of slavery are still present today. Elkins has compared Southern slavery to Nazi concentration camps in its effects upon personality.[9] Both institutions were closed and highly authoritarian societies; both produced, for the most part, total obedience to the authority figure. In concentration camps, for example, captives frequently viewed guards as father figures; correspondingly, among slaves, the master often represented a father figure. Slavery, by rewarding obedience and compliance, ate away at individual effort and achievement.

Blacks are also still struggling to overcome the "deculturation" of the slaves. White slavers threw together blacks from many different African cultures, and the slaves had no common cultural buffer to help them resist the psychological effects of slavery. The condition of slavery became their dominant institution—an institution that molded black personalities. For example, to survive within the system, slaves developed child-rearing practices that emphasized obedience over achievement.[10]

Slavery also hindered the development of a strong family life. Since many slaveowners separated families on the auction block, the slave household developed a mother-centered pattern. After the abolition of slavery, poverty in the ghetto strengthened the mother-centered tradition. Even now, about 35 percent of nonwhite families have female heads, compared to only 10 percent of white families.[11]

Abolition

In 1865 the Thirteenth Amendment abolished slavery everywhere in the United States. The Fourteenth Amendment, passed in 1867 by a Republican Congress that intended to reconstruct Southern society after the Civil War, made "equal protection of the laws" a command for every state to obey. The Fifteenth Amendment, passed in 1869, prohibited federal and state governments from abridging the right to vote "on account of race, color, or previous condition of servitude." In addition, Congress passed a series of civil rights statutes in the 1860s and 1870s guaranteeing the new black freedmen protection in exercise of their constitutional rights. The Civil Rights Act of 1875 specifically outlawed segregation by owners of public accommodation facilities. Between 1865 and the early 1880s the success of the civil rights movement was evident in widespread black voting throughout the South, the presence of many blacks in federal and state offices, and the almost equal treatment afforded blacks in theaters, restaurants, hotels, and public transportation.

Rise of white supremacy

But by 1877 support for Reconstruction policies began to crumble. In the Compromise of 1877, the national government agreed to end military occupation of the South, give up its efforts to rearrange Southern society, and lend tacit approval to white supremacy in that region. In return, the Southern states pledged their support to the Union, accepted national supremacy, and agreed to permit the Republican presidential candidate, Rutherford B. Hayes, to assume the presidency, although the Democratic candidate, Samuel Tilden, had received a majority of the popular vote in the disputed election of 1876. The Supreme Court adhered to the terms of this compromise. In the famous Civil Rights Cases of

1883, the Supreme Court declared unconstitutional those federal civil rights laws preventing discrimination by private individuals. By denying Congress the power to protect blacks from discrimination, the Court paved the way for the imposition of segregation as the prevailing social system of the South. In the 1880s and 1890s, white Southerners imposed segregation in public accommodations, housing, education, employment, and almost every other sector of private and public life. By 1895 most Southern states had passed laws *requiring* racial segregation in education and in public accommodations.

In 1896 in the famous case of *Plessy* v. *Ferguson*, the Supreme Court upheld state laws requiring segregation.[12] Although segregation laws involved state action, the Court held that segregating the races did not violate the equal protection clause of the Fourteenth Amendment so long as people in each race received equal treatment. Schools and other public facilities that were "separate but equal" won constitutional approval.

The violence that occurred during this period was almost entirely one-sided: whites attacked blacks.[13] The pattern of race relations at the turn of the century was clearly one of violent repression, exclusion of blacks from jobs and labor unions, and rigid segregation. Blacks lost most of what they had gained during Reconstruction.

Twentieth-century responses

Black response: Initial developments

NAACP and National Urban League. The first black organizations emerged from the repressive pattern of the late nineteenth century; blacks formed the National Association for the Advancement of Colored People (NAACP) and the National Urban League in 1909 and 1910, respectively. Both organizations reacted against Booker T. Washington's acceptance of the inferior status of blacks, and both worked closely with white liberals. These organizations, depending as they did on the goodwill of whites, sought black equality through court action and other legal means. They were (and still are) dominated by middle-class blacks and upper-class whites. They accepted the premise that they could effect meaningful change within the American legal system. They were (and are) conservative in that their techniques require commitment to the institutional status quo. They disavowed attempts to change or overthrow the basic political and economic structure of the society; they simply sought to integrate blacks into the existing society. In other words, they took literally the ideology and premises of the American democratic system.

Development of counterelites. When the concentration of blacks in northern cities increased the potential for mass action, a new style of violence began to emerge. The black community began to express its grievances, such as discrimination in housing and transportation. As grievances built and expression became more aggressive, a precipitating incident would occur, and blacks responded by attacking whites or their property. The northern-style riot differed substantially from southern-style violence; blacks no longer remained passive victims but became active participants. The northern-style riot made its first appearance in Springfield, Illinois, in 1908.

Perhaps the first important black counterelite was Marcus Garvey. Since the NAACP was an elitist organization both in membership and appeal, Garvey, a West Indian, organized the Universal Negro Improvement Association to articulate the latent feelings of black nationalism. Garvey's programs for a separate black nation in Africa appealed to impoverished blacks, especially as white bigotry, in the form of the Ku Klux Klan, spread north in the wake of black economic advance. Garvey was essentially a forerunner of the Black Muslims of the 1950s and 1960s and the more radical black nationalists of the late 1960s. Like the Muslims, Garvey urged his followers to practice personal frugality and establish a high level of morality. Like the nationalists, he sought to teach blacks that their color could be a source of pride rather than shame. At one time, Garvey had a following estimated at three million, but his movement collapsed in the mid-1920s. His appeal to the black masses, nevertheless, was very important, for Garvey asserted that blacks would never gain what the NAACP insisted that they could achieve: an equal share in the American economic system. As Myrdal observes, the Garvey movement "tells of the dissatisfaction so deep that it mounts to hopelessness of ever enjoying a full life in America."[14]

Court declaration of equality.   The period following the Korean War, marked by enormous legal and symbolic victories, was crucial in the development of the relationship between blacks and whites. The long labors of the NAACP paid off in the historic *Brown* v. *Board of Education of Topeka* decision in which the Court reversed the *Plessy* v. *Ferguson* doctrine of separate but equal.[15] This decision symbolized the beginning of a new era of high expectations among blacks. While elected elites had remained silent on civil rights and, in fact, exhibited substantial hostility, an appointed elite, the Supreme Court, declared that blacks and whites were equal in the eyes of the law.

However, *Brown* v. *Board of Education of Topeka* was only the beginning of the political battle over segregation. Segregation did not disappear simply because the Supreme Court declared it unconstitutional. Segregation was widespread and deeply ingrained. Seventeen states required segregation by law, and the U.S. Congress required segregation in Washington, D.C. Four other states (Arizona, Kansas, New Mexico, and Wyoming) authorized segregation at local option. Unless another political elite with equal resources could challenge the political power of the white majority in the South, the pattern of segregation was unlikely to change.

In not ordering immediate desegregation, the Supreme Court snatched the tangible portion of the victory away from blacks. The Court placed primary responsibility for enforcing this decision on local officials and school boards, in effect returning power to the white subelites in the South. As a result, during the 1950s the white South developed many schemes to resist integration. Ten years after *Brown*, only about 2 percent of the blacks in the South attended integrated schools; the other 98 percent remained in segregated schools. In short, the decision meant nothing to the overwhelming majority of blacks, whose frustrations intensified as they saw the discrepancy between the Supreme Court's intent and the behavior of local officials. Blacks had gained a legal victory, but they were impotent politically. As a result, the civil rights movement changed its focus from legal restrictions to de facto segregation and unequal socioeconomic institutions.

Politics of litigation.   Significantly, the next phase of the civil rights movement was strongly elitist. The prime players were the NAACP and the Supreme Court, both of them insulated from white and black masses. The elite orientation of the NAACP led its leaders to accept the prevailing values of white elites. It attracted the "talented tenth"—the minority of upper-class, educated blacks. It played by the "rules of the game"—litigation, not protest. White elites, especially those most removed from mass sanction, found NAACP values quite compatible with their own. The educated blacks of the NAACP sought only to remove legal barriers to equality of opportunity. Educated themselves, they regarded education as the key to success. NAACP leadership, which was economically successful on the whole, was better accepted by white elites and thus was culturally at the periphery of the black community. The NAACP's success depended largely on maintaining "good connections" with white elites, and the organizational leadership did not intend to risk its favored position by identifying with those sections of the black community unacceptable to the white elites.

Creative disorder

The civil rights movement first turned toward civil disorder in 1955, immediately after the *Brown* decision. The symbolic importance of this decision is great; and despite the paucity of tangible benefits, the decision undoubtedly increased blacks' expectations and demands. Black sociologist Kenneth Clark assesses the importance of official sanction as follows:

This [civil rights] movement would probably not have existed at all were it not for the 1954 Supreme Court school desegregation decision which provided a tremendous boost to the morale of Negroes by its clear affirmation that color is irrelevant to the rights of American citizens. Until this time the Southern Negro generally had accommodated to the separation of the black from the white society.[16]

Bus boycotts.   In 1955 a black woman refused to ride in the back of a bus in Montgomery, Alabama, lending dramatic support to Clark's hypothesis. Her act brought about the Montgomery boycott in which blacks refused to use the public transportation system until they could sit wherever they preferred; this action was the first significant step away from the NAACP's legalism. The Montgomery bus boycott also illustrated the general relationship between elites and masses. Black elites carried out the work of the NAACP; their work stimulated mass behavior, which in turn required mass-oriented leadership. Martin Luther King, Jr., who gained instant national prominence through the bus boycott, initially filled the need for mass-oriented leadership. His Southern Christian Leadership Conference (SCLC) emerged in 1957 as the first southern-originated civil rights group. Although substantially more militant than the older black organizations, it was nevertheless explicitly nonviolent. The purposes of mass demonstrations were to challenge the legality of both legal and de facto segregation and to prick the consciences of white elites.

Direct action tactics.   The tactics of the SCLC were extended by the Student Nonviolent Co-ordinating Committee (SNCC), which developed in the next phase of direct action—the sit-in demonstrations and freedom rides of the 1960s. In February 1960, at Greensboro, North Carolina, North Carolina Agricultural and Technical College students conducted the first sit-ins. As other sit-ins followed, SNCC organized to coordinate the new student protest. SNCC, unlike the SCLC, encouraged blacks to feel proud of being black. The Congress on Racial Equality (CORE), which had begun in the 1940s, emerged from quiescence to lead the freedom rides, which challenged the Jim Crow laws of transportation facilities. Many thousands of students participated in these extremely dangerous rides. Because the freedom riders refused to obey the desegregation laws, some southern whites tried to kill them.

The vigor with which blacks pursued the freedom rides and sit-ins was a clear sign that the civil rights movement was committed to direct action. However, even this new phase of the civil rights movement was not a mass movement; the participants were still relatively privileged in comparison to the black masses. The most frequent participants in the confrontations of the early 1960s were urban students with a very tolerant and optimistic attitude toward the white community. The freedom riders were not despair-driven anarchists but optimistic young people.[17] These relatively privileged youths were disappointed in the white society's unwillingness to recognize their merits.

Birmingham demonstrations. In 1963 in Birmingham, Alabama, blacks conducted prolonged demonstrations on the broadest front yet conceived by civil rights leaders. Blacks presented demands to end discrimination in public accommodations, employment, and housing to the white elite of Birmingham. Under the leadership of Martin Luther King, Jr., these demonstrations were committed to nonviolence. Probably because of the broad nature of the demands, the grass roots of the black community began to participate for the first time. All strata of the black community became active.

Civil Rights Act of 1964

The Birmingham demonstrations were another landmark in the civil rights movement. Partially because of the southern elites' repressive behavior toward these peaceful demonstrations, the Kennedy administration proposed significant civil rights legislation. Thus the Birmingham demonstration of 1963 stimulated what was to become the Civil Rights Act of 1964, Congress's first significant entry into civil rights. The act passed both houses of Congress by more than a two-thirds vote, winning the overwhelming support of both Republicans and Democrats. It ranks with the Emancipation Proclamation, the Fourteenth Amendment, and *Brown* v. *Board of Education of Topeka* as one of the most important steps toward full equality for blacks in America. The act provides:

1. That it is unlawful to apply unequal standards in voter registration procedures or to deny registration for irrelevant errors or omissions on records or applications.
2. That it is unlawful to discriminate against or segregate people on the grounds of race, color, religion, or national origin in any place of public accommodation, including hotels, motels, restaurants, movies, theaters, sports areas, entertainment houses, and other places that offer to serve the public. This prohibition extends to all establishments whose operations affect interstate commerce or whose discriminatory practices are supported by state action.
3. That the attorney general will undertake civil action for any person denied equal access to a public accommodation. An owner or manager of a public accommodation who continues to discriminate after a federal district court order is in contempt of court and subject to preemptory fines and imprisonment without trial by jury. (This mode of enforcement gave establishments a chance to mend their ways without punishment; it also bypassed southern juries, which might refuse to convict people for violations of the act.)
4. That the attorney general will undertake civil actions for people attempting orderly desegregation of public schools.
5. That the Commission on Civil Rights, first established by the

Civil Rights Act of 1957, has the power to investigate deprivations of the right to vote, to study and collect information on discrimination in America, and to make reports to the president and Congress.

6. That each federal department and agency must act to end discrimination in all programs or activities receiving federal financial assistance in any form. This action will include termination of financial assistance.

7. That it is unlawful for any employer or labor union with twenty-five or more people after 1965 to discriminate against any individual in any fashion in employment, because of race, color, religion, sex, or national origin, and that an Equal Employment Opportunity Commission will enforce this provision through investigation, conference, conciliation, persuasion, and, if necessary, civil action in federal court.

Although largely symbolic, the Civil Rights Act of 1964 did bring about tangible gains for southern blacks. The withdrawal of federal grant-in-aid money as a sanction was a remarkable innovation in federal enforcement of civil rights. When the U.S. Office of Education began to apply pressure in the South, its progress was impressive compared with the previous ten years.

The 1964 Civil Rights Act was a symbolic victory nearly equal to that of the 1954 *Brown* v. *Board of Education of Topeka* decision. One hundred years after the end of the Civil War, the three branches of the federal government had declared themselves in sympathy with black Americans.

In this phase of the civil rights movement, the NAACP's dominance diminished, and a more militant phase began. Black elites, even those who successfully challenged NAACP hegemony, were still largely of middle-class origin. By appealing to the conscience of white elites, they could extend symbolic victories to the legislative process. Although their efforts led to minimal tangible reallocations, these victories caused black elites to lose their influence over the black masses. The masses, activated by symbolic victories, began to rebel against black elites.

Continuing inequalities between blacks and whites

Blacks' economic position has improved substantially in recent years, but this improvement is not bringing the black masses appreciably closer to the white standard of living. (See table 15-1.) Comparing the ratio of white to black income allows a comparison of the condition of blacks *relative* to that of whites. Between 1947 and 1970 the gap gradually narrowed. Whereas in 1947 the median income of black families was only 51 percent of white family income, by 1970 it had risen to 64 percent. But this narrowing of the gap between black and white family incomes did not continue in the 1970s. During the recession of 1974–1975, black

TABLE 15-1.   Black income as ratio of white median family income

1947	.51	1971	.60
1964	.54	1972	.59
1965	.54	1973	.58
1966	.58	1974	.58
1967	.59	1975	.58
1968	.60	1976	.59
1969	.61	1977	.57
1970	.64	1978	.57
		1980	.56

Source: "The Social and Economic Status of the Black Population in the United States," *Current Population Reports* (1975).

family income slipped back to 58 percent of white family income. Moreover black unemployment remains about double that of whites, a ratio virtually identical to that of ten years ago. Much additional evidence points to a halt in progress toward equality. Thus the percentage of blacks below the poverty level, although reduced substantially (from 56 percent in 1959 to 29 percent in 1978), has now stabilized.

Police in the ghetto

To many ghetto dwellers, the police symbolize white oppression. "Police brutality" has become a theme with enormous emotional impact among blacks. Black novelist James Baldwin's description of the attitude of ghetto dwellers toward police is excellent:

> . . . their very presence is an insult, and it would be, even if they spent their entire day feeding gumdrops to children. They represent the force of the white world, and that world's real intentions are, simply, for that world's profit and ease, to keep the black man corralled here in his place. The badge, the gun and the holster, and the swinging club make vivid what will happen should this revolution become overt. . . . He moves through Harlem, therefore, like an occupying soldier in a bitterly hostile country; which is precisely what, and where, he is, and is the reason they walk in twos and threes.[18]

Given this state of high tension between police and ghetto residents, even a routine police action can precipitate brewing discontent into a riot. Blacks feel by a two-to-one margin that police brutality is a major cause of disorder, an idea that whites reject by an eight-to-one margin.

The police generally act to effect short-term control of riots, not to reduce the long-term problems of the ghetto. They wish to suppress riot activity vigorously and become angry when they perceive leniency in judges and courts. Many police whose beats are in the ghetto also have strong negative attitudes toward black civil rights groups and federal poverty agencies.[19] They perceive the civil rights groups as contributors to violence and the poverty agencies as misguided social reform institutions that do not understand the legitimacy of force.

The attitudes of the police are understandable in view of their recruitment and socialization processes. Police come from the social classes most likely to have antiblack biases: the lower-middle and working classes. Moreover, very few police have had college training. Since we know that education positively links with tolerance, we would expect that the police, being disproportionately representative of the uneducated classes, would be no more tolerant than other lower-class whites.

In addition to the initial antiblack bias, occupational socialization probably reinforces the attitudes of police officers. The element of danger in police officers' jobs makes them naturally suspicious. Also, since police have responsibility for enforcing rules, they depend heavily on authority and are politically and emotionally conservative.[20]

Add to these police attitudes the unusually high crime rate in ghettos, and we have the makings of another vicious circle. One officer describes the operation of this circle:

> The police have to associate with lower-class people, slobs, drunks, criminals, riff-raff of the worst sort. Most of these . . . are Negroes. The police officers see these people through middle-class or lower-middle-class eyeballs. But even if he saw them through highly sophisticated eyeballs he can't go into the street and take this night after night. When some Negro criminal says to you a few times, "Take off that badge you white mother fucker and I'll shove it up your ass," well it's bound to affect you after a while. Pretty soon you decide they're all just niggers and they'll never be anything but niggers. It would take not just an average man to resist this feeling, it would take an extraordinary man to resist it, and there are very few ways by which the police department can attract extraordinary men to join it.[21]

Busing and racial isolation in schools

In northern ghettos, de facto school segregation—segregated housing patterns coupled with neighborhood schools—has continued largely unchanged, even as integration has progressed in the South. Approximately three-quarters of all black pupils in northern cities attend de facto segregated schools (schools in which 90 percent or more of their classmates are black). Thus, while the South has made progress toward integration, segregation is actually increasing in the North.[22] Northern de facto segregation has occurred because the black population in the central cities has increased as whites have moved to suburbs and because school officials have taken little action to achieve racial balance.

In 1971 in *Swann* v. *Charlotte-Mecklenburg*, the Supreme Court finally faced the full implications of the earlier *Brown* decision for de facto segregated schools. The school board of Charlotte, North Carolina, argued that its segregated school system was the innocent by-product of a racially neutral neighborhood school policy: since neighborhoods reflect economic status and income differences between blacks and whites, it was only "natural" that some schools would be overwhelmingly white and others overwhelmingly black. The Court rejected this defense and ruled that school authorities must do whatever necessary, including busing children to different schools outside their neighborhood, to achieve integration. If an official school policy of segregation had once existed, the Court reasoned that authorities had a positive obligation to integrate the schools immediately. It soon became apparent that this decision would have greater impact in the South than in the North, because segregation had never been an official policy in the North—even though northern states had more segregation.

Political opposition to busing children to achieve racial balance in the school comes mainly from parents who fear their children will be transported into the violent crime-ridden culture of the ghetto. They

Sidney Harris. Reproduced by Special Permission of *Playboy* magazine. Copyright © 1968 by Playboy.

"I say to hell with racial imbalance—I'm through being bused in every day!"

fear exposing their children to what black children have long had to cope with—rape, robbery, extortion, mugging, dope addiction. They see ghetto schools as blackboard jungles where surviving is more important than learning. Many white parents moved to the suburbs at great cost to themselves to obtain a better education for their children, and they do not want federal judges ordering their children back to ghetto schools. Generally white parents are less fearful of busing black pupils to white schools (as long as blacks remain a minority). Thus limited one-way busing over relatively short distances is politically feasible. But the specter of large-scale two-way busing, transporting white children ten to thirty miles away from the suburbs to the ghetto, is another matter.

The widespread fear of busing seemed to lie behind the Supreme Court's five-to-four ruling, in *Millikin* v. *Bradley* (1973), striking down Detroit's plan to integrate the school system by merging it with white suburban districts. The Court held that neither Detroit nor its surrounding suburbs had intentionally segregated the schools, even though most blacks attended city schools and most whites attended suburban schools. The Court, by effectively halting busing across school-district lines, guaranteed continued segregation of northern cities. Since the suburbs are white and the central cities are black, the decision was a major victory for the white middle and upper classes. However, those whites, mostly the lower classes, living within the central city (meaning those unable to afford the exodus to the suburbs) still faced the probability of busing. The Supreme Court decision—coupled with continuing protest by central-city whites—solidified the division of metropolitan areas into black central cities and white suburbs. In 1982 two-thirds of the students in the nation's ten largest school districts were black.

By 1983 the civil rights process had come full circle. The combination of increased registration of blacks, and electoral success by blacks in large cities such as Chicago, led black leaders such as Jesse Jackson to consider seeking the Democratic nomination.

Black leaders do not necessarily agree that a black candidate is desirable, but all black leaders are taking a hard look at the electoral process as a means of achieving these goals.

The feminist movements

In recent years an increasing number of women have come to view themselves as a distinct group facing economic and social discrimination similar to that suffered by blacks.

Beginning of modern feminism

Early feminists sprang from the abolitionist movement; similarly, modern feminists found their voice initially through participation in the civil rights movement. As the movement reached its zenith in the late

1960s, active women had come to see the desirability of political activity and the necessity for cohesive organization. As Freeman explains, "The civil rights movement provided the training for many another movement's organizers, including the young women of the women's liberation movement. It would appear that the art of 'constructing' a social movement requires considerable skill and experience. Even in supposedly spontaneous social movements, the professional is more valuable than the amateur."[23] As with all other social movements, participants in the feminist movement are, as Freeman concludes, "white, middle class, and college educated."[24]

In search of group identity

Are women a "group"? That is, are their attitudes, behaviors, and problems unique to them as women? Obviously in a categoric sense, women are a group. But do they behave as an interest group? Do they, "on the basis of one or more shared attitudes, make certain claims upon other groups in society for the establishment, maintenance, or enhancement of forms of behavior that are implied by the shared attitudes?"[25]

Group self-awareness. At the elite level, the feminist movement generally appears to make its demands as if it accurately represents the views of all women. However, since women are so diverse in background and ideology, conservative women's organizations have found it easy to challenge this claim. One valuable resource in the political process is the ability of an interest group to portray itself as representative of a broad constituency; the larger the potential clientele of the group, the more difficult this stance becomes. Just as "workers," "men," or "consumers" have few attitudes in common, few attitudes are common to all women. Women do not live in ghettos like blacks. Women are rich, poor, black, white, Republican, Democratic, northern, southern, and so forth. Like men, they are too diverse to categorize. Thus while the feminist movement is analogous to the black movement in its style of leadership recruitment, analogies do not hold when we talk of group consciousness. Self-awareness in the context of one's group membership is, along with the ability of group leaders to articulate this awareness, a valuable political resource. Women have not developed this resource as fully as blacks have. Other identifications tend to overshadow shared attitudes.[26]

Spectrum of attitudes. Women do not display much cohesion in their political attitudes. Majorities of both women and men oppose busing to achieve racial equality. Majorities of both women and men favor the death penalty. On the other hand, women seem to be more opposed to the use of force. During the Vietnam war, more women were doves than were men. Women more consistently oppose war, regardless of their attitude toward women's equality; all women are also less likely than men to regard force as a legitimate method of handling urban unrest.[27] Nevertheless, over the broad array of issues that come and go during the political lives of men and women, differences between the sexes are few.

Women activists

Given the ability of politically active people to articulate ideologies and beliefs more clearly than passive ones, one would expect active women to display a more clearly discernible "women's ideology." However, not surprisingly given the diversity of women, the formal pronouncements of women's rights groups vary substantially: "The Women's Rights groups range from conservative to radical.... No simple continuum exists, however, between more and less conservative Women's Rights groups. Like any of the several segments of NOW [National Organization of Women], a given group may be conservative in some respects and quite radical in others."[28]

Political scientist Jeane Kirkpatrick (later U.S. ambassador to the United Nations) studied women delegates to the 1972 Republican and Democratic presidential nominating conventions. These women were not necessarily active in feminist groups, but they were active politically. They were also active in a variety of professional and political organizations, and most importantly, a majority were active in female civic groups. However, these women did *not* share a feminist ideology. They did not show more concern for problems related to women, such as education and child care. Further, "on most major issues of public policy, including those concerned with education and the poor, the views of women delegates were virtually identical with those of men."[29] They were no more generous than men on welfare policy; they shared men's views on busing; they were neither more generally liberal nor conservative. Kirkpatrick concluded that, to determine a woman's ideology, the candidate she supported was more indicative of her position than was her gender.

Women and work

Working women and housewives* differ in their attitudes toward sexual equality. The Survey Research Center asked respondents to place themselves on a seven-point scale based on the statement, "Some people feel that women should have an equal role with men in running business, industry, and government. Others feel that women's place is in the home." If we regard women who place themselves in the two most pro-equal

---

*The U.S. Census Bureau defines "working women" as women who are employed outside the home; "housewives" as women who, regardless of marital status, work solely in the home. This text uses the same convention in categorizing women.

rights categories as feminists, those who place themselves in the two most anti-equal rights categories as traditionalists, and the three intermediate categories as moderates, figure 15-1 illustrates the distinctions between working women and housewives.

The feminist ideology is more acceptable to working women than to housewives, even without considering additional factors such as education, type of job, and income. The experience of work seems to be more of a catalyst toward feminist thinking. A clear majority of working women cite economic necessity rather than intrinsic satisfaction as their reason to work.[30] However, women's motivation for seeking employment is not as important as the fact that once women enter the economic world, they find equality a more acceptable goal than do housewives. For example, the preference of women for male bosses does not hold for employed women. By a modest margin, employed women are less likely than men to prefer working for males.[31]

Social class and feminist ideology

The feminist movement is no exception to the rule that participants in organizational life disproportionately represent the middle to upper classes. As we saw in our discussion of interest groups, sustained group action depends on a relatively small number of people with the skills and interest to become politically oriented. Men and women participate in organizations roughly to the same degree, and in both groups degree of participation has strong links with social class.

Those women most sympathetic with the goal of equality tend to be of higher social status than women as a whole. Women scholars,

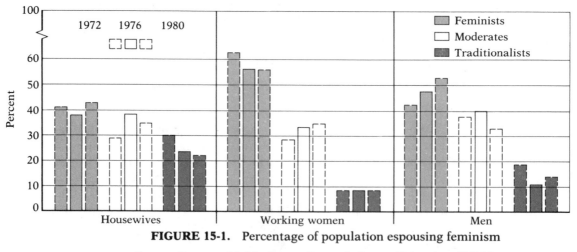

FIGURE 15-1. Percentage of population espousing feminism

Source: Data provided by Survey Research Center, University of Michigan.

active in support of feminism, have noted the class bias of the movement, some with dismay and others with sympathy. Margaret Mead, for example, "infuriated some feminists" when she described women's liberation as "essentially a middle class movement" spurred by "career drive." Similarly, Cynthia Epstein calls attention to the unrepresentative nature of women's organizations. She alleges, for example, that NOW suffers a "stigma" because its membership draws disproportionately from "college students or graduates, under 30, single, interested in professional careers, and to the political left."[32]

Unsympathetic masses. The women's movement's inability to attract lower-class recruits reflects not only the underparticipation of such classes in general but also the more conservative views of the lower classes toward changing familial and social relationships. In a similar vein, the relative absence of black women from the feminist movement probably reflects their lower socioeconomic status as well as blacks' (both female and male) reluctance to associate with a white-dominated movement for fear of co-optation. Black women approve of feminist goals more than white working-class women, but consider racial discrimination a more serious problem.

Feminists and antifeminists.   Politically active *anti*feminist groups also draw from higher social strata. Women who actively oppose the Equal Rights Amendment largely come from the middle and upper-middle classes and from the ranks of college graduates. However, unlike feminist leaders, over 70 percent of antifeminist nonworking leaders are housewives.[33] Thus both feminist and antifeminist movements draw disproportionately from the upper social strata; and, not surprisingly, Janet Boles found that activists on both sides of the ERA were from the upper middle classes.[34] As we know, the feminist movement is hardly unique in its class bias. It attracts women who are professionally oriented, highly educated, and consequently victims of severe discrimination. The antifeminist ideology appeals more to those who draw satisfaction more exclusively from the traditional family.

The ideologies of the two groups of women are quite distinct. Feminists are more liberal in their social and political ideology and are more strongly Democratic in partisan affiliation. While one cannot speak of women as a political group, one can speak of clear differences in feminists' and antifeminists' ideologies. Women are not a group, but we can identify groups of women.

The gender gap

In 1980 Ronald Reagan opposed the Equal Rights Amendment (ERA) and Jimmy Carter favored it. Reagan opposed abortion and Carter seemed to favor it. Even beyond these issues, Reagan's anti-Soviet foreign policy rhetoric and his alleged insensitivity to minorities and women seemed to offer a clear-cut choice; some analysts speculated that this sharp difference in candidates' positions might create a "gender gap" in the sexes' voting patterns. NOW, for example, referred to Reagan's "female problem" during this election, indicating their belief that women would oppose him. However, votes for major party candidates showed about the same gap between men and women in 1980 that had appeared in 1972. Women were less enthusiastic about Reagan than were men, but the election did not widen the gender gap.

Reagan had a clear lead among men in a Survey Research Center survey: 52 percent favored Reagan, and 38 percent preferred Carter. Women split almost evenly: 46 percent for Reagan, 45 percent for Carter. Reagan's greater popularity among men than among women was something of a gap, but the even split of the women's vote diluted arguments of a real gender gap.

Despite the divided vote in 1980, feminist organizations' membership jumped substantially during Reagan's first year in office. Organized groups prosper in the face of a clear threat or enemy; Reagan proved to be that threat. His continued opposition to the ERA, and that amendment's subsequent defeat further swelled feminist ranks.

Women's opposition to Reagan continued into his administration. Surveys consistently showed him less popular among women than among men. However, women's and men's positions on issues did not reveal the major gender gap many people expected. Surveys during the 1980 election showed that the ideology of women was far from damaging to the Republicans. Their economic philosophy was mixed, with modest leanings toward the philosophical positions of the Democrats. Women were less likely to want reduced government spending, but their positions were indistinguishable from men's or slightly pro-Republican on other economic issues like inflation and tax reduction. (See table 15-2.)

Pre-1980 assumptions were that women were less supportive of militant foreign policy than were men. During the Vietnam war, female hostility to the use of force was especially clear. Many sociologists explained women's greater pacificism by biology (women bear life and are more reluctant to support life-threatening policies) or by socialization (cultural and social institutions encourage girls to be more passive than boys); thus they assumed that women's pacificism was fairly well entrenched. However, recent surveys show that women are just as likely as men to believe that trying to get along with the Russians is a "big mistake." And majorities of both men and women want to increase defense spending.

Of all the "humane issues," attitudes toward the environment provide the best evidence of a gender gap. A majority of women oppose any effort to relax existing standards, while a majority of men favor relaxing them. Especially striking is the male-female difference on nuclear energy:

53 percent of the men want to build more nuclear reactors; 75 percent of the women do not. Women are somewhat more interested in reducing the income gap between rich and poor, and in increasing social security. Women are also substantially more opposed to a military draft than men.

These responses are a mixed bag, primarily because women in the 1980s are not yet the cohesive group that feminist organizations envisioned. Still, current evidence suggests that the gender gap is not entirely a media hype.

As the 1982 congressional elections approached, surveys indicated that women's dissatisfaction with Reagan was growing; his strategists were becoming increasingly troubled. A few highly visible female appointments did not assuage the anger of feminist organizations. NOW's renewed vigor led it into the elections with considerable optimism and $500,000 in contributions; others threw in another quarter of a million. Most of this money went to Democrats. However, the payoff was not as good as Democrats had hoped or Republicans had feared. Surveys indicated that women supported Democratic candidates, but so did men; however, women were *more* Democratic than men. Depending upon the survey, women's Democratic vote exceeded men's by between 3 and 6 percent. The essence of the "gap" was that majorities of men and women preferred Democrats, with women slightly more inclined in this direction.

Even though the gap was not large, it was persistent. Women's Democratic preference occurred at all levels of income and education. (See figures 15-2 and 15-3.) Both parties recognized the potential for a stable gender gap; in two successive elections, women tilted slightly away from the Republican party. Since women voted for Republicans in previous elections, future candidates are likely to campaign with this potential in mind. Women constitute 52 percent of the voting population.

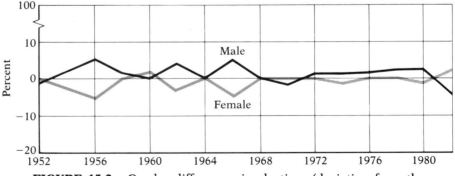

FIGURE 15-2. Gender differences in elections (deviation from the national vote for Democratic candidates for the House)

Source: University of Michigan Election Studies.

TABLE 15-2. The gender gap: Differences in opinion between men and women

Issue	Percent men	Percent women
Government should reduce spending:		
Strongly agree	8	7
Agree	35	25
Neutral	17	22
Disagree	24	30
Strongly disagree	16	16
Government should guarantee a job and a decent standard of living:		
Strongly agree	10	10
Agree	17	20
Neutral	17	24
Disagree	41	36
Strongly disagree	16	10
Is it more important for the government to reduce inflation or reduce unemployment?		
Strongly agree, reduce inflation	6	5
Agree, reduce inflation	26	23
Don't know	33	38
Agree, reduce unemployment	28	27
Strongly agree, reduce unemployment	7	8
Should we try harder to get along with the Russians, or is this a mistake?		
Strongly agree, try harder	14	13
Agree, try harder	28	27
Don't know	21	26
Agree, it's a mistake	26	26
Strongly agree, it's a mistake	11	9
N	393	440
Should we decrease or increase defense spending?		
Strongly agree, decrease	2	3
Agree, decrease	7	9
Don't know	13	20
Agree, increase	54	47
Strongly agree, increase	24	21
Should the government help minorities?		
Strongly agree, should help	6	5
Agree, should help	17	16
Don't know	26	32
Disagree, should help	37	34
Strongly disagree, should help	14	13
Should students be bused to ensure racial equality in schools?		
Strongly agree, should bus	3	3
Agree, should bus	7	6
Don't know	7	6
Disagree, should bus	25	22
Strongly disagree	58	63

TABLE 15-2. *continued*

Issue	Percent men	Percent women
Should environmental standards be relaxed?		
Keep standards as they are	46	58
Relax, with qualifications	16	13
Relax irrespective of consequences	38	30
Should we build more nuclear power plants?		
Build more	53	27
Keep existing plants, but build no more	34	53
Shut them down	13	20
Women should have an equal role with men/Women's place is in the home.		
Strongly agree, equal role	35	36
Agree, equal role	28	29
Neutral	14	18
Agree, women's place is in the home	18	12
Strongly agree, women's place is in the home	5	5
Do you approve or disapprove of the equal rights amendment?		
Strongly approve	28	31
Approve	28	30
Disapprove	19	18
Strongly disapprove	24	21
N	351	465
Abortion		
Should never be permitted	8	10
Should be permitted only if the life and health of the woman is in danger	47	45
Should be permitted if, due to personal reasons, the woman would have difficulty caring for the child	20	14
Abortion should never be forbidden	26	32

Source: Survey Research Center, University of Michigan.

Economic status of women

Evidence of economic discrimination against women is conspicuous. (See table 15-3.) Women's median income is about half that of men. To some extent, such economic disparity reflects the difficulty women have in entering high-income occupations; they must settle for more drudgery and less money. Some occupations (for example, nursing and secretarial work) are almost exclusively female; others, especially the more highly paid professions, are male dominated. However, even within occupational and educational categories, economic discrimination is evident. The average professional woman's income is 60 percent of the average professional man's; the average female college graduate's income is 63 percent of her male counterpart's. The trend, however, is clearly

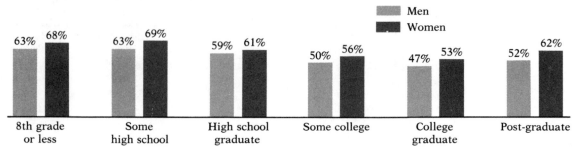

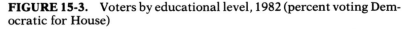

FIGURE 15-3.   Voters by educational level, 1982 (percent voting Democratic for House)

Note: Sample size = 24,438 voters as they left voting booths.

Source: Survey by ABC News, November 2, 1982. From *Public Opinion*, December/ January, 1983, p. 35.

toward equal participation in higher education. In 1974, 44 percent of the college-enrolled population was female (an increase of 6 percent since 1970), and women earned 46 percent of all bachelor's degrees, 47 percent of master's degrees, and 24 percent of the doctorates (in 1969, women earned 40 percent of the master's degrees and 13 percent of the doctorates).

The number of working women has been rising steadily since 1947 and has accelerated since 1976. Half of all adult women are employed. Greater increases are expected for younger women and for those with high educational attainment. Along with this increased work force participation, it is becoming more acceptable for mothers to work. Although women with children are less likely to enter into the job market, the percentage of employed mothers has grown substantially. The labor force work rate for women with children under six was about 12 percent in 1950; it was more than 42 percent by 1975.[35]

The dramatic increase in the number of working mothers is chang-

TABLE 15-3.   Female income as percentage of male income, 1965–1982

Year	Income of female head of family vs. male head with working wife	Income of female head of family vs. male head and nonworking wife	Income of females vs. males
1965	41	53	55
1970	41	54	54
1972	38	51	57
1973	39	50	58
1974	39	53	58
1978	38	53	59
1982	38	53	59

Source: "A Statistical Portrait of Women in the United States," *Current Population Reports* (February 1980).

ing the societal traditions that inhibited women in the past. The role of housewife, once the foundation of sex roles, holds less attraction for teenagers and young women than it once did. Since housewives are the most resistant to feminist ideology, the fact that only one in four teenage girls and young women now prefers to be a housewife becomes significant.[36]

Women:
Are 52 percent of the population;

Live an average of eight years longer than men;

Are slightly more likely than men to attend college;

Delay marriage (51 percent of women between twenty and twenty-four have never married; in 1960, 28 percent of this age group had never married);

Are more likely to head a family than in the past (women head one in seven families, an increase of 65 percent since 1970; this percentage approximates the increase in divorces);

Expect to have fewer children than in the past (of childless married women aged twenty to twenty-four 95 percent expect to have three or fewer children);

Are rapidly entering the work force (38 percent of women sixteen or older worked in 1962; 53 percent worked in 1982);

Hold 19 percent of all management jobs (up from 11 percent in 1971);

Hold 98 percent of all secretarial jobs, 97 percent of all nursing jobs, 83 percent of all librarian jobs, and 71 percent of all noncollege teaching jobs.

Changes in family structure

In addition to changes in women's role in the family, other demographic factors are eroding the family's pivotal position in American society. The marriage rate is declining, while the divorce rate is increasing. Liberalization of divorce laws, growing social acceptance of divorce or remaining single, and the broadening educational and work experience of women have contributed to these trends.[37] While divorce rates have been increasing, men and women have been remaining single longer, having fewer children, and delaying having children until later in the marriage. The net result is that fewer than half of American families are now traditional units of father, mother, and children living together in the same household.[38] As Sandra Steneel concludes, "Women are unlikely again to turn to motherhood as a full-time occupation."[39]

The increased educational attainment of women, combined with their experience at work, should certainly assist in the diffusion of the feminist ideology among American women. On balance, however, the feminist *movement* has not achieved the intensity of group identity so characteristic of the black protests. It continues to attract an active, politically sophisticated minority. This dominance by an active minority is not, of course, unique to the women's movement; all other political movements exhibit the same pattern.

Summary

Generally, established elites can depend upon mass apathy. But occasionally mass activism replaces apathy, and this activism is extremist, unstable, and unpredictable. America has experienced a long history of mass movements led by a wide variety of counterelites, from Shays's Rebellion of the eighteenth century, to recent black militancy. But the place of blacks in American society has been the central domestic issue of American politics. This chapter examines the movement for black equality in the context of elite theory to observe political activism among subservient peoples and the reaction of dominant elites to this activism. In many ways, blacks' recent political activism typifies all mass movements: it is unstable and unpredictable; it expresses resentment toward the established order; it is made up of people who seldom participate in democratic politics and do not always understand the "rules of the game"; it is highly flammable and can produce violence; it produces counterelites; and it threatens the established order.

However, we must be cautious in generalizing about mass movements based upon black experience in America. For blacks must contend not only with white *elites* but also with white *masses*. Contrary to the general assumption of elite theory, the white masses *do* have opinions about civil rights and race relations, and their opinions circumscribe elite behavior more than is normally the case. Hence the relationship between white elites and black masses is complicated by the role of the white masses. Yet elitism offers many insights into the nature of the black struggle in America and the way in which this nation has responded to black demands.

The fact that women's organizations recruit disproportionately from the middle to upper classes does not distinguish them from black organizations. The contrast comes from the inability of feminist organizations to generate the same level of intensity among the masses. Like women's organizations, black groups fight with each other; nevertheless blacks have more group consciousness than do women. As Andersen concludes: "The interests of women and the interests of men are tied to one another in a way that . . . black and white interests are not. Women are probably too cross pressured ever to constitute a lasting political movement. . . . The achievement of the movement's goals will produce increasing . . . fragmentation among women."[40] Thus, in 1980, women supported Reagan (an opponent of the equal rights amendment and a proponent of the anti-abortion amendment) and Carter equally.

1. America's prevailing myths and symbols draw from democratic theory, including recognition of minorities' rights, commitment to the value of individual dignity, and commitment to equal opportunity for all people. Although committed to these abstract ideals, white

elites over the course of American history have consistently failed to implement these ideals in public policy.

2. Centuries of slavery and segregation have left black masses poorly educated, unskilled, poorly housed, poverty-stricken, frequently unemployed, segregated, and subject to a variety of social pathologies. White elites generally expect individual blacks to solve these problems individually. Black counterelites charge that white elites created these problems and are obliged to resolve them on a wide scale.

3. White elites are willing to accept individual blacks on a near-equal basis only if blacks accept the prevailing consensus and exhibit white middle-class values. White elites are less willing to accept black masses who have not assimilated prevailing middle-class values.

4. Public-regarding liberal elites are prepared to eliminate legal barriers to provide equality of opportunity under the law for individual blacks, but they are not prepared to take massive action to eliminate absolute inequalities ("leveling"), which would bring black masses up to average white standards of living.

5. The first governmental institution to act for equality of opportunity for blacks in the twentieth century was the Supreme Court. The Court, structurally the furthest removed from the influence of white masses, was the first to apply liberal public-regarding policies to blacks. Elected elites who are more accessible to white masses were slower to act on black rights than were appointed elites.

6. Elected white elites did not respond to black requests until faced with a prolonged campaign of nonviolent civil disobedience, public demonstrations, and creative disorder and crises. Generally elites have responded by making the most minimal changes in the system consistent with maintaining stability. Often these changes are only symbolic. Elites have not contemplated revolutionary changes even when faced with massive civil disorder.

7. Elimination of legal discrimination and guaranteed equality of opportunity have largely resulted from the efforts of black middle-class groups who share a dominant elite consensus and who appeal to the conscience of white elites to extend that consensus to include blacks.

8. The successes of black elites in achieving symbolic goals have helped activate black masses, who have adopted goals that go beyond accepted elite consensus; for example, demands for absolute equality have replaced demands for equality of opportunity. New mass-oriented black counterelites have emerged to contend with established middle-class black elites. Middle-class black elites have relatively little influence with the masses in the ghettos. Mass coun-

terelites have less respect for the rules of the game than do either white elites or established middle-class black leaders.

9. Protest movements have a spillover effect; they ripple from group to group. Groups only recently beginning to protest, such as women, have not developed the group consciousness of more severely repressed groups.

10. Leaders of the women's movement are professional, educated, upper-middle-class women, whose views are not universally shared by the masses of women in America. Despite symbolic gains in the law, economic discrimination against women persists. Yet it is difficult to mobilize masses of women on behalf of feminist goals.

11. Evidence in support of a "gender gap" is mixed but suggests potential female cohesion.

NOTES

1. Frances Fox Piven and Richard A. Cloward, *Poor People's Movements* (New York: Pantheon, 1977).
2. William A. Gamson, *The Strategy of Social Protest* (Homewood, Ill.: Dorsey Press, 1975).
3. John D. McCarthy and Mayer N. Zald, "Resource Mobilization and Social Movements: A Partial Theory," *American Journal of Sociology* 82 (1977): 1212–1238. See also Steven E. Barkan, "Strategic, Tactical, and Organizational Dilemmas of the Protest Movement against Nuclear Power," *Social Problems* 72 (October 1979):19–37.
4. Michael Lipsky, *Protest in City Politics* (Chicago: Rand McNally, 1970).
5. See Piven and Cloward, op. cit., on accommodation and repression.
6. Ibid., p. 5.
7. Anthony Oberschall, *Social Conflict and Social Movements* (Englewood Cliffs, N.J.: Prentice-Hall, 1973), p. 155.
8. Gunnar Myrdal, *An American Dilemma* (New York: McGraw-Hill, 1964), vol. I, p. lxxi.
9. Stanley M. Elkins, *Slavery: A Problem in American Institutional and Intellectual Life* (New York: Universal Library, 1963).
10. David C. McClelland, *The Achieving Society* (Princeton, N.J.: Van Nostrand, 1961), pp. 376–377.
11. U.S. Department of Commerce, Bureau of the Census, *Current Population Reports*, P-20, nos. 125, 116, 106, 100, 88, 83, 75, 67, 53, 44, 33, 26 (1980).
12. *Plessy* v. *Ferguson*, 163 U.S. 537 (1896).
13. Allen D. Grimshaw, "Lawlessness and Violence in America and Their Special Manifestations in Changing Negro-White Relationships," *Journal of Negro History* 44 (January 1959):67.
14. Myrdal, op. cit., vol. II, p. 749.
15. *Brown* v. *Board of Education of Topeka*, 347 U.S. 483 (1954).
16. Kenneth B. Clark, "The Civil Rights Movement: Momentum and Organization," in Talcott Parsons and Kenneth B. Clark, eds., *The Negro American* (Boston: Beacon Press, 1966), p. 610.
17. Crane Brinton, *The Anatomy of Revolution* (New York: Vintage Books, 1965), pp. 100–105.

18. James Baldwin, *Nobody Knows My Name* (New York: Dell, 1961), p. 62.

19. *Report of the National Advisory Commission on Civil Disorders* (New York: Bantam Books, 1968), p. 306.

20. J. H. Skolnick, *Justice without Trial* (New York: Wiley, 1967), p. 61.

21. James Q. Wilson, *Varieties of Police Behavior* (Cambridge, Mass.: Harvard University Press, 1968), p. 43.

22. "Racial Isolation in the Public Schools," *A Report of the United States Commission on Civil Rights* (Washington, D.C.: Government Printing Office, 1967), pp. 3–7.

23. Jo Freeman, *The Politics of Women's Liberation* (New York: McKay, 1975), p. 70.

24. Ibid., p. 449.

25. David Truman, *The Governmental Process* (New York: Knopf, 1971), p. 33.

26. Virginia Sapiro, "Gender, Gender Roles, and Ideology in Survey Research," in Sarah Slavin Schramm, ed., *Methodological Issues in the Study of Women and Politics* (in press).

27. Sidney Verba and Norman H. Nie, *Participation in America* (New York: Harper & Row, 1972). Gerald Pomper, *Voters' Choice* (New York: Harper & Row, 1975), p. 88.

28. Maren L. Carden, *The New Feminist Movement* (New York: Russell Sage, 1974), pp. 140–141.

29. Jeane Kirkpatrick, *The New Presidential Elite* (New York: Russell Sage, 1976), p. 439.

30. *Public Opinion* (January–February 1979):38.

31. Marianne Ferber, Joan Huber, and Glenna Spitze, "Preference for Men as Bosses and Professionals," *Social Forces* (December 1979):470.

32. Cynthia Epstein, *Woman's Place* (Berkeley: University of California Press, 1970), pp. 39–40.

33. David W. Brady and Kent L. Tedin, "Ladies in Pink: Religion and Political Ideology in the Anti-ERA Movement," *Social Science Quarterly* 56 (March 1976):570.

34. Janet Boles, *The Politics of the Equal Rights Amendment* (New York: Longman, 1979), chap. 3.

35. U.S. Department of Commerce, Bureau of the Census, *A Statistical Portrait of Women in the United States*, Current Population Reports 58 (Washington, D.C.: Government Printing Office, 1980), p. 50.

36. Congressional Quarterly, *The Women's Movement*, Editorial Research Reports (Washington, D.C.: Congressional Quarterly, 1977), p. 26.

37. Department of Commerce, *Women, A Statistical Portrait*, p. 15.

38. Congressional Quarterly, op. cit., p. 18.

39. Ibid., p. 19.

40. Kristi Andersen, "Working Women and Political Participation," *American Journal of Political Science* 19 (1975):453.

SELECTED READINGS

Andersen, Kristi. "Working Women and Political Participation." *American Journal of Political Science* 19 (1975):439–453. Andersen analyzes the effects of employment and ideology on women's participation.

Banfield, Edward C. *The Unheavenly City Revisited: A Revision of the Unheavenly City.* Boston: Little, Brown, 1974. Banfield has a somewhat unusual viewpoint of the problems of the people of urban America and of the cities in which they live. He argues that the poor in America are not as unfortunate as they might first appear to be. It is only relative to the affluence of middle- and upper-class Americans that the poor seem deprived. In an absolute sense, however, they are not generally poor, especially compared to the poor of Europe or Asia. This book frequently comes up in discussions of civil rights and the problems of the poor.

Barkan, Steven G. "Strategic, Tactical, and Organizational Dilemmas of the Protest Movement against Nuclear Power." *Social Problems* 27 (1979):19–37. The author discusses the single-issue focus and civil disobedience tactics of protest organizations.

Baxter, Sandra, and Lansing, Marjorie. *Women in Politics*. Ann Arbor: University of Michigan Press, 1980. This study of women's beliefs about politics, candidates, and parties is especially helpful because of its comparative analyses.

Carden, Maren L. *The New Feminist Movement*. New York: Russell Sage, 1974. This book offers an impressionistic but informed account of the goals and membership of various kinds of women's organizations.

Clark, Kenneth B. *Dark Ghetto: Dilemmas of Social Power*. New York: Harper & Row, Harper Torchbook, 1967. Clark offers a particularly incisive analysis of the life of American blacks in urban ghetto areas and of the pathologies this life produces.

Congressional Quarterly. *The Women's Movement*. Washington, D.C.: Congressional Quarterly, 1973. This volume is an introduction to many political questions of special concern to women, including marriage laws, equal protection laws, child care, rape, and women in politics.

Epstein, Cynthia Fuchs. *Woman's Place*. Berkeley: University of California Press, 1970. Epstein discusses economic discrimination against women.

Freeman, Jo. *The Politics of Women's Liberation*. New York: McKay, 1975. This book is the best source on the origins and consequences of the women's movement.

Gamson, William A. *The Strategy of Social Protest*. Homewood, Ill.: Dorsey Press, 1975. Gamson argues that pluralist theory is not an adequate guide to protest organizations.

Kirkpatrick, Jeane. *Political Women*. New York: Basic Books, 1978. This book explores the conditions leading to women's seeking political office.

McCourt, Kathleen. *Working Class Women and Grass-Roots Politics*. Bloomington: Indiana University Press, 1977. This book describes what working-class women expect to gain from political participation.

Matthews, Donald R., and Prothro, James W. *Negroes and the New Southern Politics*. New York: Harcourt Brace Jovanovich, 1966. A pioneering work on the changing political role of southern blacks, this book considerably updates some of Myrdal's earlier comments on southern politics.

Myrdal, Gunnar. *An American Dilemma*. 2d ed. Vol. I: *The Negro in a White Nation*. Vol. II: *The Negro Social Structure*. New York: McGraw-Hill, 1964. Originally published in 1944, Myrdal's study is one of the most comprehensive analyses of the situation of blacks in America. It draws broadly from many disciplines.

Oberschall, Anthony. *Social Conflict and Social Movements*. Englewood Cliffs, N.J.: Prentice-Hall, 1973. Oberschall's book is the most authoritative and well-reasoned text on the subject.

Patterson, Ernest. *Black City Politics*. New York: Dodd, Mead, 1974. Patterson's discussions of urban organizations and political participation are especially useful.

Piven, Frances Fox, and Cloward, Richard A. *Poor People's Movements*. New York: Pantheon, 1977. The authors argue that mass demonstrations are more effective than formal organizations.

Pomper, Gerald. *Elections in America: Control and Influence in Democratic Politics*. New York: Dodd, Mead, 1968. Chapter 9 discusses the development of the civil rights movement in America. The emphasis is on the changing status of blacks in American society and the impact on American voting patterns.

Report of the National Advisory Commission on Civil Disorders. New York: Bantam Books, 1968. Popularly called the Kerner Report, this volume is the most comprehensive study of major urban riots in the United States available today. It discusses in detail the factors underlying past riots and recommends ways to avoid such confrontations in the future.

Theodore, Athena, ed. *The Professional Woman*. Cambridge, Mass.: Schenkman, 1971. This collection of essays and articles looks at the social, economic, political, cultural, and moral problems faced by women in their professional lives.

Epilogue:
Dilemmas of Politics

Revolutions come and go—but the masses remain powerless. The question then, is not how to combat elitism, or empower the masses, or achieve revolution; but rather how to build an orderly, humane, and just society.

A whole literature on mass behavior and mass psychology demonstrated and popularized the wisdom, so familiar to the ancients, of the affinity between democracy and dictatorship, between mob rule and tyranny.

—Hannah Arendt, The Origins of Totalitarianism, *1951*

If this book has left you with some uncomfortable feelings that:

> We cannot fully trust either elites or masses to preserve democratic values;

> We cannot always rely on governments, corporations, banks, television networks, and other giant institutions to protect and ensure justice;

> Ordinary individuals have a difficult task in holding these institutions responsible for their actions;

> Parties, elections, interest-group competition, and formal checks and balances do not guarantee protection of individual rights;

then the book has succeeded in its purpose: to make you feel uncomfortable about the future of democracy and the preservation of individual liberty.

Democracy is very fragile. Of the nearly two hundred nations that claim independent sovereignty in the world today, no more than two dozen qualify as democracies. Nearly four-fifths of the world's population lives under authoritarian regimes that curtail freedoms of speech and press, suppress or eliminate opposition parties, allow individuals no role in choosing their governments, and impose a single party and ideology to control all government offices and dictate public policy. Moreover, the number of democracies has declined over time, as has the number of people living under democratic governments. No unchanging law says that democracy will always exist in the United States either— or anywhere.

In chapter 1 we defined democracy as:

> Popular participation in the decisions that shape the lives of individuals in society;

Government by majority rule, with recognition of the rights of minorities to try to become majorities, including the freedoms of speech, press, assembly, and petition; and the freedoms to dissent, to form opposition parties, and to run for public office;

A commitment to individual dignity and preservation of the liberal values of life, liberty, and property;

A commitment to equal opportunity for all people to develop their individual capacities.

Pluralism offers no true substitute for democracy in its theories that:

Individual participation is antiquated in a large industrial society;

Interest-group leaders can bargain for us; we should dutifully vote in every election, even voting for the lesser of two evils when both candidates are distasteful to us;

We should join established interest groups and work within the system if we want change;

Private decisions by large corporations, banks, television networks, and other nongovernment institutions are outside the boundaries of politics and political science;

We should not expect public policy to reflect majority preferences but only the equilibrium of group interests.

To accept these notions is to lose sight of the ideal of democracy.

Democracy in world perspective

Democracy is a noble ideal. Americans take it for granted that "non-democratic" countries are less worthy than "democratic" ones. This book describes the workings of one democratic political system—the United States. This nation is one of only a handful that provide extensive legal protection for individual liberty and personal freedom. While American freedoms are not absolute, clearly the United States provides just about as much "democracy" as is possible. And, as we have suggested, even this democratic system may not be good enough. Always in the background, however, is the fact that no more than 20 percent of the world's population lives in countries that feel a legal or political obligation to protect individual freedom.

Freedom also seems to come with the highest standards of living. Throughout the world, the freest nations are those with the highest average incomes. The fear that all this wealth rests in the hands of a few people is unfounded: The wealthy, free countries also have the most equitable distribution of income. In these countries, the highest incomes are roughly twelve times the lowest incomes. While this allocation may not be ideal, it does suggest that we need not sacrifice individual freedom to achieve economic equality. Unfortunately, the least free societies do not yet make available information about income distribution in their nations; nonetheless, we can see that, while these nations are less affluent than the freer ones, they are no better at distributing income more equitably. (See table E-1.)

The American political system provides one of the highest standards of living in the world, but not the highest standard, and it provides one of the most equitable distributions of incomes but not the most equitable. But it does not stand out from other democratic nations. In preserving the symbols of democracy—frequent elections, vigorous competition, and the like—the United States is similar to Canada, Ireland, Switzerland, Austria, Japan, and Costa Rica. Actually party competition is stronger and voter participation more active in Australia, New Zealand, Denmark, Norway, Sweden, the United Kingdom, and the Netherlands. But the United States is as free as these nations, and because elections and their accompanying hoopla have minimum impact on governmental decisions, the overall differences are not great. The most totalitarian political systems are also among the poorest and least equal. Freedom, wealth, and relative equality appear to go together.

What does it mean to live in a free, partially free, or totalitarian society? Since most of us pay little attention to politics, how can we tell how free we really are? The countries at the extreme left of the continuum—the most free countries—put very few restrictions on individual behavior. Although we occasionally become irritated by zoning laws (for example, those establishing minimum floor space in housing), or angry at other minor examples of governmental coercion (compulsory social security), we rarely need to fear prosecution for our political beliefs. We can call the president an idiot or join the Communist party, the Ku Klux Klan, or the Weathermen. Only if we engage in political violence will we face prosecution. Most of us, for whom politics is a spectator sport, rarely come up against the limits of freedom. We can say what we wish, live where we wish, marry whom we wish, and spend our money as we wish. We assume that individuals are free to fail or succeed, or to make fools of themselves, in any way they wish. The government tampers with individual rights at its peril. The long litigation over the rights of criminal defendants clearly shows how seriously Americans (at least American elites) value individualism.

Partially free societies show only slightly less commitment to these values. West Germany, perhaps because of its unique past, prohibits membership in Nazi parties. The Israeli government controls access to housing. But here too, unless people join terrorist gangs or perform terrorist acts, their private and public lives are protected.

As we approach classifications III and IV in the table (away from the free end of the continuum), the distinction between public and pri-

TABLE E-1.   Freedom, economic well-being, and economic quality
(nations classified by degrees of personal freedom)

I (most free)			II			III		
Country	Average individual income	Gini index[a]	Country	Average individual income	Gini index[a]	Country	Average individual income	Gini index[a]
Australia	$ 9,120	.32	Colombia	$ 1,010	.56	Bangladesh	$ 90	.30
Austria	8,630	n.a.	Dominican Rep.	990	.49	Brazil	1,780	.65
Belgium	10,920	n.a.	Equador	1,050	.68	Honduras	530	.62
Canada	9,640	.33	Finland	8,160	.47	Kenya	380	.64
Costa Rica	1,820	.37	France	9,950	.52	Malaysia	1,370	.59
Denmark	11,900	.49	West Germany	11,730	.39	Mexico	1,640	.58
Ireland	4,210	n.a.	Greece	3,960	.38	Morocco	740	n.a.
Japan	8,810	.31	India	190	.48	Nepal	130	n.a.
Netherlands	10,230	.45	Israel	4,150	.31	Panama	1,400	.43
New Zealand	5,930	.36	Italy	5,250	n.a.	Senegal	430	.59
Norway	10,700	n.a.	Nigeria	670	n.a.	Thailand	590	.52
Sweden	11,930	.39	Papua New Guinea	660	n.a.	Average	825	.54
Switzerland	13,920	n.a.	Peru	730	.59			
United Kingdom	6,320	.39	Portugal	2,180	n.a.			
United States	10,630	.41	Spain	4,380	.39			
Average	8,981	.37	Sri Lanka	230	.38			
			Trinidad-Tobago	3,390	n.a.			
			Venezuela	3,120	.62			
			Average	3,433	.45			

TABLE 15-2. *continued*

IV			V			VII (least free)		
Country	Average individual income	Gini index[a]	Country	Average individual income	Gini index[a]	Country	Average individual income	Gini index[a]
Chile	$ 1,690	.51	Argentina	$2,230	.40	Afghanistan	$ 170	n.a.
China, Taiwan	2,800	.28	Bolivia	550	n.a.	Albania	840	n.a.
Egypt	480	.43	China, Peoples Rep.	330	n.a.	Angola	440	n.a.
El Salvador	670	.47	Chad	110	n.a.	Benin	250	n.a.
Guatemala	1,020	.29	Cuba	1,410	n.a.	Bulgaria	3,690	.21
Indonesia	378	.46	Haiti	260	n.a.	Burma	160	.38
South Korea	1,130	.36	Hungary	3,650	.24	Burundi	180	n.a.
Kuwait	17,100	n.a.	Jordan	1,180	n.a.	Central African Rep.	290	n.a.
Nicaragua	660	n.a.	Liberia	500	n.a.	Czechoslovakia	5,290	.19
Paraguay	1,070	n.a.	Pakistan	260	.33	Ethiopia	130	n.a.
Philippines	600	.49	Saudi Arabia	7,780	n.a.	Guinea	280	n.a.
Poland	3,830	.26	Syria	1,030	n.a.	Iraq	2,410	.63
Sierra Leone	250	.61	Tanzania	260	n.a.	Mauritania	320	n.a.
Singapore	3,830	n.a.	Yugoslavia	2,430	.35	Mozambique	250	n.a.
South Africa	1,720	.58	Zaire	260	n.a.	Rumania	1,900	n.a.
Sudan	370	.45				USSR	4,150	n.a.
Tunisia	1,120	.50						
Turkey	1,330	.87						
Uganda	290	.40						
Average	2,123	.45	Average	1,483	.33	Average	1,234	.35

n.a. = not available

[a]The Gini Index measures equity in personal index distribution. The higher the index, the greater the inequality; the lower the index, the greater the equality. In this table, for example, in Brazil, (Gini = .65), the wealthiest 20 percent of the population earn fifty times as much as the poorest 20 percent. In the United States (Gini = .41), the wealthiest 20 percent earn seventeen times as much as the poorest 20 percent.

vate behavior becomes sharper. A person who stays out of public life will probably not face restrictions on individual freedom. People in countries that have outlawed the Communist party, or other opposition parties, generally do not miss it; they still live and work as they please. These countries do not enjoy a very high standard of living; the masses pay less attention to politics and focus on earning a living. These governments take political prisoners, but not very many; they prohibit certain forms of expression but do little to force individual conformity to a collective goal. Visitors, or even long-term residents, in Mexico or Taiwan do not feel they are in a restrictive society. The key is to separate public from private life.

The truly totalitarian societies allow no separation of public and private life. By its nature totalitarianism requires subordination of individual preferences to those of the state and the collective society. People must do more than simply behave themselves in their public, political lives; they can participate only through the single legal party. One earns membership in this party by loyalty, not by casual registration as in the most open societies. No more than 10 percent of the populations of the Soviet Union or the People's Republic of China belong to the Communist party. Exclusion from public life does not leave people free to pursue their private lives, however. The state tells them where to live, for it carefully controls the population of major cities. The state also tells people where to work: workers cannot quit their jobs, and absenteeism is an "economic crime" that invites punishment. The state dictates where children go to school and what they study, for the needs of the state are more important than students' personal likes or dislikes. It may tell couples how many children to have, verify their personal commitment to birth control, and, if necessary, order abortion of an unwanted child. Families whose living space exceeds the legal limit may have to accept strangers into their apartment. Still, a glance at the table suggests that communist governments have achieved more equity than have noncommunist regimes allowing comparable levels of freedom. However, the figures do not reveal the benefits enjoyed by the party elite that may not be evident in income distribution data.

Inevitability of elites

Despite America's enviable position among the world's nations, we must acquire the political maturity to know that democracy remains an ideal and that elites, not masses, govern all nations. Elitism in American society is not a unique corruption of democratic ideas attributable to capitalism, war, Watergate, the military-industrial complex, or any other events or groups of people in this nation. Elitism is a necessary characteristic of all societies. Elitism has no "solution," for it is not the problem in a democracy. Many mass movements, both "left" and "right," have promised to bring power to the people. Indeed many "successful" mass movements have overthrown social and political systems, often at great cost to human life, promising to empower the masses. Hitler promised to empower *der Volk* (the people); Lenin promised "a dictatorship of the proletariat" (the workers); and Mao Tse-tung promised a revolutionary, classless "people's democracy." But invariably these movements have created new elite systems that are at least as "evil" as, and certainly no more democratic than, the systems they replaced. Revolutions come and go—but the masses remain powerless. The question, then, is not how to combat elitism or empower the masses or achieve revolution but rather how to build an orderly, humane, and just society.

Let us summarize some of the obstacles to true democracy. The sheer size of the nation and its government and corporate institutions is one of the great obstacles to democracy in America. In a large society, even assuming political equality, the individual's influence on societal decisions is so tiny as to render participation in mass democracy fruitless. As the society grows larger, the individual shrinks in influence, power, liberty, and the capacity to shape the decisions affecting his or her life. The chance that an individual in a society of 236 million people can affect the outcome of an election or any other societal decision is infinitesimal. An individual with less than one–two-hundred-millionth of a voice in the outcome of issues cannot be personally effective, even under conditions of perfect equality. Nearly half the eligible population did not vote in the 1980 presidential election. Many who abstained surely felt that their one vote in millions could not affect the outcome. This assumption is rational. Size is one obstacle to effective individual participation in politics.

But another obstacle to effective individual participation in politics is *in*equality—not only in wealth but also in education, knowledge, intelligence, and leadership. Many social democrats in America and Europe complain about inequalities *among individuals*, especially inequalities of wealth. They propose to eliminate such inequalities by taking from the rich and giving to the poor to achieve a "leveling," which they believe is essential to democracy. But the really dangerous inequalities in society are between *institutions and individuals*. If the government confiscated the wealth of every centimillionaire in America, the total would amount to less than half of one year's sales of General Motors or Exxon and less than 2 percent of the federal government's expenditures for a single year. Even very wealthy individuals are insignificant next to the wealth and power of the giant institutions of an advanced technological society. American democracy today faces the problem of controlling these giant institutions: corporations, banks, utilities, media networks, foundations, universities, and especially government itself.

Mature students of politics must confront the *iron law of oligarchy:* every political organization "becomes a minority of directors and a majority of directed."[1] As each protest movement organizes and then institutionalizes, its leadership gradually becomes a self-perpetuating oligarchy. The mass membership must delegate governing responsibilities to representatives, and by so doing it creates a governing minority distinct from the masses in behavior, role, and status. This process occurs no matter the system of accountability; delegation of authority creates a governing elite. Organization inevitably means oligarchy.

Dilemma of American politics

The dilemma of American politics today really differs little from that faced by the Founding Fathers in 1787: how to protect individuals in a majority-rule democratic system from the excesses and injustices of *both* mass majorities and elite minorities.

Nature of mass politics

The masses, being antidemocratic, are not reliable to govern democratically. Despite a superficial commitment to the symbols of democracy, the people are not attached to the ideals of individual liberty, toleration of diversity, freedoms of expression and dissent, or equality of opportunity. On the contrary, elites are more likely to hold these values. Masses are authoritarian, intolerant, anti-intellectual, nativistic, alienated, hateful, and violent. Mass politics is extremist, unstable, and unpredictable. The masses do not commit to democratic "rules of the game"; when they take political action, they frequently go outside these rules to engage in violence. Moreover, mass politics frequently reflects the alienation and hostility of the masses by concentrating on scapegoats—whether Jews, blacks, Catholics, immigrants, students, intellectuals, or any other minority—who are in some way different from the majority of the masses.

The masses are fatally vulnerable to tyranny. Extremist movements—reflecting authoritarianism, alienation, hostility, and prejudice—are more likely to grow from the masses than from elites. Hannah Arendt writes, "A whole literature on mass behavior and mass psychology demonstrated and popularized the wisdom, so familiar to the ancients, of the affinity between democracy and dictatorship, between mob rule and tyranny."[2] One cannot trust the masses, feeling in themselves the power of the majority, to restrain themselves in dealing with dissenting minorities. Tolerance of diversity comes only with years of socialization. The authoritarianism of the masses is unavoidable, given their authoritarian childhood experiences and family relationships, their limited education and restricted cultural opportunities, their monotonous job experiences, and their orientation toward immediate gratification. Efforts to reeducate or resocialize the masses are futile. Two hundred years ago Jefferson proposed universal free public education as a curative for mass ignorance, incompetence, and alienation. Today the masses in America average over twelve years of free public education, but they appear even less capable of governing wisely and humanely than did the masses of Jefferson's time.

Elite repression

Yet we have also learned that democracy is not always safe in the hands of elites, even democratically elected elites. Throughout this nation's history, elites themselves have posed threats to democracy: from the Alien and Sedition Acts, to Woodrow Wilson's "Red scare," to Roosevelt's incarceration of thousands of Japanese-Americans, to Truman's "loyalty" programs, to the Watergate "horrors." Restrictions on mass political activity—the forcible breakup of revolutionary parties, restrictions on the public appearances of demagogues, the suppression of literature expressing hatred or advocating revolution or violence, the equipping and training of additional security forces, the jailing of violence-prone radicals and their co-conspirators, and so on—are continuing threats to a democratic society.

Elite repression—its abandonment of democratic values—is a characteristic response to mass protest activity. While we may want to see Watergate as unique and unprecedented or as a product of a conservative ideology, neither perception is accurate. *All* elites are capable of repressive measures when they feel threatened by mass unrest.

Of course, repression in a free society is a contradiction. We cannot logically curtail liberty—even the liberty of a demagogue—to preserve a free society. Repression is not really a serious instrument for an elite committed to the values of individual dignity, personal freedom, and tolerance of diversity.

What is to be done?

If protest is largely futile and "working within the system" simply a diversion of energy, what *can* concerned students do to maximize their political influence? First, you can lower your expectations of short-term possibilities for change. Excessive idealism, coupled with impatience to change society *now*, leads only to bitterness and disillusionment. In the long run, these feelings may reduce rather than increase your political effectiveness. Excessive idealism can also expose you to the demagogic appeals of those politicians who exploit others' idealism for their own advantage. Understanding your personal limits in shaping the world and resolving society's problems is important. It is time to reexamine adolescent optimism about "changing the world."

Second, you must learn about the world in which you live. You will benefit from reexamining the "truths" taught in the public schools—

looking beyond the slogans of democracy (and of Marxism) to the realities of power in contemporary society. Just as this book has tried to reexamine traditional teachings about American government, concerned students should also critically reexamine the economic system, the social system, the communication system, and even the accepted "truths" of the physical and biological sciences. Developing your independent powers of social and political analysis can help you resist the floodtide of popular rhetoric, the symbolic posturing of politicians, the pseudoscience of the bureaucratic social engineers. You can learn to be wary of the politician or bureaucrat who promises to solve society's problems with a stroke of the pen: to end racism, eliminate poverty, cure the sick, prevent crime, clean the air and water, provide new energy, all without imposing heavy new taxes or further restricting individual freedom. You will learn that society's problems have no simple solutions.

Third, you will want to try to master the technological revolution rather than let it master you. For example, you should endeavor to learn about one or more aspects of technology in the pursuit of your education. If computers are going to direct your life, why not learn some computer technology yourself? The same applies to social institutions. If laws regulate your life, why not master some aspects of the law yourself, even as an undergraduate? If you are going to be the object of the administrative, managerial, and budgetary practices of large bureaucracies, why not learn something about these subjects, for self-defense if nothing else? If you are not majoring in any of the physical and biological sciences, why not explore some of these courses—perhaps on a pass-fail basis if your school permits it? The more you know about today's technology, the less impressed you will be when someone tells you that certain policies are "technological requirements."

Finally, you should become familiar with the meaning of individual freedom and dignity throughout the ages. Read about and understand the human quest for freedom in many times and cultures—from St. Thomas More to Aleksandr Solzhenitsyn, from Antigone to Galileo. You should also learn to view American democracy from a world perspective—comparing the personal freedoms we enjoy with those existing in other nations. It is one thing to struggle against mindless corporate and government bureaucracies in this country but quite another to conclude that America is "not worth saving"—especially when viewing the personal liberties of Americans in context with the personal restrictions in many other nations.

Perhaps increased suspicion and distrust of government is really a great blessing for democracy; perhaps personal freedom is most endangered when we place too much trust in government, see great idealism in its actions, and have unquestioning faith in our public leaders. Perhaps democratic values—individual dignity, freedom of speech and press, rights of dissent, personal liberty—are safer when we are suspicious of

Drawing by Bernard Schoenbaum. © 1977 The New Yorker Magazine, Inc.

government and its power and worry about its size and complexity. Perhaps the most important danger to a free people is that they "politicize" all the problems confronting them as individuals; that they blame government and "society" for the problems that beset them; and that they therefore excuse themselves from personal efforts to confront these problems. If we look to government to resolve all of our problems, our social dependency will increase, and we will assume less responsibility for our lives. The traditional democratic value is to encourage individuals to shape their own destinies.

NOTES

1. Roberto Michels, *Political Parties: A Sociological Study of the Oligarchical Tendencies of Modern Democracies* (1915; reprint, New York: Free Press, 1962), p. 70.
2. Hannah Arendt, *The Origins of Totalitarianism* (New York: Harcourt Brace Jovanovich, 1951), pp. 309–310.

The Constitution of
the United States of America

We the People of the United States, in Order to form a more perfect Union, establish Justice, insure domestic Tranquility, provide for the common defense, promote the general Welfare, and secure the Blessings of Liberty to ourselves and our Posterity, do ordain and establish this Constitution for the United States of America.

ARTICLE I

Section 1 All legislative Powers herein granted shall be vested in a Congress of the United States, which shall consist of a Senate and House of Representatives.

Section 2 The House of Representatives shall be composed of Members chosen every second Year by the People of the several States, and the Electors in each State shall have the Qualifications requisite for Electors of the most numerous Branch of the State Legislature.

No Person shall be a Representative who shall not have attained to the age of twenty five Years, and been seven Years a Citizen of the United States, and who shall not, when elected, be an Inhabitant of that State in which he shall be chosen.

Representatives and direct Taxes shall be apportioned among the several States which may be included within this Union, according to their respective Numbers, *which shall be determined by adding to the whole Number of free Persons, including those bound to Service for a Term of Years, and excluding Indians not taxed, three fifths of all other persons.*[1] The actual Enumeration shall be made within three Years after the first Meeting of the Congress of the United States, and within every subsequent Term of ten Years, in such Manner as they shall by Law direct.

[1] Superseded by the Fourteenth Amendment. Throughout, italics indicate passages altered by subsequent amendments.

The Number of Representatives shall not exceed one for every thirty Thousand, but each State shall have at Least one Representative, and until such enumeration shall be made, the State of New Hampshire shall be entitled to chuse three, Massachusetts eight, Rhode-Island and Providence Plantations one, Connecticut five, New York six, New Jersey four, Pennsylvania eight, Delaware one, Maryland six, Virginia ten, North Carolina five, South Carolina five, and Georgia three.

When vacancies happen in the Representation from any State, the Executive Authority thereof shall issue Writs of Election to fill such Vacancies.

The House of Representatives shall chuse their Speaker and other Officers; and shall have the sole Power of Impeachment.

Section 3   The Senate of the United States shall be composed of two Senators from each State, chosen by the *Legislature thereof,*[2] for six Years; and each Senator shall have one Vote.

Immediately after they shall be assembled in Consequence of the first Election, they shall be divided as equally as may be into three Classes. The Seats of the Senators of the first Class shall be vacated at the Expiration of the second Year, of the second Class at the Expiration of the fourth Year, and of the third Class at the Expiration of the sixth Year, so that one third may be chosen every second Year; *and if Vacancies happen by Resignation, or otherwise, during the Recess of the Legislature of any State, the Executive thereof may make temporary Appointments until the next Meeting of the Legislature, which shall then fill such Vacancies.*[3]

No Person shall be a Senator who shall not have attained to the Age of thirty Years, and been nine Years a Citizen of the United States, and who shall not, when elected, be an Inhabitant of the State for which he shall be chosen.

The Vice President of the United States shall be President of the Senate, but shall have no Vote, unless they be equally divided.

The Senate shall chuse their other Officers, and also a President pro tempore, in the Absence of the Vice President, or when he shall exercise the Office of President of the United States.

The Senate shall have the sole Power to try all Impeachments. When sitting for that Purpose, they shall be on Oath or Affirmation. When the President of the United States is tried, the Chief Justice shall preside: And no Person shall be convicted without the Concurrence of two thirds of the Members present.

Judgment in Cases of Impeachment shall not extend further than to removal from Office, and disqualification to hold and enjoy any Office

[2] See Seventeenth Amendment.
[3] See Seventeenth Amendment.

of Honor, Trust or Profit under the United States: but the party convicted shall nevertheless be liable and subject to Indictment, Trial, Judgment and Punishment, according to Law.

Section 4   The Times, Places and Manner of holding Elections for Senators and Representatives, shall be prescribed in each State by the Legislature thereof; but the Congress may at any time by Law make or alter such Regulations, except as to the Places of chusing Senators.

The Congress shall assemble at least once in every Year, and such Meeting shall be on the first Monday in December, unless they shall by Law appoint a different Day.[4]

Section 5   Each House shall be the Judge of the Elections, Returns and Qualifications of its own Members, and a Majority of each shall constitute a Quorum to do Business; but a smaller Number may adjourn from day to day, and may be authorized to compel the Attendance of absent Members, in such Manner, and under such Penalties as each House may provide.

Each House may determine the Rules of its Proceedings, punish its Members for disorderly Behaviour, and, with the Concurrence of two thirds, expel a Member.

Each House shall keep a Journal of its Proceedings, and from time to time publish the same, excepting such Parts as may in their Judgment require Secrecy; and the Yeas and Nays of the Members of either House on any question shall, at the Desire of one fifth of those Present, be entered on the Journal.

Neither House, during the Session of Congress, shall, without the Consent of the other, adjourn for more than three days, nor to any other Place than that in which the two Houses shall be sitting.

Section 6   The Senators and Representatives shall receive a Compensation for their Services, to be ascertained by Law, and paid out of the Treasury of the United States. They shall in all Cases, except Treason, Felony and Breach of the Peace, be privileged from Arrest during their Attendance at the Session of their respective Houses, and in going to and returning from the same; and for any Speech or Debate in either House, they shall not be questioned in any other Place.

No Senator or Representative shall, during the Time for which he was elected, be appointed to any civil Office under the Authority of the United States, which shall have been created, or the Emoluments whereof shall have been encreased during such time; and no Person holding any Office under the United States, shall be a Member of either House during his Continuance in Office.

---

[4]See Twentieth Amendment.

Section 7 All Bills for raising Revenue shall originate in the House of Representatives; but the Senate may propose or concur with Amendments as on other Bills.

Every Bill which shall have passed the House of Representatives and the Senate, shall, before it become a Law, be presented to the President of the United States; If he approve he shall sign it, but if not he shall return it, with his Objections to that House in which it shall have originated, who shall enter the Objections at large on their Journal, and proceed to reconsider it. If after such Reconsideration two thirds of that House shall agree to pass the Bill, it shall be sent, together with the Objections, to the other House, by which it shall likewise be reconsidered, and if approved by two thirds of that House, it shall become a Law. But in all such Cases the Votes of both Houses shall be determined by Yeas and Nays, and the Names of the Persons voting for and against the Bill shall be entered on the Journal of each House respectively. If any Bill shall not be returned by the President within ten Days (Sundays excepted) after it shall have been presented to him, the Same shall be a Law, in like Manner as if he had signed it, unless the Congress by their Adjournment prevent its Return, in which Case it shall not be a Law.

Every Order, Resolution, or Vote to which the concurrence of the Senate and House of Representatives may be necessary (except on a question of Adjournment) shall be presented to the President of the United States; and before the Same shall take Effect, shall be approved by him, or being disapproved by him, shall be repassed by two thirds of the Senate and House of Representatives, according to the Rules and Limitations prescribed in the Case of a Bill.

Section 8 The Congress shall have Power To lay and collect Taxes, Duties, Imposts and Excises, to pay the Debts and provide for the common Defence and general Welfare of the United States; but all Duties, Imposts and Excises shall be uniform throughout the United States;

To borrow Money on the credit of the United States;

To regulate Commerce with foreign Nations, and among the several States, and with the Indian Tribes;

To establish an uniform Rule of Naturalization, and uniform Laws on the subject of Bankruptcies throughout the United States;

To coin Money, regulate the Value thereof, and of foreign Coin, and fix the Standard of Weights and Measures;

To provide for the Punishment of counterfeiting the Securities and current Coin of the United States;

To establish Post Offices and post Roads;

To promote the Progress of Science and useful Arts, by securing for limited Times to Authors and Inventors the exclusive Right to their respective Writings and Discoveries;

To constitute Tribunals inferior to the Supreme Court;

To define and punish Piracies and Felonies committed on the high Seas, and Offences against the Law of Nations;

To declare War, grant Letters of Marque and Reprisal, and make Rules concerning Captures on Land and Water;

To raise and support Armies, but no Appropriation of Money to that Use shall be for a longer Term than two Years;

To provide and maintain a Navy;

To make Rules for the Government and Regulation of the land and naval Forces;

To provide for calling forth the Militia to execute the Laws of the Union, suppress Insurrections and repel Invasions;

To provide for organizing, arming, and disciplining, the Militia, and for governing such Part of them as may be employed in the Service of the United States, reserving to the States respectively, the Appointment of the Officers, and the Authority of training the Militia according to the discipline prescribed by Congress;

To exercise exclusive Legislation in all Cases whatsoever, over such District (not exceeding ten Miles square) as may, by Cession of particular States, and the Acceptance of Congress, become the Seat of the Government of the United States, and to exercise like Authority over all Places purchased by the Consent of the Legislature of the State in which the Same shall be, for the Erection of Forts, Magazines, Arsenals, dock-Yards, and other needful Buildings;—And

To make all Laws which shall be necessary and proper for carrying into Execution the foregoing Powers, and all other Powers vested by this Constitution in the Government of the United States, or in any Department or Officer thereof.

Section 9   The Migration or Importation of such Persons as any of the States now existing shall think proper to admit, shall not be prohibited by the Congress prior to the Year one thousand eight hundred and eight, but a Tax or duty may be imposed on such Importation, not exceeding ten dollars for each Person.

The Privilege of the Writ of Habeas Corpus shall not be suspended, unless when in Cases of Rebellion or Invasion the public Safety may require it.

No Bill of Attainder or ex post facto Law shall be passed.

No Capitation, or other direct, Tax shall be laid, unless in Proportion to the Census or Enumeration herein before directed to be taken.

No Tax or Duty shall be laid on Articles exported from any State.

No Preference shall be given by any Regulation of Commerce or Revenue to the Ports of one State over those of another: nor shall Vessels bound to or from, one State, be obliged to enter, clear, or pay Duties in another.

No Money shall be drawn from the Treasury, but in Consequence of

Appropriations made by Law; and a regular Statement and Account of the Receipts and Expenditures of all public Money shall be published from time to time.

No Title of Nobility shall be granted by the United States: And no Person holding any Office of Profit or Trust under them, shall, without the Consent of the Congress, accept of any present, Emolument, Office, or Title, of any kind whatever, from any King, Prince, or foreign State.

Section 10   No State shall enter into any Treaty, Alliance, or Confederation; grant Letters of Marque and Reprisal; coin Money; emit Bills of Credit; make any Thing but gold and silver Coin a Tender in Payment of Debts; pass any Bill of Attainder, ex post facto Law, or Law impairing the Obligation of Contracts, or grant any Title of Nobility.

No State shall, without the Consent of the Congress, lay any Imposts or Duties on Imports or Exports, except what may be absolutely necessary for executing its inspection Laws: and the net Produce of all Duties and Imposts, laid by any State on Imports or Exports, shall be for the Use of the Treasury of the United States; and all such Laws shall be subject to the Revision and Controul of the Congress.

No State shall, without the Consent of Congress, lay any Duty of Tonnage, keep Troops, or Ships of War in time of Peace, enter into any Agreement or Compact with another State, or with a foreign Power, or engage in War, unless actually invaded, or in such imminent Danger as will not admit of delay.

ARTICLE II

Section 1   The executive Power shall be vested in a President of the United States of America. He shall hold his Office during the Term of four Years, and, together with the Vice President, chosen for the same Term, be elected, as follows:

Each State shall appoint, in such Manner as the Legislature thereof may direct, a Number of Electors, equal to the whole Number of Senators and Representatives to which the State may be entitled in the Congress: but no Senator or Representative, or Person holding an Office of Trust or Profit under the United States, shall be appointed an Elector.

The Electors shall meet in their respective States, and vote by Ballot for two Persons, of whom one at least shall not be an Inhabitant of the same State with themselves. And they shall make a List of all the Persons voted for, and of the Number of Votes for each; which List they shall sign and certify, and transmit sealed to the Seat of the Government of the United States, directed to the President of the Senate. The President of the Senate shall, in the Presence of the Senate and House of Representatives, open all the Certificates, and the Votes shall then be counted. The Person having the greatest Number of Votes shall be the President, if such Number be a Major-

ity of the whole Number of Electors appointed; and if there be more than one who have such Majority, and have an equal Number of Votes, then the House of Representatives shall immediately chuse by Ballot one of them for President, and if no Person have a Majority, then from the five highest on the List the said House shall in like Manner chuse the President. But in chusing the President, the Votes shall be taken by States, the Representation from each State having one Vote: A quorum for this Purpose shall consist of a Member or Members from two thirds of the States, and a Majority of all the States shall be necessary to a Choice. In every Case, after the Choice of the President, the Person having the greatest Number of Votes of the Electors shall be the Vice President. But if there should remain two or more who have equal Votes, the Senate shall chuse from them by Ballot the Vice President.[5]

The Congress may determine the Time of chusing the Electors, and the Day on which they shall give their Votes; which Day shall be the same throughout the United States.

No Person except a natural born Citizen, or a Citizen of the United States, at the time of the Adoption of this Constitution, shall be eligible to the Office of President; neither shall any Person be eligible to that Office who shall not have attained to the Age of thirty five Years, and been fourteen Years a Resident within the United States.

In Case of the Removal of the President from Office, or of his Death, Resignation, or Inability to discharge the Powers and Duties of the said Office, the Same shall devolve on the Vice President, and the Congress may by Law provide for the Case of Removal, Death, Resignation or Inability, both of the President and Vice President, declaring what Officer shall then act as President, and such Officer shall act accordingly, until the Disability be removed, or a President shall be elected.[6]

The President shall, at stated Times, receive for his Services, a Compensation which shall neither be encreased nor diminished during the Period for which he shall have been elected, and he shall not receive within that Period any other Emolument from the United States, or any of them.

Before he enter on the Execution of his Office, he shall take the following Oath or Affirmation:—"I do solemnly swear (or affirm) that I will faithfully execute the Office of President of the United States, and will to the best of my Ability, preserve, protect and defend the Constitution of the United States."

Section 2   The President shall be Commander in Chief of the Army and Navy of the United States, and of the Militia of the several States, when called into the actual Service of the United States; he may require the Opinion, in writing, of the principal Officer in each of the executive

---

[5]Superseded by the Twelfth Amendment.

[6]See Twenty-Fifth Amendment.

Departments, upon any Subject relating to the Duties of their respective Offices, and he shall have Power to grant Reprieves and Pardons for Offences against the United States, except in Cases of Impeachment.

He shall have Power, by and with the Advice and Consent of the Senate, to make Treaties, provided two thirds of the Senators present concur; and he shall nominate, and by and with the Advice and Consent of the Senate, shall appoint Ambassadors, other public Ministers and Consuls, Judges of the supreme Court, and all other Officers of the United States, whose Appointments are not herein otherwise provided for, and which shall be established by Law: but the Congress may by Law vest the Appointment of such inferior officers, as they think proper, in the President alone, in the Courts of Law, or in the Heads of Departments.

The President shall have Power to fill up all Vacancies that may happen during the Recess of the Senate, by granting Commissions which shall expire at the End of their next Session.

Section 3   He shall from time to time give to the Congress Information of the State of the Union, and recommend to their Consideration such Measures as he shall judge necessary and expedient; he may, on extraordinary Occasions, convene both Houses, or either of them, and in Case of Disagreement between them, with Respect to the Time of Adjournment, he may adjourn them to such Time as he shall think proper; he shall receive Ambassadors and other public Ministers; he shall take Care that the Laws be faithfully executed, and shall Commission all the Officers of the United States.

Section 4   The President, Vice President, and all civil Officers of the United States, shall be removed from Office on Impeachment for, and Conviction of, Treason, Bribery, or other high Crimes and Misdemeanors.

ARTICLE III

Section 1   The judicial Power of the United States, shall be vested in one supreme Court and in such inferior Courts as the Congress may from time to time ordain and establish. The Judges, both of the supreme and inferior Courts, shall hold their Offices during good Behaviour, and shall, at stated Times, receive for their Services, a Compensation, which shall not be diminished during their Continuance in Office.

Section 2   The judicial Power shall extend to all Cases, in Law and Equity, arising under this Constitution, the Laws of the United States, and Treaties made, or which shall be made, under their Authority;—to all Cases affecting Ambassadors, other public Ministers and Consuls;—to all Cases of admiralty and maritime Jurisdiction;—to Controversies to which the United States shall be a Party—to Controversies between two or more States;—*between a State and Citizens of another State;*[7]—between Citizens of different States;—between Citizens of the same State claiming Lands under Grants of different States, *and between a State or the Citizens thereof, and foreign States, Citizens, or Subjects.*[8]

In all Cases affecting Ambassadors, other public Ministers and Consuls, and those in which a State shall be Party, the supreme Court shall have original Jurisdiction. In all the other Cases before mentioned, the supreme Court shall have appellate Jurisdiction, both as to Law and Fact, with such Exceptions, and under such Regulations as the Congress shall make.

The Trial of all Crimes, except in Cases of Impeachment, shall be by Jury; and such Trial shall be held in the State where the said Crimes shall have been committed; but when not committed within any State, the Trial shall be at such Place or Places as the Congress may by Law have directed.

Section 3   Treason against the United States, shall consist only in levying War against them, or in adhering to their Enemies, giving them Aid and Comfort. No Person shall be convicted of Treason unless on the Testimony of two Witnesses to the same overt Act, or on Confession in open Court.

The Congress shall have Power to declare the Punishment of Treason, but no Attainder of Treason shall work Corruption of Blood, or Forfeiture except during the Life of the Person attainted.

ARTICLE IV

Section 1   Full Faith and Credit shall be given in each State to the public Acts, Records, and judicial Proceedings of every other State. And the Congress may by general Laws prescribe the Manner in which such Acts, Records, and Proceedings shall be proved, and the Effect thereof.

Section 2   The Citizens of each State shall be entitled to all Privileges and Immunities of Citizens in the several States.

A Person charged in any State with Treason, Felony, or other Crime, who shall flee from Justice, and be found in another State, shall on Demand of the executive Authority of the State from which he fled, be delivered up, to be removed to the State having Jurisdiction of the Crime.

No Person held to Service or Labour in one State, under the Laws thereof, escaping into another, shall, in Consequence of any Law or Regulation therein, be discharged from such Service or Labour, but shall be

[7] See Eleventh Amendment.
[8] See Eleventh Amendment.

delivered up on Claim of the Party to whom such Service or Labour may be due.[9]

Section 3   New States may be admitted by the Congress into this Union; but no new State shall be formed or erected within the Jurisdiction of any other State; nor any State be formed by the Junction of two or more States, or Parts of States, without the Consent of the Legislatures of the States concerned as well as of the Congress.

The Congress shall have Power to dispose of and make all needful Rules and Regulations respecting the Territory or other Property belonging to the United States; and nothing in this Constitution shall be so construed as to Prejudice any claims of the United States, or of any particular State.

Section 4   The United States shall guarantee to every State in this Union a Republican Form of Government, and shall protect each of them against Invasion; and on Application of the Legislature, or of the Executive (when the Legislature cannot be convened) against domestic Violence.

ARTICLE V

The Congress, whenever two thirds of both Houses shall deem it necessary, shall propose Amendments to this Constitution, or, on the Application of the Legislatures of two thirds of the several States, shall call a Convention for proposing Amendments, which, in either Case, shall be valid to all Intents and Purposes, as Part of this Constitution, when ratified by the Legislatures of three fourths of the several States, or by Conventions in three fourths thereof, as the one or the other Mode of Ratification may be proposed by the Congress; Provided that no Amendment which may be made prior to the Year One thousand eight hundred and eight shall in any Manner affect the first and fourth Clauses in the Ninth Section of the first Article; and that no State, without its Consent, shall be deprived of its equal Suffrage in the Senate.

ARTICLE VI

All debts contracted and Engagements entered into, before the Adoption of this Constitution, shall be as valid against the United States under this Constitution, as under the Confederation.

This Constitution, and the Laws of the United States which shall be made in Pursuance thereof; and all Treaties made, or which shall be made, under the Authority of the United States, shall be the supreme

[9]See Thirteenth Amendment.

Law of the Land; and the Judges in every State shall be bound thereby, any Thing in the Constitution or Laws of any State to the Contrary notwithstanding.

The Senators and Representatives before mentioned, and the Members of the several State Legislatures, and all executive and judicial Officers, both of the United States and of the several States, shall be bound by Oath or Affirmation, to support this Constitution; but no religious Test shall ever be required as a Qualification to any Office or public Trust under the United States.

ARTICLE VII

The Ratification of the Conventions of nine States, shall be sufficient for the Establishment of this Constitution between the States so ratifying the Same.

Done in Convention by the Unanimous Consent of the States present the Seventeenth Day of September in the Year of our Lord one thousand seven hundred and eighty seven and of the Independence of the United States of America the Twelfth. In witness whereof We have hereunto subscribed our Names.

Articles in Addition to, and Amendment of, the Constitution of the United States of America, Proposed by Congress, and Ratified by the Several States, Pursuant to the Fifth Article of the Original Constitution:

Amendment I

(Ratification of the first ten amendments was completed December 15, 1791.)

Congress shall make no law respecting an establishment of religion, or prohibiting the free exercise thereof; or abridging the freedom of speech, or of the press; or the right of the people peaceably to assemble, and to petition the Government for a redress of grievances.

Amendment II

A well regulated Militia, being necessary to the security of a free State, the right of the people to keep and bear Arms, shall not be infringed.

Amendment III

No Soldier shall, in time of peace be quartered in any house, without the consent of the Owner, nor in time of war, but in a manner to be prescribed by law.

Amendment IV

The right of the people to be secure in their persons, houses, papers, and effects, against unreasonable searches and seizures, shall not be violated, and no Warrants shall issue, but upon probable cause, supported by Oath or affirmation, and particularly describing the place to be searched, and the persons or things to be seized.

Amendment V

No person shall be held to answer for a capital, or otherwise infamous crime, unless on a presentment or indictment of a Grand Jury, except in cases arising in the land or naval forces, or in the Militia, when in actual service in time of War or public danger; nor shall any person be subject for the same offence to be twice put in jeopardy of life or limb; nor shall be compelled in any criminal case to be a witness against himself, nor be deprived of life, liberty, or property, without due process of law; nor shall private property be taken for public use, without just compensation.

Amendment VI

In all criminal prosecutions, the accused shall enjoy the right to a speedy and public trial, by an impartial jury of the State and district wherein the crime shall have been committed, which district shall have been previously ascertained by law, and to be informed of the nature and cause of the accusation; to be confronted with the witness against him; to have compulsory process for obtaining witnesses in his favor, and to have the Assistance of Counsel for his defence.

Amendment VII

In Suits at common law, where the value in controversy shall exceed twenty dollars, the right of trial by jury shall be preserved, and no fact tried by a jury, shall be otherwise reexamined in any Court of the United States, than according to the rules of the common law.

Amendment VIII

Excessive bail shall not be required, nor excessive fines imposed, nor cruel and unusual punishments inflicted.

Amendment IX

The enumeration in the Constitution, of certain rights, shall not be construed to deny or disparage others retained by the people.

Amendment X

The powers not delegated to the United States by the Constitution, nor prohibited by it to the States, are reserved to the States respectively, or to the people.

Amendment XI (1798)

The Judicial power of the United States shall not be construed to extend to any suit in law or equity, commenced or prosecuted against one of the United States by Citizens of another State, or by Citizens or Subjects of any Foreign States.

Amendment XII (1804)

The Electors shall meet in their respective states and vote by ballot for President and Vice-President, one of whom, at least, shall not be an inhabitant of the same state with themselves; they shall name in their ballots the person voted for as President, and in distinct ballots the person voted for as Vice-President, and they shall make distinct lists of all persons voted for as President, and of all persons voted for as Vice-President, and of the number of votes for each, which lists they shall sign and certify, and transmit sealed to the seat of the government of the United States, directed to the President of the Senate;—The President of the Senate shall, in the presence of Senate and House of Representatives, open all the certificates and the votes shall then be counted;—The person having the greatest number of votes for President, shall be the President, if such number be a majority of the whole number of Electors appointed; and if no person have such majority, then from the persons having the highest numbers not exceeding three on the list of those voted for as President, the House of Representatives shall choose immediately, by ballot, the President. But in choosing the President, the votes shall be taken by states, the representation from each state having one vote; a quorum for this purpose shall consist of a member or members from two-thirds of the states, and a majority of all the states shall be necessary to a choice. And if the House of Representatives shall not choose a President whenever the right of choice shall devolve upon them, *before the fourth day of March next following,*[10] then the Vice-President shall act as President, as in the case of the death or other constitutional disability of the President.—The person having the greatest number of votes as Vice-President shall be the Vice-President, if such number be a majority of the whole number of Electors appointed, and if no person have a majority, then from the two highest numbers on the list, the Senate shall choose the Vice-President; a quorum for the purpose shall

[10]Altered by the Twentieth Amendment.

consist of two-thirds of the whole number of Senators, and a majority of the whole number shall be necessary to a choice. But no person constitutionally ineligible to the office of President shall be eligible to that of Vice-President of the United States.

Amendment XIII (1865)

Section 1   Neither slavery nor involuntary servitude, except as a punishment for crime whereof the party shall have been duly convicted, shall exist within the United States, or any place subject to their jurisdiction.

Section 2   Congress shall have the power to enforce this article by appropriate legislation.

Amendment XIV (1868)

Section 1   All persons born or naturalized in the United States, and subject to the jurisdiction thereof, are citizens of the United States and of the State wherein they reside. No State shall make or enforce any law which shall abridge the privileges or immunities of citizens of the United States; nor shall any State deprive any person of life, liberty, or property, without due process of law; nor deny to any person within its jurisdiction the equal protection of the laws.

Section 2   Representatives shall be apportioned among the several States according to their respective numbers, counting the whole number of persons in each State, excluding Indians not taxed. But when the right to vote at any election for the choice of electors for President and Vice President of the United States, Representatives in Congress, the Executive and Judicial officers of a State, or the members of the Legislature thereof, is denied to any of the male inhabitants of such State, being twenty-one years of age, and citizens of the United States, or in any way abridged, except for participation in rebellion, or other crime, the basis of representation therein shall be reduced in the proportion which the number of such male citizens shall bear to the whole number of male citizens twenty-one years of age in such State.

Section 3   No person shall be a Senator or Representative in Congress, or elector of President and Vice President, or hold any office, civil or military, under the United States, or under any State, who, having previously taken an oath, as a member of Congress, or as an officer of the United States, or as a member of any State legislature, or as an executive or judicial officer of any State, to support the Constitution of the United States, shall have engaged in insurrection or rebellion against the same, or given aid or comfort to the enemies thereof. But Congress may by a vote of two-thirds of each House, remove such disability.

Section 4 The validity of the public debt of the United States, authorized by law, including debts incurred for payment of pensions and bounties for services in suppressing insurrection or rebellion, shall not be questioned. But neither the United States nor any State shall assume or pay any debt or obligation incurred in aid of insurrection or rebellion against the United States, or any claim for the loss or emancipation of any slave; but all such debts, obligations, and claims shall be held illegal and void.

Section 5 The Congress shall have power to enforce, by appropriate legislation, the provisions of this article.

Amendment XV (1870)

Section 1 The right of citizens of the United States to vote shall not be denied or abridged by the United States or by any State on account of race, color, or previous condition of servitude.

Section 2 The Congress shall have power to enforce this article by appropriate legislation.

Amendment XVI (1913)

The Congress shall have power to lay and collect taxes on incomes, from whatever source derived, without apportionment among the several States, and without regard to any census or enumeration.

Amendment XVII (1913)

The Senate of the United States shall be composed of two Senators from each State, elected by the people thereof, for six years; and each Senator shall have one vote. The electors in each State shall have the qualifications requisite for electors of the most numerous branch of the State legislatures.

When vacancies happen in the representation of any State in the Senate, the executive authority of such State shall issue writs of election to fill such vacancies: *Provided*, That the legislature of any State may empower the executive thereof to make temporary appointments until the people fill the vacancies by election as the legislature may direct.

This amendment shall not be so construed as to affect the election or term of any Senator chosen before it becomes valid as part of the Constitution.

Amendment XVIII (1919)

Section 1   After one year from the ratification of this article the manufacture, sale, or transportation of intoxicating liquors within, the importation thereof into, or the exportation thereof from the United States and all territory subject to the jurisdiction thereof for beverage purposes is hereby prohibited.

Section 2   The Congress and the several States shall have concurrent power to enforce this article by appropriate legislation.

Section 3   This article shall be inoperative unless it shall have been ratified as an amendment to the Constitution by the legislatures of the several States, as provided in the Constitution, within seven years from the date of the submission hereof to the States by the Congress.[11]

Amendment XIX (1920)

The right of citizens of the United States to vote shall not be denied or abridged by the United States or by any State on account of sex.

Congress shall have power to enforce this article by appropriate legislation.

Amendment XX (1933)

Section 1   The terms of the President and Vice President shall end at noon on the 20th day of January, and the terms of Senators and Representatives at noon on the 3rd day of January, of the years in which such terms would have ended if this article had not been ratified; and the terms of their successors shall then begin.

Section 2   The Congress shall assemble at least once in every year, and such meeting shall begin at noon on the 3rd day of January, unless they shall by law appoint a different day.

Section 3   If, at the time fixed for the beginning of the term of the President, the President elect shall have died, the Vice President elect shall become President. If a President shall not have been chosen before the time fixed for the beginning of his term, or if the President elect shall have failed to qualify, then the Vice President elect shall act as President until a President shall have qualified; and the Congress may by law provide for the case wherein neither a President elect nor a Vice President elect shall have qualified, declaring who shall then act as President,

---

[11]Repealed by the Twenty-First Amendment.

or the manner in which one who is to act shall be selected, and such person shall act accordingly until a President or Vice President shall have qualified.

Section 4   The Congress may by law provide for the case of the death of any of the persons from whom the House of Representatives may choose a President whenever the right of choice shall have devolved upon them, and for the case of the death of any of the persons from whom the Senate may choose a Vice President whenever the right of choice shall have devolved upon them.

Section 5   Sections 1 and 2 shall take effect on the 15th day of October following the ratification of this article.

Section 6   This article shall be inoperative unless it shall have been ratified as an amendment to the Constitution by the legislatures of three-fourths of the several States within seven years from the date of its submission.

Amendment XXI (1933)

Section 1   The eighteenth article of amendment to the Constitution of the United States is hereby repealed.

Section 2   The transportation or importation into any State, Territory, or possession of the United States for delivery or use therein of intoxicating liquors, in violation of the laws thereof, is hereby prohibited.

Section 3   This article shall be inoperative unless it shall have been ratified as an amendment to the Constitution by conventions in the several States, as provided in the Constitution, within seven years from the date of the submission hereof to the States by the Congress.

Amendment XXII (1951)

Section 1   No person shall be elected to the office of the President more than twice, and no person who has held the office of President, or acted as President for more than two years of a term to which some other person was elected President shall be elected to the office of President more than once. But this Article shall not apply to any person holding the office of President when this Article was proposed by the Congress, and shall not prevent any person who may be holding the office of President, or acting as President, during the term within which this Article becomes operative from holding the office of President or acting as President during the remainder of such term.

Section 2   This article shall be inoperative unless it shall have been ratified as an amendment to the Constitution by the legislatures of three-fourths of the several States within seven years from the date of its submission to the States by the Congress.

Amendment XXIII (1961)

Section 1   The District constituting the seat of Government of the United States shall appoint in such manner as the Congress may direct:

A number of electors of President and Vice President equal to the whole number of Senators and Representatives in Congress to which the District would be entitled if it were a State, but in no event more than the least populous State; they shall be in addition to those appointed by the States, but they shall be considered, for the purposes of the election of President and Vice President, to be electors appointed by a State; and they shall meet in the District and perform such duties as provided by the twelfth article of amendment.

Section 2   The Congress shall have power to enforce this article by appropriate legislation.

Amendment XXIV (1964)

Section 1   The right of citizens of the United States to vote in any primary or other election for President or Vice President, for electors for President or Vice President, or for Senator or Representative in Congress, shall not be denied or abridged by the United States or any state by reason of failure to pay any poll tax or other tax.

Section 2   The Congress shall have the power to enforce this article by appropriate legislation.

Amendment XXV (1967)

Section 1   In case of the removal of the President from office or of his death or resignation, the Vice President shall become President.

Section 2   Whenever there is a vacancy in the office of the Vice President, the President shall nominate a Vice President who shall take office upon confirmation by a majority vote of both Houses of Congress.

Section 3   Whenever the President transmits to the President pro tempore of the Senate and the Speaker of the House of Representatives his written declaration that he is unable to discharge the powers and duties of his office, and until he transmits to them a written declaration to the contrary, such powers and duties shall be discharged by the Vice President as Acting President.

Section 4   Whenever the Vice President and a majority of either the principal officers of the executive departments or of such other body as Congress may by law provide, transmit to the President pro tempore of the Senate and the Speaker of the House of Representatives their written declaration that the President is unable to discharge the powers and duties of his office, the Vice President shall immediately assume the powers and duties of the office as Acting President.

Thereafter, when the President transmits to the President pro tempore of the Senate and the Speaker of the House of Representatives his written declaration that no inability exists, he shall resume the powers and duties of his office unless the Vice President and a majority of either the principal officers of the executive departments or of such other body as Congress may by law provide, transmit within four days to the President pro tempore of the Senate and the Speaker of the House of Representatives their written declaration that the President is unable to discharge the powers and duties of his office. Thereupon Congress shall decide the issue, assembling within forty-eight hours for that purpose if not in session. If the Congress, within twenty-one days after receipt of the latter written declaration, or, if Congress is not in session, within twenty-one days after Congress is required to assemble, determines by two-thirds vote of both Houses that the President is unable to discharge the powers and duties of his office, the Vice President shall continue to discharge the same as Acting President; otherwise, the President shall resume the powers and duties of his office.

Amendment XXVI (1971)

Section 1   The right of citizens of the United States, who are 18 years of age or older, to vote shall not be denied or abridged by the United States or any state on account of age.

Section 2   The Congress shall have the power to enforce this article by appropriate legislation.

Index